Twentieth-Century Gothic

Edinburgh Companions to the Gothic

Series Editors
Andrew Smith, University of Sheffield
William Hughes, Bath Spa University

This series provides a comprehensive overview of the Gothic from the eighteenth century to the present day. Each volume takes either a period, place, or theme and explores their diverse attributes, contexts and texts via completely original essays. The volumes provide an authoritative critical tool for both scholars and students of the Gothic.

Volumes in the series are edited by leading scholars in their field and make a cutting-edge contribution to the field of Gothic studies.

Each volume:
- Presents an innovative and critically challenging exploration of the historical, thematic and theoretical understandings of the Gothic from the eighteenth century to the present day
- Provides a critical forum in which ideas about Gothic history and established Gothic themes are challenged
- Supports the teaching of the Gothic at an advanced undergraduate level and at masters level
- Helps readers to rethink ideas concerning periodisation and to question the critical approaches which have been taken to the Gothic

Published Titles
The Victorian Gothic: An Edinburgh Companion
  Andrew Smith and William Hughes
Romantic Gothic: An Edinburgh Companion
  Angela Wright and Dale Townshend
American Gothic Culture: An Edinburgh Companion
  Joel Faflak and Jason Haslam
Women and the Gothic: An Edinburgh Companion
  Avril Horner and Sue Zlosnik
Scottish Gothic: An Edinburgh Companion
  Carol Margaret Davison and Monica Germanà
The Gothic and Theory: An Edinburgh Companion
  Jerrold E. Hogle and Robert Miles
Twenty-First-Century Gothic: An Edinburgh Companion
  Maisha Wester and Xavier Aldana Reyes
Gothic Film: An Edinburgh Companion
  Richard J. Hand and Jay McRoy
Twentieth-Century Gothic: An Edinburgh Companion
  Sorcha Ní Fhlainn and Bernice M. Murphy

Visit the Edinburgh Companions to the Gothic website at:
www.edinburghuniversitypress.com/series/EDCG

Twentieth-Century Gothic

An Edinburgh Companion

Edited by
Sorcha Ní Fhlainn and
Bernice M. Murphy

EDINBURGH
University Press

Edinburgh University Press is one of the leading university presses in the UK. We publish academic books and journals in our selected subject areas across the humanities and social sciences, combining cutting-edge scholarship with high editorial and production values to produce academic works of lasting importance. For more information visit our website: edinburghuniversitypress.com

© editorial matter and organisation Sorcha Ní Fhlainn and Bernice M. Murphy, 2022, 2019
© the chapters their several authors, 2022

Edinburgh University Press Ltd
The Tun – Holyrood Road
12(2f) Jackson's Entry
Edinburgh EH8 8PJ

First published in hardback by Edinburgh University Press 2022

Typeset in 10.5/13pt Sabon LT Pro
by Cheshire Typesetting Ltd, Cuddington, Cheshire,
Croydon, CR0 4YY

A CIP record for this book is available from the British Library

ISBN 978 1 4744 9012 2 (hardback)
ISBN 978 1 4744 9013 9 (paperback)
ISBN 978 1 4744 9014 6 (webready PDF)
ISBN 978 1 4744 9015 3 (epub)

The right of Sorcha Ní Fhlainn and Bernice M. Murphy to be identified as the editors of this work has been asserted in accordance with the Copyright, Designs and Patents Act 1988, and the Copyright and Related Rights Regulations 2003 (SI No. 2498).

Contents

Acknowledgements — vii

Introduction: Going to Extremes: The Gothic in the Twentieth Century — 1
Bernice M. Murphy and Sorcha Ní Fhlainn

PART I GOTHIC EVOLUTIONS

1. The Edwardian Supernatural — 15
   Emma Liggins

2. Weird Fiction in the Twentieth Century — 33
   Kevin Corstorphine

3. Gothic Modernisms — 49
   Matt Foley

4. Gothic Criticism in the Twentieth Century: Who is This Who is Coming? — 64
   Scott Brewster

PART II THE GOTHIC AND TECHNOLOGY/TRANSMEDIA CONSIDERATIONS

5. The Birth of an Evil Thought: The Gothic in Silent-Era Cinema — 83
   Murray Leeder

6. Grand-Guignol as Twentieth-Century Gothic Drama — 99
   Madelon Hoedt

7. Mid-Century Gothic Cinema (1931–79): From Monster Business to Exploitation Horror — 114
   Xavier Aldana Reyes

8. The *Unheimlich* State: Surveillance and the Digital Nation   129
   Julia M. Wright

9. Gothic Horror Films at the 'Fin-de-Millennium':
   From Nightmare Videos to Filtered Realities (1980–2000)   144
   Sorcha Ní Fhlainn

PART III KEY THEMES AND TOPICS IN TWENTIETH-CENTURY GOTHIC

10. Twentieth-Century War Gothic   165
    Agnieszka Soltysik Monnet

11. Russian Twentieth-Century Gothic: The Irrepressible Undead   180
    Muireann Maguire

12. The Gothic 1950s   196
    Steffen Hantke

13. Masks of Sanity: Psychopathy and the Twentieth-Century Gothic   213
    Bernice M. Murphy

14. Troubling Legacies: African American Women's Gothic from Zora Neale Hurston to Tananarive Due   228
    Dara Downey

15. Medical Humanities and the Twentieth-Century Gothic   243
    Laura R. Kremmel

16. Queer Gothic Literature and Culture   259
    Laura Westengard

17. 'Nightmares of the Normative': African American Gothic and the Rejection of the American Ideal   273
    Maisha Wester

18. Big Bad Wolves and Angry Sharks: The Ecogothic and a Century of Environmental Change   290
    Christy Tidwell

Notes on Contributors   305
Index   310

Acknowledgements

Much of this volume was written and edited during the greatest global crisis since the end of the Second World War: the Covid-19 pandemic, which is still unfolding as we write these acknowledgements. Throughout this project our contributors have responded to editorial queries and suggestions with insight, good humour and remarkable patience. We consider ourselves extremely fortunate to have worked with such a talented group of scholars. The editors would also like to acknowledge the invaluable aid provided by our excellent editorial assistant, Janice Deitner. Any errors or omissions contained this volume are entirely our responsibility. We would also like to thank the staff of Edinburgh University Press for their support with this book, and the Gothic Companion series editors, Professor Andrew Smith and Professor William Hughes, for their encouragement and insight. Thanks also to our peer reviewers for their helpful feedback.

Finally, we wish to thank those who helped us along the way, particularly our families, friends and Gothic familiars. Sorcha would like to thank John Gilleese, Léin Ní Longáin, Eoghan Ó Flainn and Dimitra Kitridou, and Mao, for their love and support, and, for their professional and personal encouragement, her generous and supportive friends and colleagues from the Manchester Centre for Gothic Studies and the Department of English at Manchester Metropolitan University. Bernice is grateful for the love provided by Majella, John, Eóin, Emma and Ieuan Murphy, and for the advice and support of colleagues from the School of English, Trinity College Dublin, particularly Jane Carroll, Clare Clarke, Jarlath Killeen, Darryl Jones and Stephen Matterson.

Bernice M. Murphy and Sorcha Ní Fhlainn

Introduction: Going to Extremes – The Gothic in the Twentieth Century

Bernice M. Murphy and Sorcha Ní Fhlainn

The twentieth century brought us antibiotics, air travel, vastly improved sanitation, the computer, the emancipation of women (in much of the world), the concept of the teenager and a substantial rise in global life expectancy. It also brought the 1918–19 influenza pandemic, chemical warfare, the Holocaust, climate change, overpopulation, two world wars and the atomic bomb. As Marxist historian Eric Hobsbawm put it, the century was 'an Age of Extremes'. He observed that

> An age of catastrophe from 1914 to the aftermath of the Second World War was followed by twenty-five or thirty years of extraordinary economic growth and social transformation, which probably changed human society more profoundly than any other period of comparable brevity. In retrospect it can be seen as a sort of Golden Age, and was so seen almost immediately it had come to an end in the 1970s. The last part of the century was a new era of decomposition, uncertainty and crisis [. . .].[1]

Events that took place in the last century continue to shape our lives in ways both self-evident and less immediately obvious. It is, for instance, catastrophically evident that the oil booms, pollution and consumer culture of the mid-late twentieth century were the principal causes of the global warming crisis that is now causing unprecedented wildfires, floods and temperature rises. In a less immediately obvious case of cause and effect, we might ask whether the UK's June 2016 EU membership referendum would have been a surprise victory for the 'Leave' campaign had it not been for the fact that a significant proportion of the British population is still enthralled by a sense of Britishness rooted in nostalgia for the 'glory days' of the Second World War and the lost pre-eminence of the British Empire. Or, on a similar note, would Donald J. Trump have become the 45th President of the United States in 2017 if he had not been able to evoke so crudely but effectively an idealised version of the middle-class (white) lifestyle rooted in an intensely exclusionary version of the American 1950s?

As a mode dedicated to the cultural and literary exploration of chaos, repression, violence, irrationality, the macabre, haunted architecture and haunted minds, the Gothic is uniquely positioned to dramatise and interrogate historical and cultural anxieties which mainstream literary and popular culture suppresses, overlooks or refuses to openly engage with. As David Punter argues in *A New Companion to the Gothic* (2012), what the mode shares with

> much contemporary criticism and cultural commentary ... is an overarching, even a sublime awareness of mutability, an understanding of the ways in which history itself, and certainly narratives of history, are not stable, do not constitute a rock onto which we might cling – indeed, as Gothic has always sought to demonstrate to us, there are no such rocks, there is no sure foundation.[2]

With these 'unsure foundations' in mind, it is all the more fitting that it was during the latter half of the twentieth century that the Gothic emerged as one of the liveliest and most significant areas of academic inquiry in literary, film and popular culture studies.

The sheer breadth of the mode during this period means that no single volume can explore all its complex and multifaceted manifestations. Given the breadth of our task, omissions were practically necessary. As with the messiness of century breaks, overhangs from previous centuries into new ones are acknowledged or mentioned but cannot always be fully accounted for here due to length constraints. One such omission, for instance, is Gothic video games. Important titles such as the *Resident Evil* (1996–) and *Silent Hill* (1999–) franchises have found rich cultural purchase and been the focus of sustained and valuable academic scholarship in the twenty-first century. What we will provide here instead is a twenty-first-century perspective on many of the most important themes and perspectives associated with the genre in the 'Age of Extremes' that was the twentieth century.

Since 2000, many introductory volumes, subject companions, monographs and edited collections devoted to both individual subgenres and prominent themes associated with the Gothic mode have been published. This volume is therefore not intended to serve as an introduction to an area that has already been the subject of many eminently valuable previous works. Rather, it is a lively, forward-looking, transnational and transmedia survey of the century during which Gothic Studies as a distinct academic discipline was established. The contributions featured reflect the interdisciplinary nature of the Gothic, which, during this century, migrated from literature and drama to the cinema, television and then the internet. The volume has both a chronological and thematic focus, but particular attention is paid to topics and themes related to race, identity, marginality and technology.

Fittingly, the authors of our eighteen chapters come from (and are based in) a wide range of nations, including Ireland, the United Kingdom, the United States, Canada, Switzerland and the Republic of Korea. Some – but by no means all – also appeared in the previous volume in this series, *Twenty-First Century Gothic* (2019). Our instalment has been calibrated to stand alongside this and the other earlier entries in the Edinburgh Gothic Companion series, including *American Gothic Culture* (2016) edited by Jason Haslam and Joel Faflak. However, we have also been mindful of ensuring that this collection has its own distinct and original approach. For example, the inclusion of suggested further reading at the end of each chapter is intended to facilitate further independent research. As well as providing an original and significant overview of key developments, texts and themes related to the Gothic in the twentieth century, it is our hope that this volume will provide a useful teaching tool for educators and academics who wish to provide their undergraduate and postgraduate students with a timely and accessible introduction to the key texts and topics associated with the Gothic in the twentieth century.

The volume has a broad transmedial remit: it features essays on literature, cinema, television, international cultural frameworks and the stage. There are also essays on the relationship between the Gothic in the twentieth century and relatively recent but highly significant critical areas such as the ecogothic, medical humanities, queer studies, African American studies, Russian Gothic and Gothic scholarship as an academic discipline.

Twentieth-Century Gothic is divided into three sections which position the Gothic as a multi-modal and rapidly developing discipline. The development of the mode over the twentieth century is explored in the first section, 'Gothic Evolutions'. Our opening essay, 'The Edwardian Supernatural' by Emma Liggins, argues that although it has thus far been overshadowed by discussions of the *fin de siècle* and modernism, the Edwardian supernatural is an important aspect of the twentieth-century Gothic with a distinctive take on haunted modernity. As Liggins notes, the transition period between 1900 and the outbreak of the First World War was characterised by a fascination with the supernatural and the uncanny, lost worlds, weird creatures and spiritualism. Authors such as E. Nesbit, Algernon Blackwood, H. G. Wells, Vernon Lee, Arthur Conan Doyle, Henry James and Alice Perrin all feature in her analysis, and it is argued that these authors present us with new ways of thinking about what it means, exactly, to be 'haunted' in the early twentieth-century Gothic.

In Chapter 2, 'Weird Fiction in the Twentieth Century', Kevin Corstorphine provides a historical overview of the term 'weird' as it relates to twentieth-century fiction and outlines some definitions in terms of the characteristic features of the genre, as well as the ideas underpinning its manifestations. He goes on to argue that weird fiction provides the eerie thrills of the Gothic but also an engagement with rapid developments in science, creating the perfect set of circumstances for it to proliferate in pulp magazine form in the mid-twentieth century.

Chapter 3, Matt Foley's essay on 'Gothic Modernisms', argues that this movement is an important facet of the twentieth-century Gothic. Drawing on examples from sources such as T. S. Eliot's *The Waste Land* (1922), Djuna Barnes's *Nightwood* (1936), the art and films of the European avant-garde and William Faulkner's Southern Gothic, his essay examines modernism's darker turns: the recurring depictions of transgression, haunting, the unconscious, excessive desire and somnambulism that so often preoccupied modernist artists. He suggests that in these texts (be they literature, film or painting) there is a reluctance to overtly invoke the supernatural or otherworldly. Instead, horror and terror are produced by means of an aesthetic fragmentation that reflects the alienating effects of a bleak and spiritually barren post-WWI modernity (c. 1920–40), one that is itself contradictory given the modernist desire to 'make new' aesthetics, on the one hand, and their inability to escape traumatising pasts on the other.

In the final essay in this section, 'Gothic Criticism in the Twentieth Century: Who is This Who is Coming?', Scott Brewster evokes M. R. James's famous spectre with 'a face of *crumpled linen*' to introduce the 'unsettling interlopers' which the Gothic mode champions. He traces the development of Gothic criticism during the twentieth century, identifying its main features, obsessions and contradictions. Brewster examines early accounts of the Gothic by critics such as Dorothy Scarborough, Edith Birkhead and Eino Railo, which tend to situate Gothic fiction within a broader literary history, before exploring the work of figures such as Montague Summers and Devendra Varma. The chapter then evaluates the burgeoning of Gothic scholarship pioneered by Punter's *The Literature of Terror* (1980). Throughout, Brewster's essay assesses the benefits and limitations that have arisen from the Gothic's gradual transition from marginality to the mainstream, transgression to respectability, interloper to invited guest. The chapter also asks whether this transformation actually became a new conformism that tempered, even tamed, its ability to shock, challenge or unsettle.

The volume's second section, entitled 'The Gothic and Technology/Transmedia Considerations', examines the rise of Gothic media alongside the development and advancement of technology and cultural industries during the twentieth century more generally. Particularly close attention has been paid to the rising dominance of film and its technological wonders, and the medium's positioning as a kind of Rorschach test for its audiences from the silent era to the digital future, alongside its advancement on the stage and its reach into the home through television.

In Chapter 5, 'The Birth of an Evil Thought: The Gothic in Silent-Era Cinema', Murray Leeder discusses the presence of the Gothic in the first decade of cinema, up until the conversion to sound in the late 1920s. He glosses the presence of Gothic themes in early cinema, absorbed from other media such as literature and the stage, and, while acknowledging the importance of German Expressionism, largely focusing on the American film industry. He then discusses the first adaptation of *Frankenstein* (1910) and how the film's marketing tempered the horrific elements of the plotline. Next, Leeder considers D. W. Griffith's *The Avenging Conscience* (1914), a baroque reworking of various Poe stories and poems, leading to an examination of the cycle of 'old, dark house' films of the 1920s which, Leeder argues, constitute the cycle of production of silent horror to which the Gothic label best applies. Largely stage-derived, these include Griffith's *One Exciting Night* (1922), *The Ghost Breaker* (1922), *The Bat* (1926), *Midnight Faces* (1926) and, perhaps most famously, *The Cat and the Canary* (1927). Set in Gothic mansions and often involving family dramas of inheritance, greed and deception, these films walk a delicate line between chills and laughter. Leeder also draws on Horner and Zlosnik's construction of the 'comic Gothic' to position this under-studied cycle.

Madelon Hoedt considers 'Grand-Guignol as Twentieth-Century Gothic Drama' in Chapter 6. She notes that the malleability of the Gothic mode has meant that it has always been able to adapt itself to a variety of media. Gothic drama has been a highly successful way of delivering such narratives. First gaining prominence in the late eighteenth century, alongside the first wave of Gothic novels, these plays had long theatrical runs and attracted huge audiences, as well as being on the cutting edge of developments in stagecraft and special effects. This changed in the early decades of the twentieth century. The never-ending stream of original play texts and adaptations of Gothic fiction dried up and more popular forms of performance such as spookshows and scare attractions emerged. The Grand-Guignol, the French Theatre of Horror, included both horror and comedy performances and yet focused more on realist plots than on the monsters of the Gothic. Hoedt argues that while the Grand-Guignol appears as a rupture from the Gothic dramas that preceded it, this is not the full story. The chapter positions the

Grand-Guignol as a necessary link between the spectacle and melodrama of the Gothic stage, and the psychology and gore of twentieth-century horror cinema.

Chapter 7, 'Mid-Century Gothic Cinema (1931–79): From Monster Business to Exploitation Horror' by Xavier Aldana Reyes, traces the key changes experienced by Gothic cinema during the years bookended by the success of Universal Studios' *Dracula* (1931) and *Frankenstein* (1931) and Hammer's failed attempts to modernise their Gothic horror brand. Key developments during this period included the crystallisation of the horror franchise as a viable commercial venture in the 1930s and 1940s, the rise of Gothic realism in the women's films of the 1940s, the widespread use of colour film processes in the late 1950s, and the subsequent rise of titillating and increasingly openly erotic spectacles in the exploitation cinema of Italy and Spain in the 1960s and 1970s. Alongside these medium-specific developments ran the temporal fixing of the nineteenth century as the new Gothic era, or 'Gothic cusp',[3] a fantastic or idealised version of the past that enabled the staging of ideological tensions between the barbaric past and the modern present. With the rise of pornography in the 1970s, Aldana Reyes argues, the Gothic aesthetic became unnecessary, even redundant, as concerns once channelled through the safe distance offered by retrojection were suddenly able to manifest in horror films set in contemporary times. By considering similarities and points of divergence between Universal's *Frankenstein* (1931) and Hammer's *The Curse of Frankenstein* (1957), Aldana Reyes shows both the cultural continuity of the Gothic aesthetic in this period and its evolution.

Chapter 8, by Julia Wright, is entitled 'The *Unheimlich* State: Surveillance and the Digital Nation'. It opens by referencing an important episode of one of twentieth-century Gothic TV's most notable manifestations, *Buffy the Vampire Slayer* (1997–2003), to argue that a significant section of post-1960s 'television Gothic' builds upon the early Gothic's concern with local forms of power and questions the nation-state's power as expressed through its monitoring of households. She goes on to explore three key points of friction between the state and the individual: the irreducibility of the individual to the mathematical unit; the invisible extension of state power over the individual through technological networks; and the fragmentation of the self through interactions with media and other digital forms. TV shows such as *The Prisoner* (1967–68), *Kolchak, the Night Stalker* (1974–75) and *The X-Files* (1994–2001, 2016, 2018) are discussed, and it is further argued that these Gothic television series, among other things, explore the violence inherent in digital technologies of power.

The ninth and final chapter in this section, 'Gothic Horror Films at the "Fin-de-Millennium": From Nightmare Videos to Filtered Realities (1980–2000)' by Sorcha Ní Fhlainn, explores new forms of technological circulation that informed the proliferation and aesthetics of Gothic horror films in the closing decades of the century. Ní Fhlainn's essay, marked out in distinct thematic flows, charts the rise of slashers on video and contemporary anxieties of the crumbling morality of the 1980s, through to the recuperation of horror via genre hybridisation in glossy Hollywood Gothic blockbusters. By the end of the century, the 'fin-de-millennium' gloom had pervaded postmodern horror in 'self-aware' considerations of 1980s slashers (in *Scream* [1996]), the terror of nuclear extermination and millennium-eve Satanic returns reflecting Y2K panic, and complicated notions of subjectivity and truth with the rise of found footage films. This chapter identifies the main themes and cinematic developments at the turbulent end of the twentieth century, where we identify with (and occasionally cheer for) monsters, champion outliers, and unmask doubled others, and find that our understanding of truth (and what it means to 'bear witness') is radically challenged.

In the final, and longest, section of the volume, 'Key Themes and Topics in Twentieth-Century Gothic', new areas of academic scrutiny arise as our contributors examine the core thematic demarcations of the century. Anxieties associated with and arising from the two world wars and the rise to prominence of Gothic fiction in the national literatures of both superpowers are here coupled with the emergence of Gothic thematics in narratives related to gender and sexuality, as well as those pertaining to ecocriticism, medical histories and (mal)practices, and African American literature.

In Chapter 10, 'Twentieth-Century War Gothic', Agnieszka Soltysik Monnet observes that the twentieth century was marked by two of the bloodiest global wars in history, as well as numerous colonial and resource-driven military conflicts spanning from the Philippines in 1899 to the Persian Gulf in the 1990s. The First World War and its mechanised slaughter represented both the demise of the illusion of modernity as a force of progress and enlightenment and the full maturation of the Gothic mode as a literary paradigm capable of expressing that failure. Although War Gothic has existed since the eighteenth century, it came into its full range and power only with the nightmarish conditions of the trenches and chemical weapons in the First World War. This chapter focuses on several key texts which represent the most important cultural work of War Gothic, from the war poetry of the trenches to the horror fiction and cinema of the Vietnam War, ending with a brief discussion of new developments in the Gothic representation of war at the end of the twentieth century.

Chapter 11, 'Russian Twentieth-Century Gothic: The Irrepressible Undead' by Muireann Maguire, argues that the uncanny, and particularly the undead, are a peculiarly irrepressible trope of Russian literature. Nineteenth-century Russian imitations and adaptations of European and American Gothic authors, notably Poe and Hoffmann, reached their literary apotheosis in the nightmarish fictions of Gogol and Dostoevskii. Gothic-fantastic characters and settings remained a staple of Russian symbolist and experimental prose during the early twentieth century. The Soviet era nominally introduced a period of strict realism and political orthodoxy in literature. In practice, Gothic imagery simply switched allegiance: authors used standard tropes such as the vampire, the haunted castle and the demon as propaganda against supposedly un-Soviet influences (respectively, the former bourgeoisie, repossessed properties and foreigners). Others deployed Gothic structures ironically to satirise the Soviet regime. In the aftermath of 1989, writers were again able to freely select themes and characters, triggering a resurgence of mass-market horror and fantasy fiction. Among the most successful recent examples is Sergei Luk'ianenko's *Night Watch* series of novels, begun in 1998, which follows the fortunes of various supernatural characters in contemporary Moscow. This essay offers an overview of the development of Russian Gothic fiction in the twentieth century, contrasting the representation of the undead in the work of early Soviet dissident writers such as Sigizmund Krzhizhanovskii with the politically freer, but no less culturally nuanced, portrayal of similar supernatural archetypes in the novels of Luk'ianenko. The growing number of authors who write reflectively about late and post-Soviet culture is represented by the inclusion of Anna Starobinets, who, like several of her contemporaries, also draws upon both traditional Gothic and contemporary horror tropes and themes.

Post-war America is the focus of Chapter 12, 'The Gothic 1950s' by Steffen Hantke. While the Gothic has often responded to turbulent and violent periods in European history, periods of great calm and prosperity have fostered a Gothic acutely attuned to the cost of such calm. America in the 1950s – the halcyon days of the American Century – was just such a period. To the extent that American self-assurance during the 1950s would rely on collective mechanisms of repression, Gothic motifs and strategies attached themselves to some of the historical events and accomplishments of the decade. Hantke argues that amid the popular culture of the period, Hollywood articulated these Gothic undertones. He suggests that classic films such as *The Man in the Grey Flannel Suit*

(1956) helped transform the most prominent war of the decade, the Korean War, into 'the forgotten war'. The work of canonical directors such as Nicholas Ray showed how the racial polarisation driving the nation's suburbanisation operated below the threshold of visibility until the urban riots of the following decade. In its ability to enact (and thus entrench) and reveal (and thus subvert) these mechanisms of repression, the Gothic provided a sustained note of anxiety and scepticism to reverberate along the self-assured, triumphalist tenor of 1950s American pop culture. Furthermore, as Hantke notes in conclusion, the triumphalist 'Make America Great Again' agenda which rose to ascendancy in American conservatism from 2016 onwards is rooted in an inherently sanitised and de-Gothicised version of the decade.

Chapter 13, 'Masks of Sanity: Psychopathy and the Twentieth-Century Gothic' by Bernice M. Murphy, focuses on the rise of the psychopath in the twentieth-century imagination. She begins by noting that since the end of the Second World War, Gothic fiction has been fixated on the figure of the psychopath – men and women whose (apparent) lack of empathy and refusal (or inability) to adhere to widely accepted social 'norms' and ethical constraints means that they are capable of deeply transgressive acts, including murder. In his pioneering 1941 volume *The Mask of Sanity*, psychiatrist Hervey Cleckley famously posited that psychopathy could be distinguished from 'orthodox psychoses' because while these involve visibly altered reasoning processes or 'other demonstrable personality features' and are therefore readily apparent to the outside observer, such was not the case in psychopathy. Here, Cleckley declared, '[t]he observer is confronted with a convincing mask of sanity'.[4] Using this resonant phrase as a starting point, Murphy discusses the cultural impact made by the idea of the psychopath in middle to late twentieth-century Gothic fiction, focusing on post-war texts such as Dorothy B. Hughes's 1947 novel *In a Lonely Place*, Jim Thompson's *The Killer Inside Me* (1952), William March's *The Bad Seed* (1954), John Fowles's *The Collector* (1963) and Tim Krabbé's *The Golden Egg* (aka *The Vanishing*, 1984). The cold, ruthless and scheming 'killer who hides among us' trope fitted in perfectly with the post-WWII move away from horrors of a supernatural nature to those of a very human variety, and in this chapter, the rationale behind the important place held by the psychopath in twentieth-century Gothic is established.

In Chapter 14, 'Troubling Legacies: African American Women's Gothic from Zora Neale Hurston to Tananarive Due', Dara Downey argues that Octavia Butler's 1979 neo-slavery novel *Kindred* is emblematic of a distinct ambivalence towards Gothic tropes and conventions in twentieth-century fiction by African American women. From Zora

Neale Hurston's engagement with Southern and Caribbean hoodoo, voudou and conjure in the 1920s, to Tananarive Due's visions of successful young black women haunted by the very real presence of racialised violence in the American 1990s, African American women's Gothic fiction walks a perilous line. These texts reject both the ultimate optimism of traditional Female Gothic plots and the demonisation of black characters as avatars of Gothic darkness. At the same time, she notes, they also acknowledge and dramatise the continuing usefulness of Gothic imagery and narrative tropes in excavating, and moving beyond, the horrific history of race relations in the Americas throughout the twentieth century and beyond.

In Chapter 15, 'Medical Humanities and the Twentieth-Century Gothic', Laura Kremmel looks at three intersections of the medical humanities and the Gothic: medical conspiracy and experimentation, mental institutions and contagion. She notes that in the twentieth century, medicine became involved in complex systems of technology, finance, liability and seemingly endless supplies of medications and procedures. Out of this century we get white coat syndrome (fear of hospitals and doctors), tales of surgical conspiracies, frightening treatments that invade and manipulate the body in seemingly unnatural ways, and economic systems determined to banish humanity from the art of healing. Medical conspiracy and experimentation are discussed through H. P. Lovecraft's 1920s medical characters who deviate from the system or expose its weaknesses; Stephen King's 1987 novel *Misery* and its corrupt nurse; and Robin Cook's subgenre-defining novels, specifically *Coma* (1977). Lovecraft's work also depicts mental institutions. The depiction of patients who blur the line between 'sane' and 'insane' also features in later texts such as Grant Morrison's *Arkham Asylum* (1989), and the mind as its own institution is a characteristic of Patrick McGrath's work, particularly *Spider* (1990) and *Asylum* (1996). Finally, contagion tales influence old Gothic characters and create new ones, as represented in Richard Matheson's *I Am Legend* (1954) and the film *Night of the Living Dead* (1968), texts that use monstrosity to access the human experience.

In Chapter 16, 'Queer Gothic Literature and Culture' by Laura Westengard, it is observed that since the first Gothic novel, Horace Walpole's *The Castle of Otranto* (1764), the Gothic has included themes of transgressive sexuality. In *Queer Gothic*, George Haggerty notes that cultural producers since the eighteenth century have used Gothic themes, tropes and settings 'to evoke a queer world that attempts to transgress the binaries of sexual decorum'.[5] Though Gothic themes and tropes have morphed over the years to reflect shifting cultural anxieties and desires,

Gothicism along with its inherent queerness has persisted in various forms up to the present. This chapter highlights examples of queer Gothic in twentieth-century cultural production across multiple genres and media, including queer Gothic cinema such as *Dracula's Daughter* (1936), *Rebecca* (1940) and *Suddenly Last Summer* (1959); fiction such as Shirley Jackson's *The Haunting of Hill House* (1959) and Anne Rice's *The Vampire Chronicles* (1976–); and late twentieth-century AIDS-era visual and performance art. Through these examples, Westengard examines queerness in the Gothic, gothicism in queer culture, and the function of the queer Gothic as an anti-normative orientation.

In Chapter 17, '"Nightmares of the Normative": African American Gothic and the Rejection of the American Ideal', Maisha Wester explores the ways in which African American Gothic fiction began to reject notions of the idyllic heteronormative American existence, showing that it is a simplification requiring allegiance to alienating notions of race, gender and socio-economic class. She begins by situating the 'Red Summer of 1919' (during which white Americans attacked uniformed black soldiers, firebombed black businesses and waged open warfare on black citizens) as a key turning point in Black Gothic literature. Nineteenth- and early twentieth-century writers such as slave narrative authors wrote literature testifying to the horrors of being denied humanity and citizenship, while their descendants wrote texts rooted in rejecting modern ideas of 'progress'. Drawing a portion of her title from Roderick Ferguson's essay 'Nightmares of the Heteronormative', Wester points to the ways in which heternormativity has been used as both bait and prison for African Americans, focusing on Richard Wright's 'The Man Who Lived Underground' (1945), Ralph Ellison's *Invisible Man* (1952) and Amiri Baraka's 1966 film *Dutchman*.

The volume concludes with 'Big Bad Wolves and Angry Sharks: The Ecogothic and a Century of Environmental Change' by Christy Tidwell. Tidwell begins by discussing current definitions of the rapidly evolving critical arena of the 'ecogothic', particularly as they relate to anxieties about place and space and resentful and/or rebellious non-human inhabitants, as well as the complex relationship between the human and the non-human. However, as she also notes, the ecogothic does not begin with the twentieth century but grows out of earlier ideas about the environment and humanity's relationship to it. This history, as well as shifts in environmental concerns over the century (again, primarily focusing on the US and UK), provide another way to explore key elements of the twentieth-century ecogothic. A number of ecogothic texts and themes are discussed before the chapter considers a film not usually associated with the subgenre – the 1993 blockbuster *Jurassic Park* – which is discussed in terms of its engagement with contemporary ecological crises, the spectre of human extinction, and fears that scientific and technological 'progress' has dangerously exceeded our control.

As these engaging and multifaceted chapters testify, there is much to be said about the myriad ways in which the Gothic in its various manifestations developed during the twentieth century. The era was characterised by new modes of living and new ways of thinking, violent outbursts and radical technological developments, utopian dreams and dystopian realities. Never had the world come closer to absolute (and self-inflicted) annihilation, but nor had the possibility of a better future ever seemed more practically attainable. It entirely fitting, then, that a mode which has always flourished during periods of chaos, uncertainty and possibility continued to thrive – and to evolve – in the twentieth century. It is our hope that this collection will provide an informative and engaging overview of (some) of the myriad ways in which the Gothic responded to this unprecedented 'Age of Extremes'.

Notes

1. Eric Hobsbawm, *Age of Extremes: The Short Twentieth Century, 1914–1991* (London: Abacus, 1994), p. 6.
2. David Punter (ed.), *A New Companion to the Gothic* (Oxford: Wiley Blackwell, 2012), p. 3.
3. Robert Miles, *Ann Radcliffe: The Great Enchantress* (Manchester: Manchester University Press, 1995), p. 87.
4. Hervey M. Cleckley, *The Mask of Sanity: An Attempt to Clarify Some Issues About the So-Called Psychopathic Personality* [1941], 5th edn (privately printed, 1988), p. 369.
5. George Haggerty, *Queer Gothic* (Urbana, IL: University of Illinois Press, 2006), p. 2.

Part I

Gothic Evolutions

Chapter 1

The Edwardian Supernatural
Emma Liggins

In his essay 'Some Remarks on Ghost Stories' in *The Bookman* (1929), M. R. James notes the 'astonishingly fertile' field of the ghost story, 'written with the sole object of inspiring a pleasing terror', between the late 1890s and the late 1920s. Key ingredients of the successful ghost story are, to his mind, 'malevolence and terror, the glare of evil faces, "the stony grin of unearthly malice", pursuing forms in darkness, and "long-drawn, distant screams"', not forgetting 'a modicum of blood'.[1] Gesturing to the geographies of haunting, he admires those authors who 'can make us envisage a definite time and place, and give us plenty of clear-cut and matter-of-fact detail, but who, when the climax is reached, allow us to be just a little in the dark as to the working of their machinery'.[2] This chapter investigates some of these elements of evil, terror and unearthliness in early twentieth-century ghost stories that keep the reader 'in the dark' on a number of levels.

Overshadowed by discussions of the *fin de siècle* and modernism, the Edwardian supernatural is a neglected aspect of twentieth-century Gothic, despite its distinctive take on haunted modernity. As Jerrold E. Hogle has argued, 'the Gothic is endemic to the modern ... the ever-extending tentacles of modern enterprise are always haunted by the doubts, conflicts, and blurring of normative boundaries that the Gothic articulates in every form it assumes'.[3] The 'golden age' of the ghost story, according to Ruth Heholt, encompasses both the Victorian and Edwardian eras, two periods often yoked together in critical thinking about the supernatural.[4] Yet this important transitional period from 1900 to the outbreak of the First World War was a time when the fascination with the supernatural and the uncanny, with lost worlds, weird creatures and spiritualist communications, flourished. As Victoria Margree has argued, for early twentieth-century writers:

the ghost story ... is Janus-faced, looking backwards to the nineteenth century with a sense that its demise may have been announced prematurely, while also participating in the modernist perception that real and significant changes, in both social environment and human knowledge, require the development of new ways of representing selfhood in fiction.[5]

While the dawn of the new century was heralded with predictable narratives of progress and modernity, this was undercut by images of degeneration and poverty, the decline of the British Empire, fears over the effects of mass urbanisation and technological advance, and uncertainties about the future. According to Jonathan Wild, 'the outside world reflected in the texts of this decade was a decidedly unsettled one', poised as it was between war in South Africa and the anticipation of the First World War; the death of Victoria coincided with cultural innovation and new beginnings but also contributed to the disillusionment that contributed to 'the era's restless character'.[6] In the so-called 'golden age', the greater ease of transnational exchanges also facilitated the development of new trends in Gothic, including science fiction, the weird, fairy tales and the fantastic.

Origins and Evolution of the Edwardian Supernatural

The Edwardian era is often associated with the ghost stories of M. R. James, Algernon Blackwood and William Hope Hodgson, whose early forays into the weird anticipated the popularity of H. P. Lovecraft and the American pulp magazine *Weird Tales* from the 1920s onwards. The possible meanings of the weird are useful to consider in relation to framings of the supernatural in this period, an indication of the future direction of Gothic fiction after the First World War. In *The Modern Weird Tale* (2001), S. T. Joshi defines weird writing, post-Lovecraft, not only in relation to horrific scenarios and tropes such as the vampire, the ghost, the reanimated corpse and the haunted house, but also in relation to the fear produced by the 'intrusion of the weird into the mundane world, with an emphasis on indirection and suggestion'.[7] Strangeness might take the form of a spectrum of supernatural creatures, from animal/human hybrids to tentacled monsters and unknown 'things': in 'Oh, Whistle and I'll Come to You, My Lad' (1904), one of M. R. James's best-known stories, the occupant of the hotel room by the beach is terrified by the intangibility lurking beneath the bed linen, signifying a potential resurgence of ancient evil. The strange is also manifested in animated, 'possessed' objects (often brought across geographical borders) and 'impossible' spaces, such as the afterlife or disappearing villages. In his discussion of the 'fugitive category' of weird fiction, Roger Luckhurst dates its origins in the turn of the twentieth century, associated with the Decadent movement and the development of Edwardian horror fiction; he suggests that weirdness can be as much about waywardness as about horror.[8] Women's contributions to the mode, argues Melissa Edmundson, 'complicate and expand more traditional notions of the Victorian supernatural ... [as] the spectres themselves have become more varied as a result of "living" in the modern world'.[9] The weird tale's development between the 1890s and the 1920s and this new variability of the spectral paved the way for new manifestations of the ghostly.

Examples of 'plant horror', 'an absolute rupture of the known' so significant in mid-twentieth-century science fiction and film,[10] date back to the mad botanist stories of H. G. Wells such as 'The Flowering of the Strange Orchid' (1894), and constitute a key strand of the weird tradition. Emily Alder argues that by the *fin de siècle*, 'contemporary sciences and their borderlands had helped to stimulate a particular variety of speculative fiction', which 'sometimes gets lost in the gaps between critical and generic categories'.[11] One of Algernon Blackwood's best-known weird tales is 'The Willows' (1907), in which the 'wild beauty' of the willows 'watching, waiting, listening', quickly becomes suffocating and alarming for two male travellers who spend a terrifying night on a remote island in the Danube. Humanity is dwarfed in the face of the 'alien' nature of the malevolent trees:

> their serried ranks, growing everywhere darker about me as the shadows deepened, moving furiously yet softly in the wind, woke in me the curious and unwelcome suggestion that we had trespassed here upon the borders of an alien world, a world where we were intruders ... *The willows were against us* ... What, I thought, if, after all, these crouching willows proved to be alive, if suddenly they should rise up, like a swarm of living creatures, marshalled by the gods whose territory we had invaded.[12]

This subversion of the invasion narrative shows the trees in their 'masses' huddled together, waiting to strike on the lonely island. David Punter has discussed this story in relation to the ecogothic and the notion of 'becoming-forest', linking the terrifying isolation of the uninhabited island to 'a momentary defeat for the forces of ceaseless imperialistic exploration: if the impetus behind such forces is to wipe out the right of nature to hold its own secrets'.[13] He writes of 'the pressure of the non-human, the "animal", on the surface of civilization'.[14] Alder reads the story in terms of 'quantum weird', in which 'observable reality becomes revealed as something different to what it had been', raising the possibilities of a fourth dimension and 'requiring acceptance of an entirely different conception of time, space, and matter'.[15] Work on the ecogothic has highlighted the significance of writers such as Blackwood and Wells to understandings of the Otherness of nature: 'EcoGothic investigation is well placed to examine the fear as well as the unpredictability presented by the strangeness of garden spaces ... where agency slips away into fairies, or flowers, or is undermined by the overwhelming presence of more-than-human energy in ancient orchards, trees and even water.'[16] The male narrator's fear of the trees coming to life as if commanded by an alien force anticipates John Wyndham's post-apocalyptic novel *The Day of the Triffids* (1951).

New technologies for communication and mobility, pitting the ostensibly 'old' and unknown against new ways of communicating and traversing space, channel, invite and uncannily imitate the supernatural in Edwardian fiction. 'If modern life is haunted', Fred Botting argues, 'its phantoms are not only figures of memory, guilt or indebtedness that return from the past, they are figures, fragmentary, insubstantial, fleeting, for the present's dislocation in time, space and consciousness from itself.'[17] Violet Hunt's story 'The Telegram' in *Tales of the Uneasy* (1911) achieves 'an atmosphere of the macabre and the unsettling', through the spectre's ability to reach the home of his object of desire quicker than the telegram warning of his imminent death.[18] Taking a cab ride without paying the fare, the attentive Everard Jenkins enjoys a last evening with Alice Damer before her horrifying realisation on the following day that she has 'kiss[ed] a dead man!'[19] The motorcar, 'the embodiment of Edwardian technological modernity' with its 'seductive and dangerous appeal',[20] also results in stories in which the exhilarating freedoms of the open road disintegrate into cultural anxieties about machinery out of human control.

A dark twist on the phantom coaches and train wrecks of Victorian ghost fiction, the spectral aftermath of the car crash responds to fears about the dangers of speed in new ways. Stories such as E. Nesbit's 'The Violet Car' (1910), in which a driverless phantom car haunts the landscape where a young girl was involved in a fatal hit-and-run, and Arthur Conan Doyle's 'How it Happened' (1917), in which master and chauffeur smash into the gates of a country house, may seem to show a nervous retreat from the modern. Yet Nesbit's story shows motors as both 'mov[ing] like magic' and malevolent, whereas Doyle's narrative positions the uncomprehending motorist as 'a man in a dream', only able to share the news of the 'awful smash' with a spectre.[21] This uncanny encounter with the ghost of a friend who died in the Boer War is explained by his death, positioning the dead motorist side by side with the dead soldier, both noble victims and men lost in their generation. Blackwood's chilling variation on the crash narrative, 'Transition' (1913), sees a father fatally injured on the busy London streets by a motor vehicle, described as 'a Monster ... with eyes of blazing fire'; on his spectral return to the family home bearing his Christmas gifts, he has become invisible and unheard.[22] Stories of 'supernatural invisibility', as Scarborough attests, might have 'a chilling horror more intense than that of most ghostly tales',[23] even more chilling when written from the spectral point of view. 'Spectral mobility' suggests ghosts moving 'across boundaries, between times and places'.[24] Imagining the moment of death as a painless 'transition' into another realm, these ghosts seem strangely unaware of their deaths and bemused by their failure to communicate with the living. This painless uncertainty may negate horrific deaths by war and disease but also signals the desire for spiritual communication as a form of consolation. Technology becomes destructively uncontrollable, traumatic and inadequate in these exposés of dark modernity.

The increased popularity of spiritualism, read in tandem with developments in psychoanalysis, constitutes a key context for the Edwardian supernatural. The Society for Psychical Research (SPR), established in 1882 to investigate paranormal phenomena, remained active in the new century, with members including psychologists, philosophers and novelists such as Arthur Conan Doyle and May Sinclair. The Society published reports on haunted houses, hallucinations, telepathy and dreams, though Shane McCorristine claims that the conclusions of its Census of Hallucinations (1894) were indeterminate, rather like the modern ghost story itself.[25] To be haunted is not always a consequence of seeing a ghost; as Andrew Smith writes in relation to the uncanniness of early twentieth-century ghost stories, they are 'not necessarily specifically about ghosts in any conventional sense' but may explore other images of haunting, fear and Gothic fragmentation.[26] In his essay 'The Uncanny' (1919), Sigmund Freud equates ghostliness with the 'mysterious', the 'secret' and the 'eerie', as well as with dead bodies and spiritualism, evoking a continuum between the spectral and what is hidden, strange, unsettling or out of place.[27] Margree identifies 'the psychological ghost story' as a key innovation of the early twentieth century, when writers 'negotiat[ed] modernist ideas about the (un)knowability of the psychological self'. Attention is drawn to 'what the ghosts – whether "real" or imagined by protagonists – reveal about the mental and emotional conflicts of the ghost-seers'.[28] In the forward-looking Preface to her collection *Hauntings: Fantastic Stories* (1890), Vernon Lee had already argued for the mysteriousness of the modern supernatural in sceptical times. Distancing her work from the evidence-based testimonies of the

SPR, Lee instead celebrates the 'spurious' ghosts who 'haunted certain brains', even as she locates the mysterious in 'the weird places we have seen, the strange stories we have heard'.[29] Lee's neglected collection *Pope Jacynth and other Fantastic Tales* (1904) reprints her dark fairy tale 'Prince Alberic and the Snake Lady' from 1896 alongside new stories such as 'The Lady and Death' and 'A Wedding Chest'. These strange stories about the medieval past, Faustian pacts and the violation of women's doll-like bodies address fears of feminine evil and sacred/dangerous motherhood. As Patricia Pulham has argued, in Lee's fantastic tales the past may operate as a 'safe space' of fluid sexuality and the return to the maternal body, despite the patriarchal violence it encodes.[30] By 1917, in *The Supernatural in Modern English Fiction*, Dorothy Scarborough drew on psychoanalytic terminology to confirm that 'subjective ghosts are legion in modern fiction ... evoked by the mental state of the percipients', particularly in the case of 'the mind rendered morbid by grief or remorse'.[31] Her genealogy of the ghostly recognised that objective ghosts, 'more alive than they used to be', were still very numerous, 'impressive as haunters' due to their plausibility and corporeality.[32] The psychological ghost story was a significant sign of the times.

Science, Spiritualism and the Weird: Arthur Conan Doyle and E. Nesbit

In the pages of the widely read *Strand Magazine*, established in 1891, supernatural stories shared space with topical articles on motoring, the empire, science, global travel, spiritualism and espionage – ostensibly a modern worldview but one always in dialogue with the legacies of Victorianism. Enjoying a broad readership in the early twentieth century, *The Strand* also published fiction by Richard Marsh, H. G. Wells and E. Nesbit. As one of the star contributors, Arthur Conan Doyle contributed supernatural fiction as well as his better-known crime stories. Darryl Jones has noted that a 'tension between materialism and metaphysics is ... a characteristic of the Victorian and Edwardian supernatural tale' evident in Doyle's writing.[33] New communications technology, transport systems, advances in biology and photographic reproductions all featured in the striking illustrations of the journal, showing the uncanniness of modern life.

The resurgence of interest in spiritualism at the *fin de siècle*, to be intensified in the war years, meant that séance stories became more popular. Lettice Galbraith's 'In the Séance Room' (1893), D. H. Lawrence's 'Glad

Ghosts' (1926) and Agatha Christie's 'The Last Séance' (1926) are some of the best examples of this vogue for summoning the dead to the middle-class drawing room. Aimed at 'sceptical readers' with an interest in 'the lost margin between science and the séance', according to Kevin Mills, Doyle's stories increasingly show his interest in the ambiguities of spiritualism, the occult and 'psychic revelation'.[34] His first story to directly address the 'elusive phenomena' of spiritualism, tellingly titled 'Playing with Fire' (1900), frames the séance in terms of fraudulence and experimentation.[35] Markham, the narrator, a 'man about town, anxious to be in the swim of every fresh movement', finds himself delighted by 'the soothing atmosphere of the séance with the darkened lights', where the absolute blackness of the room is contrasted to the sounds of the modern city outside the window, the barking dog, the cab with its bright lights.[36] The distancing from the civilised world is key to the supernatural encounter: 'what a gap we were bridging, the half-raised veil of the eternal on the one side and the cabs of London on the other'.[37] The supernatural appearance is preceded by the group's admiration of the paintings of mythical monsters and imaginary creatures. The story also borrows from Gothic narratives of the monstrous animal and the abhuman, as the creature called up by Mrs Delamere, the 'senseless' medium, appears to be a very material unicorn who blunders around the middle-class drawing room. The Frenchman who joins their circle might claim that 'when you imagine a thing you make a thing', yet the dark imaginings of the séance exceed expectations.[38] The soothingly luminous fog and the dark, smoky substance drifting from the table give way to the weird: '[s]omething hurtled against us in the darkness, rearing, stamping, smashing, springing, snorting ... rushing with horrible energy from one corner of the room to another'.[39] Without their matches and their technological power, the men scream in terror. In his research into apparitions and telepathy in the early twentieth century, Frank Podmore from the SPR acknowledged that 'the unique atmosphere of the spiritualist séance – the darkness, anticipation and ruses of the participants – could contribute to unconscious mal-observation and sensory hallucination among elite scientific observers'.[40] Ending with a plea to *Strand* readers, 'perhaps you may know more than we do of such occult matters, and can inform us of some similar occurrence', Doyle's story is also of its time in presenting itself as a half-disbelieving testimony of either a hoax or an inexplicable 'terrible experience'.[41]

Sharing characteristics with *fin de siècle* science fiction, Doyle's story 'The Terror of Blue John Gap' (1910) opens with the reported death of Dr James Hardcastle in 1908, before reproducing his diary entries of a terrifying journey into a Derbyshire mine and its adjacent caves from which 'you may never make your way back to the daylight again'.[42] Ridiculing local superstitions and 'weird beliefs', the doctor as the symbol of 'modern science' prefers to attribute inexplicable noises, lost sheep and pools of blood to human agency and to explain the distant roaring in terms of 'the strange reverberations which come out of an underground water system running amidst the chasms of a lime-stone formation'.[43] Scientific interest in the valuable purple minerals which give the mine its name is soon superseded by the horror of the unknown thing, the 'Terror', the 'Creature' whose unearthly cries frighten the locals. With echoes of H. G. Wells's scientist disorientated in an alien world in *The Time Machine* (1895), the doctor, 'utterly lost', finds himself unable to strike a wet match after a fall and is forced to confront what lurks in the 'absolute darkness'.[44] Subject to the invisible supernatural, the scientist senses the presence of an unseen and enormous creature and hears it drinking, 'Could it indeed be possible that some nameless thing, some dreadful presence, was lurking down yonder?'[45] The 'inconceivable monster, something utterly unearthly and dreadful', threatens 'modern science' – the potential explanation of hallucination is raised but dismissed, as 'the combat between my reason, which told me that such things could not be, and my senses, which told me that they were, raged within me'.[46] In the unmapped space of 'the horrible cavern on the hill' the unknown terror lurks – perhaps a troglodyte, or connected to 'the old world legends of dragons and other monsters'.[47] Fearing that his fellow doctor Armitage has been carried off into 'the recesses of the mountains', Hardcastle ruminates, '[w]hat an inconceivable fate for a civilized Englishman of the twentieth century!'[48] Biological explanations that 'the monstrous beast' with its fangs and huge bulb-like eyes, seemingly activated by 'the old primeval hunting-spirit', might be an old cave-bear modified by the new environment are suggestive of the powers of the past which mere modernity cannot kill.[49]

Also influenced by the unnatural terrors of the night, E. Nesbit's contributions to *The Strand* address many of the same concerns as Doyle's stories, mocking Victorian ghost story conventions as obsolete in the modern age while failing to reconcile the clash between science and spiritualism. Nesbit was also known in this period as a writer of children's fantasy fiction, including dark and disturbing fairy tales such as 'Melisande' (1901), in which the hair of the Rapunzelesque heroine grows 'at a frightful rate', filling her palace bedroom each night as she sleeps.[50] Inflected with the 'magic' of enchantment, her graphic Edwardian stories, some included in her collection *Fear* (1910), update her more traditional 1890s narratives of haunted portraits and phantom bridegrooms to feature fake ghosts, evil scientists, the shadows of suburbia and unearthly catacombs. They are often, like Doyle's, framed by a group of men expressing their disbelief in the supernatural before being forced to acknowledge the inexplicable. In 'Number 17', the commercial traveller tells the listening group in the hotel, 'We know nowadays, what with the advance of science and all that sort of thing, we know there aren't any such things as ghosts. They're hallucinations; that's what they are – hallucinations.'[51]

In 'The Power of Darkness' the two men hiding in the pitch-black Paris waxwork museum feel haunted by the half-alive exhibits; when one pretends to be an exhibit uncannily moving, the other finds 'the darkness fitted in round him very closely', as if buried alive.[52] Nesbit's foray into plant horror, 'The Pavilion' (1915), shows the 'absolute alterity' of plants, which 'menace with their wild, purposeless growth'.[53] The men at a country house party who ridicule the supernatural become victims when dared to sleep in the haunted pavilion. Built on the site of a Tudor laboratory, the pavilion acts as a host for a dangerous Virginia creeper that grows magically at night, and 'wet, sticky green stuff' becomes entangled around the dead bodies of those who sleep there.[54] The latest victim is found with 'thick twining tendrils ... about his wrists and throat', as 'a wave of green seemed to have swept from the [closed] window'; the gardener classifies these happenings as 'impossible things'.[55] In Nesbit's 'mock-Gothic' story 'The Haunted House' (1913), a bored young man recently returned to England answers an advertisement headed 'A Haunted House. Advertiser is anxious to have phenomena investigated. Any properly-accredited investigator will be given full facilities.'[56] This investigation is, however, discovered to be a front for dangerous scientific experiments, as in Nesbit's 'The Three Drugs' (1908), which sees a feverishly ambitious doctor trying to access immortality and make 'splendid superhuman life' via a new mix of chemicals.[57] Scientific myths of control are found wanting; as Alder notes, 'the ecstasy of weird experience may manifest as horror as easily as wonder'.[58] With their dark aesthetic, fascination with the limits of science and strange impossibilities, Nesbit's stories about the power of darkness and the unknown clearly border on the weird.

Haunted Geographies and the Spectre of Empire: Henry James and Alice Perrin

Early twentieth-century writers often sought to go 'beyond the haunted house', refashioning and in some instances rejecting the popular nineteenth-century Gothic trope of the domestic space troubled by the vengeful ancestral spectre.[59] Edwardian haunted geographies reflect new ways of thinking about home and family, the city and liminal space. 'The spook of to-day', according to Scarborough, 'may have a local habitation but he isn't obliged to stay there ... the modern ghost has power over certain localities rather than mere houses or apartments.'[60] However, it is not hard to find stories that borrow all the conventions of the Victorian haunted house narrative, including ancestral portraits, lost letters and unresolved crimes. As Jeffrey Weinstock notes, the 'scare tactics' of turn-of-the-century American supernatural fiction are often related to 'the uncanniness of domestic space', as 'what haunts is space itself – space that is unstable, space that is inconsistent, space that is ... "queer"'.[61] Henry James's playful story 'The Jolly Corner' (1908) shows the jaded socialite Spencer Brydon returning to his New York childhood home from a thirty-year exile in Europe in order to hunt down his alter ego, or what he might have become had he stayed in the US. The story is as much about the uncanniness of New York, now replete with skyscrapers, 'the newnesses, the queernesses', as it is about the abandoned property; for James, 'the modern, the monstrous' become two sides of the same coin.[62] The thrill of apprehending his lost self, 'the strangest, the most joyous ... duplication of consciousness', is coupled with a dread of what might have been; the 'spectral yet human' entity lurking in the house in his 'queer actuality of evening-dress' is both his 'other self' and 'the horror within him', with no explanation given for the loss of two fingers on one hand 'reduced to stumps, as if accidentally shot away'.[63] A number of Edith Wharton's ghost stories of this period, such as 'Afterward' (1910) and 'Kerfol' (1916) (and a little later, 'Mr Jones' [1928] with its phantom butler), begin with the purchasing or inheriting of old European houses, which then either reveal buried histories of persecuted women or show that investment in the old offers no solace from more haunting modern concerns such as the shadows of war. Set in Brittany, 'Kerfol' opens with an ambiguously gendered narrator experiencing 'the sheer weight of many associated lives and deaths which give a majesty to old houses', while succumbing to 'the influence of the place', an eerily silent, tomb-like and deserted spot evoking the devastation of war-torn France.[64] Such stories admit the calling up of what is repressed for their ghost-seers, as well as evoking the queer emptinesses and instabilities of both the old house and the modern dwelling.

In contrast, the supernatural is enmeshed with local superstitions and religious practices, as well as the tensions of empire, in the stories of Anglo-Indian author Alice Perrin. Resident in India as an engineer's wife from 1886 to 1902, during the period of the British Raj, Perrin wrote stories of haunted Indian bungalows and telepathic communication from ships, as the long sea voyages and global travel facilitated by the colonialist enterprise inspired new accounts of haunted space. Her collection *East of Suez* (1901), which one reviewer called a 'creepy, clever volume',[65] explores spiritual connections between survivors and those on the brink of death, with the supernatural manifested in uncanny dreams and echoes, disturbing animals that invade the home, and the crying of dead children. In 'An Eastern Echo' the English wife is jolted back in time to a chaotic scene at an Islamic festival in India where she shared a potentially erotic moment with Somerton, a man who was not her *fiancé*. Her dream-like repetition of the phrase, 'Hasan! Husain!' in her English garden occurs simultaneously with Somerton's death in a riot at the same festival two years after their interaction, an example of a 'crisis apparition', when a person's spirit appears before a loved one at the moment of their death.[66] Margree interprets this as a comforting idea for those 'separated by continents', suggesting that 'spiritual proximity persisted between loved ones even when separated by great geographical distance'.[67] It also reinforces the echoes of the East, as the English garden cannot remain disconnected from the noise and violence of the Indian festival; events in India haunt and disrupt the English family. Mrs Sinclair's joy in her motherhood is shadowed by 'the vague suspicion of something missed and unattainable . . . the undefined vibration of a regretful memory', where the indeterminacy of the 'vibration' signals what is left behind in the Indian past, 'the blinding glare of dust and heat'.[68]

The threat of violence from the colonialist past to the Anglo-Indian community can be figured through weird creatures. While exemplifying racist attitudes in some of Perrin's descriptions of Indian practices, 'The Biscobra' also foreshadows the English wife's sacrifice to her fears of the colonial Other. On arrival at her remote bungalow, with its 'uncompromising furniture', down 'a bare length of road devoid of trees', the pregnant Mrs Krey is frightened by the strangeness of India.[69] When looking at the tiny temple behind 'thick whispering leaves', which contains 'a strange, many-limbed idol smeared with red paste', she thinks 'of blood, and the Mutiny, and hideous tales of human sacrifice', equating the unknown with a mythologised threat to English women.[70] Their move to another, more 'suitable' yet 'dilapidated' dwelling, which 'had not been occupied very lately', might seem a sign of 'better times', but it is tempered by Mrs Krey's 'dread' of animals that infest the home.[71] Fearful of being left alone with the Indian bearer, or servant, Beni, she is then terrified when the 'green, scaly body' of a large biscobra, a lizard with a snake-like head, falls heavily on her shoulder, where 'it hung for one hideous second'.[72] Both hysterical wife and her newborn child die, prey to fears of Indian Otherness as figured through the animal. After their deaths the deserted bungalow is 'oppressive', 'crowded with bitter memories'.[73] Secretly visiting the moonlit cemetery where the two are buried, the bereaved husband discovers that Beni is feeding milk to a biscobra living in the grave. After Mr Krey smashes the animal's head in, with a 'cry of horror, rage and madness', the old bearer collapses lifeless, proclaiming, 'thou hast slain the soul of the child'.[74] The horror is anchored in the possible proximity between the lost Anglo-Indian 'babba' and the monstrous animal now associated with the dusty cemetery and the gaping hole next to the family grave.

Like many other women writers of the period, Perrin was also interested in domestic dynamics and mistress–servant hierarchies, examining a set of power relations inflected by race and class as well as gender. American writers such as Edith Wharton and Josephine Daskam Bacon made the figure of the servant, a staple of the Victorian ghost story, newly ominous. In Wharton's fiction dead staff continue to fulfil their duties. Haunting the servants' corridor, the automaton-like dead maid in 'The Lady's Maid's Bell' (1902) jealously guards the secrets of the house including transgressive mistress–servant intimacies. The uncertain racial identity of the new lady's maid in this story may suggest further domestic conflicts. In Bacon's disturbing story 'The Unburied' from her collection *The Strange Cases of Dr. Stanchon* (1913), the 'cursed' house, which has something 'slimy' and 'evil' at its core, appears to unleash a transgressive sexuality in its female inhabitants, who elope with married men or defy their masters.[75] This curse has particular impact on the 'wayward' black servant Mynie, whose 'self-confident' defiance of the doctor narrator and witch-like 'incantation' appear rotten and degenerate: 'I saw that girl disintegrate, decay, turn fungoid under my eyes – ugh!'[76] In the final pages, the Catholic priest acts as exorcist by burning the 'wickedest' letters from a past inhabitant hidden in the hearth in the women's bedroom.[77] Weinstock reads the story in terms of 'the repressive policing of female sexuality' to counter the panic caused by excessive desire but has little to say about the key roles of servants.[78] The 'slimy' and shocking sexual content of the letters constitutes the 'unburied' spectral legacy: '*here in the room where I wrote them, they shall live after I am gone*' – perhaps a past servant effectively buried alive for her shame.[79]

Perrin's servant story 'Chunia, Ayah' focuses on the haunted 'ayah' or nurse, traumatised by the sudden death of the young girl she cares for. The grey-haired spinster narrator, won over by the happy nature of her friend Mary's child, is also horrified by this death. The ghostly wailing child is ambiguously explained in terms of the antagonism and violence of the memsahib towards her 'sullen', 'bad-tempered' servant with what the white women call 'the face of a devil'.[80] The disembodied crying of the dead female baby, the 'high beseeching wail ... the awful pleading and despair' invites another mourning of a lost 'babba' by the ayah, who here operates as the main ghost-seer.[81] The spinster evokes other lost children by assuming that the despairing voice is that of 'some native baby ... calling hopelessly for its mother'.[82] Here the servant is the agent of death (or so it seems from Chunia's hysterical confession), yet she also evokes sympathy for her lack of agency; she is passed between the white women by Mary's absent husband, who 'beg[s] me to take the woman into my service'.[83] It is left open as to whether the haunting symbolises the 'old antipathy' of the Anglo-Indian women or the plight of lost Indian children, with no final comment on the 'saddening' sight of the mad imprisoned ayah, singing a lullaby to an 'imaginary baby'.[84] In all these stories transgressive female servants are haunted or cursed by the past histories of women, figures of a localised evil which threatens their horrified white superiors.

From haunted Indian bungalows to monstrous, noiseless cars, from dangerously alive plants to mythical creatures called up in a London séance, the Edwardian supernatural takes a myriad of forms. The modern ghost is no longer the traditional Victorian spectre, seeking retribution in the ancestral home, but a more psychological entity, nebulous, invisible, waiting in the darkness beyond the glare of electric lights. In his 1929 essay M. R. James noted the effectiveness of 'modern' ghost stories where 'the setting and the personages are those of the writer's own day',[85] a contemporaneity evident in stories by Doyle, Nesbit, Henry James and Perrin. Yet on the cusp of the First World War, the supernatural was also very much in intersection with the weird and with new forms of horror. Like the nameless thing that emerges from the dangerous gap in the Blue John Cavern, it could be a hallucination, a mockery of scientific progress, or a throwback to an earlier time made monstrous through mutation. 'To define the unease evoked by the weird', argues Luckhurst, 'requires new terminologies beyond the domesticated uncanny.'[86] The uneasy stories discussed here, and the many others ripe for discovery, all invite new readings and new ways of thinking about what it meant to be haunted in early twentieth-century Gothic.

Key Texts

Arthur Conan Doyle, *The Hound of the Baskervilles* (1901–02). On the border between the ghost story and crime fiction, this creepy Sherlock Holmes case set in Baskerville Hall on the eerie edge of Dartmoor uses Gothic tropes such as ancestral portraits, disguised identities and a mysterious ghostly hound to symbolise degeneration and biological decline.

Mary E. Wilkins Freeman, *The Wind in the Rose-Bush and other Stories of the Supernatural* (1903). An American ghost story collection that privileges the female perspective, comprising tales of child abuse, haunted objects and single women confined by ritualistic traditions in a New England setting.

Gaston Leroux, *Le Fantôme de L'Opéra* (*The Phantom of the Opera*, 1910). In this French supernatural novel, the subterranean world of the Paris Opera is haunted by the disfigured Phantom, a deceptively 'fake' ghost who figures urban decay and sexual fluidity.

Marie Belloc Lowndes, 'The Lodger' (1911). Based on the Ripper crimes of the late 1880s and adapted as one of Alfred Hitchcock's first silent films in 1927, this atmospheric story set in a disturbingly foggy London focuses on a landlady haunted by the sinister behaviour of her new lodger.

Alice and Claude Askew, *Aylmer Vance: Ghost-Seer* (1914). This story sequence by a prolific husband-and-wife duo reprises the detective as ghost-seer and clairvoyant, investigating poltergeists, vampires and demonic possession.

Melissa Edmundson (ed.), *Women's Weird 2: More Strange Stories by Women, 1891–1937* (2020). This anthology shows not only the versatility of 'women's weird' but its global significance and variations. It reprints material from the USA, Canada, New Zealand, India and Australia, including stories by Barbara Baynton, Katherine Mansfield, Sarah Orne Jewett and Bithia Mary Croker.

Further Critical Reading

Brewster, Scott, and Luke Thurston (eds), *The Routledge Handbook to the Ghost Story* (2018). A comprehensive survey of the ghost story as a dynamic, transnational mode, with chapters on individual authors and theoretical approaches, including wide-ranging discussions of 'Haunted Nations' and 'Haunted Sites'.

Downey, Dara, *American Women's Ghost Stories in the Gilded Age* (2014). A fascinating account of American women writers' gendering of the supernatural at the turn of the century, which discusses Charlotte Perkins Gilman, Mary E. Wilkins Freeman and Madeline Yale Wynne.

Hay, Simon, *A History of the Modern British Ghost Story* (2011). This genealogy foregrounds class, race and trauma in the evolution of the ghost story, with excellent chapters on 'golden age' stories and empire and the Gothic.

Bibliography

Alder, Emily, *Weird Fiction and Science at the Fin de Siècle* (Basingstoke: Palgrave, 2020).

Bacon, Josephine Daskam, *The Strange Cases of Dr Stanchon* (New York: D. Appleton & Co., 1913).

Blackwood, Algernon, 'Transition', in Tanya Kirk (ed.), *Chill Tidings: Dark Tales of the Christmas Season* (London: British Library, 2020), pp. 73–82.
Blackwood, Algernon, 'The Willows', in D. Thin (ed.), *Shadows of Carcosa: Tales of Cosmic Horror by Lovecraft, Chambers, Machen, Poe and other Masters of the Weird* (New York: New York Review of Books, 2002), pp. 179–235.
Botting, Fred, *Gothic* (Abingdon: Routledge, 2004).
Brewster, Scott, and Luke Thurston (eds), *The Routledge Handbook to the Ghost Story* (Abingdon: Routledge, 2018).
Downey, Dara, *American Women's Ghost Stories in the Gilded Age* (Basingstoke: Palgrave, 2014).
Doyle, Arthur Conan, *Gothic Tales*, ed. Darryl Jones (Oxford: Oxford University Press, 2016).
Edmundson, Melissa, 'Introduction', in Melissa Edmundson (ed.), *Women's Weird 2: Strange Stories by Women, 1891–1937* (Bath: Handheld Press, 2020), pp. vii–xxv.
Edney, Sue (ed.), *Eco-Gothic Gardens in the Long Nineteenth Century: Phantoms, Fantasy and Uncanny Flowers* (Manchester: Manchester University Press, 2020).
Freud, Sigmund, 'The Uncanny' [1919], in *The Uncanny*, trans. David McClintock (Harmondsworth: Penguin, 2003), pp. 121–62.
Harrington, Ralph, 'Transport and Trauma: Uncanny Modernities', in Scott Brewster and Luke Thurston (eds), *The Routledge Handbook to the Ghost Story* (Abingdon: Routledge, 2018), pp. 301–11.
Hay, Simon, *A History of the Modern Ghost Story* (Basingstoke: Palgrave, 2011).
Heholt, Ruth, 'Introduction: Haunted Men: Masculinity in the Ghost Stories of the Victorian and Edwardian Eras', *Victoriographies*, 4.1, 2014, pp. 1–4.
Hogle, Jerrold E., 'Introduction: Modernity and the Proliferation of the Gothic', in Jerrold E. Hogle (ed.), *The Cambridge Companion to the Modern Gothic* (Cambridge: Cambridge University Press, 2014), pp. 3–19.
Hunt, Violet, 'The Telegram', in Elizabeth Dearnley (ed.), *Into the London Fog: Eerie Tales of the Weird City* (London: British Library, 2020), pp. 23–32.
James, Henry, 'The Jolly Corner', in D. Thin (ed.), *Shadows of Carcosa: Tales of Cosmic Horror by Lovecraft, Chambers, Machen, Poe and other Masters of the Weird* (New York: New York Review of Books, 2002), pp. 237–76.
James, M. R., 'Some Remarks on Ghost Stories', *Bookman*, 71, 1929, pp. 169–75.
Joshi, S. T., *The Modern Weird Tale* (Jefferson, NC: McFarland, 2001).
Keetley, Dawn, and Angela Tenga (eds), *Plant Horror: Approaches to the Monstrous Vegetal in Fiction and Film* (Basingstoke: Palgrave, 2016).
Lee, Vernon [1890], *Hauntings and Other Fantastic Tales*, ed. Catherine Maxwell and Patricia Pulham (Peterborough, Ont.: Broadview Press, 2006).
Liggins, Emma, 'Beyond the Haunted House? Modernist Women's Ghost Stories and the Troubling of Modernity', in Emma Young and James Bailey (eds), *British Women Short Story Writers: The New Woman to Now* (Edinburgh: Edinburgh University Press, 2015), pp. 32–49.
Luckhurst, Roger, 'The Weird: A Dis/orientation', *Textual Practice*, 31.6, 2017, pp. 1041–61.

Margree, Victoria, *British Women's Short Supernatural Fiction, 1860–1930* (Basingstoke: Palgrave, 2019).

McCorristine, Shane, *Spectres of the Self: Thinking about Ghosts and Ghost-Seeing in England, 1750–1920* (Cambridge: Cambridge University Press, 2010).

Mills, Kevin, 'Conan Doyle's Sceptical Reader: Ghost Stories, Science and Spiritualism', in Scott Brewster and Luke Thurston (eds), *The Routledge Handbook to the Ghost Story* (Abingdon: Routledge, 2018), pp. 124–33.

Nesbit, E., 'Melisande', in *Nine Unlikely Tales* (London: Ernest Benn, 1901), pp. 159–92.

Nesbit, E., *The Power of Darkness: Tales of Terror*, ed. David Stuart Davies (Ware: Wordsworth, 2006).

Perrin, Alice, *East of Suez* [1901], ed. Melissa Edmundson Makala (Brighton: Victorian Secrets, 2011).

Pulham, Patricia, *Art and the Transitional Object in Vernon Lee's Supernatural Tales* (Burlington, VT: Ashgate, 2008).

Punter, David, 'Algernon Blackwood: Nature and Spirit', in Andrew Smith and William Hughes (eds), *Eco-Gothic* (Manchester: Manchester University Press, 2013), pp. 44–57.

Scarborough, Dorothy, *The Supernatural in Modern English Fiction* (New York: Knickerbocker Press, 1917).

Smith, Andrew, *The Ghost Story, 1840–1920* (Manchester: Manchester University Press, 2010).

Weinstock, Jeffrey Andrew, *Scare Tactics: Supernatural Fiction by American Women* (New York: Fordham University Press, 2008).

Wharton, Edith, *Ghost Stories*, ed. David Stuart Davies (Ware: Wordsworth, 2009).

Wild, Jonathan, *Literature of the 1900s: The Great Edwardian Emporium* (Edinburgh: Edinburgh University Press, 2017).

Notes

1. James, 'Some Remarks', pp. 169, 173.
2. Ibid., p. 174.
3. Hogle, 'Introduction', p. 7.
4. Heholt, 'Introduction: Haunted Men', p. 1.
5. Margree, *British Women's Short Supernatural Fiction*, p. 185.
6. Wild, *Literature of the 1900s*, pp. 4, 5.
7. Joshi, *The Modern Weird Tale*, p. 3.
8. Luckhurst, 'The Weird: A Dis/orientation', pp. 1047, 1050.
9. Edmundson, 'Introduction', p. x.
10. Keetley and Tenga, *Plant Horror*, p. v.
11. Alder, *Weird Fiction*, p. 3.
12. Blackwood, 'The Willows', pp. 187, 194, 195.
13. Punter, 'Algernon Blackwood', pp. 48, 49.
14. Ibid., p. 53.
15. Alder, *Weird Fiction*, p. 223.

16. Edney, 'Introduction', *Eco-Gothic Gardens*, p. 5.
17. Botting, *Gothic*, p. 154.
18. Margree, *British Women's Short Supernatural Fiction*, p. 171.
19. Hunt, 'The Telegram', p. 51.
20. Wild, *Literature of the 1900s*, pp. 5, 128.
21. Nesbit, 'The Violet Car', in *The Power of Darkness*, p. 64; Doyle, 'How it Happened', in *Gothic Tales*, p. 453.
22. Blackwood, 'Transition', p. 77.
23. Scarborough, *The Supernatural*, p. 96.
24. Harrington, 'Transport and Trauma', p. 303.
25. McCorristine, *Spectres of the Self*, p. 23.
26. Smith, *The Ghost Story*, pp. 170, 183.
27. Freud, 'The Uncanny', pp. 126, 130–1.
28. Margree, *British Women's Short Supernatural Fiction*, pp. 148, 149.
29. Lee, 'Preface', in *Hauntings*, p. 4.
30. Pulham, *Art and the Transitional Object*, p. 88.
31. Scarborough, *The Supernatural*, p. 84.
32. Ibid., pp. 86, 91.
33. Jones, 'Introduction', in Doyle, *Gothic Tales*, p. xxx.
34. Mills, 'Conan Doyle's Sceptical Reader', pp. 133, 132.
35. Doyle, 'Playing with Fire', in *Gothic Tales*, p. 384.
36. Ibid., p. 384.
37. Ibid., p. 389.
38. Ibid., p. 387.
39. Ibid., pp. 394–5.
40. McCorristine, *Spectres of the Self*, pp. 207–8.
41. Doyle, 'Playing with Fire', p. 396.
42. Doyle, 'The Terror of Blue John Gap', in *Gothic Tales*, p. 431.
43. Ibid., pp. 431, 432.
44. Ibid., p. 434.
45. Ibid., p. 433.
46. Ibid., p. 437.
47. Ibid., p. 439.
48. Ibid., p. 440.
49. Ibid., pp. 441, 442.
50. Nesbit, 'Melisande', p. 170.
51. Nesbit, 'No. 17', in *The Power of Darkness*, p. 210.
52. Nesbit, 'The Power of Darkness', in *The Power of Darkness*, p. 191.
53. Keetley and Tenga, *Plant Horror*, p. v.
54. Nesbit, 'The Pavilion', in *The Power of Darkness*, p. 96.
55. Ibid., p. 97.
56. Nesbit, 'The Haunted House', in *The Power of Darkness*, p. 232.
57. Nesbit, 'The Three Drugs', in *The Power of Darkness*, p. 53. This story first appeared as 'The Third Drug'.
58. Alder, *Weird Fiction*, p. 102.
59. Liggins, 'Beyond the Haunted House', p. 32.
60. Scarborough, *The Supernatural*, pp. 104, 105.
61. Weinstock, *Scare Tactics*, p. 21.
62. James, 'The Jolly Corner', p. 238.

63. Ibid., pp. 257, 268, 269.
64. Wharton, 'Kerfol', in *Ghost Stories*, p. 69.
65. *Vanity Fair*, 66, 17 October 1901, p. 284. Quoted in Perrin, *East of Suez*, p. 184.
66. Perrin, 'An Eastern Echo', in *East of Suez*, p. 95.
67. Margree, *British Short Supernatural Fiction*, p. 129.
68. Perrin, 'An Eastern Echo', pp. 96, 97.
69. Perrin, 'The Biscobra', in *East of Suez*, p. 166.
70. Ibid.
71. Ibid., p. 167.
72. Ibid., p. 171.
73. Ibid., p. 172.
74. Ibid., p. 174.
75. Bacon, 'The Unburied', in *The Strange Cases of Dr Stanchon*, p. 303.
76. Ibid., pp. 314, 315.
77. Ibid., p. 324.
78. Weinstock, *Scare Tactics*, p. 190.
79. Bacon, 'The Unburied', p. 325.
80. Perrin, 'Chunia, Ayah', in *East of Suez*, p. 160.
81. Ibid., p. 162.
82. Ibid., p. 162.
83. Ibid., p. 161.
84. Ibid., pp. 161, 164.
85. James, 'Some Remarks,' p. 173.
86. Luckhurst, 'The Weird: A Dis/orientation', p. 1052.

Chapter 2

Weird Fiction in the Twentieth Century
Kevin Corstorphine

Any definition of weird fiction in the twentieth century is tied to the work of H. P. Lovecraft (1890–1937). Although the weird did not begin or end with his fiction, he is a key figure because of his theorisation of the weird in the long essay 'Supernatural Horror in Literature' (1927), in which he creates a canon of authors who achieve this effect. Although gesturing towards the development of the weird impulse in the nineteenth century and its metamorphosis into the 'New Weird' in the twenty-first, this chapter will focus on the weird as it manifests in the twentieth century, centred around Lovecraft and the magazine *Weird Tales* (1923–), but expanding the definition to include a wider range of authors whose work can be considered to fall within this category. The approach is expansive and aims to avoid a reductive view of the weird as belonging only to Lovecraft and his circle, while of course acknowledging their importance. By necessity of space, not all relevant authors can appear here, but the intention is to give a sense of what is meant when readers and critics discuss the weird. Weird fiction, broadly, is a type of storytelling that attempts on some level to produce the effect of horror and may or may not adhere to Gothic conventions built up over time. In its tendencies to embrace elements of speculative and science fiction, it actively engages with the implications of developments in science while at the same time going beyond and making strange. This very strangeness, the 'weird' in the title, represents a rich seam of imagination that continues to be mined by authors in the twenty-first century, even as they go beyond the perceived limitations and certainly outdated worldviews of some its practitioners, notably Lovecraft himself.

Many of the authors here are American and flourished in the country's culture of 'pulp' magazine publishing. Weird fiction is not limited to the United States in the twentieth century, but there is a case to be made for it being somewhat of an 'American Century' for the mode. Gothic fiction, originating in Europe and coinciding with the growth of the new

American republic, hit its stride early in the country, with authors such as Edgar Allan Poe not only innovating in the form, but sowing the seeds for what would later be considered as the 'weird'. As we shall see later with Lovecraft's posthumous success, the publication of Poe's compiled *Tales of Mystery and Imagination* in 1902 was a landmark moment in the twentieth-century weird, further built on with the addition of Harry Clarke's grotesque but irresistible illustrations in the 1919 edition. I want to pick out one Poe story (not included in that collection) as a notable precursor to the weird fiction template: 'The Facts in the Case of M. Valdemar' (1845). Poe did elsewhere write on science quite sincerely, in for example *Eureka: A Prose Poem* (1848), but it is in this story that we see the marriage of his more usual psychological terror to a more existential sense of the weird, through an exploration of the margins between life and death. The narrator of the story uses mesmerism to put his friend Valdemar, who is dying of tuberculosis, into a trance at the very point of death. He then remains suspended between the states of life and death for months. When the narrator finally decides to revive the 'sleep-waker',[1] Valdemar screams that he is dead, although eerily without using his jaw or lips, and collapses into 'a nearly liquid mass of loathsome – of detestable putridity'.[2]

Poe's story illustrates several elements of what would become the twentieth-century weird. Indeed, Lovecraft holds up the tale in 'Supernatural Horror in Literature' as an example of Poe's 'permanent and unassailable place as deity and fountain-head of all modern diabolic fiction'.[3] The excess in subject matter as well as adjectives is not the only thing that Lovecraft takes from Poe's work here. He praises the 'spiritual' and 'supernatural horror' of stories such as this, in contrast to those that exemplify the 'grotesque' or a psychological 'terror'.[4] It is perhaps curious that Lovecraft, an avowed materialist, would here turn to the language of the numinous in defining the weird, but it is exactly this 'violation of the natural order' that he sees as frightening on a profound level.[5] This is in some ways a reformulation of the Gothic romance author Ann Radcliffe's terror/horror distinction, where she claims that 'terror and horror are so far opposite, that the first expands the soul, and awakens the faculties to a higher degree of life; the other contracts, freezes, and nearly annihilates them'.[6] This theorising, published in essay form as 'On the Supernatural in Poetry' (1826), is really a justification of her own style, in contrast to the gory excesses of authors such as Matthew 'Monk' Lewis and his imitators. Lovecraft finds the 'laboured mechanical explanations' of Radcliffe to be disappointing in comparison to the sense of sublimity evoked in the course of her novels. 'The true weird tale', he writes (in a swipe at the Gothic novel), 'has something more than secret murder, bloody bones, or a sheeted form clanking chains according to rule'.[7] For Lovecraft, the essence of the weird lies in something analogous to the Romantic sublime: that sense of awe so crucial in the formulation of the Gothic, that 'inspires in its perceivers a new sense of relative insignificance'.[8] Where Kant and Burke saw the sublime as a prime instigator of religious feeling, and the Romantic poets and transcendentalists would move this towards a broader conception of nature, Lovecraft's conception of the weird is one marked by a profound absence of belief, though still feeling the shock of the decline of faith characteristic of thinkers of the age.[9] This pessimistic worldview is one that would be taken up by authors such as Thomas Ligotti later in the century, and theorised by critics such as Mark Fisher, who see the potential for radical social change, viewing the presence of the weird as 'a signal that the concepts and frameworks which we have previously employed are now obsolete'.[10]

S. T. Joshi has crucially claimed that the weird tale in this period does not 'exist as a genre but as the consequence of a *world view*'.[11] This is certainly valid and goes some way towards explaining how it comes to coagulate as a set of conventions in the twentieth century. It is tempting to add that it also achieves a certain aesthetic effect, but Lovecraft's own formulation of what qualifies as weird, or as 'a literature of cosmic fear'[12] (he uses these more or less interchangeably), frustrates an effort to strictly categorise. His range of examples, characteristically, draws on folklore, religious traditions and a kind of speculative anthropology, as well as the authors he praises in the form. At times it seems that all of this is simply a matter of taste, and the weird is simply horror writing that Lovecraft thinks is *good*. Nonetheless, there is a specific effect, not directly mentioned by Lovecraft here, that gives us a concrete example of what he means and can illustrate where the philosophical and the aesthetic come together. Thomas De Quincey's essay 'On the Knocking at the Gate in Macbeth' (1823) stands alongside Radcliffe's 'On the Supernatural in Poetry' and Poe's 'The Philosophy of Composition' (1846) as one of the key moments in theorising horror prior to Lovecraft. Here De Quincey obsesses over one moment in Shakespeare's play: the 'peculiar awfulness' he feels when Duncan has been murdered and a knocking is heard.[13] The knocking, De Quincey claims, is powerful because it is concrete and belongs to the ordinary world. Prior to this, a nobleman has murdered his king, a woman has become 'unsexed', and 'another world has stepped in'.[14] The very laws of nature have been temporarily suspended, and it is only the knocking, and the resumption of everyday life, that 'makes us profoundly aware of the awful parenthesis that had suspended them'.[15] For De Quincey, there is a moment of what

Lovecraft would call cosmic horror: 'a malign and particular suspension or defeat of those fixed laws of Nature which are our only safeguard against the assaults of chaos and the daemons of unplumbed space'.[16]

Jeff VanderMeer has characterised the twenty-first-century 'New Weird' as involving a 'surrender to the weird' as opposed to having such phenomena 'hermetically sealed in a haunted house on the moors or in a cave in Antarctica'.[17] This is precisely the difference. The twentieth-century weird works within De Quincey's paradigm, where the horror stems from the creation of a fictional space where what we know to be true about the world is convincingly and horrifically made untrue, even for a moment. This is the achievement of Poe's 'The Facts in the Case of M. Valdemar'. When Valdemar screams 'Dead! Dead!'[18] through a closed mouth and we are utterly uncertain as to his status as living, dead or something in between, it creates a moment of heightened horror that is followed immediately by the catharsis of his dissolving into liquid matter: a moment that brings a shudder of realisation that the previous months were an 'awful parenthesis' leading up to this event. Nature takes over once again, and we are thrown back into the role of readers encountering a story of scientific curiosity. 'The Facts in the Case of M. Valdemar' was presented in several magazines without clarification that it was a work of fiction. As Adam Frank points out, 'while Poe did not seem actively interested in perpetrating "Valdemar" as a hoax, he played with his readers' desires to know whether it was true'.[19] The extent of the potential of mesmerism was not widely understood, and it is here that Poe uses this doubt to create a convincing breach of the reader's rationality. It is in this area of doubt, in the gap between science and the supernatural, that weird fiction finds its most natural home.

In what literary world, then, did weird fiction take root as a force in the early twentieth century? It was certainly one influenced by the flourishing of landmark horror texts in the *fin de siècle* that are widely considered to respond to the transformative scientific and social developments of the era. Indeed, most critics agree that the classic period is roughly 1880–1940, or what China Miéville has termed 'the locus classicus of the "haute weird"'.[20] Certain names are associated strongly with the earlier side of this period, including Algernon Blackwood, William Hope Hodgson and Arthur Machen. As James Machin demonstrates, however, a close examination of contemporary texts now regarded as classics of the Gothic were actually more commonly termed by variations of 'weird', including Robert Louis Stevenson's *Strange Case of Dr Jekyll and Mr Hyde* (1886) and Bram Stoker's *Dracula* (1897).[21] It is also important to note that Stevenson and Stoker, and many others of their time, regarded these kinds of stories as experiments somewhat aside from their usual output, with Henry James famously describing his (now) much-analysed classic *The Turn of the Screw* (1898) as 'rather a shameless pot-boiler'.[22] Despite this, there existed a confidence in the possibilities of the form to produce psychological depth and a sense that the form belonged to the modern age.

The American folklorist Dorothy Scarborough, in an extended essay that predates Lovecraft's 'Supernatural Horror in Literature' by a decade, discusses in similar terms what she views as the hackneyed conventions of Gothic fiction, filled with 'melancholy birds that circled portentously over ancient castles filled with gloom and ghosts'.[23] In contrast, she claims, 'the present-day artist of the uncanny knows how to strike the varied tones of supernaturalism, the shrill notes of fear, the deep diapason of awe, the crashing chords of horror'.[24] Scarborough's survey of the field covers many of the names that likewise appear in Lovecraft's essay, such as Lord Dunsany, Algernon Blackwood, Ambrose Bierce and Robert W. Chambers, as well as (and perhaps notably) important female authors absent from his list, such as Edith Wharton and Mary Wilkins Freeman. Her conclusion centres on the importance of modernity. Psychology is clearly an important part of this modernity, as shown by the allusion to the uncanny: Jentsch had published his essay *On the Psychology of the Uncanny* in 1906, and Freud's formulation of the subject would see print in 1919. Scientific progress, however, considered more broadly, is highlighted as a harbinger of greater possibilities of terror fiction. 'Science', Scarborough writes, 'is revealing wonderful facts and fiction is quick to realise the possibilities for startling situations in every field.'[25] Her assessment is less overblown than Lovecraft's but as strong a summary of the weird at the start of the twentieth century as any.

This enmeshing of science and the weird in this period is detailed extensively by Emily Alder, who argues that 'a close relationship with science is essential to the weird's existence and takes a unique form'.[26] This relationship, Alder argues, is a reciprocal one in which science and fiction feed on and reinforce each other. This is a factor characteristic of the age. The late nineteenth century gave rise to a set of practices and attitudes that would have looked strange (or indeed *weird*) to an earlier age. Developing theories in chemistry, biology and physics in the preceding decades gave rise to an experimental atmosphere in which few sacred truths remained certain. An incomplete list here might include discoveries in optics, evolution and electricity, as well as sound and image recording. Alder points to what is perhaps an inevitable culmination of these discoveries and the attempt to reconcile them with religion: the rise of 'spiritualist and occult discourses that understood all phenomena as "natural", just sometimes governed by laws we do not yet understand'.[27] Pointing also to Lovecraft's somewhat stubborn clinging to the term 'supernatural' in the title of his landmark essay on the weird, she points out that 'for "supernatural" to have any meaning, there must be a "natural" against which to define it, and in weird fiction, there is no distinction'.[28] Indeed, such was the mood at the turn of the century that the respected psychologist William James (elder brother of Henry) could claim that 'phantasms, haunted houses, trances with supernormal faculty, and even experimental thought-transference, are natural kinds of phenomenon which ought, just like other natural events, to be followed up with scientific curiosity'.[29] James was writing from a stance of dispassionate scientific inquiry, but this very curiosity, in the hand of authors of the weird, leads to terror, despair and madness.

Lovecraft's fiction puts into practice the goals he set up in his theorising of the weird. Here I will briefly touch on his famous and influential 'The Call of Cthulhu' (1928). The monstrous creature of the title usually gets all of the attention, but it is important first to set up what the story does well as a horror narrative, and why it is 'weird'. Jeffrey Andrew Weinstock has expanded on the difference between the Gothic and the weird by pointing out that for Lovecraft, 'a solitary spectral form emerging at midnight from the closet may be scary, but not especially weird'.[30] What does constitute the weird, on the other hand, is 'the prospect that ghosts are all around us, invisible to most but able to interact with the world and influence our actions'.[31] It is not so much that Lovecraft wants to do away with the supernatural altogether, but merely that he finds the set of conventions built up around its representation to be tired and boring. Weinstock confirms this by concluding that 'the frisson elicited by the uncanny upending of conventional expectation is the affective terrain of the weird tale'.[32] The first wave of Gothic fiction found a keen readership eager to partake in the pleasurable experience of reading with an awareness and appreciation of genre conventions, as parodied by Jane Austen in *Northanger Abbey* (1817), where the protagonist puts herself in a series of awkward social situations by allowing her Gothic novel-influenced imagination to run wild. It is a perpetual irony that revolutionary movements tend to settle into a new status quo, and the weird itself would build up its own set of stale conventions over time. Looking back, however, what enthusiastic writers, critics and editors saw as the potential for a new direction in horror fiction has its parallels with a broader enthusiasm for a new way of looking at the world that characterised the early twentieth century and has its parallels, in a broad sense, with modernism.[33]

The opening paragraph of 'The Call of Cthulhu' speaks directly to the ideas espoused earlier by William James, which we might call a version of logical positivism; that is, that all possible knowledge is in the realm of materialist science and can be explained in these terms. The narrator views the branches of science as something akin to the Indian parable about a group of blind men attempting to describe an elephant by feeling it, each convinced that it is a different kind of creature based on which part they touch. He writes that:

> The sciences, each straining in its own direction, have hitherto harmed us little; but some day the piecing together of dissociated knowledge will open up such terrifying vistas of reality, and of our frightful position therein, that we shall either go mad from the revelation or flee from the deadly light into the peace and safety of a new dark age.[34]

Curiosity, in this story, comes from a desire to seek the truth, but the truth is a pessimistic one. As with the shock felt in the Victorian age when evolutionary science revealed nature to be truly 'red in tooth and claw',[35] the tone and content of 'The Call of Cthulhu' suggest that there are things we might rather not know. What is important about this is not just the philosophical worldview, but how Lovecraft deploys it to create fear. The story is a layered narrative that draws from the innovations in the Gothic of the late nineteenth century, for example in Stevenson and Stoker, where found letters, clues and newspaper reports are pieced together to create a story that has plausible deniability yet allows for the possibility that the events have actually transpired. The murder of the narrator's uncle by a secret cult leads him through an investigation that eventually unearths the supposed existence of a monstrous creature, whose name is constructed of 'ominous syllables which can be rendered only as "Cthulhu"'.[36] Cthulhu lies in the submerged city of R'Lyeh, where it sends out psychic signals to the susceptible. It is just one of a race of Old Ones: ancient and powerful beings who fulfil the roles of both aliens and gods, and are far from benevolent, wishing only for power and to unleash chaos upon the human race.

The crucial point is how Lovecraft shrouds his monster in ambiguity; the account of the sailor Johansen claims outright that 'the Thing cannot be described',[37] while a bas-relief found among his uncle's possessions, as well as a statue found among the cultists, clearly represent a bizarre hybrid of human, octopus and dragon. Its physical form, however, is continually shifting and undefined, and not something that can be simply understood and defeated. As Joshi suggests, Cthulhu's very existence means that we have somehow horribly misconstrued the nature of the cosmos and our place within it; our reaction can only be horror and madness. It is worth noting at this point that this is a key element of distinction between the 'old' and 'new' weird. The newer manifestation, in its 'surrender to the weird' as VanderMeer puts it, has proved fruitful in opening up spaces of exploration from the perspectives of non-white and queer authors, who have been less comfortably situated within the mainstream narrative to begin with. Certainly, Lovecraft's personal anxieties over racial and class identities have been thoroughly examined in relation to his fictional horrors. David Simmons, for example, situates his writing within 'an American tradition . . . that seeks to configure alien, and unknowable, others as internal threats to national, political, and psychological stability'.[38]

Whatever the personal or political stance that gives birth to such abject horrors, Lovecraft is not alone in his construction of the composite, strange, yet horrifically real Cthulhu. Joshi sees Lovecraft's work as the culmination of the tradition he identifies, and indeed convincing templates for the eldritch horrors of Lovecraft's weird mode can be seen in previous texts. Arthur Machen's *The Great God Pan* (1890), for example, describes an experiment in which a surgeon operates on the brain of a young woman, Mary, in the hope of opening up her consciousness to the spirit world. Although he claims success in the experiment, he admits that her mind has been destroyed: 'she is a hopeless idiot. However, it could not be helped; and, after all, she has seen the Great God Pan.'[39] The novella centres around another young woman, Helen, who is later revealed to be Mary's child, fathered by Pan himself. After becoming implicated in scandalous events, Helen kills herself, with her death described in the following way:

> I saw a Form, shaped in dimness before me, which I will not farther describe. But the symbol of this form may be seen in ancient sculptures, and in paintings which survived beneath the lava, too foul to be spoken of . . . as a horrible and unspeakable shape, neither man nor beast, was changed into human form, there came finally death.[40]

Helen's death prefigures Cthulhu both in the reference to ancient sculptures that depict this monstrosity, and in the indeterminacy that characterises her dying form.

Algernon Blackwood produces a similar effect with his novella *The Wendigo* (1910). Here, a hunting party in the backwoods of northwestern Ontario encounter the wendigo of the title: a creature from the folklore of the Algonquin people. The wendigo is associated with cannibalism and human possession, and this occurs in the narrative, with the party's guide, Défago, seemingly taken over by its spirit. The wendigo is represented throughout the story primarily by sound, but as

Défago stumbles back to the camp there is a visual description of him that suggests the presence of the wendigo while simultaneously avoiding direct representation: 'something like a skin of horror almost perceptibly drew down in that moment over every face, and three pairs of eyes shone through it as though they saw across the frontiers of normal vision into the Unknown'.[41]

This horrific vision of something that is both beyond and yet all too real is developed at length in William Hope Hodgson's hallucinogenic account of a man who slips between dimensions in *The House on the Borderland* (1908):

> Far to my right, away up among inaccessible peaks, loomed the enormous bulk of the great Beast-god. Higher, I saw the hideous form of the dread goddess, rising up through the red gloom, thousands of fathoms above me. To the left, I made out the monstrous Eyeless-Thing, grey and inscrutable. Further off, reclining on its lofty ledge, the livid Ghoul-Shape showed—a splash of sinister colour, among the dark mountains.[42]

The tactic used by these authors is to produce horror solely by means of the suggestive power of the written word: to describe the indescribable, and in so doing convey an uneasy sense of dread that is realistic, despite the sometimes preposterous situations that are conjured up. The weird is simultaneously a *tour de force* of imagination and a mode that aspires to the strictest believability in its tone.

If the crystallisation of the weird into a genre is in large part a result of Lovecraft's writing and his association with *Weird Tales* magazine, then this does skew its definition into being associated with a certain style and aesthetic. Lovecraft's tendency towards excess in his prose (a style that his biographer L. Sprague de Camp has referred to as 'pedantically polysyllabic'),[43] and a fondness for deploying multiple adjectives in describing his horrors, has become connected with the mode, and thus the weird often excludes, for example, the ghost story writer M. R. James, despite his inclusion in Lovecraft's list of great practitioners of the form. The publication of *Ghost Stories of an Antiquary* in 1904 was no doubt a landmark in twentieth-century supernatural fiction, but as Darryl Jones points out, the ghost story exemplified and mastered by James is 'essentially Victorian' in form and outlook, and the style 'straitened, narrow, austere, limited'.[44] While this is by no means a flaw, and indeed many would characterise James as the finer stylist, this represents a traditional divergence between the classic ghost story and the weird, despite the capacity of the former to produce some of the same kinds of affective supernatural terror. It is in some ways a false dichotomy: James Machin has pointed out that 'by the 1920s [the ghost story] was a form *Weird Tales* magazine was actively defining itself against' due its perceived clichéd themes, but despite this insistence in the magazine's marketing tactics, 'it is difficult to find even a single work that fits neatly into any of these post-hoc generic distinctions'.[45] This difficulty in classification extends to the authors associated with *Weird Tales* itself, a problem perhaps inevitable for a publication set up explicitly to be eclectic and distinct from established styles of storytelling. *Weird Tales* included such authors as Seabury Quinn, Robert E. Howard, Clark Ashton Smith, Robert Bloch and August Derleth, who would notably go on to take charge of Lovecraft's posthumous reputation, establishing him as a genre writer above all else.

Derleth's invention of the term 'Cthulhu Mythos' to describe Lovecraft's fantastical 'universe' (as it might now be termed) was foundational in the marketing of not only Lovecraft's work, but genre fiction more generally. Joshi considers Derleth and Donald Wandrei's founding of Arkham House in 1939 as a move that actively encouraged a 'cult following'[46] for such work, as opposed to the wider mainstream appeal of earlier fiction, not segregated from 'literature' in a broader sense. Joshi identifies a 'critical contempt' for weird fiction as a direct consequence of this.[47] Joshi's own editorial work has gone some way to remedy this, although since the publication of *The Weird Tale* in 1990 this has been situated within a wider critical reappraisal of genre fiction in the academy and in the public sphere, connected also to the rise of critical theory. While these are in some ways unhappy bedfellows to Joshi's 'consciously antitheoretical position',[48] they share an appreciation of the philosophical aspects of weird fiction. As Carl Sederholm puts it: 'An effective weird tale may even leave readers feeling stunned and helpless, unable to process what they know to be real ... Ultimately, weird tales point readers toward fundamental problems of representation and reality.'[49] Although key studies in the philosophical implications of the weird such as Graham Harman's *Weird Realism: Lovecraft and Philosophy* (2012) and Mark Fisher's *The Weird and the Eerie* (2016) had yet to appear at the end of the twentieth century, critical reappraisals of the mode had been made by authors such as Stephen King in *Danse Macabre* (1981) and Michel Houellebecq in *H. P. Lovecraft: Against the World, Against Life* (in French, 1991).

This critical reappraisal at the start of the twenty-first century, occurring alongside the aforementioned rise of the 'New Weird', means that we are now in a position of retrospectively tracking the mode across a range of authors who might conceivably be placed within the category. The influence and cross-fertilisation of the themes and aesthetics of the weird can be seen particularly in comics such as EC's *The Vault of Horror*

(1950–55) and *Weird Fantasy* (1950–53), and the work of writers such as Alan Moore and Grant Morrison, who moved from an exploration of the latent weird themes in Marvel and DC comics to original stories that draw on and expand the weird. Films including John Carpenter's *The Thing* (1982) and the output of David Cronenberg, such as *Scanners* (1981) and *Videodrome* (1983), mined weird themes at the same time as the appearance of adaptations and mythos-adjacent titles such as Sam Raimi's *The Evil Dead* (1981) and Stuart Gordon's *Re-Animator* (1985). In fiction, the label 'horror' would become dominant as the output of Stephen King and other authors became popular with a wide audience, in addition to the stereotypical 'pimply teenager'[50] that Dale Bailey associates with pulp genre horror prior to the release of Jay Anson's *The Amityville Horror* in 1977. Although not all horror novels draw on the sensibilities of the weird, there are some notable exceptions. Joshi rightly designates Ramsey Campbell as one of the 'modern masters'[51] of the weird, and a novel such as *The Parasite* (1980), with its evocation of shifting dimensions and shuffling, malformed horrors, confirms this perspective. The writing of Thomas Ligotti is now gaining greater attention, and texts such as the collection *Songs of a Dead Dreamer* (1985) show not just a thematic and aesthetic debt to the weird but a continuation of the philosophical pessimism that infuses the Lovecraftian tradition.

The writing of Stephen King has not always been classified in terms of the weird and has been actively excluded from some examinations of the mode, but there is no doubt that King has been instrumental in popularising it to a new audience. The 1980s HarperCollins Omnibus editions of Lovecraft's fiction, for example, bear a quote from King alongside their lurid cover illustrations, claiming Lovecraft as 'the twentieth century horror story's dark and baroque prince'.[52] The following passage from *It* (1986), to give one of many possible examples, shows a clear continuation of the 'problems of representation and reality' raised through an attempt to describe the indescribable that we saw in Blackwood's *The Wendigo*, but here evoking the sense of smell rather than sound: 'Smells of dirt and wet and long-gone vegetables would merge into one unmistakable ineluctable smell, the smell of the monster, the apotheosis of all monsters. It was the smell of something for which he had no name: the smell of It, crouched and lurking and ready to spring.'[53] The key feature of a novel such as *It* is the way that it simultaneously presents a realistic portrayal of small-town American life (particularly the experience of being an adolescent) and the presence of a supernatural entity, without losing the quality of believability that characterised the earlier weird, despite the outlandishness of the plot. This formula is one that has made King's writing wildly popular across a large range of readers.

More experimentally weird is the writing of Clive Barker, whose preferred term for his fiction is the dark *fantastique*: a French term that is more inclusive than the anglophone separation of science fiction, fantasy and horror. This is a mode, as Sorcha Ní Fhlainn points out, that aims to 'reconfigure reality'.[54] The inclusion of Barker's 1984 short story 'In the Hills, the Cities' in Ann and Jeff VanderMeer's *The New Weird: An Anthology* (2008) demonstrates the evolution of the mode into something new once more: something characterised primarily by 'subversion',[55] as Barker has claimed as a driving principle.

Weird fiction in the twentieth century, perhaps appropriately, mutated across a variety of forms. It began as a diverse and multi-armed (or tentacled) attempt to refresh established conventions in horror by updating the scenarios of the Gothic and by incorporating new discoveries in science and philosophy. The first part of this distinction is aesthetic, in that the weird often eschews the aestheticisation of death into something fearful yet possessing of a certain beauty. In the case of the weird, the horror of the category-slippage of life and death and the dissolution of the body are more open and unresolved. The second part of the distinction is a similarly open narrative structure, defying the usual rational resolution of the classic Gothic novel. The third is a tendency in theme to move away from a representation of the past as something supernatural or barbaric intruding on the modern age, to the modern age itself being intrinsically linked with an assault on rational human agency. Like any set of generic conventions, these flow into one another, but through its association with specific publications such as *Weird Tales* and the posthumous cult status of H. P. Lovecraft in particular, the weird became cemented in the twentieth century as something akin to an identifiable genre, characterised by a blending of science fiction, the supernatural and horror, and with a pessimistic tone that suggests that human beings are helpless in the face of larger forces that are sometimes threatening but at best terrifyingly indifferent. It thrived in comics and cinema, and its traces could be detected in what was more usually termed horror fiction. At the turn of the twenty-first century, however, a postmodern mining of the past dug up the weird as a candidate for reinvention, and one to be put to new purposes. It remains somewhat niche, albeit highly recognised in fandom and increasingly in academia. Its influence, however, can be detected everywhere in popular culture from television and film to internet culture. The recognisability of the twentieth-century weird can now be seen in period-set video games and roleplaying games that cement its themes and aesthetics. The true form of the weird, however, was never something fixed into a set of conventions, and at the start of a new century it found new life through a generation of authors inspired by its compelling strangeness and capacity to unsettle.

Key Texts

William Hope Hodgson, *The House on the Borderland* (1908). A highly influential early work of the weird, this novel anticipates hallucinatory and dream-like prose in later horror and science fiction.

H. P. Lovecraft, *The Complete Fiction*. Lovecraft's fiction, particularly the short stories published in *Weird Tales*, remain central to twentieth-century weird fiction.

Clive Barker, *Books of Blood* (London: Sphere, 1984/1985). Published in six volumes and then in two omnibus editions, these short stories offer transgressive content beyond the gory body-horror they were first recognised for, having become a key influence on the 'new weird'.

Thomas Ligotti, *Songs of a Dead Dreamer* and *Grimscribe* (London: Penguin, 2016). Now published together, these collections of stories establish Ligotti as the inheritor of Lovecraft's mood of philosophical pessimism.

Jim Turner (ed.), *Cthulhu 2000* (London: Penguin, 1999). An excellent way to experience Cthulhu mythos stories by later twentieth-century authors of the weird including Ramsey Campbell, Poppy Z. Brite, Harlan Ellison, Kim Newman and others.

Further Critical Reading

Fisher, Mark, *The Weird and the Eerie* (2016). Fisher's readable and provocative account of the weird and its counterpoint, the eerie (characterised by an uncanny absence), gives new philosophical meaning to weird fiction and specifically its relationship to capitalism.

Houellebecq, Michel, *H. P. Lovecraft: Against the World, Against Life* (1991). The transgressive French novelist's extended essay makes a case for the importance of Lovecraft in twentieth-century literary history, focusing on his loathing of humanity and retreat from modernity.

Joshi, S. T., *The Weird Tale* (1990). The classic study of the weird tale that brought academic attention to Lovecraft and other weird authors, despite Joshi's overt resistance to the academy.

Machin, James, *Weird Fiction in Britain 1880–1939* (2018). An essential companion to the British and Irish authors who influenced Lovecraft and his peers, before becoming overshadowed by the American scene.

Simmons, David (ed.), *New Critical Essays on H. P. Lovecraft* (2013). A timely collection of essays that situates Lovecraft within wider contexts, making a solid case for the broader consideration of weird fiction in literary and cultural studies.

Bibliography

Alder, Emily, *Weird Fiction and Science at the Fin de Siècle* (Basingstoke: Palgrave Macmillan, 2020).

Bailey, Dale, *American Nightmares: The Haunted House Formula in American Popular Fiction* (Bowling Green, OH: Bowling Green State University Popular Press, 1999).

Blackwood, Algernon, 'The Wendigo', in *The Ithaqua Cycle: The Wind-Walker of the Icy Wastes* (Ann Arbor, MI: Chaosium, 1998), pp. 1–39.

Bloom, Clive, *Gothic Horror: A Reader's Guide from Poe to King and Beyond* (London: Macmillan, 1998).

Carlin, Gerry, and Nicole Allen, 'Slime and Western Man: Lovecraft in the Time of Modernism', in David Simmons (ed.), *New Critical Essays on H. P. Lovecraft* (Basingstoke: Palgrave Macmillan, 2013), pp. 73–90.

De Camp, L. Sprague, *Lovecraft: A Biography* (Garden City, NY: Doubleday, 1975).

De Quincey, Thomas, 'On the Knocking at the Gate in Macbeth', *London Magazine 1820–1824*, 8, October 1823, pp. 353–6.

Fagin, N. Bryllion, 'Another Reading of *The Turn of the Screw*', *Modern Language Notes*, 56.3, 1941, pp. 196–202.

Fisher, Mark, *The Weird and the Eerie* (London: Repeater Books, 2016).

Frank, Adam, 'Valdemar's Tongue, Poe's Telegraphy', *ELH*, 72.3, 2005, pp. 635–62.

Hodgson, William Hope, *The House on the Borderland* [1908] (New York: Ace, 1962).

Houellebecq, Michel, *H. P. Lovecraft: Against the World, Against Life* [1991] (London: Gollancz, 2008).

Hughes, William, *Key Concepts in the Gothic* (Edinburgh: Edinburgh University Press, 2018).

James, William, 'Review of *Human Personality and its Survival of Bodily Death*, by Frederick W. H. Myers (1903)', in Robert A. McDermott (ed), *Essays in Psychical Research* (Cambridge, MA: Harvard University Press, 1986), pp. 203–15.

Jones, Darryl (ed.), *M. R. James: Collected Ghost Stories* (Oxford: Oxford University Press, 2011).

Joshi, S. T., *The Evolution of the Weird Tale* (New York: Hippocampus Press, 2004).

Joshi, S. T., *The Weird Tale* (Holicong, PA: Wildside Press, 1990).

King, Stephen, *It* (London: New English Library, 1987).

Lovecraft, H. P., 'The Call of Cthulhu' [1928], in *H. P. Lovecraft: The Complete Fiction* (New York: Barnes and Noble, 2008), pp. 355–79.

Lovecraft, H. P., *H. P. Lovecraft Omnibus 1: At the Mountains of Madness and Other Novels of Terror* (London: HarperCollins, 1985).

Lovecraft, H. P., 'Supernatural Horror in Literature' [1927], in *H. P. Lovecraft: The Complete Fiction* (New York: Barnes and Noble, 2008), pp. 1041–98.

Machen, Arthur, 'The Great God Pan' [1890], in *The Great God Pan and the Inmost Light* (London: John Lane, 1894), pp. 1–110.

Machin, James, *Weird Fiction in Britain 1880–1939* (Basingstoke: Palgrave Macmillan, 2018).
Ní Fhlainn, Sorcha (ed.), *Clive Barker: Dark Imaginer* (Manchester: Manchester University Press, 2017).
Poe, Edgar Allan, 'The Facts in the Case of M. Valdemar' [1845], in *The Works of Edgar Allan Poe Volume II: Tales of the Grotesque and Arabesque* (Chicago: Stone and Kimball, 1894), pp. 322–34.
Radcliffe, Ann, 'On the Supernatural in Poetry' [1826], in Rictor Norton (ed), *Gothic Readings: The First Wave 1764–1840* (London: Continuum, 2006) pp. 311–16.
Scarborough, Dorothy, *The Supernatural in Modern English Fiction* (New York: G.P. Putnam's Sons, 1917).
Sederholm, Carl, 'The New Weird', in Maisha Wester and Xavier Aldana Reyes (eds), *Twenty-First Century Gothic* (Edinburgh: Edinburgh University Press, 2019), pp. 161–73.
Simmons, David, 'Abject Hybridity', in David Simmons (ed.), *New Critical Essays on H. P. Lovecraft* (Basingstoke: Palgrave Macmillan, 2013), pp. 13–30.
VanderMeer, Ann, and Jeff VanderMeer (eds), *The New Weird: An Anthology* (San Francisco: Tachyon, 2008).
Weinstock, Jeffrey Andrew, 'The New Weird', in Ken Gelder (ed.), *New Directions in Popular Fiction: Genre, Distribution, Reproduction* (Basingstoke: Palgrave Macmillan, 2016), pp. 177–99.
Wester, Maisha, and Xavier Aldana Reyes (eds), *Twenty-First Century Gothic* (Edinburgh: Edinburgh University Press, 2019).

Notes

1. Poe, 'The Facts in the Case of M. Valdemar', p. 333.
2. Ibid., p. 334.
3. Lovecraft, 'Supernatural Horror', p. 1067.
4. Ibid., p. 1067.
5. Ibid., p. 1083.
6. Radcliffe, 'On the Supernatural in Poetry', p. 315.
7. Lovecraft, 'Supernatural Horror', p. 1043.
8. Hughes, *Key Concepts*, p. 145.
9. Famously summed up by Nietzsche as the 'death of God' in *The Gay Science* (1882) and *Thus Spoke Zarathustra* (1883–85).
10. Fisher, *The Weird and the Eerie*, p. 13.
11. Joshi, *The Weird Tale*, p. 1.
12. Lovecraft, 'Supernatural Horror', p. 1043.
13. De Quincey, 'On the Knocking at the Gate in Macbeth', p. 353.
14. Ibid., p. 355.
15. Ibid., p. 356.
16. Lovecraft, 'Supernatural Horror', p. 1043.
17. VanderMeer, *The New Weird: An Anthology*, p. xvi.
18. Poe, 'The Facts in the Case of M. Valdemar', p. 333.

19. Frank, 'Valdemar's Tongue, Poe's Telegraphy', p. 635.
20. Machin, *Weird Fiction*, p. 10.
21. Ibid., p. 14.
22. Fagin, 'Another Reading of *The Turn of the Screw*', p. 200.
23. Scarborough, *The Supernatural in Modern English Fiction*, p. 295.
24. Ibid., p. 295.
25. Ibid., pp. 303–4.
26. Alder, *Weird Fiction*, p. 5.
27. Ibid., p. 7.
28. Ibid., p. 8.
29. James, 'Review of *Human Personality*', p. 204.
30. Weinstock, 'The New Weird', p. 179.
31. Ibid., p. 179.
32. Ibid., p. 179.
33. A topic that is expansive in its own right but examined in Carlin and Allen, 'Slime and Western Man'.
34. Lovecraft, 'The Call of Cthulhu', p. 355.
35. A common post-Darwinian assertion made famous by Tennyson in his poem 'In Memoriam A.H.H' (1850).
36. Lovecraft, 'The Call of Cthulhu', p. 355.
37. Ibid., p. 377.
38. Simmons, 'Abject Hybridity', p. 28.
39. Machen, 'The Great God Pan', p. 15.
40. Ibid., p. 101.
41. Blackwood, 'The Wendigo', p. 33.
42. Hodgson, *The House on the Borderland*, p. 134.
43. De Camp, *Lovecraft: A Biography*, p. 70.
44. Jones (ed.), *M. R. James: Collected Ghost Stories*, pp. xxix, xvii.
45. Machin, *Weird Fiction*, p. 21.
46. Joshi, *The Weird Tale*, p. 5.
47. Ibid., p. 6.
48. Ibid., p. xi.
49. Sederholm, 'The New Weird', pp. 163–4.
50. Bailey, *American Nightmares*, p. 54.
51. Joshi, *The Evolution of the Weird Tale*, p. 8.
52. Lovecraft, *H. P. Lovecraft Omnibus*, cover.
53. King, *It*, pp. 18–19.
54. Ní Fhlainn (ed.), *Clive Barker*, p. 9.
55. Barker, cited in Bloom, *Gothic Horror: A Reader's Guide*, p. 100.

Chapter 3

Gothic Modernisms
Matt Foley

The Gothic and modernism are two highly influential, often contested modes central to the twentieth-century imagination. From the mid-nineteenth century into the twentieth century, the Gothic was disseminated across genres, infecting literary and popular imaginations by transgressing spatial and temporal boundaries.[1] Critical work in the field of Gothic modernisms, my focus in this chapter, recognises and explores the Gothic registers of modernist cultural production from the late nineteenth-century 'proto-modernists' – such as Oscar Wilde, Henry James, Vernon Lee and Joseph Conrad – onwards into twentieth-century literature, film and art. So far, in reading this body of writing, scholarly work has tended towards deploying two methods that are not mutually exclusive. The first of these is to read Gothic modernisms as being represented by the macabre and haunted turns to 'high' modernist aesthetics that we find in the writings of T. S. Eliot, Virginia Woolf, James Joyce and many others – and from there to assess the resonances that modernism shares with the Gothic that came before it. The second method is to interrogate and explore the broader period of 'Gothic modernity', which Sam Wiseman suggests runs from the 1880s to the 1940s and the Second World War, by assessing the Gothic and modernism's shared spatial, technological and epistemological contexts.[2] Whether Gothic, modernist or both, writers of the period were confronted by a rapidly changing modernity through increased urbanisation, the discovery and theorisation of the unconscious, and the emergence of global conflicts on a devastating scale. Indeed, critics recognise that a pervasive ephemerality is reflected in the literature and art of the period. The relationship between the Gothic and modernism, then, is multifaceted, and both aesthetic and contextual. The Gothic is often transformed by acts of modernist experimentation, and such transformations are visible, to give but two examples, in Virginia Woolf's dislocating ghost story 'A Haunted House' (1921) and in the urban carnivalesque of Djuna

Barnes's *Nightwood* (1936). Barnes's Surrealist novel is arguably the quintessential Gothic modernist text and I turn to it at the end of this chapter. My argument here takes the long view of Gothic modernisms and reads them as a plurality, particularly in light of their formation in the late nineteenth century; their emergence in the classical, ghostly or experimental modernisms of the interwar period; and their legacies in 'new' and postmodern Gothics in the later twentieth century.

Gothic Modernisms and Gothic Studies

The emergence of Gothic modernisms as a discrete field of critical inquiry within Gothic Studies can be traced back to the early 2000s and to two landmark publications. A special issue of *Modern Fiction Studies* entitled 'Gothic and Modernism' (ed. Riquelme) appeared in the autumn of 2000, and the articles there were subsequently reworked into the edited collection *Gothic and Modernism: Essaying Dark Literary Modernity* (2008). Riquelme's introduction to the original special issue remains an immensely influential theorisation of the mode and, intriguingly, opens up the temporal limits of Gothic modernism to beyond the interwar years and well into the twentieth century, particularly by locating Oscar Wilde's *The Picture of Dorian Gray* as a precursor to late twentieth-century literatures of transgression.[3] Andrew Smith and Jeff Wallace's edited collection *Gothic Modernisms* (2001) appeared in the following year. Its delineation of Gothic modernity is somewhat tighter and more in-step with the periodisation of modernism as it is often understood in the academy. Nevertheless, Wallace and Smith's collection recognises Gothic modernisms as plural – a transmedial and transnational critical category. Here the hauntings of Virginia Woolf are considered alongside the German Expressionist cinema of Fritz Lang's *Metropolis* (1927). Cinema itself, particularly when characterised as a spectral technology, fascinated modernist writers from Woolf, to D. H. Lawrence, to Elizabeth Bowen. Indeed, modernism and the Gothic share a mutual interest in those uncanny spectres of modernity that seemed to proliferate in the early twentieth century through the adoption of new technologies, but also through the spectralisation of the self, courtesy of new discourses – psychoanalytic or otherwise – that emerged to account for the modern unconscious, sexuality and desire. Alluding to sexuality, Smith and Wallace note that the Gothic and modernism share a 'fascination with the potential erosion of moral value, and with the forms that amorality can take'.[4] Modernism and the Gothic, in turn, are both literatures of transgression, and their boundary-crossing sensibilities often meet in their mutual interest in the ghost story.

Monographs by Daniel Darvay (2016) and Sam Wiseman (2019) have revived the critical field of Gothic modernism, advancing the more localised arguments of those touchstone works from the early 2000s, such as Smith and Wallace's. As these critics all agree, on first inspection the very notion of Gothic modernisms may seem contradictory, given the rejection of the so-called 'low' and popular Gothic mode by 'high' modernist writers such as Woolf, who believed the Gothic romance no longer fit for the age of modernity.[5] This premise that the modes are oppositional was not wholly challenged during the birth of the dedicated field of Gothic Studies in the 1980s and 1990s.[6] It was only at the turn of the millennium that such a presumption was unpicked by Riquelme's introduction to his 2000 special issue. He argues that '[t]he transformations, adaptations, and other prominent traces of the Gothic in modern writing indicate the persistence of a cluster of cultural anxieties to which Gothic writing and literary modernism ... continue to respond'.[7] This sense of a *continued* response by Gothic modernisms to evolving cultural anxieties is a line of thought that I revive in this chapter.

The nature, form and scope of the modernist Gothic will no doubt remain contested for some time; nevertheless, the old assumption that Gothic and modernist sensibilities are entirely at odds has now fallen away. In discussions of literary value, privileging modernism over the Gothic is unhelpful for many reasons, but two are particularly pertinent to defining and locating Gothic modernisms in relation to adjacent critical fields. First, while it is true to say that *direct* influence from the Gothic of the late eighteenth century upon the modernisms birthed in the early twentieth century is rare – particularly in English letters – a transnational lineage can be identified between the modes. Indeed, European Gothic of the nineteenth century fed directly into the birth of the modernist project in significant and sustained ways, for instance through the poetry of Charles Baudelaire. Secondly, modernism itself is no longer narrowly defined as the cultural production of an elite few, the exclusive practice of the Bloomsbury Group or The Men of 1910. Modernism has become *modernisms* – a plurality. One outcome of this 'expansion' in modernist studies is that 'quite sharp boundaries between high art and popular forms of culture have been reconsidered', particularly in post-millennial critical work in the field.[8] A landmark moment in this expansion was the launch of the Modernist Studies Association journal *Modernism/Modernity* in 1999, only a year before the birth of the field of Gothic modernisms itself. Beyond Gothic, 'new' modernisms are many and various. Some – such as the European groups of *avant-garde* artists who came to prominence in the 1910s and 1920s and include André Breton's Surrealists – demonstrate a knowing and sustained engagement with the Gothic novel. More than this, the intellectual or taxonomical barriers often erected between modernism and genre fiction such as Gothic romance or adventure fiction have, too, been proven to be oversimplified critical constructions.

In this guise, Nicholas Daly has argued that the adventure romance of the *fin de siècle* in British and Irish writing was 'a distinctly modern phenomenon ... shaped in the same historical mould as literary modernism' and, in turn, a form of 'popular modernism'. In his model of popular modernism, Daly includes the colonial adventure fiction of H. Rider Haggard alongside Gothic writers of monstrosity such as Bram Stoker. In such an exploding of the canon, which undoes some of the assumptions we might have about modernism's distance from popular Gothic, Daly suggests that '[i]t makes more sense ... to shelf a narrative like *She* or *Dracula* with the work of modernists like Joyce and Woolf than that of eighteenth and early-nineteenth century practitioners of romance like Ann Radcliffe, or Sir Walter Scott'.[9] In the twilight of the nineteenth century, early modernists – such as the Literary Impressionists Henry James and Joseph Conrad – moved very much in the same circles as 'romance' or genre writers, including Rider Haggard and H. G. Wells. Indeed, well-known critical studies of the Gothic dating from this time – including those published in the late 1910s and 1920s, respectively, by Dorothy Scarborough and Edith Birkhead – seem less concerned with the boundaries between those writers we now recognise as modernists, on the one hand, and those who worked in genre fiction, on the other. Writing in 1921, Birkhead reads Conrad's handling of mystery and terror, particularly in his novella *The Shadow Line* (1916), as being the product of his 'romantic imagination'.[10] The oppositional distinction, then, between the modernist and romantic imaginations did not always hold up or sustain itself in the critical discourses of the time.

Studies such as Birkhead's and Scarborough's are historical reminders that literary modernism is itself a post-war critical construct. As I have suggested, scholars of Gothic modernism today often unpick, unravel and decentre readings of modernism that position it, first and foremost, as an *avant-garde* literature of 'high' experimentation. In his recent study of what he terms Gothic modernity, Sam Wiseman, for one, is at pains to point out that the critical lens he employs moves away from critical work that has privileged aesthetic experimentation as a defining factor of Gothic modernisms. Instead, Wiseman's work reads 'British-set' texts in a way that does not 'privilege the experimental aspects' of modernist works and that places modernist representations in direct comparison with the middlebrow and the popular.[11] Wiseman achieves this primarily through an analysis of place, and his argument is often concerned with the 'Gothic of the geographical edgelands, sites where country and city bleed into one another'.[12] In his reading of London as one of the urban centres of Gothic modernity, Wiseman locates Eliot's waste land alongside work by Arthur Machen, D. H. Lawrence and Nancy Cunard, whose fictions exhibit a mutual 'articulation of a metropolitan environment that feels fragile, hallucinatory, and protean, liable to shift form or dissolve altogether'.[13] This placing of Machen among the modernists goes some way to endorsing Fred Botting's recognition of the 'diffusion' of ghostliness across this period of modernity. After 1916, in particular, many of the war dead lay buried abroad and at a distance – the normal rites and rituals of mourning disrupted and placed out of joint. Ghosts tend to proliferate in a world in which mourning is delayed, made more complex, and even depersonalised. This sense of an irresolvable haunting spills beyond the page and becomes pervasive in the interwar period; modernist haunting is a cultural as well as a literary phenomenon. Questions of mourning – pertaining to its ethics – ghost the very fabric of interwar society. Botting goes so far as to argue that 'the diffusion of a sense of ghostliness' in a rapidly changing, seemingly ephemeral society 'indicates why there is no new or distinctive generic manifestation of Gothic writing at the time of modernism'.[14] Certainly, after the First World War, ghostly registers of mourning in modernist fiction proliferated. If, as Botting argues, no new, distinctly Gothic modes emerge (at least in Anglo-American literature) to represent these experiences, that does not diminish the fact that time and again modernist Gothic writing registers these anxieties in the experimental novel, the *vers libre* poem and the modern ghost story of the period.

The writing circles and networks that formed around the publication of 'modern' ghost story collections – such as Cynthia Asquith's edited ghost books (1927–57) – are further examples of what Daly has identified as the intertwining of high and popular modernisms. As Andrew Smith puts it, modernism 'subtly influenced the development of the ghost story',[15] and this development is still with us. Julia Briggs has argued provocatively that 'the history of the ghost story tails off rapidly after 1914, examples tending to become more superficial, sensational or conventional'.[16] In making this somewhat bold argument, Briggs locates the middlebrow writing of Walter de la Mare, in particular, as the best of the mode. Gothic scholarship today turns to May Sinclair or Elizabeth Bowen – whose stories were also published in Asquith's books alongside de la Mare's – to exemplify the innovations that took place after the war, but revisiting Briggs's work does remind us of the formative importance of Henry James to modernism. Penning a modern ghost story, at least in the eyes of the modernists themselves, involved refining the received genre fiction of the nineteenth century to appeal to, or more likely terrify, new and modern sensibilities. In book reviews, correspondence and prefaces, such as James's that accompanied his 1908 edition of *The Turn of the Screw* (1898), the Gothic modernists articulated a set of cultural and personal anxieties that haunted their shared culture. Such hauntings reflect the rapid development of technology in the early-to-mid twentieth century, the prevalence of spiritualist discourses at the time, and the fragmenting of the subject represented by modern psychoanalytic theories and understandings of the unconscious. Luke Thurston argues that the fragmentation of the modernist aesthetic reflects the ghosting of the signifier itself. That is, modernist spectrality haunts the edges of the field of vision and of the written word as it seeks an answer to the question: 'What counts as truth in the ontological relation between selves?'[17] The answer remains somewhat elusive, and such irresolution is typical of modernist literature. Indeed, modernist ghost stories often stage what Tzvetan Todorov referred to as the 'fantastic' – the ghostliness of the stories remains unresolved, and explicitly supernatural or everyday explanations are rarely given.

Gothic Modernist Texts

There were, then, many modernisms, which operated transnationally and included Surrealism, Imagism, the stream of consciousness novel, Vorticism, Dadaism and more. Examples of all these aesthetic forms, at times, produced hauntings; some, such as English and French Surrealism, have a clear and explicit lineage to the Gothic. Given that both modernism and the Gothic are contested and prismatic critical terms, it is only possible in what remains of this chapter, as we turn to reading more closely the contours of the Gothic modernist text, to touch the surface of Gothic modernisms as a body of work. Nevertheless, I demonstrate that this rich field of critical inquiry is relevant to unpicking and reading representations of terror and horror produced throughout the long twentieth-century Gothic. As part of this inquiry, we even might ask, what is modernist about late twentieth-century Gothic writers? As Maria Beville has noted, 'Gothic-postmodernism can be accounted for in relation to a scheme of evolution and its generic metamorphosis pertains distinctly to episodes in the development of literary history'; indeed, its relationship to Gothic modernism is not as antagonistic as we might assume.[18] To articulate but one dimension of this legacy, we might very easily extend the reach of Gothic modernisms into the post-war period by reading the work of the modernist turned postmodernist writer. Two such examples are Samuel Beckett and Jean Rhys. Beckett's postmodern staging of desolation and ghostliness is particularly connected to the modernist Gothic iconography of the waste land and the haunted self in a godless world. Desolation is evident in the bleak *mise en scène* of his absurdist drama *Waiting for Godot* (1953), while modernist modes of spectrality proliferate in his novella *Ill Seen Ill Said* (1981). More recent critical work has recognised and read convincingly a 'post-Gothic laughter' at work in Beckett's plays that stage 'laughter inappropriately, unpredictably, and often inexplicably', so that 'these otherwise human characters appear unsettlingly non-human'.[19] While such non-human laughter echoes, at least in the Irish tradition, the demonic laughter of Charles Maturin's Faustian Melmoth in that late Gothic romance *Melmoth the Wanderer* (1820), Beckett's staging resists a complete or neat interpretation of this Gothic heritage, as Hannah Simpson makes clear. Modernism's recasting of the Gothic – its transformation of Gothic concerns and motifs – wins out.

Beckett is read often as an artist working in that impasse where modernism metamorphoses into something more postmodern; Jean Rhys's *Wide Sargasso Sea* (1966) is another Gothic modernist text that we could position at this turning point. The form of Rhys's novel is fragmentary and dreamlike; in typically modernist fashion, its narration – whether focalised through Antoinette Mason or (the unnamed) Rochester – is psychologised. Reading the novel as a belated modernist text is appealing when we consider that Rhys herself moved in modernist circles in the 1920s and 1930s in London and Paris. There she produced a body of transgressive and formally complex novels and short stories that, in their critiques of masculinity and depictions of boarding house life for working girls, were perhaps too modern even for the modernists to entertain. An exile from Dominica, Rhys travelled to Europe in her late teens, where she became a chorus girl. Her literary work during the interwar period is intimately concerned with difference, desire and empire. In *Voyage in the Dark* (1934), the imagery and language of West Indian folklore – including references to the *zombi* and *obeah* – are put to economical but powerful use in Rhys's critique of an unhomely and rather cold English setting and society. It is in *Wide Sargasso Sea* – her most sustained piece of writing back against the English canon, specifically Charlotte Brontë's *Jane Eyre* (1847) – that we find a Gothic modernist text that makes a foundational contribution to postmodern and postcolonial Gothic literature. As Urmila Seshagiri has put it, Rhys's writing 'challenges the continued relevance of modernist formal accomplishments, and, simultaneously, inaugurates what would soon become the central goals of postcolonial literature in English'.[20] Indeed, Rhys's handling of modernist form – we might suggest her very Gothicising of it as a descent into entrapment – in *Wide Sargasso Sea* questions as much as it reinscribes the modernist project.

Extending, or perhaps even casting away, then, the temporal limits of Gothic modernism illuminates the influence of the mode upon some of the major categories of mid-to-late twentieth-century literature. Legacies of Gothic modernisms persist in contemporary and postmodern Gothic – for instance, in what has been termed the 'new Gothic' of the late twentieth century. This appellation is taken from the title of the influential collection of multi-authored Gothic short stories edited and selected by Patrick McGrath and Bradford Morrow in the early 1990s. In their closing comments to their introduction, McGrath and Morrow allude to the modernist moment and its relationship to the 'new Gothic' of the 1980s and 1990s in three ways. First, Sigmund Freud's psychoanalytic case studies – the modernist vignettes he published documenting the cases of his most challenging patients – are described as 'chillingly macabre' and as sharing the new Gothic's indebtedness to Poe. Secondly, McGrath and Morrow suggest that the prospect of man-made apocalypse 'redefined the contemporary psyche', and, we might argue, the nascent form of this modern, apocalyptic psyche has its roots in modernist fears of globalised and mechanised destruction on a mass scale. Thirdly, they recognise that their contemporary Gothic – the 'new' Gothic – depicts a vision of hell 'located within the vaults and chambers of our own minds' – a vision that the modernists painted frequently through their experimentation with interiority.[21] These allusions to modernist concerns form part of a line of inheritance that the authors articulate from the Gothic romance, through to the Victorian Gothic, and into their contemporary 'new' Gothic. Yet any explicit reference to the term 'modernism' is surprisingly absent. If the modernists often repress the influence of the Gothic upon their writing, then perhaps, on occasion, the 'new' Gothicists feel compelled – consciously or otherwise – to bury their modernist roots in a similar fashion.[22]

If Patrick McGrath – whose Gothic novels include *Spider* (1990) and *Asylum* (1996) – can be considered a 'quintessentially postmodern' Gothic writer,[23] one should recognise, too, that his version of postmodernism draws some of its intensity from the Gothic modernist aesthetic. Nowhere is this modernist influence clearer than in *Asylum*, which draws its mode of unreliable narration from Ford Madox Ford's *The Good Soldier* (1915). In *Asylum*, McGrath's Gothic modernist vision re-energises a narrative form borrowed from Ford's novel by infusing it with images of horror and psychosis very much indebted to the Gothic tradition of excess.

Ford, then, is one of the modernist ghosts influencing McGrath's *Asylum*; in life he was also the lover and literary champion of Jean Rhys in the 1920s, writing the foreword for her first collection *The Left Bank and Other Stories* (1927). In the 1910s, he was part of the Literary Impressionist school of writers, which brought him close to Joseph Conrad, and he later became associated with the *avant-garde* Imagist group of poets in London. His *vers libre* poem 'Antwerp' (1915) appeared in one of their collections; it paints a striking Gothic modernist vision of Belgian refugees arriving at Charing Cross after the siege of Antwerp in 1914. The atmosphere is dark and foreboding. 'Immense shafts of shadows' hang above 'the black crowd' in a haunted London. These refugees stagger rather than flow into the city. Left behind by the dead of the Belgian army, they become an atrophied crowd or mass: 'That is another dead mother, / And there is another and another and another'. The children who accompany their mothers are dressed in funereal colours, feeling their way in the gloom: 'little children, all in black, / All with dead faces, waiting in all the waiting-places, / Wandering from the doors of the waiting-room / In the dim gloom'.[24] The emphasis on waiting and dislocation here speaks to the disruptions of mourning caused by the deaths of the First World War. And these lines seem foundational to T. S. Eliot's own Gothic modernist vision of London in *The Waste Land* that would follow in 1922.

'Antwerp' was certainly read and admired by Eliot; we might speculate that it was not simply the *vers libre* form of the poem that gained his esteem. Ford's imagery is Dantean and appeals very much to Eliot's 'classicist' imagination. One of the most profound transformations that modernist Gothic undergoes, if compared to the nineteenth-century Gothic, is its predilection for a restrained rendering of terror and horror that places itself often in opposition to Romantic excesses. For the modernist critic and poet T. E. Hulme, whose understanding of classicism was influential on both Eliot and the Imagist poets of pre-war London, 'even in the most imaginative flights there is always a holding back, a reservation. The classical poet never forgets this finiteness, this limit of man.'[25] It is unsurprising, then, that the classicist Eliot would eschew the excessively Gothic roots of Djuna Barnes's novel of queer desire, *Nightwood*, which he edited and worked on in his role as a director at Faber and Faber in the 1930s. Indeed, Eliot wrote the preface to the American edition of Barnes's text as a means of recommendation. Where others might immediately recognise the Gothic, Surrealist or expressionist modes that influenced Barnes's imagination, Eliot sees in *Nightwood*:

'a quality of horror and doom very nearly related to that of Elizabethan tragedy'.[26] Revenge tragedies formed part of Eliot's 'Tradition' or canon of Western literature as he articulated it throughout his critical writing, especially in his influential 'Tradition and the Individual Talent' (1919). Eliot continues to position himself as gatekeeper and custodian of meaning in his preface to Barnes's text. His reading of *Nightwood*, though, was contested in 1937 by the American author Lewis Gannett. Taking objection to Eliot's reading, Gannet countered that the novel was a book of 'Gothic horror, not of Elizabethan tragedy'.[27]

In his overlooking of the Gothic – both in Barnes's text and in his construction of the Tradition – Eliot wilfully forgets his own childhood sensibility for Gothic horror. As a boy aged ten or so, he read Edgar Allan Poe voraciously, and many critics acknowledge that it was these Gothic horrors that prepared and primed Eliot for what he encountered later in Elizabethan tragedy.[28] Elaborating upon and strengthening in his reading the importance of this formative influence, Grover Smith has argued that Poe bequeathed to Eliot 'a primary metaphor, which Eliot would elaborate into a personal myth, the metaphor of the living death'.[29] One of the most influential critics of modernism, Michael Levenson, described Poe some time ago as the 'forgotten figure' of Eliot's *The Waste Land*, arguing that 'to remember Poe is to recover the [poem's] Gothic element that is too often explained away'.[30] Yet Eliot the critic (and the adult) was more ambiguous and bashful when it came to the influence of Poe's poetry on the modern craftsman: 'one cannot be sure', he writes in his essay 'From Poe to Valéry' (1948), 'that one's own writing has *not* been influenced by Poe'.[31] This expression of (non-)influence forms a knot – a double negative – out of which it is hard to draw a resolution. For David Punter, the revealing act of 're-remembering' Poe's influence would bring alive and resuscitate a 'foreign body' buried beneath and between the ruins of *The Waste Land*'s architecture.[32] Indeed, the nineteenth-century Gothic is an important part of the creative unconscious of modernism even if some modernists themselves – and here we may consider Woolf as well as Eliot – overtly attack or degrade it as a cultural form. The evidence is clearer than we might think; the imagery of *The Waste Land* recalls at least one nineteenth-century Gothic text – Bram Stoker's *Dracula* (1897) – in its 'bats with baby faces in the violet light' that 'beat their wings / And crawled head downward down a blackened wall'.[33]

We can contrast Eliot's performative forgetting of Poe with the more overt Gothicism of Barnes's *Nightwood*. Barnes's queer text is episodic and depicts an ensemble of Gothic outcasts and *détraqués* whose lives intertwine in modernist Paris. Felix Volkbein, the awkward protagonist of the novel's first chapter, is aligned explicitly with the figure of the Wandering Jew; Robin Vote is described in somnambulistic, vampiric and bestial imagery; while her lover Nora Flood seems one of modernism's cursed living dead: 'There is something evil in me', she confesses to the prophetic Dr Matthew O'Connor, 'that loves evil and degradation – purity's black backside.'[34] True to the tradition of the Gothic romance, Felix adopts the title of Baron as his father did before him. His family's lineage, and therefore Felix's claim to this title, is shown to be counterfeit – merely an example of Gothic fakery. Supposed portraits of Felix's grandparents are revealed to be 'reproductions of two ancient and intrepid actors' and they do not depict *bona fide* gentry.[35] Contested lineages and Gothic portraiture may recall the British Gothic – particularly *The Castle of Otranto* (1764) – but at its heart *Nightwood* is an American-European Gothic text. Avril Horner argues that Barnes's modernist appropriation of the Gothic derives 'from a French tradition of Gothic or quasi-Gothic writing' that 'begins with the *roman noir* and the *roman frénétique*' of the late eighteenth and early nineteenth centuries, and which can also be traced forward to the writings of Eugène Sue, Lautréamont, Louis-Ferdinand Céline and Georges Bataille.[36] The dream-like quality of *Nightwood* – evident, for instance, in the surreal sermons that O'Connor orates for Nora Flood to decode – also suggests an affiliation with Barnes's contemporary André Breton. The founder of Surrealism, Breton was a champion of the Gothic novel, which he lauded as an expression of the unconscious. He was particularly drawn to Maturin's *Melmoth the Wanderer* – perhaps the most influential Gothic romance for the modernists and their forebears. Oscar Wilde, for one, made many nods to his ancestor Maturin's text; Wilde was Maturin's grand-nephew by marriage.[37]

In light of these Gothic influences on continental and Irish modernisms, we might see the 'classicist' turn to Gothic modernism – that is, a privileging of the hellish visions of Dante or Elizabethan tragedy over those of the Gothic novel or Poe's short stories – as a particular phenomenon pertaining to the work of the English and Anglo-American artists of London in the interwar years: Eliot, Woolf and others. The influence of the Gothic novel survives in other forms of modernism, particularly on the continent, and so the mode retains its excessive and transgressive spurs. The study of Gothic modernisms across the long twentieth century must consider closely the work of both camps – the classicists and transgressors alike; its critical spirit closely aligning with that of 'new' modernist studies.

Further Key Texts

James Joyce, 'The Sisters', in *Dubliners* (1904). 'The Sisters' remains one of Joyce's most powerful evocations of haunting and repression in the domestic space. The story is focalised through a young, nameless narrator who is preoccupied by his memories of a dead priest.

Wyndham Lewis, *Tarr* (1918). Nowhere is modernism's distrust of Romanticism clearer than in Wyndham Lewis's pre-war novel of Paris, which he started in 1909 and revised during the war years. The city itself becomes a death house in which important debates surrounding the Vorticists' understanding of aesthetic 'deadness' are dramatised.

Robert Wiene (dir.), *The Cabinet of Dr Caligari* (1920). The German Expressionists captured the spirit of Gothic modernity like no other cinematic movement. *Caligari*'s psychologised narrative framing, its expressionistic *mise en scène* and its representation of the murderous somnambulist Cesare make it a standout example of Gothic modernism on screen.

Virginia Woolf, 'A Haunted House', in *Monday or Tuesday* (1921). Woolf's ghostly fragment is the first story in her highly influential and experimental collection *Monday or Tuesday*. The dead and the living intertwine and boundaries are transgressed in this portrait of still lives and stilted marital desire.

Elizabeth Bowen, 'The Apple Tree', in Cynthia Asquith (ed.), *When Churchyards Yawn* (1931). Collected in a Cynthia Asquith ghost book, Bowen's short story is a powerful – even hallucinatory – representation of the devastating effect that childhood trauma may have upon adult lives. Terrified by her sleepwalking, Myra's unsettling behaviour finds its roots in her past and in the suicide of a school friend.

Further Critical Reading

Riquelme, J. P. (ed.), *Gothic and Modernism: Essaying Dark Literary Modernity* (2008). The book that came from the original *Modern Fiction Studies* special issue of 2000. Its contributors' understanding of Gothic modernisms as a phenomenon of the long twentieth century is crucial to the field.

Smith, A., and J. Wallace (eds), *Gothic Modernisms* (2001). Perhaps the most influential text in the area, Smith and Wallace's edited collection includes key essays on Gothic modernisms by Sue Zlosnik and Avril Horner, David Punter, Kelly Hurley, Judith Wilt and many more.

Thurston, L., *Literary Ghosts from the Victorians to Modernism: The Haunting Interval* (2012). Thurston's monograph provides a nuanced and theoretically sophisticated reading of guests, ghosts and hospitality in Victorian and modernist ghost stories. His argument places the writing of M. R. James and Charles Dickens in conversation with Gothic modernists such as Woolf, Joyce, Bowen, May Sinclair and Henry James.

Wiseman, S., *Locating the Gothic in British Modernity* (2019). Wiseman's recent monograph articulates the myriad contexts that produce the 'Gothic modernity' of late nineteenth- and early twentieth-century British culture. In so doing, it is the first study to consider at length British genre and modernist writing of the period through their shared preoccupation with uncanny rural, urban and edgeland spaces.

Bibliography

Barnes, Djuna, *Nightwood* [1936] (London: Faber and Faber, 2001).
Beville, Maria, *Gothic-postmodernism: Voicing the Terrors of Postmodernity* (Amsterdam: Rodopi, 2009).
Birkhead, Edith, *The Tale of Terror: A Study of the Gothic Romance* [1921] (Project Gutenberg, 2004) <http://www.gutenberg.org/ebooks/14154> (last accessed 14 December 2020).
Botting, Fred, *Gothic*, 2nd edn (Abingdon: Routledge, 2014).
Briggs, Julia, *Night Visitors: The Rise and Fall of the English Ghost Story* (London: Faber and Faber, 1977).
Crawford, Robert, *Young Eliot: From St Louis to The Waste Land* (London: Jonathan Cape, 2015).
Daly, Nicholas, *Modernism, Romance, and the Fin de siècle: Popular Fiction and British Culture, 1880–1914* (Cambridge: Cambridge University Press, 1999).
Darvay, Daniel, *Haunting Modernity and the Gothic Presence in British Modernist Literature* (New York: Palgrave Macmillan, 2016).
Eliot, T. S., 'From Poe to Valéry', *The Hudson Review*, 2.3, 1949, pp. 327–42.
Eliot, T. S., 'Preface' [1937], in Djuna Barnes, *Nightwood* (London: Faber and Faber, 2001), pp. ix–xiv.
Eliot, T. S., *The Waste Land* [1922], in Lawrence Rainey (ed.), *The Annotated Waste Land with Eliot's Contemporary Prose* (New Haven, CT: Yale University Press, 2006), pp. 57–73.
Ford, Ford Madox, 'Antwerp' [1915], in Bob Blaisdell (ed.), *Imagist Poetry: An Anthology* (Mineola, NY: Dover Publications, 1999), pp. 61–4.
Horner, Avril, '"A detour of filthiness": French Fiction and Djuna Barnes's *Nightwood*', in Avril Horner (ed.), *European Gothic: A Spirited Exchange, 1760–1960* (Manchester: Manchester University Press, 2002), pp. 230–51.
Hulme, T. E., *Speculations: Essays on Humanism and the Philosophy of Art* [1924], ed. Herbert Read (London: Routledge and Kegan Paul, 1965).
Mao, Douglas, and Rebecca L. Walkowitz, 'The New Modernist Studies', *PMLA*, 123.3, 2008, pp. 737–48.
McGrath, Patrick, and Bradford Morrow, 'Introduction', in Patrick McGrath and Bradford Morrow (eds), *The New Gothic: A Collection of Contemporary Gothic Fiction* (London: Pan, 1992), pp. xi–xiv.
Morin, Christina, *Charles Robert Maturin and the Haunting of Irish Romantic Fiction* (Manchester: Manchester University Press, 2017).
Punter, David, 'Hungry Ghosts and Foreign Bodies', in A. Smith and J. Wallace (eds), *Gothic Modernisms* (Basingstoke: Palgrave, 2001), pp. 11–28.
Riquelme, J. P., 'Toward a History of Gothic and Modernism: Dark Modernity from Bram Stoker to Samuel Beckett', *Modern Fiction Studies*, 46.3, 2000, pp. 585–605.

Riquelme, J. P. (ed.), *Gothic and Modernism: Essaying Dark Literary Modernity* (Baltimore: Johns Hopkins University Press, 2008).

Seshagiri, Urmila, 'Modernist Ashes, Postcolonial Phoenix: Jean Rhys and the Evolution of the English Novel in the Twentieth Century', *Modernism/Modernity*, 13.3, 2006, pp. 487–505.

Simpson, Hannah, '"Strange Laughter": Post-Gothic Questions of Laughter and the Human in Samuel Beckett's Work', *Journal of Modern Literature*, 40.4, 2017, pp. 1–19.

Smith, Andrew, *Gothic Literature*, 2nd edn (Edinburgh: Edinburgh University Press, 2013).

Smith, Andrew, and Jeff Wallace, 'Introduction', in Andrew Smith and Jeff Wallace (eds), *Gothic Modernisms* (Basingstoke: Palgrave, 2001), pp. 1–10.

Smith, Grover, 'Eliot and the Ghost of Poe', in Shyamal Bagchee (ed), *T. S. Eliot: A Voice Descanting* (London: Palgrave Macmillan, 1990), pp. 149–63.

Thurston, Luke, *Literary Ghosts from the Victorians to Modernism: The Haunting Interval* (Abingdon: Routledge, 2012).

Wilt, Judith, 'The Ghost and Omnibus: The Gothic Virginia Woolf', in Andrew Smith and Jeff Wallace (eds), *Gothic Modernisms* (Basingstoke: Palgrave, 2001), pp. 62–77.

Wilt, Judith, *Ghosts of the Gothic: Austen, Eliot and Lawrence* (Princeton, NJ: Princeton University Press, 1980).

Wiseman, Sam, *Locating the Gothic in British Modernity* (Clemson, SC: Clemson University Press, 2019).

Woolf, Virginia, 'Gothic Romance' [1920], in *Collected Essays of Virginia Woolf*, ed. Andrew McNeillie, 6 vols (New York: Harcourt, 1988), vol. 3, pp. 304–7.

Zlosnik, Sue, 'Foreword', in Matt Foley and Rebecca Duncan (eds), *Patrick McGrath and his Worlds: Madness and the Transnational Gothic* (New York: Routledge, 2019), pp. ix–xiii.

Notes

1. Botting, *Gothic*, p. 104.
2. Wiseman, *Locating the Gothic*, p. 3.
3. Riquelme, 'Toward a History of Gothic and Modernism', p. 593.
4. Smith and Wallace, 'Introduction', p.3.
5. Woolf, 'Gothic Romance', p.306.
6. Studies of the Gothic or the ghost story that were in their time outliers in literary studies – i.e. that pre-date the wider 'birth' of Gothic studies after David Punter's *The Literature of Terror* (1980) – do include modernist writers in the Gothic conversation. Julia Briggs's *Night Visitors: The Rise and Fall of the English Ghost Story* (1977) and Judith Wilt's *Ghosts of the Gothic: Austen, Eliot and Lawrence* (1980) are two such examples.
7. Riquelme, 'Toward a History of Gothic and Modernism', p. 589.
8. Mao and Walkowitz, 'New Modernist Studies', pp. 737–8.
9. Daly, *Modernism, Romance and the Fin de siècle*, pp. 145–50
10. Birkhead, *The Tale of Terror*, n.p.

11. Wiseman, *Locating the Gothic*, p. 4.
12. Ibid., p. 5.
13. Ibid., p. 117.
14. Botting, *Gothic*, p. 149.
15. Smith, *Gothic Literature*, p. 132.
16. Briggs, *Night Visitors*, p. 165.
17. Thurston, *Literary Ghosts*, p. 168.
18. Beville, *Gothic-postmodernism*, p. 17.
19. Simpson, 'Strange Laughter', p. 2.
20. Seshagiri, 'Modernist Ashes', p. 487.
21. McGrath and Morrow, 'Introduction', pP. xiii–xiv.
22. Patrick McGrath is explicit about his debt to modernism elsewhere in his critical writing, and many reflections on modernist texts can found in his literary archive at the University of Stirling.
23. Zlosnik, 'Foreword', p. ix.
24. Ford, 'Antwerp', lines 113, 115–18.
25. Hulme, 'Romanticism and Classicism', pp. 119–20.
26. Eliot, 'Preface', p. xiv.
27. Cited in Horner, 'A detour of filthiness', p. 231.
28. Crawford, *Young Eliot*, pp. 45–6.
29. Smith, 'Eliot and the Ghost of Poe', pp. 150–1.
30. Cited in Punter, 'Hungry Ghosts', p. 15.
31. Eliot, 'From Poe to Valery', p. 327; original emphasis.
32. Punter, 'Hungry Ghosts', p. 15.
33. Eliot, *The Waste Land*, lines 379–81.
34. Barnes, *Nightwood*, p. 122.
35. Ibid., p. 6.
36. Horner, 'A detour of filthiness', p. 230; original emphasis.
37. Morin, *Charles Robert Maturin*, p. 5.

Chapter 4

Gothic Criticism in the Twentieth Century: Who is This Who is Coming?

Scott Brewster

Throughout the twentieth century, Gothic criticism returned constantly to questions concerning the history, characteristics and purpose of the form: what are its typical features; what effects does it seek to produce; is it conservative or radical; is it a thing of the past, or is it still a thing of the present? This chapter charts the development of Gothic criticism across nine decades, assessing the answers it proposed to these questions and dwelling on some landmarks along the way. To dramatise these recurrent preoccupations of the Gothic, let us first turn to a fictional moment that summons a terror from the past. In M. R. James's 'Oh, Whistle, and I'll Come to You, My Lad' (1903), on a seaside holiday the curious scholar Parkins unearths an enigmatic whistle in a ruined Templar preceptory. Walking back to his lodgings along the beach, a site of residual patterns and unpredictable change, Parkins notices an 'indistinct personage' that leaves him uncomfortable on 'that lonely shore',[1] although his encounter with this stranger is yet to come. After translating an inscription on the whistle as 'Who is this who is coming?', Parkins blows it and calls up unexpected company. The whistle reaches across time and space: its soft note possesses 'a quality of infinite distance' and conjures 'a vision of a wide, dark expanse at night'.[2] The spirit that subsequently manifests in Parkins's bedroom is speechless and assumes only 'a horrible, an intensely horrible, face *of crumpled linen*',[3] but it produces a sense of claustrophobic intimacy and presentness. James's wraith, signifying nothing and arriving as much from the future as from the remote past, figures the type of Gothic terror traced by this essay. Since generic definitions loom large in accounts of the Gothic – an attempt to homogenise, make homely the countenance and habits of this strange, often unsettling form – it might be worth observing that James deplored the 'weltering and wallowing' excesses of the Gothic, preferring instead 'a modicum of blood, shed with deliberation and carefully husbanded'.[4] Nonetheless, the mixture of anticipation and dread, excitement and unease in his tale encapsulates the recurrent preoccupations of Gothic criticism in the twentieth century: whether the literature of terror speaks to the present, whether it wears a companionable, even familiar face, and whether it is fascinated, or unnerved, by the terror that awaits. The Gothic as a mode opens on to the unprecedented, the incalculable – a disquieting interloper at once behind and ahead of us.

The earliest twentieth-century accounts of the Gothic, by critics such as Dorothy Scarborough, Edith Birkhead and J. M. S. Tompkins, concentrate mainly on generic survey and the Gothic's place within a broader literary history. In the main, Gothic fiction is viewed as a minor part of the novel tradition and 'a historically circumscribed phenomenon'.[5] To some degree, this criticism concerns recovery, shining fresh light on neglected or forgotten texts and treating them seriously, rather than as a source of academic embarrassment. Michael Sadleir's *The Northanger Novels: A Footnote to Jane Austen* (1927), which concentrates on the 'horrid' novels mentioned in *Northanger Abbey*, nonetheless implies by its subtitle that the Gothic is a marginal interest for the literary critic. Chris Baldick and Robert Mighall dismiss the modest aspirations and 'shame-faced antiquarianism' exhibited by these works, but this view is unduly severe.[6] In fact, it plays out a Gothic trope, portraying this small group of critics as sober, preoccupied with the abstruse and prone to distraction by curios, behaving in a manner reminiscent of James's scholars (and James himself). What is more attuned to the Gothic, we might conclude, than assigning value to old materials and quaint or superannuated views of the world?

Dorothy Scarborough's *The Supernatural in Modern English Fiction* (1917), notable for its energy and wit, regards the Gothic and the ghost story as components of the broader category of supernatural literature, which 'reveals and transforms the world we live in'.[7] Scarborough sets the tone for subsequent scholarly examinations of Gothic romance by rehearsing its settings, plots, tropes, themes, and the relationship between the explained and unexplained supernatural. In her account, Gothic romance crumbled to dust long ago: it denotes 'the eighteenth-century novel of terror dealing with medieval materials' and is merely a precursor of supernaturalism in modern English literature.[8] The Gothic popularised romance and extended its readership, but its machinery 'creaked audibly', and the form proves only a minor impetus to a supernaturalism that developed a 'special power' in later fiction.[9] Modern ghosts sensibly eschew the more absurd and egregious trappings of the Gothic, freeing themselves from mouldering vaults and 'clanking chains'.[10] Ghosts in the early twentieth century are in rude health, 'more active, more alive than they used to be',[11] and also more formally varied than their Gothic antecedents. Supernatural fiction in its contemporary guise derives its vitality both from rendering spectres more terrible *and* from 'the levelling influence that makes them more human', a realism comparing favourably to the 'charnel shudders' of the Gothic.[12] Scarborough concludes by remarking that '[t]he slashing sword has been displaced by the psychographic pen' in the modern ghost story.[13] This invocation of Freud anticipates Eino Railo's *The Haunted Castle* (1927) and Mario Praz's *The Romantic Agony* (1933), which draw on psychoanalysis to situate the Gothic as the dark counterpart of Romanticism, an approach later informing Robert Kiely's *The Romantic Novel in England* (1972). Here we see glimpses of a theoretical emphasis that increasingly characterises approaches to the Gothic in the latter part of the century.

Edith Birkhead's *The Tale of Terror: A Study of the Gothic Romance* (1921) also regards Gothic romance as merely one strand of a wider tradition: although the tale of terror assumes particular literary significance at the end of the eighteenth century, it 'appeals to deeply rooted instincts' and belongs to 'every age and clime'.[14] Birkhead rehearses a standard narrative by claiming that, in the 1820s, Gothic literature 'lost its individuality and was merged into other forms'.[15] Charles Robert Maturin is viewed as 'the last of the Goths', and Walter Scott constructs romance from 'the stuff of real life'; 'the terrors of the invisible world only fill the stray corners' of a fiction 'solidly built on Scottish soil'.[16] Yet Birkhead also charts the sustained influence of Gothic romance on literature from both sides of the Atlantic through to the early twentieth century. The Gothic therefore represents a continuing legacy, rather than a timebound moment in literary history. In her conclusion, Birkhead observes that interest in the contemporary tale of terror 'has already been transferred from "bogle-wark" to the effect of the inexplicable, the mysterious and the uncanny on human thought and emotion',[17] signalling a heightened formal self-consciousness upon which later criticism will focus.

J. M. S. Tompkins's *The Popular Novel in England, 1770–1800* (1932) locates the Gothic as a specifically English form within a broader European context and ascribes it social and political significance. The Gothic in the 1790s represented 'a natural reaction' away from 'a long period of sobriety in literature', and in a moment of 'revolutionary excitement' and growing demand for reading material among the lower middle classes these factors combined 'to intensify the appeal of the terrible and increase the opportunities of gratifying it'.[18] Tompkins highlights the contribution made by the Gothic to the development of literary suspense, but does not view it as formally or thematically innovative. Gothic romance 'appropriated and refurbished the stock-in-trade of the sentimental novel', these home-grown influences enhanced by the German *schauerroman* (horror story, shudder-novel), with its 'wild extravagance of sentiment and incident'.[19] In depicting the Gothic as a creature solely of its time, Tompkins nevertheless acknowledges that it also deployed anachronism as a deliberate aesthetic strategy. Following the lead of Clara McIntyre, who pointed out that most early Gothic novels were not set in the medieval period, Tompkins emphasises that characters in Gothic fiction 'are not in the least Gothic. They are projections of eighteenth-century ideals.'[20] Sturdily Protestant, market-savvy and banishing filth and 'physical horror',[21] this version of the Gothic appears the antithesis of the radical, subversive force represented in late twentieth-century criticism.

Montague Summers's idiosyncratic, sometimes reactionary *The Gothic Quest* (1938) restores many obscure Gothic texts to the public domain, but largely offers plot summary and literary-historical detail rather than rigorous evaluation, aside from a vehement attack on Surrealist claims upon the Gothic in his closing chapter. David Punter declares Summers's book 'all but useless as an introduction to the Gothic', in turn 'seriously marred by tendentiousness' and 'special pleading', and overwhelmed by his bibliographical material.[22] Summers himself is equally uninhibited in his assessment of Gothic criticism. With haughty disdain, he decries the standard of current scholarship, especially the 'deplorably jejeune output of the Universities', a malaise attributable to lack of access to 'sufficient material', including 'romances which are really significant and historically important'.[23] Summers grants more elevated purpose to Gothic novelists than his predecessors; they rendered 'infinite service' by allowing readers respite from 'the relentless oppression and carking cares of a bitter actuality'.[24] As the 'Novel of Escape', Gothic romance offered 'counter-excitement' to the 'lowering shadows' of war and revolutionary upheaval at home and abroad in the late eighteenth century. Summers detects a distorted reflection of this pattern in the present, with readers reaching for crime fiction and thrillers as a 'precious anodyne' against impending crisis. Such 'unwholesome rubbish' contrasts with Gothic fiction which, even when dealing with lurid themes, never sinks to the level of this contemporary 'dull draff'.[25] Summers's conviction about the Gothic's lofty ambitions reconciles him to its more lubricious pleasures: in Matthew Lewis's *The Monk* (1796), 'pictures of voluptuous passion are necessary to the narrative' and 'the violence of the orgasm but serves to balance and throw in high relief the charnel horrors'.[26]

Notwithstanding this salacious subject matter, the Gothic novel remains 'an aristocrat of literature',[27] a contention that pays little heed to the decidedly bourgeois disposition of its earliest form. Noting that the great Gothic novelists never exhibited the 'slightest sympathy for socialism', Summers strenuously separates Gothic romance from any association with the 'ugly' and 'murderous' term 'Revolution': his use of 'quest' in the title denotes 'the spiritual as well as the literary and artistic seeking for beauty'.[28] To counter the Surrealist Andre Breton's assertion that the Gothic guides its readers from the tyranny of the past to an enlightened present, Summers proclaims his suspicion of an 'official intimacy', confirmed to him by an '[i]mpartial and most trustworthy authority',[29] between Surrealism and communism, a sinister alliance reminiscent of the workings of the Inquisition in Ann Radcliffe's *The Italian*. In contrast, Gothic romance offers us a consoling vision of 'the peace and plenty, the culture and stability of the past' that appears 'entirely preferable to the turmoil, the quarrels, the artistic sterility and chaotic depression of the present'.[30] In admonishing Breton's dangerous radicalism, however, Summers conjures a late 1930s Europe that recalls the political and cultural anxiety to which, he claimed earlier, the early Gothic novel offered an antidote. Summers strives to preserve the purity of the Gothic's originary moment and distance it from his own time, but he cannot mask his dread that a different, more turbulent past has returned to haunt the present. Ironically, in such circumstances, Breton's visionary Gothic, leading us out of darkness, may seem an inviting prospect.

Devendra Varma's *The Gothic Flame* (1957) attempts to guide us to that light. By identifying the historical development and staple generic features of Gothic romance, but also its psychic and spiritual dimensions, Varma's study brings together the disparate concerns of his critical forebears. Discernibly introspective about an emerging critical tradition, Varma first makes peace with the Surrealists; Herbert Read's foreword claims that Varma has 'rescued a dream literature from oblivion', demonstrating in the manner of Edmund Burke that 'the Gothic flame is capable of tempering the soul to a purity beyond the range of our dingy realism'.[31] Tompkins's introduction charts changing attitudes to a form that no longer merits only 'amused tolerance' from literary historians,[32] and makes bold claims for how criticism has shaped this re-evaluation. Freudian psychoanalysis and Surrealism have added 'a new dimension to the study of Gothic writing', connecting it 'to the psychological condition of literate Western Europe at the end of the eighteenth century' and more broadly 'to the permanent nature of man'.[33] The Gothic constitutes an intimate part of us, especially at moments of historical pressure; it is homely, familiar, even homeopathic. For Tompkins, Varma 'sees the Gothic writers as restoring the sense of the numinous to a literature cramped by rationalism and bleached by exposure to unvarying daylight'.[34]

Despite his high-minded mission to disclose its timeless, visionary capacity, Varma confines the Gothic to a 'neglected and dim period' between Fielding and Richardson and the fiction of Austen and Scott, before it disintegrated after 1830.[35] Yet it is also 'a vital thing, a potential force in the literature of today'.[36] The Gothic certainly remains a 'residuary' influence on Varma's approach: he attributes the revival of interest in Gothic fiction to Elkin Matthew's catalogue of old books purchased from 'country halls and old mansions' after the First World War,[37] a bibliographical (and commercial) endeavour that, in a familiar Gothic trope, unleashes the recrudescent power of the past. Similarly, his definition of the Gothic relies on unresolved oppositions, an abiding characteristic of the form. The Gothic represents the barbaric, a 'wildness of thought and roughness of work' appealing to the 'rebel minds of the mid-eighteenth century' who rejected neoclassical restraint. As such, it is Dionysian rather than Apollonian, favouring 'communion with nature and irrational primitive forces' over 'the artistic instinct for order and individuation'.[38] Simultaneously, however, the Gothic is animated by 'holy serenity', offering 'a sense of infinity to our finite existence'.[39] While it appeals 'to the night-side of the soul', it evokes in us 'the same feelings that the Gothic cathedrals evoked in medieval man'; like Summers, Varma ascribes 'sacred purpose' to the Gothic.[40] Continuity and devotion, rather than disruption and transgression, are the watchwords.

In varying ways, critics in the first half of the century identified many features of the Gothic – its ambivalent appeal, its ability to respond to cultural 'anxiety', its capacity for reinvention across different historical moments, and its visionary purpose – that continued to preoccupy criticism in later decades. Although treated primarily as an intriguing byway in the history of English letters, the Gothic is active rather than moribund, its traces still discernible in the present day. In the spirit of the Gothic revival, Gothic fiction is akin to an inspiring ruin, although its transgressive potential is strictly limited. Darkness is tamed, subversion curbed, and excesses are primarily attributed to poor taste in these early accounts. From the late 1970s, however, criticism charts a new direction. Shorn of eccentric trappings, and acquiring greater methodological rigour, it no longer views the Gothic as a relic or peripheral interest; although still visionary or poetic, it is also a dark and evolving form. In this period, too, the Gothic undergoes the transition from marginality to the academic mainstream.

As William Hughes observes, David Punter's *The Literature of Terror* (1980) constitutes 'a – possibly *the* – major landmark in the development of a systematic and theoretically informed Gothic scholarship', while Jerrold E. Hogle deems it the book that 'most helped to launch world-wide acceleration in the study of Gothic'.[41] Subsequently published as a two-volume second edition in 1996 – underscoring the mode's marketability and prominence in university curricula – Punter's foundational work saw Gothic Studies begin to acquire institutional status. In his original preface, Punter expresses his dissatisfaction with existing approaches to the Gothic, including Marxism's restriction to realist literature. Freud is his main point of reference, since psychoanalysis 'contains an implicit aesthetic dimension and centres upon an analysis of fear'.[42] Punter defines the Gothic in 'sociocultural, thematic, formal, psychological' terms, highlighting features such as '[a] particular attitude towards the recapture of history', 'a mode of revealing the unconscious' and 'connections with the primitive, the barbaric, the tabooed'.[43] Its continued resonance can be understood most clearly in terms of terror: 'exploring Gothic is also exploring fear and seeing the various ways in which terror breaks through the surfaces of literature'.[44]

While still providing elements of generic and historical overview, *The Literature of Terror* signals a conceptual reflexivity that prefigures the diversity of theoretical approaches to the Gothic over the next two decades. In the preface to the second edition, Punter acknowledges the 'flood of critical material' since the original book appeared, which has 'modified or overturned' critical assumptions about what the Gothic is and revised notions of the canon associated with the term.[45] Punter had contributed to this canonical revision in the first version of the book by including a chapter on Gothic film, and this formal and theoretical transformation is illustrated visually in the second edition. Each volume's cover is adorned with cinematic images – volume I shows Christopher Lee in *Dracula* (1958), while volume 2 pictures Anthony Quinn and Gina Lollobrigida in *The Hunchback of Notre Dame* (1956) – that acknowledge the Gothic's move beyond the literary.

In Volume 2, a new chapter on contemporary manifestations of the Gothic is somewhat hesitant about its diversification into fashion, popular music and digital media, a development typifying the 'systemic coagulation of production and consumption which the Gothic itself predicts and reflects'.[46] Nonetheless, the discussion does encompass horror film, graphic novels and cyber-gothic. Punter's revised chapter on theory and the Gothic deploys Freud and Marx to examine how the Gothic 'enacts psychological and social dilemmas'.[47] The form returns 'constantly, and hauntedly' to paranoia, barbarism and taboo, and its terror hinges on 'a dialectic of power and impotence'.[48] Generally resistant to 'realist aesthetics', the Gothic deals in ambiguity and removes the 'illusory halo of certainty from the so-called "natural" world'.[49] Ideologically, the Gothic is presented as torn between conservatism and radicalism, the past and the future. Strikingly, given that it would subsequently be celebrated for its transgressive, countercultural tendencies, Punter stresses that the Gothic does not advocate sexual liberation: rather, it is 'too tentative, too hesitant about its perceptions'.[50] Similarly, he argues that 'Gothic can at one and the same time be categorised as a middle-class and an anti-middle-class literature', since it is centred on a 'dialectic of comfort and disturbance'.[51] At once threatening and sustaining, the Gothic 'both confronts the bourgeoisie with its limitations and offers it modes of imaginary transcendence',[52] invoking the escapism proposed by Summers over fifty years previously.

Punter's main definitions – opposition to realism, anxieties about power, class tensions and psychic conflict – underpin much of the criticism that followed *The Literature of Terror*. In particular, significant capital is invested in tracing bourgeois ambivalence. In the first issue of the journal *Gothic Studies* in 1999, another milestone in the development of the field, Hogle suggests that now we see the Gothic 'as a complex symbolic realm where conditions and quandaries that we want to "throw off" from ourselves (what the middle class wants to "other" from itself in the urban West) face us in half-repulsive, half-attractive spectres or monstrosities'.[53] Equally, while earlier critics had adopted Freud to read the Gothic, psychoanalysis became a dominant paradigm from the later 1970s, with the bourgeois psyche again the central arena. Elizabeth MacAndrew sees Gothic literature as akin to nightmare, while, for Coral Ann Howells, Gothic 'projects a peculiarly fraught fantasy world of neurosis and morbidity'.[54] Its timeless psychosexual drama simultaneously embodies fears and offers 'a retreat from insoluble problems',[55] a manoeuvre strikingly similar to that performed by psychoanalysis. This romance between the Gothic, its criticism and psychoanalysis represents a classic case study of intertwined, mutually reinforcing and transferential passions.[56] William Patrick Day proposes that the Gothic, like psychoanalysis, responds 'to the problems of selfhood and identity, sexuality and pleasure, fear and anxiety as they manifest themselves in the nineteenth and early twentieth centuries'.[57] In a similar vein, Anne Williams identifies Freud as the true heir of Walpole and Radcliffe, and the most profoundly Gothic creator of narrative in the twentieth century.[58] The Gothic and psychoanalysis share 'a common cultural matrix' and '[i]nstead of using Freud to read Gothic, we should use Gothic to read Freud'.[59]

Yet it is Freud's least certain act of reading that casts the longest shadow over Gothic criticism. The ubiquity of his essay 'The Uncanny'

(1919) has encouraged a common tendency 'to conflate the uncanny *with* the Gothic'.[60] Enigmatic companion rather than informing model, however, the uncanny constitutes an odd starting point for critics: it functions, one might say, rather like James's whistle. A 'class of the frightening which leads back to what is known of old and long familiar',[61] associated with the compulsion to repeat and the uncertain boundaries between the living and the inanimate, Freud's uncanny also involves the novel and the unforeseen. An inheritance from earliest times, the uncanny denotes a feeling, experience or ambivalence that endures, even thrives, in the modern world. Surprising, disturbing, transformative, the uncanny comes from the future as well as the past.

Feminist literary theory also focused on the family romance staged by the Gothic. Published in 1976, the same year that Punter started writing *The Literature of Terror*, Ellen Moers's *Literary Women* established the important category of Female Gothic, reflecting the impact of second-wave feminism and implicitly acknowledging the women who pioneered Gothic criticism in the early twentieth century. The project to recover and re-evaluate women's role in the Gothic tradition was part of a wider movement in Anglo-American feminist criticism to reinscribe women writers into literary history. Female Gothic gave a crucial impetus to Gothic criticism, which had hitherto been relatively unreflective about gender. Indeed, as Lauren Fitzgerald claims, feminist literary criticism can be said to have 'rescued' and institutionalised Gothic Studies.[62] While Moers prompted crucial examinations of women's entrapment and coercion in patriarchal culture, and showed how Gothic texts written by women could foreground the rejected other of Realism and Romanticism,[63] Female Gothic was also criticised from within feminism for fashioning a heroine in its own heteronormative, white image (exemplified by the othering of Bertha Mason in *Jane Eyre*), and rehearsing rather than challenging the bourgeois 'property plot'.[64] Moers's category was regarded by some as essentialist, especially as male writers could explore 'the implications, for Victorian culture, of the "female" Gothic plot', and was also seen as complicit with 'victim feminism'.[65] Others noted that women Gothic novelists in the period were actively concerned with readerships and questions of financial and creative autonomy,[66] rather than overshadowed by the strictures of patriarchal society.

These critiques of Female Gothic for saying too little about difference or agency, allied to new approaches in gender studies and the development of queer theory, led to a more expansive and fluid conception of how the Gothic could accommodate or marginalise diverse sexualities and identities. Eve Kosofsky Sedgwick, a major theorist of the queer in the 1980s and 1990s, consistently draws on the Gothic novel to explore closeted desire and the uncanniness of heterosexual masculinity, as well as 'the terms of a dialectic between male homosexuality and homophobia'.[67] As Stephen Bruhm argues, the Gothic became 'a perfect mode for the interrogation of sexual power and sexual pleasure. Like the queer episteme, the Gothic disrespects the borderlines of the appropriate, the healthy, or the politically desirable.'[68]

Gothic criticism also began to deploy postcolonial theory in a more sustained fashion. While the Gothic is marked by orientalism from its early moments, late Victorian Gothic offers the most intense expression of the terror of colonial expansion. Patrick Brantlinger's account of 'Imperial Gothic' identifies two main fears lying at its heart: 'going native', and what might come back from the 'margin' to the 'centre'. Although viewing both imperial romance and the Gothic as 'childish and subrational',[69] Brantlinger establishes interpretative paths for subsequent analyses. In an influential reading, Stephen Arata deploys *Dracula* to illustrate the concept of 'reverse colonization', the fear that 'the "civilized" world is on the point of being colonized by "primitive" forces'.[70] Such narratives, Arata contends, 'provide an opportunity to atone for imperial sins, since reverse colonization is often represented as deserved punishment'.[71] Judie Newman observes that the Gothic is crucial for postcolonial theory: through its ability to 'retrace the unseen and unsaid of culture', it is 'very well adapted to expressing the untold and unspeakable stories of colonial experience'.[72] In this vein, Punter's *Postcolonial Imaginings* (2000) analyses postcolonial experience in terms of haunting, wounds, silence and dispossession.

A number of studies in the 1990s also showed the Gothic to have been thoroughly enmeshed in scientific and cultural debates about racial, sexual and bodily difference. In their examination of the discursive construction of monstrosity that the Gothic serves *and* challenges, J. Halberstam contends that nineteenth-century literature is 'a Gothic tradition', due to the 'changing technologies of subjectivity that Foucault describes'.[73] Importantly, given the tendency to treat the Gothic as timeless romance, fantasy or psychodrama, Halberstam asserts that '[m]onstrosity (and the fear it gives rise to) is historically conditioned rather than a psychological universal'.[74] Kelly Hurley shows how, in the *fin de siècle*, the Gothic borrows liberally from evolutionary theory, criminal anthropology and early theories of the unconscious. Just as scientific discourses dismantled conventional ideas of the human, so Gothic narratives rendered supernatural 'the specific content of scientific theories and scientific anxiety in general',[75] exploring the disconcerting implications of these ideas. In this period of 'cultural stress', the Gothic negotiates 'unmanageable realities for its audience'.[76]

Fred Botting's *Gothic* (1996), an overarching account of the mode, reflects this proliferation of theoretical perspectives, and is also marked by a playful tone that appears comfortable with the myriad guises that the Gothic continues to assume. Published in the same year as the second edition of *The Literature of Terror*, and part of the commercially successful Routledge Critical Idiom series, it set another institutional stamp on Gothic criticism. Botting claims that 'Gothic signifies a writing of excess', and that the form is shaped by 'a dynamic of limit and transgression that both restores and contests boundaries'.[77] Gothic scholarship mirrors this testing of limits: recent critical practices 'have moved Gothic texts from previously marginalised sites designated as popular fiction or literary eccentricity'.[78] Emphasising how the Gothic's relation to identity, sexuality, power and empire is being explored in nuanced ways in the late twentieth century, Botting anticipates 'future examinations of the ways Gothic texts produce, reinforce and undermine received ideas about literature, nation, gender and culture'.[79] His conclusion discusses Francis Ford Coppola's 1992 cinematic version of *Dracula*, in which the Gothic seems drained of energy and longing to be put out of its misery. Yet, just as it lingers on the brink of extinction, Botting reflects that this may be the 'prelude to other spectral returns'.[80] Given this instinct for survival, it is unsurprising that this prediction of continued vitality would be borne out, not least by the vigorous renewal of the vampire bloodline in the twenty-first century. As has usually been the case for the Gothic, in its end is its resurgence. Here, the gaze of Gothic criticism turns to a future whose uncertainty is to be embraced.

On the cusp of a new century, however, a more resistant note was struck. In their much-cited essay 'Gothic Criticism', appearing in Punter's *A Companion to the Gothic* (2000) – itself another critical landmark in Gothic Studies – Baldick and Mighall perceive this journey from mystery to enlightenment as symptomatic of a voguish, wish-fulfilling view of the past. Gothic criticism 'has abandoned any credible historical grasp upon its object, which it has tended to reinvent in the image of its own projected intellectual goals of psychological "depth" and political "subversion"'.[81] Such an approach misguidedly presents the Gothic as a liberatory revolt against bourgeois rationality. Current critical interest in the Victorian Gothic falls prey to the 'anxiety model', in which Gothic texts reveal middle-class fears about the progressive future (represented, in fact, by contemporary criticism) rather than the return of a primitive past. Inspired primarily by Marxism, feminism and psychoanalysis, Gothic criticism besieges the anxious bourgeois, a figure who is merely 'a fantasy projected by vengeful frustration' at the resilience and 'well-fed complacency' of the middle class.[82] Scornful of such critical anachronism, Baldick and Mighall nonetheless endorse the 'dissynchronicity' of Dracula with the Victorian world, an 'out-of-placeness' that makes him properly Gothic.[83] This argument only holds, of course, if we overlook the threat posed in Stoker's novel by the Count's eager embrace of modernity, and his ability to navigate the networks of power, property and finance in imperial London. In denying Gothic criticism the 'anachronistic emphases'[84] enjoyed by Gothic fiction, Baldick and Mighall paint most critics as unable to interrogate the reinvented pasts and imagined futures they encounter. The Gothic, however, lives in a time out of joint, and that untimeliness must also be the time of critical reading.

Lucie Armitt has observed that a 'paradoxical combination of exuberance and darkness is one of the sustaining features of the Gothic as it survives into and through the twentieth century'.[85] As a new century approached, Gothic and its criticism looked back to the past and forward to an uncertain future, poised somewhere between pleasurable anticipation and dis-ease. In Colorado, the massacre at Columbine High School in 1999 bestowed new visibility, and grim seriousness, on Goth subculture and the Gothic aesthetic.[86] There were also fears that the millennium bug would send us back to a pre-digital stone age, a Gothicised danger that never materialised, although the anxiety that an advanced machine age, supposed to lay superstition and chance finally to rest, harboured its own destruction suggested the pervasiveness of the uncanny. What was to come in September 2001 wore the face of an unfamiliar terror, even if its causes and effects were both old and new. 9/11 was an event that became characterised variously as unprecedented, incalculable, sublime, traumatic and uncanny. Many of these terms, of course, are associated with the Gothic, and this event, testing belief in several senses, would provoke critical debate about how contemporary Gothic might 'bring out and keep at bay our deepest ambivalences towards the worst of cultural traumas'.[87] Gothic criticism, therefore, returns to that defining question: in that lonely walk along the shoreline, does the Gothic look behind or ahead, searching for a familiar face or peering into a future faintly visible on the horizon?

Key Texts

David Punter, *The Literature of Terror Vol. 1: The Gothic Tradition*, and *Vol. 2: The Modern Gothic* (1980). This landmark study moves beyond generic and historical overview to establish the main theoretical foundations for Gothic criticism in the following decades, and can be argued to have inaugurated Gothic Studies as a scholarly field.

Chris Baldick and Robert Mighall, 'Gothic Criticism' (2000). A provocative and entertaining assessment of Gothic criticism, especially in the latter part of the twentieth century.

Anna Powell and Andrew Smith (eds), *Teaching the Gothic* (2006). Chapters in this volume provide succinct accounts of the main branches of Gothic scholarship. It includes a survey by William Hughes of the development of Gothic criticism since the late eighteenth century and a chapter by Jerrold E. Hogle on theorising the Gothic.

Lucie Armitt, *Twentieth-Century Gothic* (2011). This study devotes a chapter (pp. 144–59) to the main preoccupations of Gothic criticism across the twentieth century.

Jerrold E. Hogle and Robert Miles (eds), *The Gothic and Theory: An Edinburgh Companion* (2019). While focused predominantly on theoretical developments in the twenty-first century, this volume explores the conversation between the Gothic as a mode and diverse theoretical and philosophical perspectives since the eighteenth century. In his introduction, Hogle traces the gradual institutionalisation of Gothic criticism across the twentieth century.

Further Critical Reading

Hogle, Jerrold E., and Andrew Smith, 'Revisiting the Gothic and Theory: An Introduction' (2009). Hogle and Smith offer a succinct overview of the main theoretical trends in Gothic Studies since the mid-1960s that have transformed the Gothic from a marginal to a mainstream scholarly field. They show how Gothic has interacted with theory since its earliest moments; while this process has involved the theorising of Gothic and the 'Gothic-ising of theory', the relationship between theory and Gothic has also proven mutually enriching.

Hughes, William, *Key Concepts in the Gothic* (2018). A crisp and accessible account of the central terms, theoretical perspectives and forms associated with the Gothic from the eighteenth century to the present.

Punter, David (ed.), *A New Companion to the Gothic* (2012). This revised and expanded volume, containing thirty-six essays, provides a comprehensive account of the historical and global development, as well as the formal diversity, of the Gothic tradition. It also assesses various conceptual approaches to Gothic, including the postcolonial, queer theory and psychoanalysis, and includes the essay by Baldick and Mighall on Gothic criticism discussed in this chapter.

Bibliography

Arata, Stephen, 'The Occidental Tourist: *Dracula* and the Anxiety of Reverse Colonization', *Victorian Studies*, 33.4, 1990, pp. 621–45.

Armitt, Lucie, *Twentieth-Century Gothic* (Cardiff: University of Wales Press, 2011).

Baldick, Chris, and Robert Mighall, 'Gothic Criticism', in David Punter (ed.), *A Companion to the Gothic* (Oxford: Blackwell, 2000), pp. 209–28.
Birkhead, Edith, *The Tale of Terror: A Study of the Gothic Romance* (London: Constable, 1921).
Botting, Fred, *Gothic* (London: Routledge, 1996).
Brantlinger, Patrick, *Rule of Darkness: British Literature and Imperialism, 1830–1914* (Ithaca, NY: Cornell University Press, 1988).
Brewster, Scott, 'Gothic and the Question of Theory', in Glennis Byron and Dale Townshend (eds), *The Gothic World* (Abingdon: Routledge, 2014), pp. 308–20.
Bruhm, Stephen, 'Gothic Sexualities', in Anna Powell and Andrew Smith (eds), *Teaching the Gothic* (Basingstoke: Palgrave Macmillan, 2006), pp. 93–106.
Clery, E. J., *Women's Gothic: From Clara Reeve to Mary Shelley* (Tavistock: Northcote, 2000).
Day, William Patrick, *In the Circles of Fear and Desire: A Study of Gothic Fantasy* (Chicago: University of Chicago Press, 1985).
Fitzgerald, Lauren, 'Female Gothic and the Institutionalization of Gothic Studies', *Gothic Studies*, 6.1, 2004, pp. 8–18.
Freud, Sigmund, 'The Uncanny' [1919], in *Penguin Freud Library Vol. 14: Art and Literature* (Harmondsworth: Penguin, 1990), pp. 335–76.
Halberstam, J., *Skin Shows: Gothic Horror and the Technology of Monsters* (Durham, NC: Duke University Press, 1995).
Hoeveler, Diane Long, *Gothic Feminism: The Professionalisation of Gender from Charlotte Smith to the Brontës* (University Park, PA: Pennsylvania State University Press, 1998).
Hogle, Jerrold E., 'The Gothic–Theory Conversation: An Introduction', in Jerrold E. Hogle and Robert Miles (eds), *The Gothic and Theory: An Edinburgh Companion* (Edinburgh: Edinburgh University Press, 2019), pp. 1–30.
Hogle, Jerrold E., 'History, Trauma and the Gothic in Contemporary Western Fictions', in Glennis Byron and Dale Townshend (eds), *The Gothic World* (Abingdon: Routledge, 2014), pp. 72–81.
Hogle, Jerrold E., 'Introduction: Gothic Studies Past, Present and Future', *Gothic Studies*, 1.1, 1999, pp. 1–9.
Hogle, Jerrold E., and Robert Miles (eds), *The Gothic and Theory: An Edinburgh Companion* (Edinburgh: Edinburgh University Press, 2019).
Hogle, Jerrold E., and Andrew Smith, 'Revisiting the Gothic and Theory: An Introduction', *Gothic Studies*, 11.1, 2009, pp. 1–8.
Howells, Coral Ann, *Love, Mystery and Misery: Feeling in Gothic Fiction* [1978] (London: Athlone, 1995).
Hughes, William, *Key Concepts in the Gothic* (Edinburgh: Edinburgh University Press, 2018).
Hurley, Kelly, *The Gothic Body: Sexuality, Materialism, and Degeneration at the Fin de Siècle* (Cambridge: Cambridge University Press, 1996).
James, M. R., *Collected Ghost Stories*, ed. Darryl Jones (Oxford: Oxford University Press, 2011).
James, M. R., 'Some Remarks on Ghost Stories', in *Collected Ghost Stories*, ed. Darryl Jones (Oxford: Oxford University Press, 2011), pp. 410–16.

Kiely, Robert, *The Romantic Novel in England* (Cambridge, MA: Harvard University Press, 1972).
MacAndrew, Elizabeth, *The Gothic Tradition in Fiction* (New York: Columbia University Press, 1979).
McIntyre, Clara F., 'Were the "Gothic Novels" Gothic?', *PMLA*, 36, 1921, pp. 652–64.
Milbank, Alison, *Daughters of the House: Modes of the Gothic in Victorian Fiction* (London: Macmillan, 1992).
Moers, Ellen, *Literary Women* (New York: Doubleday, 1976).
Newman, Judie, 'Postcolonial Gothic: Ruth Prawer Jhabvala and the Sobhraj Case', in Victor Sage and Allan Lloyd Smith (eds), *Modern Gothic: A Reader* (Manchester: Manchester University Press, 1996), pp. 171–87.
Powell, Anna, and Andrew Smith (eds), *Teaching the Gothic* (Basingstoke: Palgrave Macmillan, 2006).
Punter, David, *The Literature of Terror Vol. 1: The Gothic Tradition*, 2nd edn (London: Longman, 1996).
Punter, David, *The Literature of Terror Vol. 2: The Modern Gothic*, 2nd edn (London: Longman, 1996).
Punter, David, *Postcolonial Imaginings: Fictions of a New World Order* (Edinburgh: Edinburgh University Press, 2000).
Punter, David (ed.), *A New Companion to the Gothic* (Oxford: Blackwell, 2012).
Praz, Mario, *The Romantic Agony* (Oxford: Oxford University Press, 1933).
Railo, Eino, *The Haunted Castle: A Study of the Elements of English Romanticism* (London: Routledge, 1927).
Sadleir, Michael, *The Northanger Novels: A Footnote to Jane Austen* (Oxford: Oxford University Press, 1927).
Scarborough, Dorothy, *The Supernatural in Modern English Fiction* (New York: G. P. Putnam's Sons, 1917).
Sedgwick, Eve Kosofsky, *Between Men: English Literature and Male Homosocial Desire* (New York: Columbia University Press, 1985).
Spooner, Catherine, 'Goth Culture', in David Punter (ed.), *A New Companion to the Gothic* (Oxford: Blackwell, 2012), pp. 350–65.
Summers, Montague, *The Gothic Quest* (London: Fortune Press, 1938).
Tompkins, J. M. S., *The Popular Novel in England, 1770–1800* (London: Constable, 1932).
Varma, Devendra, *The Gothic Flame: Being a History of the Gothic Novel in England* (London: Arthur Barker, 1957).
Williams, Anne, *Art of Darkness: A Poetics of Gothic* (Chicago: University of Chicago Press, 1995).

Notes

1. James, *Collected Ghost Stories*, p. 81.
2. Ibid., p. 83.
3. Ibid., p. 92.
4. Ibid., p. 415.

Gothic Criticism in the Twentieth Century 79

5. Punter, *Literature of Terror Vol. 1*, p. 13.
6. Baldick and Mighall, 'Gothic Criticism', p. 209.
7. Scarborough, *The Supernatural in Modern English Fiction*, p. 3.
8. Ibid., p. 6.
9. Ibid., pp. 52, 53.
10. Ibid., p. 106.
11. Ibid., p. 91.
12. Ibid., p. 300.
13. Ibid., p. 283.
14. Birkhead, *Tale of Terror*, p. 15.
15. Ibid., p. 221.
16. Ibid., pp. 93, 156.
17. Ibid., p. 228.
18. Tompkins, *Popular Novel in England*, p. 221.
19. Ibid., pp. 294–5, 298.
20. McIntyre, 'Were the "Gothic Novels" Gothic?'; Tompkins, *Popular Novel in England*, p. 295.
21. Tompkins, *Popular Novel in England*, p. 272.
22. Punter, *Literature of Terror Vol. 1*, p. 15.
23. Summers, *Gothic Quest*, p. 11.
24. Ibid., p. 198.
25. Ibid., p. 13.
26. Ibid., pp. 222, 223.
27. Ibid., p. 397.
28. Ibid., pp. 400, 398.
29. Ibid., p. 411.
30. Ibid., p. 398.
31. Read, 'Foreword', in Varma, *Gothic Flame*, p. viii.
32. Tompkins, 'Introduction', in Varma, *Gothic Flame*, p. xi.
33. Ibid., p. xiii.
34. Ibid., p. xv.
35. Varma, *Gothic Flame*, p. 3.
36. Ibid., p. 205.
37. Ibid., p. 6.
38. Ibid., p. 209.
39. Ibid., pp. 231, 212.
40. Ibid., p. 15.
41. Hughes, *Key Concepts*, p. 9; Hogle, 'The Gothic–Theory Conversation', p. 8.
42. Punter, *Literature of Terror Vol. 1*, pp. vi, vii.
43. Ibid., pp. 16, 4.
44. Ibid., p. 18.
45. Ibid., p. viii.
46. Punter, *Literature of Terror Vol. 2*, p. 145.
47. Ibid., p. 197.
48. Ibid., p. 184.
49. Ibid., pp. 182, 183.
50. Ibid., p. 191.
51. Ibid., p. 203.

52. Ibid., p. 197.
53. Hogle, 'Introduction: Gothic Studies Past, Present and Future', p. 1.
54. MacAndrew, *Gothic Tradition in Fiction*, p. 3; Howells, *Love, Mystery and Misery*, p. 5.
55. Howells, *Love, Mystery and Misery*, p. 7.
56. Brewster, 'Gothic and the Question of Theory', p. 314.
57. Day, *Circles of Fear and Desire*, p. 181.
58. Williams, *Art of Darkness*, p. 240.
59. Ibid., p. 243.
60. Armitt, *Twentieth-Century Gothic*, p. 146.
61. Freud, 'The Uncanny', p. 340.
62. Fitzgerald, 'Female Gothic', p. 9.
63. Williams, *Art of Darkness*, p. 8.
64. Fitzgerald, 'Female Gothic', p. 10.
65. Milbank, *Daughters of the House*, pp. 12–13; Hoeveler, *Gothic Feminism*, p. 7.
66. Clery, *Women's Gothic*, p. 23.
67. Sedgwick, *Between Men*, p. 92.
68. Bruhm, 'Gothic Sexualities', p. 94.
69. Brantlinger, *Rule of Darkness*, p. 251.
70. Arata, 'The Occidental Tourist', p. 623.
71. Ibid., p. 623.
72. Newman, 'Postcolonial Gothic', p. 171.
73. Halberstam, *Skin Shows*, p. 2.
74. Ibid., p. 6.
75. Hurley, *The Gothic Body*, p. 6.
76. Ibid., p. 5.
77. Botting, *Gothic*, pp. 1, 9.
78. Ibid., p. 17.
79. Ibid., p. 20.
80. Ibid., p. 180.
81. Baldick and Mighall, 'Gothic Criticism', p. 209.
82. Ibid., pp. 225, 226.
83. Ibid., p. 221.
84. Ibid., p. 220.
85. Armitt, *Twentieth-Century Gothic*, pp. 144–5
86. Spooner, 'Goth Culture', p. 355.
87. Hogle, 'History, Trauma and the Gothic', p. 76.

Part II

The Gothic and Technology/Transmedia Considerations

Chapter 5

The Birth of an Evil Thought: The Gothic in Silent-Era Cinema
Murray Leeder

The silent era of film, running roughly from the medium's public debut in 1895 through to the late 1920s, seems so long ago – almost unimaginably so. As cinema is a modern medium, forever marked with newness, its earliest phases feel illegitimate, almost impossible. Gothic tropes now characterise even its most mundane of expressions; reviewing a programme of 1914 films for *The Guardian*, Peter Bradshaw describes the experience as 'more like a séance than anything else: an eerie summoning of ghosts from the early days of cinema and the twentieth century'.[1] This says little enough about the films themselves but a lot about our position relative to them; they now seem alien and uncanny. It is perhaps for that reason that, with the possible exception of comedy, there is no type of silent film that proved to have a longer cultural afterlife than its horrific, Gothic, gruesome versions. The Gothic label tends to adhere most strongly to four cycles of silent-era films, and I will briefly list each of these in turn.[2]

First, and earliest, is early cinema and the trick films, especially those of Georges Méliès. Méliès was a Paris-based magician and impresario who saw in the new medium a vehicle for the magical theatre's wondrous appearances, disappearances, animations, explosions and transformations. Made well before the genres of science fiction, fantasy and horror were understood as separate, Méliès's trick films had elements of them all, and a great many of them – including the first, *Le Manoir du diable* (*The House of the Devil*, 1896) – use the backdrop of stock Gothic locales such as haunted castles, graveyards and laboratories. One stock scenario that proved to have particular traction was that of a traveller checking into a haunted hotel and being comically beset by ghostly forces. Among the most famous of these were Méliès's *L'auberge ensorcelée* (*The Bewitched Inn*, 1897), *Uncle Josh in a Spooky Hotel* (1900) by Edwin S. Porter, *La maison hantée* (*The Ghost House*, 1906) by Segundo de Chomón and *The Haunted Hotel*

(1907) by J. Stuart Blackton. These works are quintessential examples of what Tom Gunning famously called 'the cinema of attractions', meaning that they prioritise spectacle and impact over narrative integration.[3] They would fade around 1910 in the face of increased audience demand for narrative complexity and the institution of the feature as the industry's principal product, yet many of their techniques and themes remained, simply less dominant.

The second cycle is German Expressionism, with its distorted, dreamlike landscapes that represent mental states, and its frequent supernatural themes. Key Expressionist films include *Das Cabinet des Dr Caligari* (*The Cabinet of Dr Caligari*, 1920), *Der Golem* (*The Golem*, 1920), *Nosferatu: Eine Symphonie des Grauens* (*Nosferatu*, 1922), *Orlacs Hände* (*The Hands of Orlac*, 1924), *Geheimnisse einer Seele* (*Secrets of a Soul*, 1926) and ultimately *Metropolis* (1927). In the latter, the most Gothic imagery and themes are associated with Dr Rotwang (Rudolf Klein-Rogge), the prototypical cinematic mad scientist, in whose twisted laboratory the famous set piece of the creation of the robot Maria takes place. An earlier and very influential German work was the doppelgänger tale *Der Student von Prag* (*The Student of Prague*, 1913), which was analysed by the psychoanalyst Otto Rank and mentioned via a footnote in Sigmund Freud's famous 1919 essay on the uncanny.[4]

Another significant cycle encompasses Hollywood melodramas of the 1920s that involve disfigurement and monstrosity, emblematised by the ten collaborations of director Tod Browning and actor Lon Chaney (most notably, *The Unknown* [1927]) and by the expensive 'horror-spectaculars'[5] such as *The Hunchback of Notre Dame* (1923), *The Phantom of the Opera* (1925) and *The Man Who Laughs* (1928). These are often less overtly Gothic in terms of their look but involve twisted psychological themes that match the physiognomy of their unfortunate characters. Somewhat related to this cycle through its use of monstrous make-up and themes of duality are the numerous adaptations of Stevenson's *Strange Case of Dr Jekyll and Mr Hyde* (1886). The year 1920 alone saw three of these, two in the United States (the famous one with John Barrymore and another starring Sheldon Lewis) and F. W. Murnau's unauthorised *Der Janus-Kopf* in Germany.

Lastly, and perhaps least discussed, is the cycle of serio-comedic 'old, dark house' films in the 1920s. These films concern inheritances, take place in a crumbling Gothic mansion criss-crossed with secret passages and chambers, and almost inevitably feature a ghost or monster that ends up being revealed as a scheming human in disguise; they are in almost every way the inheritors of the Radcliffean Gothic and the ancestors of *Scooby-Doo* (1969–76). Most of these are adaptations, largely with theatrical but also including some literary sources, and some were popular enough to be filmed more than once. Mary Roberts Rinehart's novel *The Circular Staircase* (1908) was adapted both into a film of that title in 1915 and the stage play *The Bat* in 1920 (co-written with Avery Hopwood), which was itself adapted into the film *The Bat* (1926); *The Bat* was filmed again in 1930 and 1959. Paul Dickey and Charles W. Goddard's play *The Ghost Breaker* (1909) was adapted in 1914 and 1922. Others, such as *Midnight Faces* (1926), had original screenplays but were nonetheless strongly steeped in the conventions of Gothic stage melodramas. Probably the best regarded of these was Paul Leni's *The Cat and the Canary* (1927), to which we will return, based on John Willard's 1922 play of the same name. This is one cycle that continued over into the sound period with relatively little pause; there was a sound remake of *The Cat and the Canary*, the lost *The Cat Creeps* (1930), and James Whale's *The Old Dark House* (1932). Bob Hope would star in two different remakes of silent films from the late stages of this cycle: *The Cat and the Canary* (1939) and *The Ghost Breakers* (1940). Throughout this cycle, the comedy is woven into the narrative harmoniously with horror. Horner and Zlosnik propose that the Gothic can be thought of as a 'a spectrum that, at one end, produces horror-writing containing moments of comic hysteria or relief and, at the other, works in which there are clear signals that nothing is to be taken seriously'.[6] The old, dark house films are firmly in the later type, operating in an unserious mode of spookiness while stopping short of outright farce.

Nonetheless, we can also note that one need only very slightly extend the confines of the old, dark house cycle to include more overt works of slapstick featuring the most famous comedians of the silent era (Buster Keaton in *The Haunted House* [1921], Harold Lloyd in *Haunted Spooks* [1920], Harry Langdon in *The First Hundred Years* [1924], the children of Our Gang in *Shivering Spooks* [1926]), as well as many more similar films starring relatively forgotten comedians (for example, *Ghost Hounds* [1917], *Grab the Ghost* [1920] and *Money to Burn* [1922]). The format also lent itself to animation. The first recurring animated character, Colonel Heeza Liar, starred in *Colonel Heeza Liar, Ghost Breaker* (1915). In *Felix the Ghost Breaker* (1923), Felix the Cat eventually unmasks a purported ghost as a living man trying to frighten a farmer into selling his property to him. The faker is punished by being kicked to the moon by a donkey. In the mixed-format *KoKo's Haunted House* (1928), KoKo the clown and his canine Fitz are actively tormented by their animators.

Trouble in Mind

Emphasising these four cycles (the trick film, German Expressionism, the disfigurement melodramas and the old, dark house film) has an obvious drawback, since there are plenty of important Gothic films peripheral to them. Some are from different national contexts (for example *Häxan* [1922] by Danish director Benjamin Christensen and *Kurutta Ippēji* [*A Page of Madness*, 1926] by Japan's Teinosuke Kinugasa). My treatment here will not give equal weight to all of these but will focus on the theme of Gothic interiority, and a tendency in silent film to blend cinematic spaces with mental spaces through motifs of projection, shadowing and mirroring. I have discussed elsewhere[7] the extent to which early cinema, and cinema in general, inherited the mantle of the eerie shows of the Phantasmagoria, originating in the late eighteenth century. Exhibitors such as Étienne-Gaspard Robert (under the stage name 'Robertson') and Paul de Philipstal (as 'Philidor') mixed rear-projected magic lanterns with stunning images of ghosts, skeletons, demons and the like; Robertson screened his shows in the quintessentially Gothic locale of an abandoned Capuchin convent. Terry Castle refers to the eighteenth century as witnessing the 'invention of the uncanny'. The era of the Gothic novel's invention was also that of the internalisation of the supernatural into the mind, where once external forces were turned into phantasmatic 'inner pictures'.[8] The very term 'phantasmagoria', Castle notes, drifted from describing this external spectacle to referencing:

> the phantasmic imagery of the mind. This metaphoric shift bespeaks ... a very significant transformation in the human consciousness over the past two centuries ... the spectralization or 'ghostifying' of mental space ... Thus in everyday conversation we affirm that our brains are filled with ghostly shapes and images, that we 'see' figures and scenes in our minds, that we are 'haunted' by our thoughts.[9]

David J. Jones has also shown how significant the magic lantern was to the development of Gothic literature.[10] Pepper's Ghost, the projection trick that debuted at London's Royal Polytechnic Institution in 1862, provided wispy, airy reflected ghosts for the adaptation of Gothic tales such as Dickens's 'The Haunted Man' (1848), the new optical technology and familiar Gothic narratives complementing each other perfectly.[11] The literary Gothic and its visual (and phonic, etc.) equivalents have never been neatly cleaved off from each other. Throughout this chapter, I will emphasise the extent to which those linkages of projection, doubles, shadow and the spaces of the mind continue into silent-era cinema's Gothic expressions.

Let us take, for example, the first adaptation of one of the canonical Gothic novels, Mary Shelley's *Frankenstein* (1818). 1910 is often placed at the centre of a transitional period, when the trick film and other short forms based around spectacle and display declined in favour of narrative integration.[12] That year also saw the fascinating Thomas Edison production of *Frankenstein*, directed by J. Searle Dawley. Sixteen minutes long, it interestingly incorporates elements of the trick film, including the spectacular creation sequence in a vat of fire, threaded into a loose narrative adaptation of Mary Shelley's novel. Frankenstein's workshop looks much like the set of a Méliès trick film, with objects painted on the walls and an inanimate skeleton conspicuously prominent in frame. Spurned by his creator, the monster (Charles Ogle) confronts Frankenstein (Augustus Phillips) in a room dominated by a huge mirror at the right of the frame. We see the monster enter through the reflection of a door, and his later attempt to attack Frankenstein is interrupted when he sees his own horrifying reflection. He later invades Frankenstein's wedding night but is apparently expelled by Frankenstein's love for Elizabeth (Mary Fuller). In the final scene, introduced by the intertitle 'THE CREATION OF AN EVIL MIND IS OVERCOME BY LOVE AND DISAPPEARS', the monster goes back to the mirror to confront his own visage. After contorting melodramatically, he disappears via a substitution splice, though his image remains in the reflection. Frankenstein enters the room, spots the reflection, and then it too disappears, replaced by Frankenstein's own reflection via a graphic match.

The creation sequence has rightfully drawn the lion's share of commentary on this *Frankenstein*, but in a sense its ending is just as interesting and more ambiguous. Following a summary published in *The Edison Kinetogram*, we are to understand the ending thus:

> under the effect of love and his better nature, the monster's image fades and Frankenstein sees himself in his young manhood in the mirror. His bride joins him, and the film ends with their embrace. Frankenstein's mind now being relieved of the awful horror and weight it has been labouring under for so long.[13]

This conservative 'love conquers all' interpretation, forced or even trite though it may be, is nonetheless interesting for framing the film as essentially being a psychodrama about Frankenstein's mind – the monster is created by his 'evil idea' and ultimately sent away by his force of will. When read as a reflexive commentary on its medium, this *Frankenstein* not only invocates creation, but also cinema's uncanny potentialities.

The Expressionist masterpiece *The Cabinet of Dr Caligari* is, of course, silent cinema's go-to example of this dreamlike Gothic filmmaking, complete with the much-disliked twist ending that reveals much of the film to have been the ravings of a madman. However, I want to draw attention to an earlier and far less discussed example from none other than the man long discursively enshrined as the Father of Film: D. W. Griffith.

The Gothic Griffith

Griffith's star has, of course, waned in recent decades. This is in part because of the increasing acknowledgement of other film pioneers, but has more to do with the rightful distaste aroused by the flagrant racism of his most famous film, *The Birth of a Nation* (1915). Before he made *The Birth of a Nation*, a celebratory account of the foundation of the Ku Klux Klan, Griffith had directed hundreds of shorts for the Biograph Company, covering a range of genres, including Gothic melodramas such as *The Sealed Room* (1909). Griffith's fondness for melodramatic emotional display innately gives his work affinities with the Gothic, and these come to the fore most strongly in certain of his features. His immediate prior feature to *The Birth of a Nation* was *The Avenging Conscience: or "Thou Shalt Not Kill"* (1914). *The Avenging Conscience*, though swiftly eclipsed in Griffith's career, was highly praised at the time, notably by the poet and pioneering film theorist Vachel Lindsay.[14] It has attracted relatively little scholarship despite its fascinating place in film history and contains many moments that anticipate *The Birth of a Nation*, including a climactic suicide, a vision of Jesus and an armed standoff in a remote cabin. It is based on Edgar Allan Poe, both in terms of details of his personal life and in terms of motifs drawn from his numerous stories and poems, sometimes overtly cited in intertitles. Griffith had earlier made the short *Edgar Allen Poe* (1909) [sic]; Henry B. Walthall, star of both *The Avenging Conscience* and *The Birth of a Nation*, would also play Poe in the biopic *The Raven* (1915).[15]

The Avenging Conscience involves the romance of Walthall's nameless character and the young Annabel (Blanche Sweet). Their engagement is blocked by his cruel, eye-patch-wearing uncle and guardian (Spottiswoode Aitken), and he is haunted by visions of murder. In one almost proto-Eisensteinian montage sequence, Walthall's character watches a spider kill a fly and observes ants swarming a larger insect, leading him to conclude that nature itself condones murder. The intertitles proclaim, 'THE BIRTH OF THE EVIL THOUGHT'. He strangles his uncle and conceals the body behind a wall in prime Poe fashion. Haunted by guilt, however, he begins to hallucinate his uncle's superimposed ghost; meanwhile, a blackmailer (an evil Italian proletarian, one of Griffith's bigoted racial and class-based portrayals) threatens to uncover his crime. In a development more of Griffith than Poe, the nephew sees visions of Christ on the cross and of the tablet inscribed with the commandment 'THOU SHALT NOT KILL'. The film's centrepiece draws on 'The Tell-Tale Heart' (1843), as a police detective visits the nephew, who focuses intently on a drumming pencil and a tapping shoe. Close-ups and use of the iris's focused gaze show us his perspective, being maddened by the repeated, heartbeat-like noises which, of course, we do not hear.

What follows is an impressive display of Gothic excess. The nephew's conscious mind unravels completely, and he sees an image of demons crawling through a fiery inferno. Contorting his face mightily before the befuddled detective, he then sees an image of himself behind roiling smoke, bound with rope and being stroked by a laurelled skeleton. Finally, he sees, via superimpositions, his crime re-enacted, as spectres of himself and the uncle appear to restage the initial strangulation. The nephew punctuates the point by jumping about the room strangling air while mugging like an ape. He then flees and the film enters a much more familiar Griffith scenario – chases and gunfights – with a local posse breaking into his hideaway from outside. The nephew hangs himself, and, upon witnessing his fate, his lover also dramatically commits suicide by jumping off a cliff.

The film is not over, however: the nephew awakes in a chair, grabbing at his neck, and is greeted by his uncle. The uncle is not only still alive but is actually benign, and he quickly gives his assent to the marriage. This literal 'all just a dream' ending is capped with a lengthy idyll, showing Pan and a series of children dressed as wood sprites, intercut with footage of a cougar, a panther and some rabbits. Presumably paying tribute to Poe's neoclassical affinities and framed as the visualisation of a poem that the nephew is reading, this sequence is a bewildering over-correction to the Gothic imagery on display earlier in the film. However, the 'just a dream' copout allows another reading of *The Avenging Conscience*, making an already interior film – which itself contains dream sequences! – into an almost completely oneiric one. During the dream-phase of the film, we watch Annabel raise a curtain. A superimposed skyscape appears, which covers not just the window but the entire half of the screen, even the space beyond the window, and also visually manifests a split second before she raises the curtain to reveal it. Even if this is simply a clumsy effect, it holds the implication that the skyscape provides a glimpse into the stormy, Brontëan landscape of her mind. In the film's final scene, intercut with the aforementioned neoclassical parade, the same effect recurs, awkwardly positioning a roiling cloudbank over the two lovers. The overt display of romance and tranquillity at the culmination of this intensely moralistic narrative unfolds beneath an impression of turmoil, literally superimposed above.

The Avenging Conscience would not be the last of Griffith's forays into the Gothic. In 1926 he adapted Maria Corelli's novel *The Sorrows of Satan*. He also made *One Exciting Night* (1922), an entry in the old, dark house cycle. The Griffith Papers held jointly by the Library of Congress and the Museum of Modern Art contain correspondence with a law firm in New York City, comparing the script against more than a dozen Gothic stage melodramas to avoid actionable similarities. The Gothic was clearly a topic of special interest to Griffith. One could argue, however, that there are traces of it even in *The Birth of a Nation*, and not only because of its many echoes of *The Avenging Conscience*. In one unsettling scene, the protagonist, Colonel Benjamin Cameron (Walthall), watches white children don sheets to scare a black child. Cameron's face lights up and an intertitle announces 'THE INSPIRATION', again transposing supernatural imagery with a mental state. The KKK's white robes and hoods, the film argues, are scooped directly from the stock aesthetic of the ghost. Linda Williams observes that this sequence inverts the scene in *Uncle Tom's Cabin* (1852) where Cassy and Emmeline escape from Simon Legree by posing as the ghost of the enslaved woman that he murdered;[16] just as Stowe's novel has been re-evaluated as a work of the American Gothic,[17] it may be prudent to do the same for *The Birth of a Nation*, which continues to haunt the Hollywood film industry to this day.

Claws and Cages: *The Cat and the Canary*

The fullest realisations of the formal potential of silent film come from the late silent era. Several significant film theorists, notably Rudolf Arnheim,[18] saw sound as a major step backward for a medium that had developed an intricate silent visual language; while few today would go so far as that, there was clearly at least a temporary regression in formal sophistication, which led to the stiff and stagey feel of so much early sound cinema. For a variety of reasons, *The Cat and the Canary* stands almost as the apex of silent Gothic cinema, especially for its melding of the expressionistic style imported from Germany with the conventions of the old, dark house comedies. Before leaving Germany, director Paul

Leni directed *Das Wachsfigurenkabinet* (*Waxworks*, 1924), an anthology film built around the dummies in the wax museum, which includes a terrifying and effective episode about Jack the Ripper. Leni would subsequently direct *The Man Who Laughs*, based on Victor Hugo's novel,[19] and another comedic Gothic film, *The Last Warning* (1928), before dying of sepsis in 1929.

The Cat and the Canary takes place in a huge Gothic mansion overlooking the Hudson River, where millionaire Cyrus West is dying. After the introductory intertitle, we see an exterior of the jagged, many-turreted house. Superimposed in front of it we then see a halo of light that contains the convalescing West. Another dissolve shows him surrounded by massive outlines of empty medicine bottles. Another intertitle tells us that his 'greedy relatives, like cats around a canary, had brought him to the verge of madness –' We then see him surrounded by oversized black cats, superimposed feline spectres that snarl and swat in his direction. A document now partially obstructs the image: the handwritten 'Last Will and Testament of Cyrus West. To be opened twenty years after my death.' It disappears to show West apparently dead, and then, over the image of the house again, a monstrous hand reaches out and draws the image back to the front of the frame. It now reads 'This envelope is <u>never</u> to be opened if the terms of my will are carried out.' In just a few minutes, the film establishes its premise, the core themes of inheritance and madness, while mapping the spooky and stylish aesthetic of the film to follow.

An intertitle informs us that West's ghost is rumoured to walk the mansion's halls. We then see POV-coded mobile camerawork, putting us in the implicit perspective of an unseen force roaming through a hallway. We are then told that 'on the night when the will was to be read, there was something more tangible than a ghost in the house'. We see a flashlight shining through the room and more fluid camerawork that ends at a safe, where a gloved hand reaches forward to put in a combination. It remarkably anticipates the POV camerawork associated with *Halloween* (1978) and the other films of the first slasher cycle.

The Cat and the Canary is overstuffed with every old, dark house archetype, up to and including the claim of an escaped lunatic prowling the premises: 'He's a maniac who thinks he's a cat, and tears his victims like they were canaries!' Gorgeously made, *The Cat and the Canary* features all of the dreamy, almost surreal qualities associated with silent Gothic films, turning cinematic space into a torturous labyrinth of the mind. The camerawork remains swift and mobile. Lighting throws huge expressive shadows on to the walls; sometimes they look like cages or vicious claws. Even the intertitles get in on the act: they shiver and tremble when words such as 'GHOSTS!' are spoken. When West's relatives arrive for the midnight reading of his will on the twentieth anniversary of his death, they cluster séance-like around a table. A giant painting of Cyrus adorns the wall, and we occasionally get playful POV shots from its apparent perspective. The supernatural is suggested and implied throughout even though, like most films of its ilk, *The Cat and the Canary* proves to be a work of the Todorovian fantastic-uncanny mode,[20] where supernatural themes are eventually ruled out. The motivations are in the end all too human (and distinctly Gothic): greed, as a scheming cousin plots to drive the rightful heir Annabelle West (Laura La Plante) to madness and thus secure the inheritance for himself. As Simone Natale notes, the stock aesthetic for ghostliness, the superimposition, appears throughout *The Cat and the Canary* but not to depict actual ghosts; rather, they suggest mental images and impressions, such as Cyrus surrounded by medicine bottles and cats.[21] At one point, the film's comic hero, Paul Jones (Creighton Hale), becomes frightened at an omen of death and a skull appears superimposed next to his head.

As Natale also notes, superimpositions are also occasionally associated with sound, to remind us that even though we cannot hear diegetic noises, the characters can, and react to sound cues. A knocking at the door is conveyed by a superimposition, as is the sudden chiming of a clock. Conversely, dialogue is occasionally not conveyed by intertitles; this is the case during the reading of the will, where the lawyer's mouth is even shot in close-up but his words go unreported. The complicated relationship of silent – or perhaps better, 'mute' – films to sound ones is thus played with on a formal level. Robert Spadoni notes that had *The Cat and the Canary*

> been a sound film . . . [it] would have been a feast of noises . . . like the host of visual techniques Leni deployed, to make the viewers jumpy. The *Motion Picture News* predicted that the film would 'score best when presented mostly with mechanical sound effects rather than customary musical accompaniment.' We can easily imagine what some of those sound effects must have been: creaking hinges, banging doors, shrieking women, howling cats.[22]

Viewers might well have experienced this and other films in a sound-immersed landscape, though one that emerged from their theatrical space rather than cinema's mechanical apparatus. One could say that sound itself is treated as a ghostly force in its simultaneous presence in and absence from the cinematic world.

The Haunting of the Silent Period

The process of cinema converting to sound was uneven in ways that belie the neat periodisation favoured by many film histories. The late 1920s and early 1930s saw a number of Gothic films released both in sound and silent versions, to accommodate cinemas not yet converted for sound. A film such as *The Terror* (1928) tends to slip through both silent- and sound-oriented histories, predating as it does *Dracula* (1931), which is often positioned as the ur-work of the classical cycle of Gothic horror talkies of the 1930s. *Dracula* too was released in a silent version. On a less literal level, there are personnel and thus aesthetic continuities. *Dracula*'s cinematographer was Karl Freund, a German émigré who had shot *The Golem* and *Metropolis*; he would later direct *The Mummy* (1932) and *Mad Love* (1935). Art director Charles D. Hall and make-up maestro Jack Pierce were veterans who helped establish the style of the sound horror film. Some European examples, notably Carl Theodor Dreyer's *Vampyr* (1932), verge on being silent films with sound. Tod Browning's infamous *Freaks* (1932) gestures to the silent style with a single intertitle that introduces the film's grotesque wedding banquet sequence.

Much later, traces of the silent-era Gothic remain. Tim Burton's early films such as *Beetlejuice* (1988) and *Edward Scissorhands* (1990) are filled with Gothic ambience drawn from silent films, especially German Expressionism. In his intricate silent film pastiches, Guy Maddin often draws upon Gothic imagery as he grapples with deep and often very personal psychological and melodramatic themes. And more recently, creators in a variety of media have almost compulsively reframed the silent era through a Gothic lens. It has been revisited in narratives such as *Shadow of the Vampire* (2000), which places a real vampire on the set of *Nosferatu*, and *Playback* (2012), in which the early cinema pioneer Louis Le Prince is reimagined as an immortal haunting force. John Carpenter's *Cigarette Burns* (2005) concerns the investigation of a demonic silent film, and various literary works also chart the relationship between silent film and things Gothic and supernatural (for example, Gemma Files's *Experimental Film* [2015] and Jonathan Skariton's *Séance Infernale* [2018]). A number of music videos, including Rob Zombie's 'Living Dead Girl' (1999), 'Square Hammer' by Ghost (2016), Sufjan Stevens's 'You Are the Blood' (2009), Delaney Davidson's 'One Step Ahead' (2020) and Marilyn Manson's 'Cryptorchid' (1996), draw on silent horror aesthetics to create various shades of creepiness. Silent films are cited in more recent horror films such as *The Babadook* (2014), and there have been full-scale pastiches, such as *The Call of Cthulhu* (2005), which imagines what an adaptation of Lovecraft's famous story might have looked like in the year of its publication, 1926. In a comic mode, *Portlandia* (2011–18) had a sketch in which a woman is encouraged by a postman to watch *The Cabinet of Dr Caligari* only to find that she's under a curse and now has to trick someone else into watching it. Arguably, in the public's imagination, the entire silent period has been Gothicised.

Key Texts

Le Manoir du diable (*The House of the Devil*, 1896). The first Georges Méliès trick film, using a stock Gothic scenario to explore the transformative potential of the new medium.

Frankenstein (1910). Produced by Thomas Edison, this was the first adaptation of Shelley's novel, melding spectacle and narrative in a dreamlike package.

Der Student von Prag (*The Student of Prague*, 1913). Based on Poe's story 'William Wilson' (1839), a haunting study of doubling and obsession.

The Avenging Conscience (1914). D. W. Griffith's extended Poe homage ranges from violent melodrama to soporific romance to Gothic horror.

Das Cabinet des Dr Caligari (*The Cabinet of Dr Caligari*, 1920). Twisted, artificial and oneiric, the exemplary text of German Expressionism.

The Haunted House (1921). A slapstick comedy in which Buster Keaton's bank teller stumbles into a fake haunted house set up by a gang, with madcap results.

Nosferatu, eine Symphonie des Grauens (1922). The earliest surviving adaptation of *Dracula*, featuring the iconic make-up design on Max Schreck's Count Orlok.

Felix the Ghost Breaker (1923). Felix the Cat is comically beset by supernatural forces.

The Phantom of the Opera (1925). A spectacular mega-production anchored by the sensitive performance of Lon Chaney; most famous for the iconic unmasking scene.

The Cat and the Canary (1927). The consummate 'old, dark house' mystery, bringing Leni's European sensibility to an exciting mystery story.

The Unknown (1927). This fascinating melodrama about deformity and desire has become the most famous of Tod Browning's numerous collaborations with Lon Chaney.

La chute de la maison Usher (1928). The dreamy, poetic Poe adaptation by critic and experimental filmmaker Jean Epstein.

Further Critical Reading

Aldana Reyes, Xavier, *Gothic Cinema* (2020). A readable and persuasive survey that gives early chapters to numerous aspects of the silent-era Gothic.
Jones, David Annwn, *Re-Envisaging the First Age of Cinematic Horror: 1896–1934: Quanta of Fear* (2018). A paradigm-redefining work emphasising the production of fear by films from cinema's first decades.
Kinnard, Roy, *Horror in Silent Films: A Filmography, 1896–1929* (1995). An extensive catalogue.
Phillips, Kendall R., *A Place of Darkness: The Rhetoric of Horror in Early American Cinema* (2018). Phillips emphasises the interplay between supernatural beliefs and the rationalistic scientific mindset in US silent cinema.
Rhodes, Gary D., *The Birth of the American Horror Film* (2018). Sorted thematically by topics such as witches, devils, murders and executions, and mad scientists, Rhodes's book has a global scope and an impressive depth.
Soister, John T., and Henry Nicolella, *American Silent Horror, Science Fiction and Fantasy Feature Films, 1913–1929* (2012). An extremely thorough archival treatment of numerous silent films, many with Gothic elements and some of which are extremely obscure.

Bibliography

Aldana Reyes, Xavier, *Gothic Cinema* (New York: Routledge, 2020).
Arnheim, Rudolf, *Film as Art* (Berkeley, CA: University of California Press, 1957).
Bradshaw, Peter, 'A Night at the Cinema in 1914 Review – Ghosts from the Early Days of Film', *The Guardian*, 31 July 2014, <http://www.theguardian.com/film/2014/jul/31/a-night-at-the-cinema-in-1914-review-bfi> (last accessed 21 October 2021).
Brubaker, Ed, and Doug Mahnke, *Batman: The Man Who Laughs* (New York: DC Comics, 2008).
Castle, Terry, *The Female Thermometer: 18th-Century Culture and the Invention of the Uncanny* (Oxford: Oxford University Press, 1995).
Conrich, Ian, 'Before Sound: Universal, Silent Cinema, and the Last of the Horror-Spectaculars', in Stephen Prince (ed.), *The Horror Film* (New Brunswick, NJ: Rutgers University Press, 2004), pp. 40–57.
Denson, Shane, *Postnaturalism: Frankenstein, Film, and the Anthropotechnical Interface* (New York: Columbia University Press, 2014).
Freud, Sigmund, 'The "Uncanny"', in *The Standard Edition of the Complete Psychological Works of Sigmund Freud. Vol. XVII (1917–1919)* (London: Hogarth Press, 1964), pp. 219–52.
Groth, Helen, 'Reading Victorian Illusions: Dickens's *Haunted Man* and Dr. Pepper's "Ghost"', *Victorian Studies*, 5.10, 2007, pp. 43–65.
Gunning, Tom, 'The Cinema of Attractions: Early Film, its Spectator and the Avant-Garde', in Thomas Elsaesser and Adam Barker (eds), *Early Cinema: Space, Frame, Narrative* (London: BFI, 1990), pp. 56–62.

Horner, Avril, and Sue Zlosnik, *Gothic and the Comic Turn* (Basingstoke: Palgrave Macmillan, 2005).
Jones, David Annwn, *Re-Envisaging the First Age of Cinematic Horror: 1896–1934: Quanta of Fear* (Cardiff: University of Wales Press, 2018).
Jones, David. J., *Sexuality and the Gothic Magic Lantern: Desire, Eroticism and Literary Visibilities from Byron to Bram Stoker* (Basingstoke: Palgrave Macmillan, 2014).
Keil, Charlie, *Early American Cinema in Transition: Story, Style, and Filmmaking, 1907–1913* (Madison, WI: University of Wisconsin Press, 2001).
Kinnard, Roy, *Horror in Silent Films: A Filmography, 1896–1929* (Jefferson, NC: McFarland, 1995).
Leeder, Murray, *The Modern Supernatural and the Beginnings of Cinema* (Basingstoke: Palgrave Macmillan, 2017).
Leeder, Murray, '"Visualizing the Phantoms of the Imagination": Projecting the Haunted Minds of Modernity', in Murray Leeder (ed.), *Cinematic Ghosts: Haunting and Spectrality from Silent Cinema to the Digital Era* (New York: Bloomsbury Academic, 2015), pp. 39–57.
Lindsay, Vachel, *The Art of the Moving Picture* (New York: Macmillan, 1915).
Liu, Faith, '"An Authentic Ghost Story": Manipulating the Gothic in *Uncle Tom's Cabin*', *Palgrave Communications*, 3, 1 June 2017, <https://www.nature.com/articles/palcomms201741> (accessed 8 November 2021).
Natale, Simone, 'Specters of the Mind: Ghosts, Illusion, and Exposure in Paul Leni's *The Cat and the Canary*', in Murray Leeder (ed.), *Cinematic Ghosts: Haunting and Spectrality from Silent Cinema to the Digital Era* (New York: Bloomsbury Academic, 2015), pp. 59–75.
Neibauer, James L., 'Gothic Cinema during the Silent Era', in Richard Hand and Jay McRoy (eds), *Gothic Film* (Edinburgh: Edinburgh University Press, 2020), pp. 11–20.
Phillips, Kendall R., *A Place of Darkness: The Rhetoric of Horror in Early American Cinema* (Austin, TX: University of Texas Press, 2018).
Rhodes, Gary D., *The Birth of the American Horror Film* (Edinburgh: Edinburgh University Press, 2018).
Soister, John T., and Henry Nicolella, *American Silent Horror, Science Fiction and Fantasy Feature Films, 1913–1929* (Jefferson, NC: McFarland, 2012).
Spadoni, Robert, *Uncanny Bodies: The Coming of Sound Film and the Origins of the Horror Genre* (Berkeley, CA: University of California Press, 2017).
Stern, Seymour, 'Griffith and Poe', *Films in Review*, 2.9, 1951, pp. 23–8.
Todorov, Tzvetan, *The Fantastic: A Structural Approach to a Literary Genre* (Cleveland, OH: Press of Case Western Reserve University, 1973).
Williams, Linda, *Playing the Race Card: Melodramas of Black and White from Uncle Tom to O.J. Simpson* (Princeton, NJ: Princeton University Press, 2001).

Filmography

The Avenging Conscience (dir. D. W. Griffith, USA, 1914).
The Birth of a Nation (dir. D. W. Griffith, USA, 1915).

Das Cabinet des Dr Caligari (*The Cabinet of Dr Caligari*, dir. Robert Weine, Germany, 1920).
Der Student von Prag (*The Student of Prague*, dir. Stellan Rye, Germany, 1913).
The Cat and the Canary (dir. Paul Leni, USA, 1927).
Felix the Ghost Breaker (dir. Otto Messmer, USA, 1923).
Frankenstein (dir. J. Searle Dawley, USA, 1910).
The Haunted House (dir. Edward F. Cline and Buster Keaton, USA, 1921).
La chute de la maison Usher (dir. Jean Epstein, France, 1928).
Le Manoir du diable (*The House of the Devil*, dir. Georges Méliès, France, 1896).
Metropolis (dir. Fritz Lang, Germany, 1927).
Nosferatu, eine Symphonie des Grauens (dir. F.W. Murnau, Germany, 1922).
The Phantom of the Opera (dir. Rupert Julian, USA, 1925).
The Unknown (dir. Tod Browning, USA, 1927).

Notes

1. Bradshaw, 'A Night at the Cinema', n.p.
2. There has been a spate of recent publications on the topic of silent-era horror and Gothic cinema. Examples include Gary D. Rhodes's *The Birth of the American Horror Film* (2018), Kendall R. Phillips's *A Place of Darkness: The Rhetoric of Horror in Early American Cinema* (2018), Xavier Aldana Reyes's *Gothic Cinema* (2020), and James L Neibauer's 'Gothic Cinema during the Silent Era' (2020).
3. Gunning, 'The Cinema of Attractions'.
4. Freud, 'The "Uncanny"', p. 226.
5. Conrich, 'Before Sound', p. 40.
6. Horner and Zlosnik, *Gothic and the Comic Turn*, p. 4.
7. Leeder, *The Modern Supernatural*; Leeder, 'Visualizing the Phantoms of the Imagination'.
8. Castle, *The Female Thermometer*, p. 7.
9. Ibid., pp. 141–3.
10. Jones, *Sexuality and the Gothic Magic Lantern*.
11. Groth, 'Reading Victorian Illusions'.
12. Keil, *Early American Cinema in Transition*.
13. Qtd. in Denson, *Postnaturalism*, p. 120.
14. Lindsay, *The Art of the Moving Picture*.
15. Poe adaptations would also be popular for avant-garde filmmakers in both the US (Charles Klein and Leon Shamroy's *The Telltale Heart* [1928], James Sibley Watson and Melville Webber's *The Fall of the House of Usher* [1928]) and in France (Jean Epstein's *La chute de la maison Usher* [1928]).
16. Williams, *Playing the Race Card*, pp. 129–32.
17. Liu, '"An Authentic Ghost Story"'.
18. Arnheim, *Film as Art*.
19. The look of Gwynplaine (Conrad Veidt) in *The Man Who Laughs* would inspire the appearance of the Joker in the *Batman* comics. Ed Brubaker would pay homage to this lineage with the one-shot comic *Batman: The*

Man Who Laughs (2005), and Scott Synder would later introduce the horrifying Batman/Joker hybrid called 'the Batman Who Laughs'.
20. Todorov, *The Fantastic*.
21. Natale, 'Specters of the Mind', p. 70.
22. Spadoni, *Uncanny Bodies*, p. 55.

Chapter 6

Grand-Guignol as Twentieth-Century Gothic Drama
Madelon Hoedt

The malleability of the Gothic mode has meant that it has always been able to adapt itself to a variety of media. In particular, Gothic drama has been a highly successful way of delivering its narratives. First gaining prominence in the late eighteenth century, alongside the first wave of Gothic novels, these plays achieved long runs and huge audience numbers, as well as being on the cutting edge of developments in stagecraft and special effects. This situation changed in the early decades of the twentieth century: the never-ending stream of original play texts and adaptations of Gothic fiction dried up and, in the second half of the century, appeared to give way to the efforts of filmmakers and more commercial forms of performance such as spookshows and scare attractions. Between these two eras sits, perhaps uncomfortably, the Théâtre du Grand-Guignol, the French Theatre of Horror. Offering a selection of one-act plays, the Grand-Guignol included both horror and comedy performances and focused on realist plots over Gothic monsters. More horror than terror, more natural than supernatural, the Grand-Guignol appears as a rupture from the Gothic dramas that preceded it, yet the situation is more complex.

The aim of this chapter is to offer an analysis of the Grand-Guignol as the meeting point between the conventions of the eighteenth- and nineteenth-century Gothic drama and as pre-empting the concerns of later horror films and performances. By providing a brief overview of the developments that came before and after, as well as some insights into the productions staged in early twentieth-century Paris, the chapter will position the Grand-Guignol as a necessary connection between the spectacle and melodrama of the Gothic stage, and the psychology and gore of twentieth-century horror cinema.

The history of the Théâtre du Grand-Guignol is not bereft of episodes of mystery and sensationalism, and is notable for its longevity. The venue and company were in operation in France between 1897 and

1962, a lifespan of nearly seventy years, but this is also a history which has, in many ways, been lost to the ages. As Hand and Wilson note, 'the Grand-Guignol has been virtually ignored by academics and today has the status of one of the world's great forgotten theatres',[1] citing its position as a popular form of entertainment as one of the causes for this neglect. This sentiment is echoed in Deák, who goes so far as to say that the Grand-Guignol has been disregarded as 'an insignificant form of entertainment'.[2] As a result, publications on the topic are few and far between, and often appear in French, creating a potential barrier for Anglophone researchers. Despite these hurdles, a number of scholars have examined the Theatre of Horror in greater detail, with Mel Gordon's *The Grand Guignol: Theatre of Fear and Horror* (1998) and the 2002 book by Richard Hand and Michael Wilson, titled *Grand-Guignol: The French Theatre of Horror*, being the most thorough of these studies. Others, such as Deák and Gerould (1984), offer a more compact overview of the form and its origins. It should be noted that much of this work is quite sensationalist in tone, yet such an account may well be appropriate for a theatre such as the Grand-Guignol, adept as it was at creating its own myths.

The story of this theatre truly starts, for Gordon, Hand and Wilson, with Oscar Méténier, the founder of the original Théâtre du Grand-Guignol in 1897. Co-founder of the Théâtre Libre, together with Antonin Antoine, in 1887, Gerould describes Méténier as being one of the figures at the centre of 'the Naturalist controversy at the end of the last century'.[3] Moving away from the heightened performance and Manichean worldviews found in melodrama, naturalism is more interested in the portrayal of the lives of everyday people. As Gerould explains,

> In their desire to show life as it is, the Naturalists in the theatre insisted on direct observation, research and documentation; precise notation of fact; and objectivity of technique. They applied to drama the discoveries and methods of 19th-century science, particularly those of experimental medicine, to produce authentic case histories and clinical studies.[4]

Although Méténier's efforts with Antoine predated the founding of the Grand-Guignol by roughly a decade, it is worth mentioning this connection, as the naturalist sensibility would remain an influence in the programming of the Grand-Guignol. Gerould describes how, in the earliest years of the new theatre, 'it was a direct offshoot of the Théâtre Libre and attracted many of Antoine's authors. Alternating farces with serious drama, Méténier specialized in staging short, often sensationalistic plays in which scrupulous attention was paid to realistic details.'[5]

When Méténier stepped down less than two years later, handing over the stewardship of the Grand-Guignol to Max Maurey, what the latter inherited 'was not a theatre of horror *per se*, but a successful house of naturalism, dedicated to the true-to life representation of a society dehumanized by capitalism and bourgeois morality'.[6]

What Maurey found were several elements that proved fertile ground for the formula of terror to follow, recognising the aspects of Méténier's work that possessed 'popular and commercial viability'.[7] The early programming of the Grand-Guignol, and indeed of other naturalist theatres of the time, consisted of a programme of one-act plays often spanning multiple genres and topics so as to appeal to the largest possible audience.[8] In the case of the Théâtre Libre and the Grand-Guignol both, these offerings included *comédie rosse*, defined by Gerould as plays which take 'sardonic pleasure in undermining the high ideals of traditional religious morality by showing how harsh economic facts and biological drives render those ideals hollow and inoperative'.[9] The plots of such plays often found their origins in the *faits divers*, a particular brand of illustrated newspaper story from the late nineteenth century. In these short narratives, readers were treated to accounts of true crime and 'their frequently bizarre denouements'.[10] Although Gordon notes the connection between these newspaper items and (Gothic) melodramas, he also points out three key differences, each of which would persist in the Grand-Guignol programming: the brevity of the *faits divers*; the lack of a happy ending; and the plots, which were drawn from life rather than offering supernatural or saccharine fantasies.[11]

Ultimately, Gordon notes, 'the *fait divers* prefigured exactly what the Grand Guignol would be on the stage'.[12] Indeed, the stewardship of Maurey can be seen as a distinct turning point in the choice of stories: as Gordon explains, 'if Méténier focused on extreme naturalistic "slice of life" sketches, Maurey's interest pointed toward something different: what one critic referred to as the "slice of death" drama'.[13] Both the style of programming and its subject matter became a big influence in Maurey's leadership between 1898 and 1915. Recognising the value of varied programming as a tool not only to attract patrons, but to heighten their experience, Maurey refined the device known as *la douche écossaise*, a hot and cold shower, alternating between horror plays and more comedic offerings. This style of programming provided the audience with 'an emotional rollercoaster ride', in which 'the horror plays were all the more successful for the comic relief provided by the comedies (and vice versa)'.[14] A second key contribution of Maurey to the success of the Grand-Guignol and its status as a popular entertainment was his eye for publicity stunts, thus creating 'a theatrical genre that became shrouded in its own mythology'.[15]

Performances at the Theatre of Horror were not confined to the stage alone, but extended to Maurey's persona and appearance, as well as the running of the theatre. A famous anecdote relates to Maurey's decision to add a house doctor to the permanent staff to aid those who had become unwell due to the horrors performed onstage.[16] Gordon adds to this a description of a cartoon that circulated in 1904, in which a member of the audience shouts for a doctor but is informed by Maurey that the doctor himself has fainted; a similar drawing from the same period highlights a supposed order from the Police Commissioner that all those attending a performance are required to undergo a medical check before being allowed inside the Theatre of Horror.[17] Key here is that Maurey's efforts to convince his audience of the reality of the horrors staged in the Grand-Guignol were not down to publicity alone but were emphasised further by a range of production techniques, all of which helped to create and uphold its mythology.[18] Maurey's amalgam of marketing, close attention to special effects and the power of careful scripting and pacing collectively underpin the current understanding of the Theatre of Horror.

When Camille Choisy took over in 1915, many aspects of Maurey's successful formula remained in place, and as argued by Hand and Wilson, this was when the Grand-Guignol entered its golden age.[19] Choisy retained the contributions of Méténier and Maurey, while continuing to innovate aspects of staging, acting and special effects. He expected his performers 'to inhabit real characters with a full range of powerful and animalistic impulses', while navigating the complicated technical effects: 'Each Grand Guignol actor had to possess a double skill in stage concentration and sleight-of-hand trickery.'[20] This resulted in what Gordon describes as 'a particular and discernible style of performance'.[21] Embodied by L. Paulais and Paula Maxa, the most revered male and female leads in the history of this theatre, Choisy's era saw some of the more memorable plays and performances of the Grand-Guignol. This golden age finished in 1928, when, due to financial issues, stewardship of the theatre was handed to Jack Jouvin, followed by the departure of Choisy, Maxa and Paulais. The tight ensemble began to splinter, with some setting up theatres to rival the Grand-Guignol. Although Hand and Wilson note that it would be 'unfair to lay the blame for the decline of the Grand-Guignol entirely at the door of Jack Jouvin',[22] it was from this point onwards that the popularity of the theatre started to suffer. Hand and Wilson offer several arguments that might explain this decline, from the management style of Jouvin and his need to navigate the landscape left by Choisy and Maxa, to the introduction of cinema with the start of the Universal Monster cycle in the early 1930s, and even political factors: the Theatre of Horror survived two world wars, but its audience was perhaps left with less of an appetite for staged terrors. Although the Grand-Guignol remained open following the departure of Jouvin in 1937, the managers who followed could not recover its success, and the Theatre of Horror shut its doors in 1962.

Interestingly, in these works by Gordon and Hand and Wilson, any mention of a connection between the Grand-Guignol and the Gothic is largely absent, and the same is true when surveying further research on the form.[23] Across these sources the Grand-Guignol is primarily described as a novelty, a breaking away from theatre traditions in terms of both the content of its plays and the way in which its productions were realised through acting and stagecraft. My argument here, however, is that although the form includes these realist elements, its productions remain very aware of their predecessors, borrowing from and leaning into storylines that would not have looked out of place on the Gothic stage. The innovation of the Grand-Guignol, as with so much of the horror genre, grew from the works that came before it, and in turn, its incorporation of naturalist aspects paved the way for the examples of psychological horror that came after.

The Gothic in its theatrical form started to appear almost as soon as the Gothic emerged as a distinct mode, alongside the first wave of novels in the second half of the eighteenth century. Indeed, some of the earliest Gothic novelists, such as Harold Walpole and Matthew 'Monk' Lewis, can be counted among the first wave of Gothic playwrights. Lewis, in particular, saw considerable success with his play *The Castle Spectre* (1797), which was performed and revived across London theatres almost as soon as it was written. Others, such as Joanna Baillie, wrote almost exclusively for the (Gothic) stage, further emphasising the success of the form in the theatrical mode. The appetite of audiences for such material continued in the nineteenth century, as texts moved into what Diane Long Hoeveler has termed the Victorian Gothic drama, divided into an early (1820–50), middle (1850–80) and late period (1870–1910), each defined by specific developments.[24] Hoeveler describes how the early period focused primarily on the revival of older works, such as a renewed run of *The Castle Spectre*, and on melodramatic adaptations of existing books such as Mary Shelley's *Frankenstein* (1818), John Polidori's *The Vampyre* (1819) and Victor Hugo's *The Hunchback of Notre-Dame* (1831). The middle period proved central to the development of special effects onstage. Examples of this include the evolution of the vampire trap and the Corsican trap, a device that allowed actors to move across the stage, slowly ascending and seemingly gliding into view,[25] and the introduction of Pepper's Ghost, a means by which ghostly figures could be projected onto the stage. These were readily adopted by Gothic plays to add to the spectacle of the performances. The late period focused on so-called star vehicles, specific productions made famous by those who appeared in them, such as Henry Irving in *The Bells* in 1871 and the performance of Richard Mansfield in *Strange Case of Dr Jekyll and Mr Hyde* in 1888.

In addition, Hoeveler notes the prevalence of adaptations during this period, drawing particular attention to the rapid pace with which stage versions followed the publication of novels, and to the liberties that were often taken with the source material to create a more sensational offering on the stage. What is shared across these developments in Gothic drama is an adherence to the conventions found in Gothic fiction. In *The Literature of Terror* (1996), David Punter lists such characteristics: 'an emphasis on portraying the terrifying, a common insistence on archaic settings, a prominent use of the supernatural, the presence of highly stereotyped characters and the attempt to deploy and perfect techniques of literary suspense are the most significant'.[26] These ideas are echoed by Andrew Smith: 'the early Gothic appears to be highly formulaic, reliant on particular settings, such as castles, monasteries, and ruins, and with characters, such as aristocrats, monks, and nuns, who, superficially, appear to be interchangeable from novel to novel'.[27] These recognisable tropes and spaces reappear on the Gothic stage: in part, this was due to the previously noted number of adaptations, yet even original works such as Lewis's *The Castle Spectre* and Baillie's *De Montfort* (1798) feature ruined castles, long-buried family secrets and the ghosts of those who have departed.

This understanding of the Gothic is used as a point of comparison with the Grand-Guignol and appears to highlight the disconnect between the two. As Hand and Wilson note, 'When talking of a "Theatre of Horror" one might imagine the monster-iconography and Gothic extravaganzas (ironic or otherwise) on display in Richard O'Brien's *The Rocky Horror Show* (1975), Andrew Lloyd-Webber's *Phantom of the Opera* (1986), and even Anne Rice's *Interview with the Vampire* (1976).'[28] Instead, they argue, the Grand-Guignol is removed from such productions, leaving behind the familiar conventions and excesses of the heyday of Gothic drama. Hand and Wilson identify it as a realist form, noting that 'the Grand-Guignol steers well clear of all things supernatural, [pushing] the human subject into monstrosity'.[29] Similarly, Deák draws attention to the contemporaneity of the Grand-Guignol as opposed to the archaic settings commonly found in Gothic fiction, noting that '[i]t is interesting to notice that Grand Guignol avoided historical themes and that, in an attempt to actualize the plays, they incorporated technological innovations (electrical appliances, cars, submarines, telephones) as dramatic elements'.[30]

This emphasis on modern concerns is echoed by Hand and Wilson: 'Maurey's team, led by de Lorde, sought to exploit contemporary fears'[31] in a move away from the style and themes established by Méténier at the end of the nineteenth century, but arguably also removed from the melodramas that dominated the preceding decades. These contemporary fears were realised in appropriate spaces: 'bedrooms, brothels, the ramparts of besieged consulates, lighthouses, rooms in museums, sitting rooms, boats, opium dens, doctors' surgeries, operating theatres and so on'.[32] These observations seem not merely to place the Grand-Guignol in a different theatrical tradition, moving away from the heightened emotions of melodrama to more realistic portrayals in the naturalist mode; it also updated its subject matter, abandoning castles and doublets in favour of lab coats and surgeries. In this way, scholars have positioned the Grand-Guignol as a clear departure from, almost an opposite to, Gothic drama, with innovations in stagecraft, acting and the content covered by the plays presented at the Theatre of Horror as the main changes.

With regard to stagecraft and acting, there is evidence that the Grand-Guignol continued to innovate and develop. As Deák points out, 'Grand Guignol represents a highly-specialized genre, which involved innovative mise en scène techniques', further highlighting the role its managers played in these developments: 'Choisy did not hesitate to intensify the horrors presented on stage ... Spectacular mise en scène use of light and sound effects were, under his directorship, carried further than ever before – to such an extent that mise en scène took priority over literary elements.'[33] Similarly, Gordon and Hand and Wilson devote ample time to the discussion of the effects used in the theatre, drawing attention to the continued innovation and indeed importance of stagecraft in the Grand-Guignol.[34] It would appear, then, that spectacle remained as central to the small Parisian stage as it had been for the Gothic dramas of the nineteenth century. At the same time, however, the difference in approach and the emphasis on realism found here changed the way in which these effects were used. Deák notes the precision required by the performers to manage the extreme situations central to the form:

> An ambiguity in text, or a lack of precision in stage business or effects could have turned a horror scene into comedy. Of primary importance were the credibility of mise en scène and, at the same time, the ability to create an atmosphere of susceptibility in which the spectators' critical faculties were surpressed [sic] and their imaginations channelled in the right direction.[35]

Here Deák hints at the fact that realism in the Grand-Guignol was not necessarily concerned with the scientific verisimilitude advocated by naturalism but was rather engaged with making things *seem* real. This relationship of the form with realism is discussed in more detail by D'Arcy, who comments on 'the balance between the realism of the event and the intertextuality of what is implied or evoked', explaining how 'an audience's sense of "what is real" or "what is sufficiently and convincingly real" whilst watching bloody horror performances is often as fluid as the blood itself'.[36]

Such observations add complexity to the representation of the Grand-Guignol as a straightforward realist form, and the same is true for the acting conventions used in its performances. Where melodramatic acting is defined by codified gestures and heightened emotional displays, naturalism is more concerned with 'a methodical analysis of human behavior, heredity, and environment'[37] as defining factors in the actions and motivations of characters and the source for the human monsters displayed on the Grand-Guignol stage. However, melodrama still has a place here, as noted by Deák:

> The typical play was always realistic in setting and circumstances. Only after verisimilitude was established, was the first motif of fear, the first hint of the sensational introduced ... The brutal event, the importance of realistic detail, and the moral detachment from the theme, came from the naturalistic heritage of the Grand Guignol, but the importance of atmosphere, extreme emotions, the elements of the unknown and mysterious had much in common with melodrama.[38]

In its portrayal of contemporary horrors, the Grand-Guignol would lean on its naturalist heritage, while at the same time continuing to borrow from the melodramatic tradition as found in Gothic drama to deal with the extreme events portrayed onstage: 'The Grand-Guignol is a form that seems to break away from conventional naturalism as often as it embraces it.'[39] Deák explains how these two tendencies had to be balanced by the performer: 'The verisimilitude of the situation demanded concentration on realistic detail and a rather realistic approach, but in the expressions of horror, in the situations of torture, madness, and violent death, actors had to be able to produce a rather difficult scale of expressions and sounds.'[40] In their relationship to both tradition and innovation, the stagecraft and acting style of the Grand-Guignol show an awareness of and affinity with the nineteenth-century staged horrors that preceded it.

A similar tension is found when examining the narratives presented by the Grand-Guignol, which so far have been defined as focusing on contemporary and, more specifically, 'real' fears. Looking to the lives of the lower classes and true-crime stories for inspiration, the Theatre of Horror left behind the historical themes often found in Gothic plays. Arguably, much of the Gothic work from the eighteenth and early nineteenth centuries was preoccupied with its settings of castles and ruins, and its narratives were often fantastical in nature: Botting simply states that 'Gothic texts are not realistic'.[41] At the same time, the Gothic often used such settings to provide a reflection for current concerns, and Botting draws attention to 'Gothic fiction's engagement with cultural and inter-cultural concerns, particularly at the end of the nineteenth century', highlighting the way in which Gothic narratives adapted to their time.[42] Similarly, the preoccupation of the Grand-Guignol with science and discovery is found in landmark Gothic texts from across the nineteenth century, such as *Frankenstein* (1818) and *Dracula* (1897), which focus on the clash between the scientific mind and older forces, in some ways paving the way for the Grand-Guignol's plots of mad doctors and hideous experiments. Arguably, these observations relate to Gothic fiction more generally; however, as I previously pointed out, the Gothic drama of the nineteenth century, specifically, was defined by adaptations of novels, with plays often hitting the stage as soon as the books hit the shelves. Such a trend can also be detected in the Grand-Guignol, with Hand and Wilson noting its status as 'a significant theatre of adaptation' and drawing attention to efforts to bring to the stage 'adaptations of fiction, cinema and even historical events'.[43] A list of horror plays, provided by Gordon, makes mention of adaptations of work by authors such as Rudyard Kipling, Guy de Maupassant, Octave Mirbeau, Edgar Allan Poe and Robert Louis Stevenson.[44] In addition, Gordon and Hand and Wilson highlight stage adaptations from films such as *Das Cabinet des Dr Caligari* (*The Cabinet of Dr Caligari*, 1920) and *Les Yeux sans visage* (*Eyes Without a Face*, 1960) as part of the Grand-Guignol repertoire. Although Gordon only includes brief summaries of some seventy plays out of the thousands of scripts presented at the Grand-Guignol, his list offers some insight into the type of material that would find its place on this stage and shows a similar synergy between the theatre and other media as that found in nineteenth-century Gothic drama.

More interesting than the comparison of the source material for scripts is the role of the supernatural. Portrayals of ghosts onstage were often central to the spectacle offered by Gothic dramas and appeared as part of the earliest performances, such as the aforementioned *The Castle Spectre*. Although often subject to contemporary debates on whether the supernatural should be displayed in such a way, the Gothic stage remained haunted by its ghostly apparitions. The roots of the

Grand-Guignol in naturalism and its focus on human over paranormal monsters appeared to remove these phantasms, as pointed out by Hand and Wilson, yet this relationship is more complex.[45] An interesting example is a play entitled *The Coffin of Flesh* (de Lorde and Bauche, 1924), described in Gordon as a marriage between science and the supernatural: four doctors, in a search to determine whether the soul can live without a body, form a club to stage séances and investigate paranormal phenomena.[46] When one of them dies from a stroke upon encountering the ghost of his mother, the others proceed to experiment on him in an attempt to induce a novel state between life and death. The script is mentioned by Deák in relation to a description from writer Andre de Lorde on 'how to stage the appearance of a ghost',[47] arguably showing that such images were part of the Grand-Guignol repertoire. *The Closed Door* (Francheville, 1910) shows a similar indebtedness to supernatural themes, with the ghost of a doctor's wife exacting her revenge on his new spouse.[48] Other texts, such as *The Haunted House* (Bonis-Charancle, 1903) and *The Kiss of Blood* (Aragny and Neilson, 1929), lean into the motif of the explained supernatural. In *The Haunted House*, the audience is introduced to a lawyer and two married couples, the Avenels and the Ravans, who are spending a night in a supposedly haunted house. In their conversation at the start of the play, they invoke 'all the signifiers of a haunted house yarn', in which 'the macabre history of the house and the continuing rumours surrounding it seem to be setting the scene for a supernatural manifestation'.[49] Lights have been seen in the house, and the clanking of chains has been heard, but as midnight strikes, the only figure that appears is a real man: Fulbert, the rightful owner of the property. Fulbert refutes any claims of supernatural phenomena and attempts to remove the unexpected visitors, but is interrupted by 'a piercing scream . . . followed by a burst of laughter'.[50] The denouement of the play reveals that Genevieve, Fulbert's wife, is the source of these noises and an example of the Gothic 'mad woman in the attic': her demeanour changed by an unidentified illness, she was found cheating on her husband, who imprisoned her in the abandoned house. When the visitors attempt to set her free, Fulbert produces a knife and kills Genevieve to ensure she is his forever.

The plot of *The Kiss of Blood* includes a similar focus on jealousy and revenge: Joubert attends the clinic of Doctor Leduc and his assistant Volguine, complaining of an unbearable pain in his right index finger and imploring the doctor to amputate the digit. Naturally, the doctor refuses, and instead attempts to fool Joubert into thinking the operation has been performed by tying back the finger and bandaging his hand. Upon the discovery of the deceit, Joubert gets hold of a scalpel and severs the digit himself. Leduc finds himself intrigued by the case, and in the second half of the play the audience finds him and Volguine visiting Joubert at home. His servant, Maria, informs them that Joubert's wife has recently died, and of the impact it has had on him and the household: 'And this house, in the middle of nowhere, now has the air of death about the place. At night, when the wind rustles the trees, it sounds like voices crying.'[51] This mansion, like Fulbert's, is presented as haunted, and when Joubert appears, he reveals this to be the case: after he shoots his wife Hélène in a fit of jealousy and dumps her body in the Seine, she continues to visit him and to punish him for murdering her. Indeed, the severing of his finger, 'the finger that pulled the trigger',[52] is done by Joubert as a result of this haunting and, according to him, at the behest of the ghost of his deceased wife. At the climax of the piece, it is revealed that Hélène is not dead, but has been driven mad by her husband's attempt on her life and is using the pretence of the supernatural to exact her vengeance on him. Under her influence, Joubert finds himself forced to cut off his right hand with an axe, leading to his death.

Although these are only a selection of examples from a repertoire that reportedly includes thousands of scripts, these instances do indicate an understanding on the part of the Grand-Guignol and its writers of the language of the Gothic and the supernatural, as well as a clear engagement with this material. The primary denizens of its stage might have been human monstrosities, informed by passion and revenge, yet elements of stagecraft, acting and scripting discussed here provide evidence of an awareness of existing horror (theatre) traditions. By contrast, it is the monstrous humans of the Theatre of Horror that live on and are reflected in developments in horror cinema across the twentieth century. Leaving behind the Gothic monstrosities of Universal and later Hammer Studios, films such as *Psycho* (1960) and *Peeping Tom* (1960) as well as earlier examples such as *M* (1931) seem to carry on the tradition of the monstrous human once found on the Parisian stage. Similarly, its penchant for spectacle and mythmaking, of taking the show outside the theatre, set the scene for the many publicity stunts found in horror across the twentieth century, from the rigged cinemas of William Castle to the supposed reality of *The Blair Witch Project* (1999). As a popular theatre that was nearly lost to history, the mythology of the Grand-Guignol still intrigues, drawing audiences back to the dark alleys of Paris, and to the horrors presented on this tiny stage.

Key Texts – Modern Discussions of the Grand-Guignol

Carl Grose, *Grand-Guignol* (2009). An original play that has been described as a 'cheerfully gory celebration of the theatre' (Lyn Gardner for the *Guardian*, 2014). Invoking the real people behind the Theatre of Horror, Grose's text plays with the conventions of the Grand-Guignol as well as those of modern horror on the stage.

Penny Dreadful (season 1, 2014). During its first season, the Grand-Guignol theatre is central to the *Penny Dreadful* series. Although its location is moved from Paris to London, and it is linked more closely to the Victorian period that precedes the real Theatre of Horror, the history behind the theatre and the invocation of its name in a mainstream show is certainly noteworthy.

The Most Assassinated Woman in the World (2018). A French thriller film which explores the mythology of the theatre, linking the fictional murders committed onstage to real-life crime cases. Although this element of the plot is arguably rather clichéd, the film does excel in its depiction of the Grand-Guignol, its culture and its theatre space.

Agnes Pierron, *Le Grand Guignol: Le Théâtre des peurs de la Belle Epoque* (1997). Never translated from French, and now somewhat of a rarity, Pierron's work is considered a seminal volume. Providing some historical commentary, most turn to this book for its reproduction of 55 original Grand-Guignol scripts, reproduced with introductory notes to contextualise the work.

Mel Gordon, *The Grand Guignol: Theatre of Fear and Terror* (rev. edn, 1998). The first comprehensive overview of the Grand-Guignol in English. Although Gordon's book might appear more sensationalist than academic, his writing fits the style of the Theatre of Horror. The work is notable for its detailed overview of the plots of seventy Grand-Guignol plays, as well as the inclusion of two scripts.

Richard Hand and Michael Wilson, *Grand-Guignol: The French Theatre of Horror* (2002); *London's Grand Guignol and the Theatre of Horror* (2007); *Performing Grand-Guignol: Playing the Theatre of Horror* (2016). Those interested in this form could do worse than picking up one of the titles produced by Hand and Wilson. A combination of analysis, comments on performance practice and translations of scripts, these three books are an excellent way into further study of the Grand-Guignol.

Further Critical Reading

Cox, Jeffrey, *Seven Gothic Dramas, 1789–1825* (1994). This collection contains seven key dramatic Gothic texts, as well as a long and comprehensive introduction on the form that preceded the Grand-Guignol.

Hoedt, Madelon, 'Gothic Drama and the Uncanny Stage' (2021). This essay offers a brief introduction to the form, from its inception in the late eighteenth century through to modern-day incarnations. It also references a number of key texts on the various modes of Gothic drama for those interested in learning more.

Jones, Kelly, Benjamin Poore and Robert Dean, *Contemporary Gothic Drama: Attraction, Consummation and Consumption on the Modern British Stage* (2018). An edited collection on the role and shape of the Gothic as found in contemporary performance, which provides an interesting overview of the variety of work produced in the twentieth century that is influenced by the form.

Saglia, Diego, 'Gothic Theater, 1765–Present' (2013). This essay charts the development of Gothic drama without taking a historical approach. Instead, Saglia demonstrates the shifting nature of the form along three key themes, thus offering a new take on how to study Gothic drama.

Bibliography

Botting, Fred, *Gothic* [1995], 2nd edn (Abingdon: Routledge, 2014).

Cox, Jeffrey, *Seven Gothic Dramas, 1789–1825* (Athens, OH: Ohio University Press, 1994).

D'Arcy, Geraint, 'Blood Effects in Grand-Guignol and Horror Performance: Making the Right Kind of Splash', *Horror Studies*, 9.1, 2018, pp. 21–36.

D'Arcy, Geraint, 'The Corsican Trap: Its Mechanism and Reception', *Theatre Notebook*, 65.1, 2011, pp. 12–22.

Deák, Frantisek, 'The Grand Guignol', *The Drama Review*, 18.1, 1974, pp. 34–52.

Gerould, David, 'Oscar Méténier and "Comédie Rosse": From the Théâtre Libre to the Grand Guignol', *The Drama Review*, 28.1, 1984, pp. 15–28.

Gordon, Mel, *The Grand Guignol: Theatre of Fear and Terror*, rev. edn (New York: Del Capo Press, 1998).

Hand, Richard J., 'Half-Masks and Stage Blood: Translating, Adapting and Performing French Historical Theatre Forms', in Katja Krebs (ed.), *Translation and Adaptation in Theatre and Film* (Abingdon: Routledge, 2014), pp. 143–61.

Hand, Richard, and Michael Wilson, 'The Grand-Guignol: Aspects of Theory and Practice', *Theatre Research International*, 25.3, 2000, pp. 266–75.

Hand, Richard, and Michael Wilson, *Grand-Guignol: The French Theatre of Horror* (Exeter: University of Exeter Press, 2002).

Hand, Richard, and Michael Wilson, *London's Grand Guignol and the Theatre of Horror* (Exeter: University of Exeter Press, 2007).

Hand, Richard, and Michael Wilson, *Performing Grand-Guignol: Playing the Theatre of Horror* (Exeter: University of Exeter Press, 2016).

Hoedt, Madelon, 'Gothic Drama and the Uncanny Stage', in Clive Bloom (ed.), *The Palgrave Handbook of Steam Age Gothic* (Basingstoke: Palgrave Macmillan, 2021), pp. 453–64.

Hoeveler, Diane Long, 'Victorian Gothic Drama', in William Hughes and Andrew Smith (eds), *The Victorian Gothic* (Edinburgh: Edinburgh University Press, 2012), pp. 57–71.

Jones, Kelly, Benjamin Poore and Robert Dean, *Contemporary Gothic Drama: Attraction, Consummation and Consumption on the Modern British Stage* (Basingstoke: Palgrave Macmillan, 2018).

Jurković, Tanja, 'Blood, Monstrosity and Violent Imagery: Grand-Guignol, the French Theatre of Horror as a Form of Violent Entertainment', *[sic] – a journal of literature, culture and literary translation*, 1, 2013, <https://www.sic-journal.org/Article/Index/208> (last accessed 27 July 2021).

Jurković, Tanja, 'Grand-Guignol: Inside Showtime's Penny Dreadful Demimonde', in Clive Bloom (ed.), *The Palgrave Handbook of Contemporary Gothic* (Basingstoke: Palgrave Macmillan, 2020), pp. 865–77.

Punter, David, *The Literature of Terror: The Gothic Tradition*, vol. 1 (Harlow: Longman, 1996).

Saglia, Diego, 'Gothic Theater, 1765–Present', in Glennis Byron and Dale Townsend (eds), *The Gothic World* (Abingdon: Routledge, 2013), pp. 354–65.

Smith, Andrew, *Gothic Literature*, 2nd edn (Edinburgh: Edinburgh University Press, 2013).

Notes

1. Hand and Wilson, *Grand-Guignol*, p. ix.
2. Deák, 'The Grand Guignol', p. 34.
3. Gerould, 'Oscar Méténier', p. 16.
4. Ibid., pp. 15–16.
5. Ibid., p. 18.
6. Hand and Wilson, *Grand-Guignol*, p. 5.
7. Ibid., p. 6.
8. Deák, 'The Grand Guignol', p. 35.
9. Gerould, 'Oscar Méténier', p. 16.
10. Gordon, *The Grand Guignol*, p. 7.
11. Ibid., pp. 7–8.
12. Ibid., p. 8.
13. Ibid., pp. 17–18.
14. Hand and Wilson, *Grand-Guignol*, p. 11.
15. Ibid., p. 11.
16. Deák, 'The Grand Guignol', p. 37; Hand and Wilson, *Grand-Guignol*, p. 12.
17. Gordon, *The Grand Guignol*, p. 19.
18. Hand and Wilson, *Grand-Guignol*, p. 12.
19. Ibid., p. 16.
20. Gordon, *The Grand Guignol*, pp. 24, 26.
21. Ibid., p. 24.
22. Hand and Wilson, *Grand-Guignol*, p. 21.
23. D'Arcy, 'Blood Effects'; Deák 'The Grand Guignol'; Gerould, 'Oscar Méténier'; Hand, 'Half-Masks and Stage Blood'; Hand and Wilson, 'The Grand-Guignol: Aspects of Theory and Practice'; Hand and Wilson, *London's Grand Guignol*; Jurković, 'Blood, Monstrosity and Violent Imagery'; Jurković, 'Grand-Guignol'.
24. Hoeveler, 'Victorian Gothic Drama', pp. 57–71.
25. The Corsican trap takes its name from the melodramatic play *The Corsican Brothers* (1852), adapted for the stage by Dion Boucicault. For more detail on this mechanism, see D'Arcy, 'The Corsican Trap'.

26. Punter, *The Literature of Terror*, p. 1.
27. Smith, *Gothic Literature*, p. 3.
28. Hand and Wilson, *Grand-Guignol*, p. x.
29. Ibid., p. x.
30. Deák, 'The Grand Guignol', p. 43.
31. Hand and Wilson, *Grand-Guignol*, p. 15.
32. Ibid., p. 32.
33. Deák, 'The Grand Guignol', pp. 34, 38.
34. Gordon, *The Grand Guignol*, pp. 44–7; Hand and Wilson, *Grand-Guignol*, pp. 52–66.
35. Deák, 'The Grand Guignol', p. 39.
36. D'Arcy, 'Blood Effects', pp. 35, 22.
37. Gordon, *The Grand Guignol*, pp. 8–9.
38. Deák, 'The Grand Guignol', p. 39.
39. Hand and Wilson, *Grand-Guignol*, p. 35.
40. Deák, 'The Grand Guignol', p. 42.
41. Botting, *Gothic*, p. 12.
42. Ibid., pp. 17, 13.
43. Hand and Wilson, *Grand-Guignol*, p. 14.
44. Gordon, *The Grand Guignol*, pp. 53–105.
45. Hand and Wilson, *Grand-Guignol*, p. x.
46. Gordon, *The Grand Guignol*, p. 84.
47. Deák, 'The Grand Guignol', p. 42.
48. Gordon, *The Grand Guignol*, p. 81.
49. Hand and Wilson, *Performing Grand-Guignol*, p. 53.
50. Bonis-Charancle, in Hand and Wilson, *Performing Grand-Guignol*, p. 65.
51. Aragny and Neilson, in Hand and Wilson, *Grand-Guignol*, p. 259.
52. Ibid., p. 259.

Chapter 7

Mid-Century Gothic Cinema (1931–79): From Monster Business to Exploitation Horror
Xavier Aldana Reyes

The period between the early 1930s, when Universal Pictures' *Dracula* (1931) and *Frankenstein* (1931) premiered, and the late 1970s, when the European exploitation boom died out, is arguably the most significant to the history of the Gothic in the twentieth century. Numerous films, from *The Black Cat* (1934) and *I Walked with a Zombie* (1943) to *The Innocents* (1961) and *The Vampire Lovers* (1970), are still hailed as landmarks in cinema history by journalists and critics, and these five decades were also responsible for the emergence of the horror genre as a journalistic label and its consolidation as a specific type of filmic experience. The impact of some of the most significant films of this era has been such that there is no form of popular culture left untouched by them, from literature to television, video games and even breakfast cereals. The various figures in the monster pantheon that surfaced in the 1930s may have originated in nineteenth-century literature and have previously found a long life on the stage, but their transition to cinema immortalised them. In particular, the design and make-up for Count Dracula and Frankenstein's monster, as well as the performances by Bela Lugosi and Boris Karloff, would become so iconic that they remain denotative of Gothic horror to this day. Together with Dr Jekyll and Mr Hyde, they form a 'foundational triptych' for the Gothic that has generated hundreds of copycats, sequels and parodies.[1] Universal films also popularised other monsters, such as the Wolf Man and the Mummy, that would become horror staples despite not deriving from literary sources or having solid cinematic precedents.

Gothic cinema experienced key changes during the years bookended by the success of *Dracula* and *Frankenstein* and Hammer Film Productions' failed attempts to modernise their Gothic horror brand and eventual hibernation. These developments include the institutionalisation of the horror franchise as a viable commercial venture and the entrenchment of the monster as a visual source of fear in the 1930s and 1940s; the widespread use of colour film processes in the late 1950s and the 1960s; and the subsequent rise of openly erotic spectacles in Europe's exploitation films in the 1960s and 1970s. By considering the points of divergence and concentrating on the similarities between two adaptations of Mary Shelley's *Frankenstein* (1818) – Universal's *Frankenstein* and Hammer's *The Curse of Frankenstein* (1957) – this chapter illustrates the continuity and cultural role of the Gothic in this period. While the basics of the story remained similar, *The Curse of Frankenstein*'s heightening of violence, cinematographic spectacle and eroticism speaks to the Gothic's enduring pursuit of transgression from the relatively safe distance provided by a largely fantastic retrojected past. Once horror grew mainstream and daring enough to set its titillating nightmares in the present and the Gothic became redolent of archaism and prone to caricature, the latter decreased in popularity and embraced the creative potential of postmodern irony and pastiche.

Mid-Century Developments: New Monsters, Effects and Markets

As Murray Leeder's chapter in this volume shows, the Gothic had manifested in cinema well before the 1930s. The 'trick' films of directors such as Georges Méliès, the first narrative films (often adaptations of stage plays or novels, such as J. Searle Dawley's *Frankenstein*, from 1910) and the old, dark house mysteries of the 1920s relied on chiaroscuro lighting, editing and special effects such as superimpositions and stop-motion photography for audience effect. Thanks to German cinema, the early roster of recurring characters (imps and devils, ghosts and ghouls, witches and alchemists) expanded to incorporate Faustian doppelgängers, vampires and golems. Early German cinema, and Expressionism in particular, can be seen as having developed what I have termed 'monster-framing': films such as *Der Student von Prag* (*The Student of Prague*, 1913), *Der Golem* (*The Golem*, 1915) or *Nosferatu, eine Symphonie des Grauens* (*Nosferatu*, 1922) show a markedly different approach to the presentation of monsters as sources of horror.[2] In *Nosferatu*, the moment in which the first mate of the *Empusa* (Wolfgang Heinz) recoils in fear after awakening the vampire Count Orlok (Max Schreck) would be solidified by Christine's (Mary Philbin) reaction shot in the face reveal scene in *The Phantom of the Opera* (1925). Universal Pictures, the studio behind the latter film, had previously made the Jewel production *The Hunchback of Notre Dame* (1923), a successful historical melodrama that has retrospectively been seen as one of the first proto-horrific American films because of Lon Chaney's involvement.[3] Universal would go on to develop *The Man Who Laughs* (1928), also after a Victor Hugo novel, before attempting a more straightforward horror mystery in their remake of the old, dark house mystery *The Cat and the Canary* (1927), the now lost *The Cat Creeps* (1930). Given the number and importance of these predecessors, it would be disingenuous to suggest that Gothic cinema was born in the 1930s. However, it is indeed possible to think of the years that run from the early 1930s to the 1980s as the period during which the Gothic came of age and crystallised primarily as an aesthetic mode beholden to the horror genre (the 'Gothic horror' subgenre). The Gothic also flourished outside horror, in melodramas and film noir, helping visualise the Female Gothic that had thrived in the writings of Ann Radcliffe, the Brontë sisters and Daphne du Maurier.[4]

When *Dracula* was eventually adapted to the big screen from the stage, following profitable theatrical British and American productions, there was little indication that the film would do as well as it did. In fact, all but one of Universal's initial reading reports for Bram Stoker's novel were unfavourable, and the studio representative who attended the 1927 Broadway premiere was ambiguous about its filmability.[5] Despite this, *Dracula* had massive ticket sales and made the largest profit of all the studio's releases in 1931.[6] This commercial success was important for at least two reasons. The first is that *Dracula* was a 'talkie'. Its lack of atmospheric diegetic music and rather static camerawork might make the film appear a little wooden to contemporary viewers, but, as Robert Spadoni has pointed out, its stage origins encouraged the punctuation of action 'with loud sounds and noises'.[7] The soundscape is not made up of tense moments climaxing with a sonic shock, or 'buses' – after the bus scare in *Cat People* (1942) – but of uncanny details, such as Lugosi's hissing and snarling, Renfield's mad laughter, or the creaking of coffins in the scene where the vampires awaken. From then on, Gothic moods would progressively rely on acoustic cues and mood enhancers.

The second reason *Dracula*'s success matters is that it was Universal's first film where the supernatural agent (the vampire) was not ultimately dispelled as fancy or explained away as the work of meddling thugs in disguise. Not all Universal's horror films would feature a supernatural monster. The Edgar Allan Poe films of the 1930s, namely *Murders in the Rue Morgue* (1932), *The Black Cat* and *The Raven* (1935), are good examples. Yet the studio's most famous valuable assets, and those that would be turned into franchises in the late 1930s and throughout the 1940s, were all dependent on them in concept and title. As Kyle Edwards has argued, what would make characters such as Dracula so appealing is that they were 'presold properties that required little marketing'.[8]

Frankenstein came hot on the heels of *Dracula* and hoped to capitalise on its success. The film's gigantic and initially speechless monster, memorably played by a melancholic and heavily made-up Karloff, is less likely to engender fear than pity among twenty-first-century viewers. Like many of Universal's early 'horrors', however, the film simultaneously embraced the thrill of its potential spookiness. Promotional materials for exhibitors, including lobby cards and publicity articles, emphasised *Frankenstein*'s 'eerie', 'thrilling' and 'startl[ing]' qualities.[9] Tellingly, its brief prologue, in which actor Edward Van Sloan explains to the camera that the then owner of Universal (Carl Laemmle) would like to offer audiences 'a word of friendly warning', cautions that the film 'will thrill [them]; it may shock [them]; it may even horrify [them]'. This gimmick acted as more than a pre-emptive measure; as with the exploits once used to sensationalise Grand-Guignol theatre productions, such as having nurses on the premises for those who might faint, Van Sloan's description of the film's possible effects necessarily enhanced them. Importantly, this prologue began actively connecting the aesthetics of the Gothic (chiaroscuro lighting, shadow-enhancing techniques, dramatic sets) with unsettling affective experiences.

In 1932 the BBFC (British Board of Film Classification) introduced the 'H' (for 'Horrific') advisory certificate, which indicated that no children under 16 should be present at screenings, to protect viewers from the films that had followed *Dracula* and *Frankenstein*. In time, the certificate would be applied to films such as *Son of Frankenstein* (1939), *The Ghost of Frankenstein* (1942) and *The Return of the Vampire* (1943). As has been noted by other critics, it is also important to remember that, although 'horror' might not have denoted 'a specific cycle' or 'a stable generic category', it was definitely used regularly in journalism from 1931 to 1933 to describe a given '"type" of film'.[10] The 'discursive framework' we now associate with it, a series of 'aesthetic and narrative choices and expectations', may thus be understood to have begun then.[11] Of even more importance to this chapter is the fact that, at least initially, what we now retrospectively classify as early 'horror' was predominantly of the Gothic variety. In other words, the origins of the horror genre hark back quite directly not just to the British literary tradition but also to a specifically Gothic aesthetic.[12]

The settings in *Dracula* and *Frankenstein* are temporal hotchpotches that mix past and present. *Dracula* is set in the 1930s, and scenes such as the one at a London theatre introduce modern settings and characters. By contrast, the Transylvania that Renfield (Dwight Frye) visits at the beginning of the film is a credulous and anachronistically feudal place. The entrance to Castle Dracula is the best example of Hollywood's sense of the architectonic Gothic: the vast open space, which resembles a ruined cathedral, dwarfs the visitor, is crepuscular, and connotes decay (the huge cobweb Renfield is forced to remove with his walking stick) and danger (the various predatory animals, from bats to wolves and spiders, that can be seen or heard). As Dwight enters the lived-in spaces, a suit of armour and huge candelabra suggest past glories, the opulence of aristocratic nobility and bygone times (candles instead of electricity, rather austere and grand interiors), much like the vampire's attire. Similarly, *Frankenstein* is set around the end of the nineteenth century – supposedly in 1899 or shortly before, as this is the year that the story returns to in *Bride of Frankenstein* (1935) – but its Bavarian Alps setting, especially its angry peasant mob and castle, are evocative of the Middle Ages. Frankenstein's watchtower best encapsulates this tension between archaism and modernity. His high-end laboratory, full of all the latest scientific bric-a-brac and electric machinery, contrasts starkly with the building's catacomb feel and expressionistic windows. The Gothic in these films acts as a distancing safeguard that usefully locates the fantastic in the superstitious and outmoded past, away from the pragmatic present, itself depicted as realistic.

The Gothic is also regularly a catalyst for repressed desire, from the sexual (Dracula) to the creationist (Frankenstein), and articulates forms of social transgression that must be somehow punished or policed. From here on, the Gothic would not simply stage Manichean battles between good and evil. It would also channel the dark side of the human psyche, usually literalised in the body and actions of the physical or moral monster. In fact, it is possible to read the eugenic discourses and racial discrimination typical of the early twentieth century in the construction of Universal's monsters.[13]

The late 1930s and 1940s saw the entrenchment of monsters, themselves attached to a terrible place, as the prevalent source of threat in horror films. Universal had produced sequels to both *Dracula* and *Frankenstein* by 1936, but following a successful 1938 double-bill run of the originals at the Regina Theatre in Beverly Hills (which initially also included RKO's *Son of Kong*, from 1933), the studio adopted a more Fordian mode of Gothic horror production. This period saw Universal returning repeatedly to the same characters and premises and eventually mashing various properties together in films such as *Frankenstein Meets the Wolf Man* (1943), *House of Frankenstein* (1944) and *Abbott and Costello Meet Frankenstein* (1948), which pitted Dracula, Frankenstein and the Wolf Man against the famous American comedy duo. This last film was naturally more light-hearted, even if fear was not completely averted, and points to the steady transformation of the Gothic monster from horror-inducing behemoth to sympathetic figure and stand-in for social prejudice throughout the twentieth century. Other studios with smaller budgets, the so-called Poverty Row studios (Monogram, PRC and Republic), copied Universal and produced a long string of very cheap horror films, although few of those were aesthetically Gothic. In this respect, these productions reflect the more general direction of horror in this decade. By the 1950s, old-fashioned, crypt-dwelling vampires had been largely replaced by atomic age oversized beasts and hostile space invaders. Even the Female Gothic cycle of the 1940s, best exemplified by *Rebecca* (1940) and *Gaslight* (1944), which substituted the Gothic castle with old mansions and supernatural antagonists with Bluebeards and tyrannical patriarchs, had begun to dry up by 1949.

When British company Hammer Film Productions decided to shoot a new treatment of Mary Shelley's *Frankenstein* as a period colour Gothic, little did they suspect that the resulting film would be a terrific brand-defining success. *The Curse of Frankenstein*, a stark departure from their previous black-and-white science fiction films, was swiftly followed by *Dracula* (1958). Terence Fisher came back as director, as did actors Peter Cushing and Christopher Lee. Key to Hammer's success was the return to the classical formula of the monster as the *pièce de résistance* and to an expeditious production model that saw them make more than fifty horror films in less than twenty years. Particularly innovative was Hammer's approach towards sexuality and violence. Although some of their cinematic offerings might seem tame by contemporary standards, it is worth remembering that *Dracula*, like the vast majority of Hammer films, received an X certificate (16+) and was accused of being sadistic by the British press.[14] In fact, the 2013 restored version of *Dracula* featured extended versions of the scene in which Dracula seduces Mina and of his disintegration at the end, both of which were originally cut by the BBFC for being too erotic and graphic. Arguably, this is precisely what defined the Hammer formula and the Gothic that would follow, both in the UK and abroad: pent-up sexuality and gore. The horror genre found the Gothic, traditionally a disavowing negotiator of transgression, to be an ideal vehicle for films that would increasingly be more concerned with pushing the boundaries of the acceptable than with eliciting fear. The temporal fixing of the nineteenth century as the new Gothic era, or 'Gothic cusp', a fantastic or idealised version of the past that enabled the staging of ideological tensions between the barbaric old and the modern new, would also be reinstated during the 1950s and 1960s.[15]

If Britain was responsible for starting a trend, continental Europe, especially Italy in the late 1950s and 1960s and Spain in the late 1960s and early-to-mid-1970s, exploited and augmented it. By 1961, the year when the breakthrough *La maschera del demonio* (*Black Sunday*, 1960) was exhibited in the US, Italy had already released the sexy vampire parody *Tempi duri per i vampiri* (*Uncle Was a Vampire*, 1959), which included a cameo by Christopher Lee, and *L'amante del vampiro* (*The Vampire and the Ballerina*, 1960) and *L'ultima preda del vampiro* (*The Playgirls and the Vampire*, 1960), horror films with stripping musical numbers and female nudity. The nipple flashed in *Il mulino delle donne di pietra* (*Mill of the Stone Women*, 1960), Italy's first colour horror film, would soon be overshadowed by much more depraved explorations of sexual taboos. Necrophilia, sadism and lesbianism (portrayed as sexual deviance) would all be strong ingredients in Gothic films such as *L'orribile segreto del Dr Hichcock* (*The Horrible Dr Hichcock*, 1962), *La frusta e il corpo* (*The Whip and the Body*, 1963) and *Danza macabra* (*Castle of Blood*, 1964).

Spain would not lag behind. Jesús (Jess) Franco's *Gritos en la noche* (*The Awful Dr Orlof*, 1962), funded by producers who had allegedly been persuaded of the value of investing in horror after a screening of Hammer's *The Brides of Dracula* (1960), would be followed by Paul Naschy vehicles such as *La marca del hombre lobo* (*Frankenstein's Bloody Terror*, 1968) and *La noche de Walpurgis* (*The Werewolf Versus the Vampire Woman*, 1971). 1972 was a peak year for Spanish horror, with 25 per cent of all films released belonging to the genre.[16] That Italy and Spain, countries which had not previously been responsible for any major horror cycles, suddenly went into creative overdrive speaks not just to their capacity to capitalise on commercial fads, but to the importance of the Gothic at this cultural juncture.

The Gothic in the 1960s and 1970s, and until the rise of pornography in the late 1970s and the subsequent decoupling of sex from horror, mostly manifested as one of many variants of horror and cognate genres. *Gialli* (violent pulp thrillers) and serial killer films, although set in the present and not requiring supernatural interventions, operated in comparable ways, by using the trappings of horror and noir to sublimate a repressed eroticism. In quite a number of cases, the heady coupling of gore and titillation ended up in an indefensible sensationalisation of rape and murder that betrays misogyny. Where the Gothic had an important role to play was, paradoxically, in channelling progress, aligning monsters such as vampiric witches, *giustizieri* (punishers) or warlocks as stalwarts of the ossified past.[17] For example, a film such as *La noche del terror ciego* (*Tombs of the Blind Dead*, 1972) set the licentious, modern Spaniards of the present against the forces of darkness personified by a group of reanimated and bloodthirsty Knights Templar. As with the slashers that would flourish soon after, such scenarios allowed for a critique and literal punishment of a more debauched and morally loose present time. As it had done in literature before, the Gothic in the mid-twentieth century continued to explore the tensions between the permissible and the transgressive and prod the limits of the morally sanctionable. Once actual hardcore films made 'horrotica' (or sex horrors) a redundant hybrid, the Gothic aesthetic became unnecessary.[18] The concerns its temporal distancing once codified would travel into horror films set in contemporary times.

Frankenstein vs. *The Curse of Frankenstein*: Gothic Transgression and Its Cultural Work

A viewing of Universal's *Frankenstein* and Hammer's *Curse of Frankenstein* back-to-back is likely to bring to light a number of obvious differences. The former is shot in black-and-white and makes brilliant use of shadows; the latter is sumptuously shot in Eastmancolor and is brightly lit throughout. The former is light on gore, with the 'abnormal' brain scene sticking out as the only moment where a disembodied organ is spotted; the latter relishes its anatomical formaldehyde curios and features a shocking sequence in which the monster is gruesomely shot in the eye. The former makes no concession to eroticism; the latter endows Elizabeth (Hazel Court) with a generous décolletage. The former is told omnisciently; the latter takes the shape of a long confession from Frankenstein. Some of these changes have to do with the evolution of cinema itself. *Frankenstein* was shot when the 'talkie' had just begun to take over the silent film and years before colour processes became prevalent. Twenty-six years is a long time in film history, so it makes perfect sense that these adaptations would differ in great measure from each other. Focusing on their common ground and on elements that were carried over, however, paints a more interesting picture that reveals how these films may be seen as pioneering in their own rights. It also enables a reading of their shared interest in transgressing the boundaries of the socially acceptable and of the pursuit of cinematic spectacle as indicative of Gothic horror's cultural role during the mid-twentieth century.

Frankenstein's most famous line is, ironically, one that original audiences would not have heard. As Victor (Colin Clive) notices the first sparks of life stirring in his monstrous creation, he reacts deliriously to this impossible conquering of nature. 'In the name of God', he cackles, 'now I know what it feels like to be God!' The sacrilegious line, initially censored, nevertheless captures the film's main moral dilemma: should humankind's creationist whims ever be indulged, or are they mere vainglorious and reckless attempts to supersede the limitations of material existence? After all, Victor does at one point ask Dr Waldman (Van Sloan) if he has ever been tempted to do something 'dangerous' himself, and posits that few advances would have been made had other individuals not wanted to 'find out what lies beyond'. In other words, scientific advance partly lies with the apparently irresponsible gall of those who deliberately tread where they should not, who ask too many questions and seek to penetrate the mysteries of the natural world – and who will therefore inevitably be judged to be insane. In this sense, one of *Frankenstein*'s most controversial aspects, its challenge to the all-knowingness of a divine creator, aligns it with the Gothic's interest in prodding the limits of the modern and the outdated. The mad scientist's guiding principles here are as driven by the will to improve the human condition as they are by a daringness that seems too familiar to dismiss as eccentric or characteristic of Victor alone. Arguably, one of the reasons the Frankenstein myth has survived into the twentieth century in the form of ethical quandaries emerging from advances in artificial intelligence is precisely because it speaks to an aspect of human nature that has only been accentuated by access to more complex forms of technology.[19] *Frankenstein* did not merely re-present the age-old conflict between the stasis of tradition and the shock of the new, a conflict mirrored by its chiaroscuro compositions. In doing so, it also challenged the status quo.

Whale's *Frankenstein* is well known for its forward-looking messages, but also for its production values, especially the cinematography of the 'it's alive!' scene. If Rotwang's laboratory in *Metropolis* (1927), with its contrasting and old-fashioned exterior and underground catacombs, had already provided a snapshot of the paraphernalia that would become *de rigueur* in future mad scientist films, *Frankenstein* took this to the next level. The film's best-known moment is a smorgasbord of dials, whirring and electricity; its syncopated pace and bloated length are completely ancillary to the narrative and mostly anticipatory. The monster's birth is prolonged and requires labour; it is also laden with the prospect of failure. The reanimation scene is a purely cinematic take on the affective histrionics of the literary Gothic, of the excessive style its writers have often been derided for. Clive's acting is just as dramatic, conveying a form of ecstasy that also intimates lunacy. Much like the Gothic as a mode, the scene is aesthetically bombastic and travels into the dark side of the human psyche, into its most selfish and treacherous recesses.

The Curse of Frankenstein covers the same ground. Friend Paul (Robert Urquhart) questions the 'horror' of Victor's (Peter Cushing) experiments early on, guessing at the unethical methods by which his friend is sourcing the monster's body. Upon glimpsing the creation, Paul deems it 'horrible', a statement Victor misunderstands. When he explains that the features are not important, that the fact that he will be creating a being that lives and breathes is what matters, Paul appeals to his kindness. Doctors work for 'the eventual good of mankind', he remarks, and '[t]his [the experiment] can never end in anything but evil'. Victor rejects this prognosis. When 'a benevolent mind' is inserted into the creature, his features will assume 'wisdom and understanding'. Whether this is actually the case is not known, as the brain is damaged in a fight, and this results in the monster becoming violent and dangerous. There are echoes of archaic pseudoscience here (for instance, phrenology), but the film poses a number of timeless questions. Is evil innate? Does it reside in the mind? And is one man's wisdom and understanding another one's damnation or idea of hell? The monster in this film, as in many other adaptations of *Frankenstein*, turns out to be a failed project that refuses to let go or be forgotten. It becomes a carnal reminder of the doctor's selfish drive and lack of humanity.

By the time *The Curse of Frankenstein* was released, creationist delusions had become a staple of mad science cinema and were no longer frowned upon, but Hammer's film pushed the envelope in other ways. Besides Elizabeth's obvious eroticisation through costuming, it is important to note how Justine (Valerie Gaunt), the sympathetic housekeeper in Shelley's novel, is recast as Victor's mistress. The character serves a purpose: her circumstances signal that wife-cheating Victor is not as clean-cut as we may have been led to believe. Additionally, when Justine gets pregnant and demands that he marry her, Victor shows no compassion and sets the monster upon her. Her untimely demise neatly embodies the duplicitous nature of the Gothic. On the one hand, the film twice punishes licentiousness – Justine's death will be followed by Victor's execution at the end of the film. On the other, the film exploits the very taboo it endeavours to curtail. Like sin, or evil, the monster exteriorises the ugliness of Victor's repressed libido, as well as his ambitious nature. This would become a constant in the various sequels to *Dracula* and *Frankenstein* throughout the 1960s and 1970s, the second golden period of Gothic horror. In its conglomeration of the human and the 'Other', the monster, whether used in a more complex manner (1967's *Frankenstein Created Woman*) or in a more regressive and sexist one (1971's *Dr Jekyll and Sister Hyde*), would act as a vessel for changing attitudes towards the normative and for constructions of alterity. Evolving attitudes towards gender, sexuality, race and class can be traced in the horror that monsters elicit through their extraordinary corporeality and behaviours.

Much as the nameless monster has come to be read as Frankenstein's interdependent double, it is possible to think of the Gothic during the mid-twentieth century as the dark, uninhibited mirror image of acceptable society. In cinema, the Gothic does not just manifest at the temporal level, through monsters and times riddled with credulity, fear and the horror of the morally barbarous, but also in an aesthetic that enhances feelings of fear, anguish, suspense and discombobulation through suggestive shadowplay, stark colours, suspenseful build-up or bursts of gory shock. For all its emphasis on effect, the Gothic is simultaneously humane and candid in its approach to the human condition, channelling whims and anxieties that more realist modes dare not approach. Unsurprisingly, the traditional Gothic would evolve to become a catalyst for social injustice in the 1980s and beyond, filtering the plights of marginalised communities and identities.

Key Works

Dracula's Daughter (1936). Although it was substantially revised after the original script was refused Production Code approval, this film offered as overt an engagement with queer sexuality as the era would see. Countess Marya Zaleska (Gloria Holden) is also a great example of an early cinematic vampire unhappy with her lot.

Rebecca (1940). Hitchcock's first American film is a great example of how the Gothic manifested outside the horror genre. The film contains all the elements of the Female Gothic: a secretive husband, a naïve yet plucky heroine, a resentful housekeeper and a disorienting haunted estate.

Les Yeux sans visage (*Eyes without a Face*, 1960). France was also an important player during the 1960s and 1970s, if often as co-producer. This fascinating and elegantly visceral surgical horror about a doctor obsessed with returning to his daughter the beauty he stole in a car accident is a little gem that inspired further face-grafting horrors.

House of Usher (1960). Roger Corman's Poe cycle in the United States was more psychological than Hammer's Gothics. As Corman told his producers, in this film 'the house is the monster', and Usher's obsession is excellently reflected by the cinematography and *mise en scène*. The capacity for setting to channel warped psyches is definitely one of the period's important developments.

La maschera del demonio (*Black Sunday*, 1960). An influential Italian classic that demonstrated that resorting to old formulas and black-and-white photography could still be effective. This film paved the way for more erotic and violent continental spectacles and, importantly, for their international importing.

Further Critical Reading

Aldana Reyes, Xavier, *Gothic Cinema* (2020). This book's medium-specific approach to the Gothic explores in more detail the main films to emerge from the period and the technological developments that shaped the film industry. It also defines the aesthetic parameters of Gothic cinema more broadly.

Hanson, Helen, *Hollywood Heroines: Women in Film Noir and the Female Gothic Film* (2007). Quite possibly the most thorough book on the Female Gothic cycle of the 1940s. This study is great for its detailed eye to genre and social context, especially Hanson's reading of certain films as both reflective of changing gender roles and potentially empowering for female viewers.

Hutchings, Peter, *Hammer and Beyond: British Horror Film* (2021 [1993]). This is one of the most important explorations of Hammer and British horror. Hutchings manages to synthesise and streamline what could otherwise seem a disparate filmic output, explaining clearly what was unique about the British industry of the period and Hammer's formula.

Rigby, Jonathan, *Euro Gothic: Classics of Continental Horror Cinema* (2016). Roberto Curti and Antonio Lázaro-Reboll's respective monographs are more thorough in their grounding of the specific national coordinates of Italian and Spanish Gothic horror, but Rigby's compendium is currently the most comprehensive survey of European horror film.

Skal, David J., *The Monster Show: A Cultural History of Horror* (2001 [1993]). This classic book offers one of the best analyses of the role of monsters and horror film in American culture. Skal does a brilliant job of connecting certain horror strands to key historical and cultural moments like the two World Wars, the fears engendered by the Cold War and the AIDS pandemic.

Bibliography

Aldana Reyes, Xavier, *Gothic Cinema* (Abingdon: Routledge, 2020).

Edwards, Kyle, '"House of Horrors": Corporate Strategy at Universal Pictures in the 1930s', in Richard Nowell (ed.), *Merchants of Menace: The Business of Horror Cinema* (London: Bloomsbury, 2014), pp. 13–30.

Elliott, Kamilla, 'Gothic – Film – Parody', in Catherine Spooner and Emma McEvoy (eds), *The Routledge Companion to Gothic* (Abingdon: Routledge, 2007), pp. 223–32.

Friedman, Lester D., and Allison B. Kavey, *Monstrous Progeny: A History of the Frankenstein Narratives* (New Brunswick, NJ: Rutgers University Press, 2016).

Hanson, Helen, *Hollywood Heroines: Women in Film Noir and the Female Gothic Film* (London: I.B. Tauris, 2007).

Hearn, Marcus, *The Hammer Vault: Treasures from the Archive of Hammer Films* (London: Titan Books, 2011).

Hutchings, Peter, *Hammer and Beyond: British Horror Film* [1993] (Manchester: Manchester University Press, 2021).
Jancovich, Mark, 'Bluebeard's Wives: Horror, Quality and the Paranoid Woman's Film in the 1940s', *The Irish Journal of Gothic and Horror Studies*, 12, 2013, pp. 20–43.
Matellano, Víctor, *Spanish Horror* (Madrid: T & B Editores, 2009).
Miles, Robert, *Ann Radcliffe: The Great Enchantress* (Manchester: Manchester University Press, 1995).
Peirse, Alison, *After Dracula: The 1930s Horror Film* (London: I.B. Tauris, 2013).
Phillips, Kendall R., *A Place of Darkness: The Rhetoric of Horror in Early American Cinema* (Austin, TX: University of Texas Press, 2018).
Pirie, David, *A New Heritage of Horror: The English Gothic Cinema* (London: I.B. Tauris, 2009).
Rigby, Jonathan, *Euro Gothic: Classics of Continental Horror Cinema* (London: Signum Books, 2016).
Riley, Philip J. (ed.), *Frankenstein* (Absecon, NJ: MagicImage Filmbooks, 1989).
Skal, David J., *Hollywood Gothic: The Tangled Web of* Dracula *from Novel to Stage to Screen* [1990] (New York: Faber and Faber, 2004).
Skal, David J., *The Monster Show: A Cultural History of Horror* [1993], rev. edn (New York: Farrar, Straus and Giroux, 2001).
Smith, Angela M., *Hideous Progeny: Disability, Eugenics, and Classic Horror Cinema* (New York: Columbia University Press, 2011).
Spadoni, Robert, *Uncanny Bodies: The Coming of Sound and the Origins of the Horror Genre* (Berkeley, CA: University of California Press, 2007).
Tohill, Cathal, and Pete Tombs (eds), *Immoral Tales: Sex and Horror Cinema in Europe 1956–1984* (London: Titan Books, 1995).
Vieira, Mark A., *Hollywood Horror: From Gothic to Cosmic* (New York: Harry N. Abrams, 2003).
Worland, Rick, *The Horror Film: An Introduction* (Oxford: Blackwell Publishing, 2007).

Filmography

Abbott and Costello Meet Frankenstein (dir. Charles T. Barton, USA, 1948).
The Black Cat (dir. Edgar G. Ulmer, USA, 1934).
Bride of Frankenstein (dir. James Whale, USA, 1935).
The Brides of Dracula (dir. Terence Fisher, UK, 1960).
The Cat and the Canary (dir. Paul Leni, USA, 1927).
The Cat Creeps (dir. Rupert Julian, USA, 1930).
Cat People (dir. Jacques Tourneur, USA, 1942).
The Curse of Frankenstein (dir. Terence Fisher, UK, 1957).
Danza macabra (*Castle of Blood*, dir. Antonio Margheriti [as Anthony Dawson], Italy/France, 1964).
Daughter of Dracula (dir. Lambert Hillyer, USA, 1936).
Der Golem (*The Golem*, dir. Henrik Galeen and Paul Wegener, Germany, 1915).

Der Student von Prag (*The Student of Prague*, dir. Paul Wegener and Stellan Rye, Germany, 1913).
Dr Jekyll and Sister Hyde (dir. Roy Ward Baker, UK, 1971).
Dracula (dir. Tod Browning, USA, 1931).
Dracula (dir. Terence Fisher, UK, 1958).
Frankenstein (dir. J. Searle Dawley, USA, 1910).
Frankenstein (dir. James Whale, USA, 1931).
Frankenstein Created Woman (dir. Terence Fisher, UK, 1967).
Frankenstein Meets the Wolf Man (dir. Roy William Neill, USA, 1943).
Gaslight (dir. George Cukor, USA, 1944).
The Ghost of Frankenstein (dir. Erle C. Kenton, USA, 1942).
Gritos en la noche (*The Awful Dr. Orlof*, dir. Jesús Franco, Spain/France, 1962).
House of Frankenstein (dir. Erle C. Kenton, USA, 1944).
House of Usher (dir. Roger Corman, USA, 1960).
The Hunchback of Notre Dame (dir. Wallace Worsley, USA, 1923).
I Walked with a Zombie (dir. Jacques Tourneur, USA, 1943).
Il mulino delle donne di pietra (*Mill of the Stone Women*, dir. Giorgio Ferroni, Italy/France, 1960).
The Innocents (dir. Jack Clayton, UK, 1961).
L'amante del vampiro (*The Vampire and the Ballerina*, dir. Renato Polselli, Italy, 1960).
L'orribile segreto del Dr Hichcock (*The Horrible Dr Hichcock*, dir. Riccardo Freda [as Robert Hampton], Italy, 1962).
L'ultima preda del vampiro (*The Playgirls and the Vampire*, dir. Piero Regnoli, Italy, 1960).
La frusta e il corpo (*The Whip and the Body*, dir. Mario Bava [as John M. Old], Italy/France, 1963).
La marca del hombre lobo (*Frankenstein's Bloody Terror*, dir. Enrique L. Eguiluz, Spain/West Germany, 1968).
La maschera del demonio (*Black Sunday*, dir. Mario Bava, Italy, 1960).
La noche de Walpurgis (*The Werewolf Versus the Vampire Woman*, dir. León Klimovsky, Spain/West Germany, 1971).
La noche del terror ciego (*Tombs of the Blind Dead*, dir. Amando de Ossorio, Spain/Portugal, 1972).
Les yeux sans visage (*Eyes Without a Face*, dir. Georges Franju, France/Italy, 1960).
The Man Who Laughs (dir. Paul Leni, USA, 1928).
Metropolis (dir. Fritz Lang, Germany, 1927).
Murders in the Rue Morgue (dir. Robert Florey, USA, 1932).
Nosferatu, eine Symphonie des Grauens (*Nosferatu*, dir. F. W. Murnau, Germany, 1922).
The Phantom of the Opera (dir. Rupert Julian, USA, 1925).
The Raven (dir. Lew Landers [as Louis Friedlander], USA, 1935).
Rebecca (dir. Alfred Hitchcock, USA, 1940).
The Return of the Vampire (dir. Lew Landers, USA, 1943).
Son of Frankenstein (dir. Rowland V. Lee, USA, 1939).
Son of Kong (dir. Ernest B. Schoedsack, USA, 1933).
Tempi duri per i vampiri (*Uncle Was a Vampire*, dir. Steno, Italy/France, 1959).
The Vampire Lovers (dir. Roy Ward Baker, UK, 1970).

Notes

1. Elliott, 'Gothic – Film – Parody', p. 223.
2. Aldana Reyes, *Gothic Cinema*, p. 78.
3. Worland, *The Horror Film*, pp. 50–5.
4. See Hanson, *Hollywood Heroines*; Jancovich, 'Bluebeard's Wives'.
5. Skal, *Hollywood Gothic*, pp. 165–6.
6. Vieira, *Hollywood Horror*, p. 35.
7. Spadoni, *Uncanny Bodies*, p. 56.
8. Edwards, '"House of Horrors"', p. 25.
9. See Riley (ed.), *Frankenstein*, n.p.
10. Peirse, *After Dracula*, p. 8.
11. Phillips, *A Place of Darkness*, p. 5.
12. Pirie, *A New Heritage of Horror*, pp. 1–13.
13. Smith, *Hideous Progeny*, pp. 1–31.
14. Hearn, *The Hammer Vault*, p. 20.
15. Miles, *Ann Radcliffe*, p. 87.
16. Matellano, *Spanish Horror*, p. 22.
17. Aldana Reyes, *Gothic Cinema*, pp. 191–6.
18. Tohill and Tombs (eds), *Immoral Tales*, p. 5.
19. Friedman and Kavey, *Monstrous Progeny*, pp. 185–200.

Chapter 8

The *Unheimlich* State: Surveillance and the Digital Nation
Julia M. Wright

In the first episode of the third season (1998–99) of *Buffy the Vampire Slayer*, titled 'Anne', Buffy has run away from her large suburban home and is working in a diner in a poor part of Los Angeles. In an exterior shot, Buffy leans out of the only window in her one-room apartment as the camera takes in the badly damaged pavement on the street below and a police car, siren blaring, passing through the nearby intersection. In the first diner scene, two homeless youths come in and dump out the coins they have collected to try to buy some food. The central homeless character of the episode is Lily, a young woman with a traumatic past who is constantly reinventing and renaming herself. Buffy too lives under a pseudonym, Anne, so her 'watcher' Giles and her mother cannot find her. The evildoers of the week are kidnapping homeless youths and putting them to work in a hell dimension where they are forced to repeat that they are 'no one'. Kidnapped as well, Buffy eventually responds to the demand that she answer, 'I am no one', by cheerily replying, 'I'm Buffy the Vampire Slayer. And you are?' In one famous segment of the long fight scene that follows, she fights the demons with a hammer and sickle as the main demon yells in exasperation, 'They don't fight back – that's how it works!' She not only fights back, but Lily does too, reversing, for a moment, the excessive passivity and docility that the episode suggests is typical of young women pushed beyond the secure bounds of suburban domesticity.

Thus far, the episode's thinly Marxist critique is straightforward. But there is an odd moment about 16 minutes into the episode when the direction switches to documentary realism, as a series of dissolves depicting homeless youths are used as a visual bridge between Buffy gazing at the urban wasteland outside her window and her friends as they lounge on well-padded furniture at their favourite club. The direction takes viewers from 'bare life' to bar life in under a minute.[1] After the focus returns to Los Angeles, Buffy frees some of the enslaved youths and then returns home to Sunnydale, after giving Lily her job, her apartment and her Los Angeles moniker, Anne. It is as if the images of homeless youths are not only extra-diegetic but also incomprehensible to televisual narrative. They remain outside the space of the resolution as well as the narration.

The focus on the homeless as 'no one' resonates with twentieth-century Gothic concerns about the state's interest in counting its people in uniform ways – as units rather than individuals. Building on early Gothic's concern with more local formations of power (over castles, monasteries and aristocrat-run estates), a significant thread of television Gothic, especially in the wake of the turbulent 1960s, has questioned the nation-state's power as expressed through its monitoring of households. Against the Enlightenment fantasy of a public sphere that openly monitors the state, as discussed by Habermas, such Gothic works represent either the failure of this fantasy or its inversion in a public that is secretly monitored by the state. The growth in surveillance technologies has made computers and cameras the correlates of hidden passageways and peepholes in early literary Gothic, while the state's accumulation of data on its people approaches the sublime. From the earliest modern censuses, states have collected data on individuals, but the modern state's technologies now go well beyond address, gender and employment, violating Enlightenment concepts of a private sphere and thus threatening the integrity of the sovereign individual that the Enlightenment theorised. Here, I explore three points of friction between the digital and the individual in US Gothic television: the irreducibility of the individual to the mathematical unit; the invisible extension of state power over the individual through technological networks; and the fragmentation of the self through interactions with media and other digital forms.

Accounting for the Modern State

Consider Patrick McGoohan's *The Prisoner* (1967–68), produced in the UK but also aired in Canada and the US: a spy for the state, the Prisoner resigns and declares that he will not be 'pushed, filed, stamped, indexed, briefed, debriefed or numbered', a process that is represented as machine-driven. After his resignation, he is forcibly transferred from his London home to a house in a village where he is denied freedom, individuality and his name, in a plot broadly parallel to the youths kidnapped into a hell dimension in *Buffy*. In the village, nationality and names are alike unknown – everyone instead is designated only by a number. The Prisoner refuses to submit to this, just as Buffy rejects her subjugation as 'no one' in the factory. This is echoed with a twist in the opening sequence for *The Prisoner* in which the prisoner asks, 'Who is Number One?' or, in the usage of the series, 'No. 1' – no one.[2] At the end of the series, 'No. 1' is revealed to be the Prisoner, looping the series around the same conundrum as 'Anne': what does it mean to be 'no one', to be beyond recognition by the modern (Gothic) state's accounting?

The rare extra-diegetic moment in 'Anne' is partly social commentary that echoes a fairly large body of television episodes in which homelessness is confronted as a significant social failure, especially in the influential series *The X-Files* (1993–2002).[3] As Emily Horton notes of the larger history, 'Gothic literature's repeated repudiation and subversion of established domestic structures ... mak[e] homelessness a central Gothic theme and motif'.[4] Horton also makes the essential point that the representation of homelessness as the condition of heroic rebellion or of 'a critical reaffirmation of hybrid and marginal experience'[5] contributes to the erasure of material difficulties such as hunger, cold, violence and untreated illness that 'Anne' momentarily reflects and allegorically resolves. Anne, moreover, is the name of the companion of the narrator of Thomas De Quincey's *Confessions of an English Opium-Eater* (1821). De Quincey notes in introducing her that 'the stream of London charity flows in a channel which, though deep and mighty, is yet noiseless and underground; not obvious or readily accessible to poor houseless wanderers'.[6] Without a surname or a street address, Anne is untraceable after she and the narrator are separated, despite his overtly Gothic wish 'to haunt—to way-lay—to overtake—to pursue [her] into the central darkness of a London brothel, or ... into the darkness of the grave'.[7] A century and a half later in the television movie *The Night Stalker* (1972), the trope reappears: throughout the movie, Carl Kolchak is depicted as sharing his home with Gail; at the end, when he is being run out of town, he tries to call her but is told she is an 'undesirable element' who has already been told to leave, and that he will not be able to find her. Other echoes of De Quincey's lost girl run through Gothic television, including Laura Palmer in *Twin Peaks* (1990–91), Mulder's abducted sister in *The X-Files*, the spectral sister in *American Gothic* (1995–96), and both Buffy and Lily in 'Anne'.

These lost girls all reflect the failure of state authority to count, monitor and control the domestic space that is supposed to house them. This is the *unheimlich* state, both uncanny and, like patriarchal power in many early Gothic texts, fragile in its dominance.[8] Anthony D. Smith has tied the emergence of nationalism to the development of the civic bureaucracy in the eighteenth century, one of its first tasks being to identify and locate populations – in the first US census of 1790, and the first British census of 1801, both rooted in counts of households.[9] As Kathrin Levitan notes of this early census era's emphasis on 'understanding and controlling the urban poor', British 'Census takers consistently invoked an image of people who were wandering, who did not fit into groups, and who were difficult to both control and count'.[10] Henry Mayhew's study of the London poor, key to urban Victorian Gothic,[11] is an extension of this crucial Enlightenment development in the operations of the nation-state: regular information-gathering guided and interpreted via demographics and statistics to inform public policy, including by identifying recalcitrant populations. Malthus's work, also considered in relation to the Gothic, contributed to the arguments for this first British census.[12]

However, we need to take the history of state information-gathering back further to William Petty and his use of data collection to facilitate Oliver Cromwell's genocidal dominance of Ireland. Petty led the Down Survey (1656–58), the first state-run survey in Ireland to be numerically rather than verbally descriptive, and turned a thousand ex-soldiers into surveyors with identical sets of instruments and instructions.[13] As Aaron James Henry has detailed, the Down Survey meant that 'Fields, meadows, mountains, bogs, parishes, houses and families were transformed from accumulated objects into like units, and then were compressed into the ordered arrangement of the map. Together these processes structured "ratio" as a form of political detail.'[14] This is the foundation of the mathematical regime of the twentieth-century state in which population, Gross Domestic Product, employment rates and so on – and percentage fluctuations as key ratios – are critical to the state and its purported priorities.

The failure of this scientific regime of surveillance to control the nation – and especially its girls – through domestic units is a recurring concern of 1960s Gothic television. In the first episode of *The Addams Family* (1964–66), 'The Addams Family Goes to School', a truant officer shows up to investigate why the children have never been to school. The truant officer and the postman appear first, setting up the normalcy that the family disrupts as a governmental one. On arriving at the Addams' home, the truant officer is let in by the daughter Wednesday, then directed to the mother Morticia, who is in charge of the children, who directs him to the father Gomez as the one responsible for 'the law', after which Gomez directs him to the grandmother because she covers 'education'. Arguing for the importance of schooling, the truant officer pleads with Gomez, the only male in this educational chain, 'But they've got to go to school! Everybody sends their kids to school! . . . Surely you want your youngsters to be like other children?' Gomez explains, 'We have our own Board of Education.' The very first episode thus establishes the house as the site of a doppelgänger state, with familiar government departments run by different family members in different rooms and, like any Kafkaesque bureaucracy, booting hapless visitors from one department to another. The fundamental point of the episode is the friction that arises from the transfer of children from the private home, with its own rules and its own governance, to the state, with another set of rules and another system of governance in which children are made to conform to national, normative discourses. It is these normative discourses that the conclusion of the episode critiques: Morticia objects to her children being exposed to violent fairy tales at school and persuades the truant officer that they contribute to a violent society. Daniel Cho and Tyson Lewis have traced a similar critique of uniformity in 1990s Gothic depictions of Homeowners' Associations '[f]rom the *X-Files* to *Buffy the Vampire Slayer*' where the '"demonic" quality is none other than the privileging of the homes' uniformity over the individuality of the modern subject'.[15] Standard units are required for the state's mathematics to work, and hence its discipline: as the Prisoner shouts in every episode, 'I am not a number. I am a free man.'

A key device that appears in the series *Kolchak, the Night Stalker* (1974–75) embodies this very particular concern with the friction between units and individuals. In an early episode, 'The Energy Eater', Kolchak works with Jim Elkhorn, an Indigenous man who teaches Kolchak local Indigenous history as he pursues a series of murders. They retrieve X-ray images from the site of a supernatural event and overlay them to match lines and contours, often down the middle of an image; they tape the assembled X-rays together and hang the collected piece from a string across the middle of the room. Together, the overlapping X-rays show a single, enormous eye, belonging to the supernatural being that the episode strongly associates with the settler erasure of Indigenous peoples and histories. A quarter of a century later in *Angel* (1999–2004), the same device appears. In 'Apocalypse, Nowish', two members of the team, Gunn and Wesley, try to interpret hundreds of pages of a printout of another character's mind: Gunn realises that the printout is not intelligible as text but as shapes, and so he tells Wesley, 'You're looking too close.' Again, a team then works to piece pages together, overlapping to connect lines and shapes, to create a giant image: a square with a giant X, termed 'the Eye of Fire'. From X-rays to a computer-generated X, both are technologically produced records of individual interiority – and they are records that are meaningless until they are pieced together into a giant 'eye' or 'I'. In a recent iteration of the device, for the third episode of *Lovecraft Country* (2020), 'Holy Ghost', it is once again the connection between the records that signifies, not the individual records themselves, and once again characters uncover that which the dominant group erases – a history of science that brutalises and murders African Americans. This Gothic convention thinks of documentation otherwise than the state: instead of an individual record that represents an individual as a unit that is comparable to all other units, it stresses lines of connection that are simply not visible on a per-record level nor calculable via 'political arithmetic', as Petty terms it.

This trope appears in other forms. The plot of the second Kolchak television movie, *The Night Strangler* (1973), is broadly that of one of the more compelling first-season episodes of *The X-Files*, 'Squeeze' (1993). In both, a human being artificially prolongs his life by consuming body parts of victims at intervals (thirty years in *The X-Files*, twenty-one years in *The Night Strangler*) and continues, over a century, to live at the same address. Both serial killers, operating across multiple generational cycles, fall outside of norms and practices that can be captured by census data and police work. The investigators need to go into the archives to look for repetitions on a very different temporal scale to find the monster: old records, old newspapers. In tracing this broader archival history, Mulder also notes that 'fingerprinting was just coming into its own in 1903', papering over a gap in the fingerprint record with the history of those records. As with the printouts in *Angel*, the pattern is missed if they 'look too close'. In these Gothic series, then, the modern state's system of record-keeping is ineffective, its focus on norms and units preventing it from seeing the more meaningful patterns that connect individuals and events.

Data Collection

Such calls to look more closely at intersections and overlaps, rather than calculating interchangeable units and ratios, depart from more familiar literary Gothic tropes, particularly Burkean obscurity. A century after the Down Survey, Irish thinker Edmund Burke wrote in his *Philosophical Enquiry into the Origin of our Ideas of the Sublime and Beautiful* (1757),

> To make any thing very terrible, obscurity seems in general to be necessary. When we know the full extent of any danger, when we can accustom our eyes to it, a great deal of the apprehension vanishes ... Those despotic governments which are founded on the passions of men, and principally upon the passion of fear, keep their chief as much as may be from the public eye.[16]

The Down Survey is legible in this context as an effort to 'know the full extent of any danger' – to control the fears of the 'despotic government' by laying the population open to a manageable view so 'we can accustom our eyes to it'. In post-1950s American Gothic, this alignment between the tyrannical state and its accumulation of data is crucial. The state's capacity to 'know the full extent' of its population emerges from this body of work as the Gothic nightmare of the US libertarian fantasy of regularity without regulation, exemplified by the figure of the 'invisible hand' in Adam Smith's *Wealth of Nations* (1776). As Stefan Andriopoulos suggests, the 'invisible hand' is a Gothic trope which serves to mythically instate a moral order that 'render[s] external interventions by the state unnecessary. [Smith] can reject the mercantilist demand for state intervention only by a hidden recourse to supernatural intervention.'[17] The bureaucratic state denies the libertarian utopia by repudiating its providential reliance on the invisible hand through endless counting machines and forms with yes/no questions. In this context, what is important is less *The X-Files*' interest in government conspiracy than its early interest in the digital surveillance tools that help to advance that conspiracy.

In 1993 *The X-Files*' first-season episode, 'Ghost in the Machine', mixed *2001: A Space Odyssey* (1968) with government efforts to obtain Artificial Intelligence. The episode repeatedly depicts a computer exercising control through digital surveillance. Early in the episode, for instance, the computer stalls the elevator while Scully and Mulder are in it. There is a computer-controlled camera and microphone in the elevator, so when Scully picks up the elevator's emergency phone and identifies herself, the computer gets the information it needs to locate her home address. It then hacks her modem to gain control of her personal computer. This is both political critique and a recognition of the Gothic resonances of this kind of invisible control. After all, Dracula's supernatural connection to Mina offers a similar flow of information in Bram Stoker's 1897 novel, itself widely discussed in terms of advances in information technology and the bureaucratic state. Winthrop-Young suggests, for instance, that Stoker's novel 'is one of the first texts to address ... the volatile relationship between freedom from below, control from above, and ever-increasing heaps of information'.[18] 'Ghost in the Machine' imagines what we now call a 'smart building', in which a computer runs all the elements, from security to elevators to plumbing, in the name of efficiency. The centralisation of information in one system is precisely the threat that the episode explores: each of the computer's interventions draws on the systems integration that defines its normal functioning. For the murder in the opening scene, for instance, the computer accesses the phone systems, plumbing and an electronic lock.

By the second season of the series, the writers were exploring networked systems beyond building design. In 'Blood', a government experiment combines pesticides and digital displays to stoke people's phobias. 'Blood' was widely recognised for reflecting growing concern about mass shootings, but it also addresses gendered violence and refers explicitly to 'suicide by cop' and 'the spree killer'. In broad terms, 'Blood' reflects on violence associated with mental health crises and poor impulse control but looks for systemic causes – decisions made by the state. The episode echoes the repetitiveness of digital forms (as series of 1s and 0s, go-to loops, and so on) by repeating the same plot sequence over and over: someone under stress because of an anxiety, an electronic display with increasingly violent messages, and then violence. Displays include a zipcode-entry machine, an elevator, a cash machine (ATM), a calculator and television screens in a department store that show news clips from Charles Manson to the assault on Rodney King. Throughout the episode, technology clutters rooms and fills the televisual frame, stressing the ubiquity of electronic screens and their connection to unseen networks. In one scene, Scully's laptop is visible with multiple cables hooking it to other devices and the internet, while in the next Mulder's laptop is shown without any visible cables, its ports shrouded in darkness, echoing the conventional Gothic device of the woman as overly available to intrusion.

A pivotal scene involves the agents' discussion of the use of subliminal messages to control behaviour, such as to 'deter shoplifting'. In this conversation, state interest in digital tools is not linked to capturing information to better understand the population, but to manipulating behaviour to produce the kind of awe that is key to the Gothic:

> MULDER: It's a fact that some department stores use subliminal messages in their ambient music to deter shoplifting. And the Russians have been using advanced electroencephalographic techniques to control behaviour...
> SCULLY: Controlled by who? By the government? By a corporation?... Why would they intentionally create a populace that destroys itself?
> MULDER: Fear. It's the oldest tool of power. If you're distracted by fear of those around you, it keeps you from seeing the actions of those above.

The sublime has become the subliminal in its capacity to control. At the end of the episode, Mulder receives verbal messages through his mobile phone's numeric display, reinforcing the implication that the state is using non-state electronic networks to extend its power.

In 'Blood', the conspiracy not only erodes privacy, but also psychological integrity and autonomy – and it is explicitly directed at the purported core of American society. Mulder notes that 'The killers were all middle-income, responsible people. None with a history of violence.' Moreover, 'given their backgrounds, the perpetrators would be, statistically, more likely the victims of violent crimes, rather than the originators'. This returns to the fundamental contradiction between the libertarian state and the bureaucratic state. 'Middle-income, responsible people' are self-governing, law-abiding, capitalist subjects – the Smithian fantasy of a population in which self-interest necessarily works to the benefit of the public interest. The *X-Files* episode 'Blood' imagines electronic surveillance eroding the white middle class's privacy and hence autonomy through the obscure operations of the digital state that treats them as interchangeable units.

Fragments and Iterations

The Gothic anthology series of the 1950s and 1960s drew deep from the well of Gothic literature. In the first season of *Alfred Hitchcock Presents*, Hitchcock calls attention to these debts, noting in his introduction that the plot of the episode 'Into Thin Air' (1955) will be 'familiar because it is a classic of its kind. Many, many people have borrowed this legend, quite profitably, too', before listing 'two novels' and mentioning his own movie, *The Lady Vanishes* (1938). The long-running Gothic soap opera *Dark Shadows* (1966–71) relied heavily on British literary tropes, beginning with a heroine evocative of Victorian fiction,[19] and only turning to the supernatural fare of vampires, werewolves and zombies late in its first season. The anthology format itself recalls Victorian Gothic tropes of narrative fragmentation and iteration.

In the 1996 *X-Files* episode, 'Jose Chung's "From Outer Space"', author Jose Chung interviews various characters for a book on alien abduction. While the focus on alien abduction aligns it with science fiction, the episode is formally Gothic: it is fragmented, giving different pieces of narrative from different perspectives, and sometimes the same event from different perspectives or different states of consciousness. The emphasis on interviews highlights the longstanding Gothic interest in perspective and the unreliability of memory, most notably in Anne Rice's *Interview with the Vampire* (1976). The episode also draws on the nineteenth-century Gothic interest in mesmerism in a series of scenes depicting or discussing hypnotism, and in this sense returns to the central concern of 'Blood', that is, the fragility of individual sovereignty. As Chung interviews Scully, they begin talking about one of his earlier books, *The Caligarian Candidate* (clearly alluding to *The Manchurian*

Candidate, a 1959 novel by Richard Condon that became an influential movie in 1962). Chung tells Scully,

> I was interested in how the CIA, when conducting their ... mind-control experiments back in the '50s, had no idea how hypnosis went ... As a storyteller, I'm fascinated how a person's sense of consciousness can be so transformed by nothing more magical than listening to words – mere words.

Such a transformation undoes the unitary individual on which the Enlightenment and government data collection is founded.

This episode first aired on 12 April 1996. A few weeks earlier, on 23 February 1996, the network aired 'Pusher', yet another episode about mind control: Mulder notes, 'Suggestion is a powerful force. The science of hypnosis is predicated on it, as are most TV commercials. I mean, they're designed to plant thoughts in your head.' These three episodes – 'Blood', 'Pusher', 'Jose Chung' – all circulate around the Gothic concern with the sovereignty of the individual that lies at the foundation of ideas of the sovereignty of the state back to Enlightenment political thought, especially John Locke's work.[20] Put another way, we might think of the homology between the two kinds of sovereignty as a doppelgänger: each kind of sovereignty is threatened by the other kind precisely because they are so nearly alike that they cannot logically coexist. In 'Jose Chung's "From Outer Space"', this Gothic concern is specifically tied to a cover-up of government medical experiments: hypnosis is used to replace memories of state abduction with a narrative of alien abduction. Both 'Blood' and 'Pusher' refer to subliminal advertising as proof that mind control is possible, and in both Scully tries to highlight the triviality of consumer decisions in comparison to other choices: in 'Pusher', she responds, 'Inducing someone to buy hair color is a little different than inducing them to drive in front of a speeding truck.'

This is where all three episodes come together and connect to Agamben's notion of 'bare life'. In 'Jose Chung', Scully asks a teenager if he and his date had 'consensual sexual intercourse'; he replies, 'If her father finds out, I'm a dead man.' The threat 'You're a dead man' is then repeated by a Man in Black, a cliché character in conspiracy theories, and by Scully and Mulder, who are misidentified in some interviews as Men in Black. Agamben, partly responding to Michel Foucault's concept of biopolitics, suggests that 'life originally appears in law only as the counterpart of a power that threatens death'.[21] The 'Jose Chung' episode returns to this, like Freud circling back to a neighbourhood in his essay on the uncanny, not only in the circulation of death threats in the virtual space of unreliable memories but also in the discovery of 'a real live dead alien body' that turns out to be a dead man zipped into an alien costume. The autopsy of the dead man is edited into a misleading video titled 'Dead Alien!', a counterfeit counterpart to Chung's book as 'non-fiction science fiction'; they are both designed to make money, in terms worth considering in relation to Jerrold Hogle's essays on the counterfeit in the Gothic.[22] Doubles, iterations, layered memories, hypnotism and subliminal messages that alter consciousness and direct the will – all of these undo the individual, putatively 'free' subject of American politics.

In other words, the 'truth' is refracted into 'versions of the truth', discussed by Chung and Scully in an early scene, and those versions then proliferate through scenes that replay the same event in different versions – Scully leaning against the wall in one version, a military officer in the same pose in the same room in another. There are no longer facts, or 'real' bodies that can be classified as dead or alive (digitally, zeroes or ones), or even clear government pathways to the recording of data. Petty's vision of uniform surveyors creating a uniform and complete account of the nation is exposed as fictional, even utopian, revealing instead overlapping images with lines of continuity and pieces that are discontinuous, like the composite 'eyes' of *Kolchak* and *Angel*.

This framework also has larger implications for *The X-Files*, recalling Eddie Robson's point that Mulder's 'sense of freedom is curtailed because he lacks certain truths that are important to him, chiefly the fate of his abducted sister'.[23] Many of the 'truths' he lacks are precisely those that configure the subject of, and to, the state with which he is in conflict. The possibility that the Smoking Man, who has no name for most of the series, may be Mulder's biological father undermines the foundations of Mulder's government identity as well as the fiction of a knowable domestic order. The clones, especially of Mulder's sister, de-individualise identity through a proliferation of units that shake the foundations of his quest to find his lost sister. Even the emergence of the surveillance of Mulder's home in 'E.B.E.', an episode that starts with military surveillance, highlights not just his struggle with the state but also the increasing uncanniness of his home in relation to it. The government conspiracies for which the series is well known organise as the central character-driving crisis of the early seasons the impossibility of a reliable census of the Mulder family unit. This domestic uncertainty is tied to the impossibility of securing the Mulder homes: Mulder's apartment, his mother's home and the family home (when the siblings were children) are all repeatedly transgressed through the course of the series.

The *X-Files* catchphrase, 'Trust No One', accretively echoes the Gothic concern with the collection of public data in which each person is just a 'one', a unit subject to 'political arithmetic', reverberating from the absent but ruling 'No. 1' in *The Prisoner* to Buffy, the 'chosen one', who is 'no one' in 'Anne'. All of these images of non-identity echo strangely in a digital world of ones and zeroes. To be 'no one' is to be zero, or 'off' in binary language – materially unconnected, without any current flowing through it. These Gothic television series explore the irreducibility of human experience to data as wielded by the state, and thus the violence inherent in digital technologies of power.

Key Works

David Levy (creator), *The Addams Family* (ABC, 1964–66). Gothic satire of early family sitcoms, based on the cartoons of Charles Addams.

Jeff Rice (creator), *Kolchak, the Night Stalker* (ABC, 1974–75). This short-lived series offered a Gothic twist on the film-noir tropes of the detective and investigative journalist, and influenced a number of later Gothic series.

Chris Carter (creator), *The X-Files* (Fox, 1993–2018). This popular series mixed science fiction, Gothic and detective modes, veering between extraterrestrial, supernatural and governmental threats within a broadly Gothic style.

Joss Whedon (creator), *Buffy, the Vampire Slayer* (WB and UPN, 1997–2003). This influential series, based on a movie and later continued in graphic novels, offered a Gothic version of conventional teen dramas.

Joss Whedon (creator), *Angel* (WB, 1999–2004). This series was a spin-off from *Buffy* but, especially in its early seasons, replaced the teen drama elements with conventions from film noir set in Los Angeles.

Further Critical Reading

Haslam, Jason, and Joel Faflak (eds), *American Gothic Culture: An Edinburgh Companion* (2016). Useful essays that address film and literature as well as television.

Jowett, Lorna, and Stacey Abbott, *TV Horror: Investigating the Dark Side of the Small Screen* (2013). Comprehensive overview of a number of relevant series.

Ledwon, Lenora, '*Twin Peaks* and the Television Gothic' (1993). Foundational early essay on TV Gothic.

Sanders, Steven M., and Aeon J. Skoble (eds), *The Philosophy of TV Noir* (2008). Useful essays on mystery series related to the Gothic, going back to the 1950s.

Bibliography

Agamben, Giorgio, *Means without End: Notes on Politics*, trans. Vincenzo Binetti and Cesare Cazarino (Minneapolis, MN: University of Minnesota

Press, 2000).

Andriopoulos, Stefan, 'The Invisible Hand: Supernatural Agency in Political Economy and the Gothic Novel', *ELH*, 66, 1999, pp. 739–58.

Burke, Edmund, *Enquiry Concerning the Origin of our Ideas of the Sublime and Beautiful* [1757], ed. Adam Phillips (Oxford: Oxford University Press, 1998).

Cho, Daniel, and Tyson Lewis, 'Home Is Where the Neurosis Is: A Topography of the Spatial Unconscious', *Cultural Critique*, 64, 2006, pp. 69–91.

De Quincey, Thomas, *The Confessions of an English Opium-Eater*, ed. Joel Faflak (Peterborough, Ont.: Broadview Press, 2009).

Freud, Sigmund, 'The Uncanny' [1919], in *The Standard Edition of the Complete Psychological Works of Sigmund Freud*, trans. James Strachey (London: Hogarth Press, 1955), vol. 17, pp. 219–52.

Habermas, Jürgen, *The Structural Transformation of the Public Sphere*, trans. Thomas Burger and Frederick Lawrence (Cambridge, MA: MIT Press, 1994).

Haslam, Jason, and Joel Faflak (eds), *American Gothic Culture: An Edinburgh Companion* (Edinburgh: Edinburgh University Press, 2016).

Henry, Aaron James. 'William Petty, the Down Survey, Population and Territory in the Seventeenth Century', *Territory, Politics, Governance*, 2, 2014, pp. 218–37.

Hogle, Jerrold E., '*Frankenstein* as Neo-Gothic: From the Ghost of the Counterfeit to the Monster of Abjection', in Tilottama Rajan and Julia M. Wright (eds), *Romanticism, History, and the Possibilities of Genre: Re-forming Literature, 1789–1837* (Cambridge: Cambridge University Press, 1998), pp. 176–210.

Horton, Emily, 'A Voice Without a Name: Gothic Homelessness in Ali Smith's *Hotel World* and Trezza Azzopardi's *Remember Me*', in Siân Adiseshiah and Rupert Hilyard (eds), *Twenty-First Century Fiction: What Happens Now* (New York: Palgrave Macmillan, 2013), pp. 132–46.

Jowett, Lorna, and Stacey Abbott, *TV Horror: Investigating the Dark Side of the Small Screen* (London: I.B. Tauris, 2013).

Ledwon, Lenora, '*Twin Peaks* and the Television Gothic', *Literature/Film Quarterly*, 21, 1993, pp. 260–70.

Levitan, Kathrin, *A Cultural History of the British Census: Envisioning the Multitude in the Nineteenth Century* (New York: Palgrave Macmillan, 2011).

McDonagh, Josephine, *Child Murder and British Culture, 1720–1900* (Cambridge: Cambridge University Press, 2003).

Mighall, Robert, *A Geography of Victorian Gothic Fiction* (Oxford: Oxford University Press, 2003).

Robson, Eddie, 'Gothic Television', in Catherine Spooner and Emma McEvoy (eds), *The Routledge Companion to Gothic* (New York: Routledge, 2007), pp. 242–50.

Sanders, Steven M., and Aeon J. Skoble (eds), *The Philosophy of TV Noir* (Lexington, KY: University of Kentucky Press, 2008).

Smith, Anthony D., 'Neo-classicist and Romantic Elements in the Emergence of Nationalist Conceptions', in Anthony D. Smith (ed.), *Nationalist Movements* (London: Macmillan, 1976), pp. 74–87.

Tuite, Clara, 'Frankenstein's Monster and Malthus' "Jaundiced Eye": Population, Body Politics, and the Monstrous Sublime', *Eighteenth-Century*

Life, 22, 1998, pp. 141–55.

Wheatley, Helen, *Gothic Television* (Manchester: Manchester University Press, 2006).

Winthrop-Young, Geoffrey, 'Undead Networks: Information Processing and Media Boundary Conflicts in Dracula', in Donald Bruce and Anthony George Purdy (eds), *Literature and Science* (Amsterdam: Rodopi, 1994), pp. 107–29.

Wright, Julia M., *Men with Stakes: Masculinity and the Gothic in US Television* (Manchester: Manchester University Press, 2016).

TV

Borchert, Rudolph, and Arthur Rowe (writers), 'The Energy Eater', *Kolchak, the Night Stalker* (ABC, 13 December 1974).

Cockrell, Marian (writer), 'Into Thin Air', *Alfred Hitchcock Presents* (CBS, 1955).

De Knight, Steven S. (writer), 'Apocalypse Nowish', *Angel* (WB, 17 November 2002).

Gansa, Alex, and Howard Gordon (writers), 'Ghost in the Machine', *The X-Files* (Fox, 29 October 1993).

Gilligan, Vince (writer), 'Pusher', *The X-Files* (Fox, 23 February 1996).

Green, Micha (writer), 'Holy Ghost', *Lovecraft Country* (HBO, 30 August 2020).

Jacobs, Seaman, and Ed James (writers), 'The Addams Family Goes to School', *The Addams Family* (ABC, 18 September 1964).

Matheson, Richard (writer), *The Night Stalker* (ABC, 11 January 1972).

Matheson, Richard (writer), *The Night Strangler* (ABC, 16 January 1973).

McGoohan, Patrick (creator), *The Prisoner* (ITV, 1967–68).

Morgan, Darin (writer), 'Jose Chung's "From Outer Space"', *The X-Files* (Fox, 12 April 1996).

Morgan, Glen, and James Wong (writers, with story by Darin Morgan), 'Blood', *The X-Files* (Fox, 30 September 1994).

Morgan, Glen, and James Wong (writers), 'E.B.E.', *The X-Files* (Fox, 18 February 1994).

Morgan, Glen, and James Wong (writers), 'Squeeze', *The X-Files* (Fox, 24 September 1993).

Whedon, Joss (writer and director), 'Anne', *Buffy the Vampire Slayer* (Fox, 29 September 1998).

Notes

1. I refer here to Giorgio Agamben's influential term 'bare life'.
2. The Prisoner's house in the village has two signs at the door: 'Private' and 'No 6'.
3. The series was later followed by a movie (2008) and two further seasons (2016, 2018).
4. Horton, 'A Voice Without a Name', p. 135.

5. Ibid., p. 136.
6. De Quincey, *Confessions*, p. 71.
7. Ibid., pp. 83–4, 72.
8. See Freud, 'The Uncanny'.
9. Smith, 'Neo-classicist and Romantic Elements', pp. 74–87.
10. Levitan, *Cultural History of the British Census*, p. 4.
11. See, for example, Mighall, *Geography of Gothic Fiction*.
12. See, for example, McDonagh, *Child Murder and British Culture*; Tuite, 'Frankenstein's Monster'.
13. Henry, 'William Petty', pp. 222–4.
14. Ibid., p. 226.
15. Cho and Lewis, 'Home Is Where the Neurosis Is', p. 77. For an exemplary instance, see 'Arcadia', a 1999 episode of *The X-Files*.
16. Burke, *Enquiry*, p. 54.
17. Andriopoulos, 'The Invisible Hand', p. 747.
18. Winthrop-Young, 'Undead Networks', p. 107.
19. Wheatley, *Gothic Television*, p. 150.
20. For a discussion of television Gothic and specifically masculine agency, see Wright, *Men with Stakes*.
21. Agamben, *Means without End*, pp. 7, 5.
22. See, for example, Hogle, '*Frankenstein* as Neo-Gothic'.
23. Robson, 'Gothic Television', p. 248.

Chapter 9

Gothic Horror Films at the 'Fin-de-Millennium': From Nightmare Videos to Filtered Realities (1980–2000)
Sorcha Ní Fhlainn

Near the end of the second act of Wes Craven's *Scream* (1996), a scene begins in a packed video store with Randy (Jamie Kennedy) restocking the horror section. The store is busy, having had a surge of interest in the 'mass murder' section following the recent murders of two local teenagers and with an unknown killer on the loose. The town of Woodsboro is terrorised, and the natural solution for its horror-literate teens is to throw parties and watch scary movies. Given his fluency in the genre, Randy acts as the sage librarian of all horror history collected in the store. Randy is soon cornered by classmates Stu Redmond (Matthew Lillard) and Billy Loomis (Skeet Ulrich), who each, in turn, accuse the other of being the local spree killer. After declaring that the police are wasting time by not revisiting the slasher classic *Prom Night* (1980) to solve the mystery, Billy and Stu suggest that Randy may have his own motive for being the killer. For Randy, the answer to this accusation is apt: 'It's the millennium. Motives are incidental.'

Scream, as a high point in the 1990s horror renaissance, is an ironic film that trades on insider fan knowledge of tropes and conventions, enamoured with the subgenre it critically unpacks. Thoroughly savvy about the filmic influence of video and slasher culture of the 1980s, *Scream* functions as a mid-1990s social document that simultaneously points to the jaded and well-worn ideas of the previous decade, while also articulating a distinct unease about the unpredictable and gloomy future rampant in 1990s discourse. Randy's comment about the millennium points directly to this precarious sense of unease as the turn of the century neared. As *Scream* deftly demonstrates, horror film culture would shift from dangerous knowledge to (video store-gleaned) survival guide, radically transforming its place in corporate Hollywood culture in the process. This chapter will examine various distinctive movements from 1980–2000 that dominated the sociopolitical landscape and aesthetic shifts of Gothic horror films – horror films that include significant

Gothic narrative elements and aesthetics. The chapter addresses this fragmented terrain, moving from video panics and the slasher film to Hollywood Gothic and fantasies of Armageddon, to the rise of found footage. Furthermore, I will examine two highly successful and culturally important films – *A Nightmare on Elm Street* (1984) and *The Blair Witch Project* (1999) – as short case studies to foreground the fragmented, excessive and gloomy qualities of the final two decades of the twentieth century onscreen.

Fred Botting observes in his seminal study of the Gothic mode that while the Gothic felt excessively worn out by the mid-1990s, such exhaustions and endings often open up new and surprising possibilities.[1] The screen terrors of the 1980s and 1990s were highly fragmented, including abject gore and body horror onscreen; anxieties about digital technology and sentience; fear of nuclear conflagration as a result of Cold War tensions; the widespread use of the web and cyberculture; public panics about censorship, screen violence and video games; and the perceived prevalence of and fascination with serial killers in the popular imaginary (including, but not limited to, Ted Bundy, the 'Night Stalker' Richard Ramirez and Jeffrey Dahmer). Despite the thematic fragmentations that pervaded cinema at the end of the twentieth century (from serial killers to ghosts, vampires and zombies, to demonic forces and urban legends), Gothic and horror titles – often delineated between Gothic's subtle, suggested and uncanny offerings and horror's more overt violence, sadism and bleak worldview – have enjoyed a 'steady commingling' since the 1970s.[2] One of the most interesting aspects of the shift in Gothic film's ability to capture the imagination came about through its distribution and consumption, ranging from unrated video releases that threatened to expose children to 'depraved' materials, through to conjuring up audience interest in 'real' found footage films in the burgeoning age of digital marketing. The thematic arrangement of this period is therefore challenging to consolidate, given the explosion in Gothic horror titles during the period and the variety of subgenre film styles that emerged. However, elements of the Gothic travelled into mainstream horror entertainment throughout this period, from supernatural slashers and Faustian bargains to terrifying physical transformations; horror films at the end of the twentieth century, whether distributed on video tape or captured on handheld video camera, are frequently underpinned by disturbing and Gothic intrusions of the past and a sickening, inescapable feeling that threatens our feelings of safety and reassurance.

New Gothic Nightmares of the Video Age

The expansion of screen horror was largely facilitated by technological innovation, with the migration of film viewing into the home via cable television, VCR ownership and video rental stores, which became a primary distribution model in film viewing alongside theatrical release and televisual broadcast. 1980s horror films were a 'low' form of cultural entertainment that would, with the popular prevalence of video store circulation, be at the vanguard of a revolutionary technological shift in how we consumed film and gained access to a wider array of titles. As Daniel Herbert observes, 'Video stores changed the way [people] treated movies and thus changed "movie culture" or the ways in which people socialize around movies and collectively make movies meaningful ... they had a newly physical presence in the world and were treated as commodities.'[3] This also made video a valuable commodity by which viewers could gain generic fluency, enabling repetitive viewing, pausing, rewinding and recontextualising the image free from a linear viewing experience, while also enabling in-depth knowledge and fan culture. This economic model also drove the prevalence of the 'sequel' in production terms, accelerating more content to be created for video release, while whetting viewers' appetites for extended instalments and expanded screen narratives. As Stephen Prince observes, 'sequels were like brand labels, and the studios sought to brand audience loyalty by developing characters and film properties that could be manufactured in perpetuity'.[4] This branding was highly profitable in horror productions, giving rise to ongoing instalments in quick succession, with varying levels of financial success and narrative coherence. Between 1978 and 2000 alone, the most popular slasher franchises flourished (in film and across other media platforms including games, novels, comics, and TV adaptations), with *Halloween* (1978–) extending to five films, the *Nightmare on Elm Street* (1984–) franchise featuring seven titles, and *Friday the 13th* (1980–) consisting of nine titles.[5] Gothic film, as Spooner observes about the wider reach of the Gothic at the 'fin-de-millennium', is extremely canny and self-aware, steeped in the history of replication, and commercially savvy.[6]

This explosion of horror film availability, however, was subject to its own scandals and calls for regulation. In the UK, due to a legal loophole, the burgeoning unregulated video rental market had made unclassified titles available to rent. The 'video nasties' crisis introduced film bans by the Director of Public Prosecutions (DPP) under the Obscene Publications Act 1959. The DPP's lists featured a disorganised assortment of ultra-low budget exploitation and grindhouse films – often with lurid shock covers and stills, with promises to horrify in the marketing blurbs. Julian Petley notes that 'one of the most remarkable aspects of the "video nasty" panic was the speed and intensity with which a few horror videos came to be seen as nothing less than harbingers of the apocalypse'.[7] Spearheaded by conservative crusaders including Mary Whitehouse,[8] the British tabloid media further fuelled this moralistic campaign with shock warnings of susceptible youths (read: working-class children) gaining access to such tapes, which being 'brought into British homes might ... infect impressionable minds'.[9] Video became one of the most progressive technological means to access new and previously unavailable titles and to build one's own personal archive and viewing preferences beyond the reach of self-declared moral guardians. Thus, as Kim Newman notes, 'like all new technology, the video recorder was suspect',[10] a veritable gateway to youth corruption in the family home.

Invasions into the familial space by demonic forces were thematically twinned in US and UK culture at the time. In the US, the prevailing and concurrent moral panic was the Satanic Panic crisis. The most infamous example of this crisis centred on the McMartin pre-school trial (1984–90), a lawsuit which was based on allegations of satanic rituals, blood sacrifices and sexual defilement.[11] Thematically inspired by the McMartin trial's central concern about children in peril, Wes Craven's script for *A Nightmare on Elm Street* used the universal experience of nightmares to stage and explore repressed traumas. Craven was also inspired by *Los Angeles Times* reports of multiple deaths of Asian Pacific Rim males who had died in their sleep following vivid and violent nightmares. Noting the similarity with '"bangungut syndrome" – named after the Filipino word for nightmare', the terror of dying while asleep became a source of genuine threat.[12] A few of the victims had hidden coffee pots from concerned family members and tried in vain to stave off their need to sleep and dream. Craven's 1984 film channelled these real-world panics and traumas into the then popular slasher film cycle, producing a highly influential Gothic counternarrative to the Reaganite American dream of prosperity and security. Slasher films such as *A Nightmare on Elm Street*, as John Kenneth Muir aptly comments,

> arrived in movie theatres during a time when teens wondered if there would be a tomorrow. Can it come as a total surprise that this generation's entertainment of choice concerns a crucible of survival in which only the clever, the moral, the resolute, and the resourceful manage to survive an apocalyptic world that seemed stacked against them?[13]

Representing 1980s excesses of violence, familial horrors and Gothic revenge, *A Nightmare on Elm Street* best exemplifies the traumatic repressions of the Reagan revolution. Krueger as the horror icon of the decade distinctly targets the youth of Elm Street, draining away the vitality of the future generation to feed the economic and hedonistic appetites of the present.[14]

According to Adam Rockoff, by 1984 slasher films had undergone a distinct evolution, from their inception with precursors *Psycho* (1960) and *Black Christmas* (1974) to gamechanger *Halloween* (1978), through to the increased gore of *Friday the 13th* (1980) and *My Bloody Valentine* (1981).[15] A distinctive formula underpins the slasher film, as examined in seminal studies by Carol J. Clover and Vera Dika.[16] The killer, typically male and subjectively wronged or twisted by some earlier event, returns to stalk, terrorise and kill the teenagers of suburban America. The popularity of these titles informed a type of profitable traumatic replay of the killer's compulsion to kill as a form of moral, economic or social retribution. The success of these series hinges upon the spectacle of the returning iconic killer and the ingenuity and brutality with which the teenage victims, in a ritualistic form of 'compulsive repetitiveness', are dispatched.[17] Crucially, it is the star status of the returning killer, as opposed to the survivor/s, that marks out the slasher's enduring appeal.[18] Emerging as the killer's nemesis is the 'Final Girl', a modern-day update of the Gothic heroine who stands apart from her peers, runs away, fights back, cleverly misdirects and eventually overcomes the killer's games of death.[19]

A Nightmare on Elm Street signals the full flourishing of the slasher in presenting one of the decade's most grotesque horror icons, Freddy Krueger (Robert Englund), as a unique 'killer with personality', with signature mordant quips, and bearing a bladed glove signifying sexual menace. Krueger is introduced as a spectral killer who was, years earlier, charged for a series of child murders. Freed on a legal technicality at trial, Krueger was hunted down by the parents of Elm Street who meted out vigilante justice by burning him to death. Targeting the teens of Elm Street in revenge, Krueger returns via the dream world beyond the reach of their (often disbelieving) parents and authority figures. Tina (Amanda Wyss) and Nancy (Heather Langenkamp) describe experiencing similar nightmares of being pursued by a burn-scarred man in a filthy red and green striped jumper with knives for fingernails. Tina's brutal murder during a sleepover is blamed on her delinquent boyfriend Rod (Nick Corri), but Nancy is convinced that her friend died at the hands of Krueger and must eventually confront Krueger's menace alone. Nancy is, as Carol J. Clover states, the 'grittiest of Final Girls', and goads

Krueger into a game of pursuit to drag him into reality.[20] She injures and misdirects him with her impressive self-made booby-trapped doors and makeshift weapons, setting him alight, but he still spectrally and impossibly reappears after each tussling round. At the climax of this battle, Krueger kills Nancy's mother Marge (Ronee Blakley) in her bed, taking revenge for her part in the vigilante mob that burned him alive. Nancy discovers that her fear fuels his horrific supernatural powers; in their final confrontation, she demands restoration of the friends and family he has murdered, and turns her back on him, taking back her power and declaring, 'You're nothing. You're shit.' Casting off his power as abject psychic excess, this negation of Krueger's phantasmagorical power and her demand for restoration works, at least temporarily, as the film's coda concludes with a brightly shot scene on the family's front porch in which Nancy is reunited with her mother and her friends. Like most slasher icons, Freddy endures, at least in spirit, in a set-up for future sequels: he foils Nancy's perfect ending by trapping her and her friends in Glen's car, while her mother, newly converted to sobriety, is sucked through the front door. Craven's final image, that of young girls skipping while singing the film's nursery rhyme theme that forewarns 'Freddy's coming for you', reminds us that Freddy's legacy, and the fear he instils in the town (and the film's 1980s teen audience), endures.[21]

A Nightmare on Elm Street added a distinct Gothic undercurrent to what was considered a cheap subgenre to produce, particularly in its successful use of in-camera effects, optical trickery, 'rubber reality' special effects and make-up.[22] The nightmare set pieces in particular capture the disorienting terror of being hunted and offer a destabilising viewing experience through the blending of everyday and surrealist scenes. While caught in the dream world with Freddy, familiar and everyday spaces are corrupted and rendered uncanny (rotating bedrooms, steamy boiler rooms, bottomless bathtubs, permeable walls) as 'complex visions of unbridled, hellish, nightmare worlds' with an intense and heightened sense of claustrophobia.[23] As James Kendrick observes, the Gothic surrealism in the oneiric space disturbs both the audience and the viewer, as

> Freddy is literally omnipresent within his victims' dreamscapes ... He can be simultaneously on both ends of the frame, which is depicted in one of Tina's dreams when she is shown running from Freddy on the left side of the screen, only to run smack into him on the right side.[24]

This dream space terror transgresses the 'everyday' aesthetics of the typical slasher film as proposed by Clover, and enables Craven to fill the frame with impossible Gothic violations of space.[25] This trend of nightmarish intrusion into the real world comes to full fruition in a metatextual postmodern examination of the film series and its cultural influence in Craven's final instalment, *Wes Craven's New Nightmare* (1994).

Our mode of viewing and engaging with our cultural monsters also shifted in this period. While the slasher (and its sequels) ruled at the box office, video steadily grew throughout the 1980s to become the dominant mode of viewing, according to Caetlin Benson-Allott, who notes that '[s]ince 1988, US audiences have watched the majority of their movies on a video platform'.[26] As a portable home entertainment apparatus, video transformed how we privately consume films, while Gothic horror films articulated anxieties about the wider world and our place within our communities. Serving as some of the most popular social documents, horror films in the age of Reagan took on an appropriate Gothic shape. Films charting graphic monstrosity, transformations and economic insecurities found expression in narratives about werewolves (*The Howling* and *An American Werewolf in London* [both 1981]),[27] vampires (*The Hunger* [1983], *Fright Night* [1985], *Near Dark* and *The Lost Boys* [both 1987])[28] and hauntings in suburban America (*The Amityville Horror* [1979], *Poltergeist* [1982], *Beetlejuice* [1988]). The flourishing of horror often dwelled on the era's obsession with aesthetics and surfaces, the pursuit of physical perfection contrasted through the lens of body horror and toxicity,[29] and growing concern about Reaganomics, consumerism and its neoliberal consequences (especially evident in *The Stuff* [1985], *Society* [1989] and *American Psycho* [2000]). The body horrors of David Cronenberg (*Videodrome* [1983] and *The Fly* [1986]), Clive Barker (*Hellraiser* [1987] and *Nightbreed* [1990]) and John Carpenter (*The Thing* [1982]) spoke to instabilities around issues of sexuality and gender, HIV+ infection, and the body-as-text. Furthermore, films concerning reproductive rights and the moral policing of the poor, migrants and people of colour can be explicitly seen in Gothic science fiction films, particularly around themes of Alien invasion (*Aliens* [1986], *Alien Nation* [1988] and *They Live* [1988]).

Other prevalent societal nightmares shadowed the anxieties of nuclear war and the advancement of technology. While 'Protect and Survive' public bulletins and pamphlets in the UK anticipated such possibilities in the late 1970s and early 1980s,[30] Gothic science fiction fantasies imagining apocalyptic futures, radiation poisoning, government cover-ups and nuclear conflagration featured in films and TV movies including *The Day After* (1983), *Threads* (1984) and the animated feature *When the Wind Blows* (1986). Glimpses of humanity's terrible fate at the hands of mechanised extermination appeared in *The Terminator* (1984), viscerally expanded upon in its 1991 sequel, *Terminator 2: Judgment*

Day, in a graphic sequence during which we witness the razing of Los Angeles, and the conflagration of franchise heroine Sarah Connor (Linda Hamilton). This iconic dream sequence immediately recalls the horrors of Hiroshima and Nagasaki in 1945, and situates humanity's nuclear destruction as a fated, contemporary event. The terrifying possibilities of nuclear meltdowns onscreen were underpinned by the actual nuclear disasters at Three Mile Island (in Pennsylvania, 1979) and Chernobyl (in Ukraine, 1986), and the political amplification of Cold War tensions between the USA and the USSR.

In the aftermath of the Cold War, following the fall of the Berlin Wall in 1989, there was a brief newfound sense of optimism: Francis Fukuyama posited that we had reached 'the End of History', a theory that foregrounded liberal democracies as an end point in the evolutionary progress of government. Despite this shift in geopolitical relations, Fukuyama warned that we should be mindful of technology as a threat to humanity beyond our control.[31] Fantasies of Armageddon in popular film continued into the 1990s and broadly bifurcated into two parallel narrative forms, feeding into anxieties that the future would be undone by Artificial Intelligence (AI), or sparked by the supernatural return of ancient evil at the threshold of the millennium. Two prime examples of these competing fantasies of Armageddon were released in the summer of 1999 at the height of Y2K paranoia: in *The Matrix*, humanity is trapped in a virtual simulation, enslaved by machine overlords to be used as biological batteries; in *End of Days*, the hard body icon of 1980s action cinema, Arnold Schwarzenegger, returns to thwart Satan's plan to inaugurate a new dark age on the eve of the third millennium.

Hollywood Gothic and Independent Cinema

In the early 1990s formulaic slashers had been bled dry, with cycles nearing exhaustion and audiences jaded with their familiar plots and machinations. With the mixing of the Hollywood thriller and the literary adaptation, the Hollywood Gothic cycle (1990–96) began a process of recuperation for Gothic titles and horror/thriller hybrid films in more traditional and conservative film circles. Glossed up as literary adaptations with all-star casts, many Gothic horror titles were recategorised as hybrid thrillers to eschew any connection with horror's 'lowbrow' 1980s splatter aesthetics. Oscar-winning releases, including *Misery* (1990) and Coppola's *Dracula* (1992), quickly led to the development of *Interview with the Vampire* (1994), *Mary Shelley's Frankenstein* (1994), *Wolf* (1994) and *Mary Reilly* (1996), each underpinned by significant budgets and helmed by celebrated directors. These titles came into vogue alongside the psychological thriller – the most celebrated of all being *The Silence of the Lambs* (1991), with its infamous serial killers, Hannibal Lecter and Buffalo Bill, serving as direct descendants of Stoker's Dracula and Shelley's Victor Frankenstein, respectively.[32] Trading 1980s slashers for 1990s 'inspired by true crime' serial killers, *The Silence of the Lambs* singularly inaugurated a slew of popular psychological police procedural films in the early to mid-1990s. The best of those that followed its form, including *Copycat* (1995) and *Se7en* (1995), utilise the trope of a gifted if troubled cop and/or FBI psychologist who is pitted against a brilliant and disturbed killer in a deadly game of cat and mouse.

Apparently having no external enemy abroad left to fight following the Cold War, American paranoia turned inward, focusing on the horrors to the homeland, from alien invasions and serial killers to criminal conspiracies, feeding into a growing distrust of public institutions and law enforcement in series such as *The X-Files* (1993–2002). Doubles and duplication abounded with the rise of screen duos on both sides of the law: Detectives Somerset (Morgan Freeman) and Mills (Brad Pitt) lead the investigation into a series of apocalyptic murders in *Se7en*, as do both Mulder (David Duchovny) and Scully (Gillian Anderson) on TV and in film (*The X-Files: Fight the Future* [1998]), while serial killers and final girls also doubled up in *Scream* (1996) and *Scream 2* (1997), reviving the slasher subgenre through a hyper-postmodern lens that was evidently fluent in 1990s horror theory.[33] However, knowing the rules of the slasher film would not ensure one's survival in this age of postmodern reinvention.

Gothic doubling (exposing divided shadow selves of public icons, or people of significant privilege, including O. J. Simpson, Michael Jackson and President Clinton) ran riot in the culture at large throughout the 1990s. The media was saturated with dark disclosures and allegations in both public discourse and cinematic texts. As Mark Edmundson observes of the destabilising nature of doubling during the Gothic 1990s:

> the conventions of Gothic horror are making their way into, and decisively shaping, many apparently nonfictional forms. On broadcast news, in the most respected daily papers, on TV talk shows, in our modes of therapy ... in our medical and environmental discourses, and even in advanced brands of intellectual analysis, the Gothic mode is ascendant. Not only do the 90s media seem to seek out Gothic tales to bring to the centre of cultural consciousness, they also sometimes rework events until they assume the proper Gothic shape.[34]

Knowing 'the truth' was no longer a state of truly believing in the evidence presented by those in authority either. For Edmundson, 'gothic thrives in a world where those in authority – the supposed exemplars of the good – are under suspicion'.[35] Thus, the domains of horror television, exposé infotainment, tabloid journalism, reality TV and burgeoning internet culture all fuelled a sense of profound doubt in the public imagination, offering alternative viewpoints that critiqued more traditional spheres of power and authority.

This duality also enabled an emerging counterculture in filmmaking, considered as a collective 'cinema of outsiders' by Emanuel Levy in his seminal study on the movement,[36] which actively competed with big budget studio releases in shaping film culture outside of studio constraints. Film festivals such as Sundance provided edgier, often noncommercial means for new filmmakers – the first generation raised on video culture – and those working outside the studio system to secure distribution for their micro-budget films. This shift towards new 'indie films', including *Cube* (1997) and international subversive critiques such as *Funny Games* (1997) and *Ringu* (1998), offered an aesthetic and tonal counterweight to Hollywood Gothic productions.[37] As Peter Biskind observes,

> [Independent] films were anything Hollywood was not. If Hollywood made movies, indies made 'films'. If Hollywood sold fantasy and escapism, indies thrived on realism and engagement. If Hollywood avoided controversial subjects, indies embraced them. If Hollywood movies were expensive, indie films were cheap.[38]

Following a decade of revisionist and ironic slashers, paranoia in the American heartland feeding conspiracy-led distrust, and titles that profoundly fed into millennial anxieties about the imminence of the end times – including *In the Mouth of Madness* (1994), *The Devil's Advocate* (1997), *Stigmata* (1999) and *The Ninth Gate* (1999) – *The Blair Witch Project* (1999) debuted at Sundance to critical and commercial acclaim with its ingenious synthesis of Gothic conventions and found footage documentary.

Blair Witches and Filtered Realities

The Blair Witch Project was arguably the most divisive Gothic film to emerge during the 1990s. Presented as found footage recovered a year after their disappearance in 1994, the film concerns three student filmmakers, Heather Donohue, Michael Williams and Joshua Leonard (all of the actors used their real names), who trek into the woods near Burkittsville, Maryland while shooting a documentary about the legend of the Blair Witch. Interviewing locals about the legend, stories emerge about local murders and the disappearance of children, with various interviewees identifying the local woods as haunted. Another local tale, relayed by two fishermen, concerns Robin Weaver, a young girl who vanished for three days and returned telling a story about a woman 'whose feet never touched the ground'. Yet another story tells of children being murdered in twos, with one forced to wait in the corner of a room facing the wall as the other is killed. As Heather, Josh and Mike continue to hike into the woods, they reach Coffin Rock, a place where a ritualistic murder of five men took place in the nineteenth century. The woods seem alive with stories of death. Soon the group begin to squabble and become disorientated, seemingly walking in circles on their daily hikes. Eventually admitting they are lost, and running low on provisions, they attempt to abandon the project to get home and discover they cannot find a way out. In frustration, Mike discards the map and seals their fate. Their campsites become sites of terror and confusion every night: a cairn of stones, which Josh disturbs, signals another presence, as does the sound of twigs snapping and footsteps. In quick succession, the horror escalates further; they discover wooden stick figures decorating the trees, while at night their tents are shaken, their items are disturbed, covered in slime or taken, and each member of the group grows increasingly furious with the other. When Josh inexplicably disappears, Mike and Heather are convinced they can hear him screaming during the night, and later discover his teeth in a bloodied bundle of sticks and plaid fabric. In the film's most famous sequence, Heather's tearful cathartic confession to camera in extreme close-up is emotionally agonising as she realises aloud, 'We're going to die out here.' Following a voice presumed to be Josh's, Heather and Mike find a ruined house, which bears the bloody handprints of children on its crumbling walls. In the basement, as Heather enters following weird cries and screams, we see Mike facing the corner, his camera now discarded, and Heather's camera falls to the ground. Subjectivity has now collapsed entirely, and the final indistinguishable frames blur to the whirring sound of running video tape.

The film quickly divided audiences on its release: its unstable framing, ambient noises and folk horror urban legends unsettled many reviewers (including Roger Ebert), while others found its lack of resolution and the absence of the Blair Witch (or any other monstrous figure) onscreen to be profoundly unsatisfying. Nonetheless, the film confirmed independent cinema's ability to upend Hollywood's polished productions in a decade that saw the ascent of indie films and attendant minor studios (Miramax, October Films, Artisan Films etc.). This success was partly due to the clever hybridisation of the film's traditional and digital promotional strategies. With an abundance of ancillary materials, including the manufactured legend of the Blair Witch and a supporting documentary, missing posters for the three actors (who had been declared dead online), maps, interviews and active online message boards, these promotional layers all added to the lore that this was a true story. As J. P. Telotte notes, this strategy also

> offered to those who had not yet seen the film but who might have heard some of the hype, as well as to those who had already seen it, a path of further investigation and a source of other, similarly creepy sensations – in effect, a different context for viewing the film.[39]

The film's 'chance' discovery as lost film reels, drawing on the literary Gothic trope of the discovered manuscript, documents the filmmakers' final days in the woods in a realist tone that felt altogether new and raw. Its aesthetic tone of dread and disorientation, amplified by strange cuts and edits between monochrome and colour camera footage, uneven shifts between locations, jarring day-to-night transitions, and unseen assailant/s, marks out *The Blair Witch Project* as a thoroughly postmodern film. There is an abundance of technology and information available but an 'apparent inability to see truth'.[40] As Muir observes, the film 'asks us to fill in the blanks, to imagine the horrors that our eyes didn't actually witness'.[41] Moreover, *The Blair Witch Project* acts as an important bridge between horror exploitation videos of the past, evoking the infamous *Cannibal Holocaust* (1980) – the first found footage horror film and banned 'video nasty' – but also laying the groundwork for the found footage boom of the early 2000s.

Gothic cinema's advances and alchemical potency, from real-life unregulated video tapes and viral nightmarish video circulation (in *Ringu*) to recovered 'real' found footage, traversed radical shifts from 1980 to the end of the twentieth century. In each step of this progression – from the advancement of 'dangerous' consumerist technologies to viral marketing campaigns and realist filmmaking strategies – Gothic horror films have confronted viewers with the prevalent cultural fear of the moment, and have worked through our shared nightmares accordingly. *The Blair Witch Project* reminds viewers that resolution is not always possible and that in the age of technological accessibility, people can vanish without a trace and the truth may never be (narratively) resolved; that smug assuredness does not guarantee survival; and that ancient evils and moral panics – brought about by folkloric legends, Satanic forces and prophecies of doom – still endure and retain mysteries of their own. While the twenty-first century's horror culture channelled gloom and rage in the aftermath of 9/11, informing found footage and survivor films (*28 Days Later* [2002], *REC* [2007], *Cloverfield* [2008]), new ludic games of death (the *Saw* franchise [2004–]) and spectacles of torture (*Hostel* [2005]) in quick succession, the continuation of these successful subgenres nonetheless owes a significant debt to the slasher franchises (and their sequels) and the industry outsiders who shaped Gothic film at the end of the twentieth century.

Key Films

The Shining (1980). Stanley Kubrick's adaptation of Stephen King's novel is a masterclass in Gothic cinema (debuting the now-ubiquitous use of the floating Steadicam down the hotel's chilling corridors and hedge-maze). The film focuses on the disintegration and isolated madness of the Torrance family as they spend the winter in the labyrinthine, haunted Overlook Hotel.

Hellraiser (1987). In his directorial debut, Clive Barker adapts his Faustian bargain themed novella *The Hellbound Heart* (1986) to the screen in full body-horror glory. With the use of a mysterious puzzle box, Frank Cotton opens the gates to hell. Rebirthed on earth, Frank is then pursued by the mysterious Cenobites, who relish in fleshly pleasures and pain and want his debt to be repaid in full.

The Silence of the Lambs (1991). Jonathan Demme's film, adding prestige to Gothic cinema with its Oscar sweep, fuses Gothic literary conventions with the police procedural in this adaptation of Thomas Harris's 1988 novel. A masterful example of 1990s doubling onscreen, FBI trainee Clarice Starling must consult with Hannibal 'the Cannibal' Lecter to stop another serial killer who is skinning women.

In the Mouth of Madness (1994). Rounding off John Carpenter's informal 'Apocalypse' trilogy (also comprising *The Thing* [1982] and *Prince of Darkness* [1987]), this film posits a 'plague of insanity' brought forth by horror writer Sutter Cane, who has mysteriously vanished while preparing his latest manuscript. One of the finest films about dangerous books and the fragility of our perception of reality in 1990s cinema.

Ringu (1998). In Hideo Nakata's adaptation of Koji Suzuki's 1991 novel, journalist Reiko Asakawa encounters a mysterious cursed videotape with the power to kill, tracing the origins of the curse to a mysterious girl who vanished decades earlier and possessed frightening psychic powers. An excellent example of video's unregulated circulation and the terror of viral technology.

Further Critical Reading

Benson-Allott, Caetlin, *Killer Tapes and Shattered Screens: Video Spectatorship from VHS to File Sharing* (2013). This study advances considerations of apparatus theory and the importance of portability in understanding modes of viewing Gothic and horror films since the 1980s.

Botting, Fred, *Gothic* (1995; 2nd edn, 2013). Botting's seminal study significantly advances understanding of the intricate and intertextual nature of the Gothic mode across film, fiction and popular culture. The final chapter in the 2013 updated edition, 'Consuming Monsters', is particularly useful, with new sections on Ludogothic and Cybergothic.

Derry, Charles, *Dark Dreams 2.0: A Psychological History of the Modern Horror Film From the 1950s to the 21st Century* (2009). Significantly expanded from its original 1977 edition, this psychological study of the evolution of the horror film is particularly useful in examining the repetitive cycles and psychological unease that underpins the horror genre, specifically from the Cold War to the War on Terror.

Kendrick, James, *Hollywood Bloodshed: Violence in 1980s American Cinema* (2009). Kendrick's book is one of the finest on 1980s popular cinema and is extremely useful for understanding the fascination with and explicit nature of screen violence during the decade.

Phillips, Kendall R., *Dark Directions: Romero, Craven, Carpenter, and the Modern Horror Film* (2012). Phillips's study situates the cinema of Romero, Craven and Carpenter as the horror auteurs of a frustrated and disillusioned generation. Collectively, these directors shaped popular horror cinema from New Hollywood to the end of the century.

Shary, Timothy, *Generation Multiplex: The Image of Youth in American Cinema since 1980* (2002; rev edn, 2014). Shary's book examines the rise of the multiplex and the modern blockbuster for and about young audiences. It provides a particularly useful account of the popularity and reception of the teen slasher film. A masterful study of blockbuster American cinema and teen film culture.

Spooner, Catherine, *Contemporary Gothic* (2006). Spooner's study examines the significant debates and cultural expressions of Gothic culture in the late twentieth and early twenty-first centuries. Strongly recommended for students and scholars at all levels, this book advances the final chapter in Botting's *Gothic* by way of its important examination of contemporary Gothic culture in consumerism and mass entertainment.

Bibliography

Abbott, Stacey, *Celluloid Vampires: Life after Death in the Modern World* (Austin, TX: University of Texas Press, 2007).

Aldana Reyes, Xavier, 'Gothic Cinema from the 1970s to Now', in Richard J. Hand and Jay McRoy (eds), *Gothic Film: An Edinburgh Companion* (Edinburgh: Edinburgh University Press, 2020), pp. 77–86.

Auerbach, Nina, *Our Vampires Ourselves* (Chicago: University of Chicago Press, 1995).
Barker, Martin (ed.), *The Video Nasties: Freedom and Censorship in the Media* (London: Pluto Press, 1984).
Benson-Allott, Caetlin, *Killer Tapes and Shattered Screens: Video Spectatorship from VHS to File Sharing* (Berkeley, CA: University of California Press, 2013).
Biskind, Peter, *Down and Dirty Pictures: Miramax, Sundance, and the Rise of Independent Film* [2004] (London: Bloomsbury, 2007).
Botting, Fred, *Gothic* [1995], 2nd edn (London: Routledge, 2013).
Clayton, Wickham (ed.), *Style and Form in the Hollywood Slasher Film* (Basingstoke: Palgrave, 2015).
Clover, Carol J., 'Her Body, Himself', *Representations*, 20, 1987, pp. 187–228.
Clover, Carol J., *Men, Women, and Chainsaws* [1992] (Princeton, NJ: Princeton University Press, 2015).
Curry, Bill, 'Medical Riddle: Hmong Deaths in U.S.', *Los Angeles Times*, 27 February 1981, <https://www.washingtonpost.com/archive/politics/1981/02/27/medical-riddle-hmong-deaths-in-us/8601cef2-a502-4438-b4ba-7e754ab52659/> (last accessed 21 June 2021).
Derry, Charles, *Dark Dreams 2.0: A Psychological History of the Modern Horror Film From the 1950s to the 21st Century*, 2nd edn (Jefferson, NC: McFarland, 2009).
Dika, Vera, *Games of Terror: 'Halloween', 'Friday the Thirteenth' and the Films of the Stalker Cycle* (Cranbury, NJ: Fairleigh Dickenson University Press, 1990).
Edmundson, Mark, *Nightmare on Main Street: Angels, Sadomasochism, and the Culture of Gothic* (Cambridge, MA: Harvard University Press, 1997).
Egan, Kate, *Trash or Treasure? Censorship and the Changing Meanings of the Video Nasties* (Manchester: Manchester University Press, 2007).
Fahy, Thomas, *Dining with Madmen: Fat, Food, and the Environment in 1980s Horror* (Jackson, MS: University Press of Mississippi, 2019).
Fukuyama, Francis, *The End of History and the Last Man* [1992] (New York: First Free Press, 2006).
Haberman, Clyde, 'The Trial that Unleashed Hysteria Over Child Abuse', *The New York Times*, 9 March 2014, <https://www.nytimes.com/2014/03/10/us/the-trial-that-unleashed-hysteria-over-child-abuse.html> (last accessed 5 July 2021).
Herbert, Daniel, *Videoland: Movie Culture at the American Video Store* (Berkeley, CA: University of California Press, 2014).
Kendrick, James, *Hollywood Bloodshed: Violence in 1980s American Cinema* (Carbondale, IL: Southern Illinois University Press, 2009).
Kendrick, James, 'Razors in the Dreamscape: Revisiting "A Nightmare on Elm Street" and the Slasher Film', *Film Criticism*, 33.3, 2009, pp. 17–33.
Levy, Emanuel, *Cinema of Outsiders: The Rise of American Independent Film* (New York: NYU Press, 1999).
Mann, Craig, *Phases of the Moon* (Edinburgh: Edinburgh University Press, 2020).
Muir, John Kenneth, *Horror Films of the 1980s. Vol. 1: 1980–1984* (Jefferson, NC: McFarland, 2007).

Muir, John Kenneth, *Horror Films of the 1990s* (Jefferson, NC: McFarland, 2011).
Newman, Kim, 'Turning Nasty', *Sight and Sound*, 31.5, 2021, pp. 33–5.
Ní Fhlainn, Sorcha, *Postmodern Vampires: Film, Fiction and Popular Culture* (Basingstoke: Palgrave, 2019).
Ní Fhlainn, Sorcha, 'Screening the American Gothic: Celluloid Serial Killers in American Popular Culture', in Joel Faflak and Jason Haslam (eds), *American Gothic Culture* (Edinburgh: Edinburgh University Press, 2016), pp. 187–202.
Ní Fhlainn, Sorcha, 'Sweet, Bloody Vengeance: Class, Social Stigma and Servitude in the Slasher Genre', in Holly Lynn Baumgartner and Roger Davis (eds), *Hosting the Monster* (Amsterdam: Rodopi, 2008), pp. 179–96.
Petley, Julian, '"Are We Insane?" The "Video Nasty" Moral Panic', *Recherches sociologiques et anthropologiques*, 43.1, 2012, <https://doi.org/10.4000/rsa.839> (last accessed 5 July 2021).
Petley, Julian, *Film and Video Censorship in Modern Britain* (Edinburgh: Edinburgh University Press, 2011).
Phillips, Kendall R., *Dark Directions: Romero, Craven, Carpenter, and the Modern Horror Film* (Carbondale, IL: Southern Illinois University Press, 2012).
Prince, Stephen, 'Introduction: Movies and the 1980s', in Stephen Prince (ed.), *American Cinema of the 1980s* (Oxford: Berg, 2007), pp. 1–21.
Protect and Survive, bulletin, The National Archives, <https://www.nationalarchives.gov.uk/films/1964to1979/filmpage_warnings.htm> (last accessed 21 June 2021).
Roche, David, *Making and Remaking Horror in the 1970s and 2000s: Why Don't They Do It Like They Used To?* (Jackson, MS: University Press of Mississippi, 2014).
Rockoff, Adam, *Going to Pieces: The Rise and Fall of the Slasher Film, 1978–1986* (Jefferson, NC: McFarland, 2002).
Shary, Timothy, *Generation Multiplex: The Image of Youth in American Cinema since 1980* [2002], rev edn (Austin, TX: University of Texas Press, 2014).
Spooner, Catherine, *Contemporary Gothic* (London: Reaktion, 2006).
Telotte, J. P., '*The Blair Witch Project* Project: Film and the Internet', *Film Quarterly*, 54.3, 2001, pp. 32–9.
Wee, Valerie, 'The *Scream* Trilogy, "Hyperpostmodernism", and the Late-Nineties Teen Slasher Film', *Journal of Film and Video*, 57.3, 2005, pp. 44–61.

Filmography

28 Days Later (dir. Danny Boyle, UK, 2002).
Alien Nation (dir. Graham Baker, USA, 1988).
Aliens (dir. James Cameron, USA/UK, 1986).
American Psycho (dir. Mary Harron, USA/Canada, 2000).
An American Werewolf in London (dir. John Landis, USA/UK, 1981).
Amityville Horror, The (dir. Stuart Rosenberg, USA, 1979).
Beetlejuice (dir. Tim Burton, USA, 1988).

Black Christmas (dir. Bob Clarke, Canada, 1974).
The Blair Witch Project (dir. Daniel Myrick and Eduardo Sánchez, USA, 1999).
Bram Stoker's Dracula (dir. Francis Ford Coppola, UK/USA, 1992).
Cannibal Holocaust (dir. Ruggero Deodato, Italy, 1980).
Cloverfield (dir. Matt Reeves, USA, 2008).
Copycat (dir. Jon Amiel, USA, 1995).
Cube (dir. Vincenzo Natali, Canada/USA, 1997).
The Day After (TV movie, dir. Nicholas Meyer, USA, 1983).
The Devil's Advocate (dir. Taylor Hackford, Germany/USA, 1997).
End of Days (dir. Peter Hyams, USA, 1999).
The Fly (dir. David Cronenberg, USA/UK/Canada, 1986).
Friday the 13th (dir. Sean S. Cunningham, USA, 1980).
Fright Night (dir. Tom Holland, USA, 1985).
Funny Games (dir. Michael Haneke, Austria, 1997).
Halloween (dir. John Carpenter, USA, 1978).
Hellraiser (dir. Clive Barker, UK, 1987).
Hostel (dir. Eli Roth, USA/Czech Republic, 2005).
The Howling (dir. Joe Dante, USA, 1981).
The Hunger (dir. Tony Scott, UK/USA, 1983).
In the Mouth of Madness (dir. John Carpenter, USA, 1994).
Interview with the Vampire (dir. Neil Jordan, USA, 1994).
The Lost Boys (dir. Joel Schumacher, USA, 1987).
Mary Reilly (dir. Stephen Frears, USA/UK, 1996).
Mary Shelley's Frankenstein (dir. Kenneth Branagh, USA/Japan/UK, 1994).
The Matrix (dir. Lana Wachowski and Lilly Wachowski, USA/Australia, 1999).
Misery (dir. Rob Reiner, USA, 1990).
My Bloody Valentine (dir. George Mihalka, Canada, 1981).
Near Dark (dir. Kathryn Bigelow, USA, 1987).
Nightbreed (dir. Clive Barker, USA/UK/Canada, 1990).
A Nightmare on Elm Street (dir. Wes Craven, USA, 1984).
The Ninth Gate (dir. Roman Polanski, France/Spain, 1999).
Poltergeist (dir. Tobe Hooper, USA, 1982).
Prince of Darkness (dir. John Carpenter, USA, 1987).
Prom Night (dir. Paul Lynch, Canada, 1980).
Psycho (dir. Alfred Hitchcock, USA, 1960).
REC (dir. Jaume Balagueró and Paco Plaza, Spain, 2007).
Ringu (dir. Hideo Nakata, Japan, 1998).
Saw (dir. James Wan, USA, 2004).
Scream (dir. Wes Craven, USA, 1996).
Scream 2 (dir. Wes Craven, USA, 1997).
Se7en (dir. David Fincher, USA, 1995).
The Silence of the Lambs (dir. Jonathan Demme, USA, 1991).
Society (dir. Brian Yuzna, USA/Japan, 1989).
Stigmata (dir. Rupert Wainwright, USA/Mexico, 1999).
The Stuff (dir. Larry Cohen, USA, 1985).
They Live (dir. John Carpenter, USA, 1988).
Threads (TV movie, dir. Mick Jackson, UK/Australia/USA, 1984).
The Terminator (dir. James Cameron, UK/USA, 1984).
Terminator 2: Judgment Day (dir. James Cameron, USA, 1991).

The Thing (dir. John Carpenter, USA/Canada, 1982).
Videodrome (dir. David Cronenberg, Canada, 1983).
Wes Craven's New Nightmare (dir. Wes Craven, USA, 1994).
When the Wind Blows (dir. Jimmy T. Murakami, UK, 1986).
Wolf (dir. Mike Nichols, USA, 1994).
The X-Files (TV series, created by Chris Carter, USA/Canada, 1993–2002).
The X-Files: Fight the Future (dir. Rob Bowman, USA, 1998).

Notes

1. Botting, *Gothic*, p. 180 – this sentiment concludes the first edition of Botting's study. It has since been revised and expanded to include later iterations of the Gothic and its confrontation with the digital on screen in the twenty-first century in its 2014 second edition.
2. Aldana Reyes, 'Gothic Cinema from the 1970s to Now', p. 77.
3. Herbert, *Videoland*, pp. 2–3.
4. Prince, 'Introduction: Movies and the 1980s', pp. 2–3.
5. In the post-millennial period, these series would all undergo further reimaginings, cross-over films, prequels and/or reboots. See Roche, *Making and Remaking Horror in the 1970s and 2000s*.
6. Spooner, *Contemporary Gothic*, pp. 22–3.
7. Petley, '"Are We Insane?" The "Video Nasty" Moral Panic', para. 30.
8. For much more on the video nasties crisis, see Barker (ed.), *The Video Nasties*; Egan, *Trash or Treasure?*; and Petley, *Film and Video Censorship in Modern Britain*.
9. Newman, 'Turning Nasty', p. 34.
10. Ibid., p. 34.
11. Haberman, 'The Trial that Unleashed Hysteria Over Child Abuse'.
12. Curry, 'Medical Riddle'.
13. Muir, *Horror Films of the 1980s*, p. 18.
14. Ní Fhlainn, 'Sweet, Bloody Vengeance', pp. 179–96.
15. Rockoff, *Going to Pieces*, pp. 5–50.
16. For more on the foundational aesthetic, stylistic, and gender paradigms that underpin slasher studies, see Clover, 'Her Body, Himself', and her seminal study *Men, Women and Chainsaws*; Dika, *Games of Terror*; and for later considerations of the slasher and its influence, Clayton (ed.), *Style and Form in the Hollywood Slasher Film*.
17. Clover, *Men, Women, and Chainsaws*, p. 22.
18. See Ní Fhlainn, 'Screening the American Gothic', pp. 187–202.
19. Clover, *Men, Women, and Chainsaws*, pp. 35–41.
20. Ibid., p. 38.
21. This debt to Craven's influential films is evident in the *Fear Street* (2021, Netflix) trilogy too. While its first instalment, *Fear Street Part One: 1994*, calls out to Craven's final *Nightmare on Elm Street* film, *New Nightmare* (1994), as the beginning of the hyper-postmodern slasher film, it also positions its opening murders as a direct (at times, replicating shot-for-shot) homage to Craven's *Scream* (1996).

22. Craven used the term 'rubber reality' (Muir, *Horror Films of the 1980s*, p. 11) to mean in-camera practical and malleable effects, which includes make-up, costuming, tricks with props and puppetry.
23. Derry, *Dark Dreams 2.0*, p. 211.
24. Kendrick, 'Razors in the Dreamscape', p. 24.
25. Clover, *Men, Women, and Chainsaws*, p. 22.
26. Benson-Allott, *Killer Tapes and Shattered Screens*, p. 1.
27. See Mann, *Phases of the Moon*.
28. See Auerbach, *Our Vampires Ourselves*; Ní Fhlainn, *Postmodern Vampires*; Abbott, *Celluloid Vampires*.
29. For more on this, see Fahy, *Dining with Madmen*.
30. *Protect and Survive* bulletin.
31. Fukuyama, *The End of History and the Last Man*, pp. 86–8.
32. Ní Fhlainn, *Postmodern Vampires*, pp. 121–31.
33. Wee, 'The *Scream* Trilogy', pp. 44–61.
34. Edmundson, *Nightmare on Main Street*, pp. 5–6.
35. Ibid., p. 20.
36. See Levy, *Cinema of Outsiders*.
37. Both *Funny Games* and *Ringu* would be remade in the US in the 2000s as part of a wider trend to remake international horror titles.
38. Biskind, *Down and Dirty Pictures*, p. 19.
39. Telotte, 'The *Blair Witch Project* Project', p. 35.
40. Muir, *Horror Films of the 1990s*, p. 603.
41. Ibid., p. 603.

Part III

Key Themes and Topics in Twentieth-Century Gothic

Chapter 10

Twentieth-Century War Gothic
Agnieszka Soltysik Monnet

It is commonly accepted that war has had a significant influence on modern art and culture – for example, the role of the First World War in the development of Anglo-American modernism – but the relationship between modern war and the Gothic is even more closely intertwined. From the earliest Gothic texts to the most recent horror films, war has been a tacit or explicit subject of dread, graphic description or psychological investigation. As the twentieth century experienced two global wars and many regional ones – touching countless people across the planet and taking millions of lives in often horrific and utterly dehumanising ways never previously imagined – the Gothic mode played an exceptionally important role in the representation and impact of these traumatic and dislocating experiences in both literature and film. In this chapter I will be focusing mainly on British and American culture produced in English but will occasionally mention how War Gothic has appeared in other national contexts, since the reach of the Gothic as a language and toolbox for portraying the violence, horror and haunting after-effects of war has followed the international reach of both the novel and the horror film. After a brief look at the origins of War Gothic in the eighteenth century, I will trace its development in the twentieth century with a special focus on the Gothic war poetry of the First World War and the long afterlife of WWI and WWII trauma culture in the last decade of the century.

Origins and Overview

War Gothic includes a family of devices that run from gallows humour and graphic body horror to more subtle Gothic metaphors of ghostliness and haunting as a means of depicting the mental injuries produced by war.[1] The original English Gothic has traditionally been linked to the

Age of Revolutions (especially the French Revolution), but its roots are even more firmly planted in the first real world war, known in Britain as the Seven Years' War (1756–63) and in the United States as the French and Indian War (1754–63).[2] This conflict, fought by a large number of belligerents including France, Britain, Spain, Prussia, Russia, Austria, Sweden, India and the Iroquois Confederacy, left somewhere between 900,000 and 1,400,000 people dead across the globe, including large numbers of civilians. Historical events often work their way into literature and art very indirectly, and this global war was no exception. The first Gothic novel, written by Horace Walpole, does not refer to the war explicitly, but the breathless plot of *The Castle of Otranto* (1764) begins with a young man crushed to death by a giant steel helmet, gesturing tacitly to the massive death toll of young men that had just occurred. In the decades that followed, against the backdrop of the American and French Revolutions, the Gothic developed into the dominant aesthetic toolbox for stories of violence both inside and outside the home.[3]

Although war was rarely the explicit subject of the Gothic, the traumas of revolutionary war clearly fed into the dislocations and violence in the work of early Gothicists such as Matthew 'Monk' Lewis, Charles Brockden Brown and Mary Shelley. Mobs, cruelty, murder, tyranny and political allegory abound in these first novels. The nineteenth century turned out to be a period of frequent warfare in Europe, the UK and the US, and the rising importance of the Gothic across English and American (and more generally European) literature can be correlated to the cumulative impact of the Napoleonic Wars, the American Indian Wars and the Crimean War, to name just the biggest and longest conflicts. The literature of sentiment, satire and other popular genres simply did not have the traction that the increasingly accepted literature of the Gothic, Dark Romanticism, and what we could call Dark Naturalism – realism strongly infused with horror – was able to achieve in the depiction of both physical and mental trauma. These trends, present throughout the antebellum and Victorian periods, germinated into the War Gothic fiction of the US Civil War and the First World War.

In a sense, the story of mechanised, industrial-era warfare is the story of War Gothic achieving dominance as a literary mode. In the United States this happened in the wake of the Civil War and had its most fully realised form in the work of Ambrose Bierce in the 1890s. Known as a writer of both Gothic and 'weird tales', Bierce is first and foremost a chronicler of war. In 'Chickamauga' (1889), Bierce uses a child protagonist to show the way conventional stories of battle make the young dream of becoming war heroes, only to violently undercut this myth with the reality of broken bodies and dehumanised men crawling away from battle like wounded animals, the child driven half-mad by the discovery of his own home destroyed and his mother dead.[4]

Bierce also pioneered the use of the Gothic to render the many ways in which war's traumas affect people's minds, a full century before PTSD was recognised as a legitimate mental condition. In 'A Tough Tussle' (1888), a Union soldier finds himself trapped for the night with a dead Confederate soldier. The strain of this close confinement with a corpse seems to drive the protagonist mad because in the morning he is found dead with a wound to the heart from his own sword, and the rotting corpse has been repeatedly stabbed as well.[5] We are given to understand that the soldier fought the dead man in what the title calls a 'tough tussle' throughout the night before somehow killing himself, as if his disordered mind had created this final battle and fought both his own part and that of his enemy. The psychological strain of combat situations – scarcely credited by physicians and officers as even 'real' until the Vietnam era – here works itself into literature by veterans through Gothic devices such as doppelgängers, ghosts, descents into madness and the uncanny.

For the UK and the rest of Europe, the real horror of modern warfare began in 1914, and poetry was the first genre to be impacted by the killing because of its portable nature. Young men in the trenches started to describe their disillusionment and the nightmare conditions of their experience almost immediately, including Alan Seeger, Isaac Rosenberg, Wilfred Owen, Siegfried Sassoon and Robert Graves. The bitterness, the bleakness and the disillusionment of these veteran-poets stamped a Gothic face on the meaning of war for an entire generation. (I will return to this extraordinary body of work in the next section.) Gothic-infused fiction about the war began to emerge only midway through the 1920s, beginning with Ernest Hemingway's *In Our Time* (1925), which included short inter-chapters full of graphic body horror and death, and William Faulkner's *Soldiers' Pay* (1926), about a severely injured, almost catatonic war veteran being escorted home. Universally feted and even envied, the injured soldier is a silent and uncanny figure who has clearly been damaged beyond any repair or possibility of normal life, much like Hemingway's own 'Soldier's Home', a story from *In Our Time* about an oddly affectless young veteran.[6] An entire generation of men came home 'hollow' and broken, as T. S. Eliot's poem 'The Hollow Men' (also 1925) poignantly suggested.[7]

Interwar cinema was also impacted by the war, and the years of mass death and mutilation led to the emergence of what we now consider the best of modern cinema horror, including German Expressionist films such as *The Cabinet of Dr Caligari* (1920), *Nosferatu* (1922) and

Waxworks (1924), and the American classic *Phantom of the Opera* (1925). The idea of the body as an empty husk, the face as a disfigured mask, and of people as mindless and uncanny monsters would become leitmotifs in these films and influence the horror film cycle of the 1930s, including *Frankenstein* (1931), *Dracula* (1931) and *The Mummy* (1932). The entire generation of great horror directors of this period, such as Fritz Lang, F. W. Murnau, Tod Browning and James Whale, were all clearly grappling with memories and legacies of the First World War.[8] One film that brought the war and the Gothic together with particular effectiveness was Abel Gance's *J'Accuse* (1919), which features an extraordinary scene of an entire field of dead soldiers rising up from their graves in order to march on the nearest town to see if its inhabitants are conducting themselves in a manner worthy of the sacrifices that had been made for them (spoiler alert: they are not).

Less well known than the First World War were the many colonial wars that were fought throughout these early decades of the twentieth century, including the Boer War, the Philippine–American War and the occupation of Haiti.[9] This last effort, which saw US troops in Haiti from 1915 to 1934, created lucrative conditions for American businesses, introduced American-style Jim Crow laws to the only nation in the world born of an anti-slavery revolution, and produced the earliest literary accounts and Hollywood films about zombies. In the first Hollywood zombie movie, Victor Halperin's *White Zombie* (1932), a Creole plantation owner, played by Bela Lugosi, enslaves the wills of political enemies, rivals, labourers and a white woman whom he covets. The cultural work of the figure of the zombie is complex, clearly originating in the legacy of slavery and the forced dispossession of labourers of their free will, but it proved surprisingly adaptable. Within a few years of Halperin's first film, for instance, a movie imagining zombie soldiers was made. Also by Halperin, *Revolt of the Zombies* (1936) begins its story during the First World War and imagines a French colonial priest using a secret formula to turn men into soulless automatons. When the priest's formula is stolen, a group of Allied representatives must travel to Cambodia to find and destroy the formula, but one of the men – also French – finds it before the others and begins to use it to create a private army.

Soon after, *Revenge of the Zombies* (1943) inaugurated a conceit that would never die: zombification in the service of Hitler. Popular throughout the entire twentieth century, Nazi zombies distill into a single unsettling image several overlapping fears: of dehumanising medical experiments such as those conducted by scientists of the Third Reich, of the mindlessness of enemy soldiers, and of the loss of individual autonomy in military service more generally. Soldiers occupy an ambivalent position in modern culture, hailed as heroes for their self-sacrifice but often suspected of naive simple-mindedness in their obedience to orders, or worse yet, of secret blood lust and an attraction to violence. The Nazi zombie trope served as a powerful analgam of all these anxieties and would keep returning in various guises well into the twenty-first century.

The Second World War, when it finally came after years of fascist build-up in Germany and Italy, created its own unique war culture of dread and anxiety, especially in England because of the bombing campaigns of 1940 and 1941. One of the most interesting examples of British wartime Gothic writing was the work produced by Mervyn Peake, who wrote the first instalments of his neo-Gothic fantasy series *Titus Groan* (1946) and *Gormenghast* (1950) during the war and immediately afterwards. Peake also produced a number of poems and illustrations that captured the bleak, violent and demystifying spirit of Gothic war art typical of artists who refused to be enlisted into triumphant or propagandistic artwork.

Similarly dark themes continued after the war with the many unsettling examples of film noir that were produced in this period. The war fed into these films in subtle and indirect ways, in keeping with the general overarching dynamic of repression and denial that descended in the post-war years, making frank discussions of the war impossible and consigning veterans to a heavy silence.[10] Yet the horror that veterans had witnessed lingered under the surface of post-war prosperity and created an undercurrent of tension and unease. Nicholas Ray's *In a Lonely Place* (1950) allows this fear of the veteran's violence to become visible. Humphrey Bogart plays a veteran – now a Hollywood scriptwriter – who is strangely out of tune with other people and the normal range of human emotions, with a history of violence and a latent potential for rage. When he is suspected of murder early in the film, an attractive neighbour provides an alibi and they fall in love. Yet Bogart's ability to hide his violent propensities gets harder and harder to maintain, and the film ends with him choking his fiancée nearly to death, instantly ending their love affair. Although he is cleared of the murder of which he had originally been accused, the film shows that he is nevertheless guilty of *being capable of it*. With this bleak ending, *In a Lonely Place* joins the larger work of the film noir genre at this time in reminding spectators that the war had been much darker than post-war culture was willing to admit. Although veterans were largely silent, these darkly psychological thrillers and Gothicised crime stories often did the work of cultural memory – indirectly and figuratively – at a time when more explicit treatment of the war was not possible.

With the extraordinary violence unleashed by the United States in Vietnam, subtlety and repression were thrown aside, and this war inaugurated a new era of War Gothic literature and popular culture. Like the First World War, the Vietnam War was largely seen as illegitimate and therefore the gap between its stated purpose and its realities created opportunities for many kinds of irony. The Gothic naturally filled these ironic spaces with bitter humour, graphic bodily injury and grim metaphor. One of the earliest instances of Vietnam War Gothic was a 1974 film, *Deathdream* (also known as *Dead of Night*), based loosely on W. W. Jacobs's 'The Monkey's Paw' (1902), about a dead soldier who is willed back to life by the power of his mother's desire that he return. The young soldier comes home, but his odd and uncanny manner gradually becomes more unsettling until it is revealed that he needs to murder people for their blood in order to stay 'alive'. The protagonist has elements of both the zombie and the vampire, tropes that serve as Gothic metaphors for the violence of the troubled veteran which would become a standard feature of popular culture in the 1970s and 1980s.

The literature of the Vietnam War was also keyed to the Gothic mode from the start, including Ron Kovic's memoir *Born on the Fourth of July* (1976) and veteran-writer Gustav Hasford's novel *The Short-Timers* (1979), both of which use body horror, Gothic metaphors and madness, as well as Larry Heinemann's *Paco's Story* (1986), narrated by a young soldier's ghost. Tim O'Brien, probably the best-known writer to emerge from the war, wrote a harrowing mystery novel – *In the Lake of the Woods* (1994) – about a veteran with repressed PTSD whose wife disappears from their vacation cabin, who begins to suspect that he has brutally murdered her himself. We gradually learn that he had participated in My Lai-style massacres in Vietnam, and fragments of these past events begin to emerge along with confused glimpses of his wife's harrowing last moments, demonstrating the power of Gothic themes of self-alienation and evil doppelgängers to figuratively render the psychological disorders and repression linked to war trauma for perpetrators as well as victims.

The Vietnam War continued to cast its long shadow over the last decades of the twentieth century, with highly influential films such as *Jacob's Ladder* (1990), loosely inspired by Ambrose Bierce's 'An Occurrence at Owl Creek Bridge' (1890), about a veteran who returns to the US and begins to hallucinate and/or remember shocking images from a possibly drug-induced massacre during the war. The film includes images of asylum horror and uncertainty about reality that influenced a generation of subsequent Gothic/horror films, including *Silent Hill* (1999), *The Sixth Sense* (1999), *The Jacket* (2005) and *Black Swan*

(2010). The Vietnam War also impacted the 1970s horror and slasher film cycle, starting with George Romero's *Night of the Living Dead* (1968), which ends with the sound of a helicopter and the sight of a pile of burning bodies, and more explicitly in the militaristic *Day of the Dead* (1985). More allegorically, the alien horror film *Predator* (1987) is widely regarded as using the 'invisible enemy' trope associated with counter-insurgency warfare in the Vietnam War as a metaphorical depiction of the disorientation experienced by US soldiers in the Vietnamese jungles.

The last decades of the twentieth century saw more Nazi war horror such as *The Frozen Dead* (1966), *The Boys from Brazil* (1978) and *The Keep* (1983). While many if not most Nazi horror films are extremely schlocky, the popular fascination with Nazis and the Holocaust also produced more mainstream horror such as Stephen King's 1982 novella *Apt Pupil*, about an American teenager who discovers a Nazi criminal secretly living in his neighbourhood and begins to extort both lurid stories and increasingly unhinged flashbacks of Nazi behaviour from him. The story was made into a major Hollywood film starring Ian McKellen in 1998 and showed the enduring fascination with Nazism that would continue unabated.

The First World War, a collective trauma that had quickly been buried in the past when the global Depression hit in 1929 and even more so when the Second World War broke out, also emerged in this last decade of the twentieth century as a theme for several extraordinary Gothic examinations. British writer Pat Barker's trilogy *Regeneration* (1991), *The Eye in the Door* (1993) and *The Ghost Road* (1995) is set in Craiglockhart War Hospital where the psychiatrist W. H. R. Rivers treated shell-shocked soldiers such as Wilfred Owen and Siegfried Sassoon. In *Gods and Monsters* (1998), Bill Condon crafts a Gothic film study of an ageing James Whale in Hollywood increasingly tormented by memories of the trenches as a series of strokes has loosened these long-repressed memories.

Hollow Men

In this section I will focus on some of the poetry that came out of the First World War. No other war has been written about and remembered in quite such explicitly Gothic terms as 'the Great War'. From the very first poems of the war, such as Alan Seeger's 'I Have a Rendezvous with Death' (1915), to the haunting masterpieces of Anglo-American modernism, T. S. Eliot's *The Waste Land* (1922) and 'The Hollow Men'

(1925), death is omnipresent, uncanny, impersonal and yet strangely intimate. Death has so much force and agency that it seems more alive than the men who fight the war, and this most important of boundaries – that between life and death – seems to dissolve into uncertainty in the trenches.

Among the first to fall was Alan Seeger, a classmate of Eliot's at Harvard, who had spent two years in Greenwich bohemia before moving to Paris and falling in love with France, as legend has it. A closer scrutiny of his life and poetry can raise questions in the twenty-first-century reader about what or who else Seeger might have loved to make him long so ardently for death. This was a period of intense homophobia and Seeger came from a devoutly Christian family, and one wonders if there might not have been more than simply an enthusiasm for chivalry behind the themes of his two most famous poems: 'I Have a Rendezvous with Death' and 'Ode in Memory of the American Volunteers Fallen for France', both published posthumously in 1916. If, like Hart Crane and other gay poets of the era, Seeger sought death as an escape from an intolerable life of stigma, this was a secret that he took to his grave. However, as an American, Seeger should not even have been in the war yet, since the United States would only join the Allied powers in 1917. Seeger enlisted in the French Foreign Legion with other American volunteers, thus making the latter poem an uncanny eulogy for himself.

It is, however, the other poem that Seeger is best remembered for: 'I Have a Rendezvous with Death'. The poem begins with the line that became its title, comparing his seemingly inevitable death to a romantic 'rendezvous', a strangely sexualised image that only gets stranger as the poem progresses. A comparison with a 'date' at some 'disputed barricade' evokes a nocturnal meeting that could as easily be between two queer soldiers or sentinels as between a soldier and his fate. The allegorisation of Death is no less strange for being a 'he' who takes his hand (a trope of queer literature that dates back to Walt Whitman) and leads him into his 'dark land' (an image that easily lends itself to a sexual reading, especially when coupled with the closed eyes and 'quenched' breath). Queer or not, the poem is uncanny in its erotic longing for a midnight encounter with a personified 'Death', a desire that was tragically fulfilled for Seeger one afternoon during the Battle of the Somme in 1916.

Another early poem – even more famous and widely popular – is 'In Flanders Fields' by Canadian physician Lieutenant-Colonel John McCrae. Written in 1915 after the Battle of Ypres in French Flanders, McCrae's poem would also become strangely prophetic and uncanny when he died three years later. Although it is recited by schoolchildren around the world, the poem is far darker and more Gothic than it appears at first glance. A reminder to honour the dead, it is spoken from beyond the grave – or more accurately, from within their graves – by 'the Dead' themselves. The fallen 'Dead' tell us that they now lie in Flanders fields and that they 'shall not sleep' if the living 'break faith' with them. The question of how civilians could ever be vigilant, grateful and faithful enough to fully honour the men who died 'for' them is an uncomfortable one, as Abel Gance's 1927 film suggested. Thus, the prospect of the 'Dead' lying awake in their graves in those blood-red poppy-covered fields is very real and one of the many ways in which the dead of the First World War seemed disturbingly undead in the years that followed.

The poetry of the trenches also delved into graphic body horror and deliberately shocking displays of how war dehumanises wounded soldiers that far outstripped these subtler evocations of intimacy with death. The purpose of these types of explicit descriptions of injury was always to demystify and disenchant war by showing its 'truth'. The hope was that illusions of noble deaths and patriotic glory would wither in the face of the gruesome violations that occurred in combat. The point of poetry like this (as with prose) was to show that the human being becomes a mere thing, a piece of meat, when he dies, giving the lie to illusions of glorious death on the battlefield. Far from being exalted in death, the soldier becomes obscene, as parts of his body meant never to be seen, such as the liquid insides, are exposed to the witness's gaze. Among the most important – and again, widely known and read – of these kinds of War Gothic poems is Wilfred Owen's 'Dulce et Decorum Est', written in 1917 and published posthumously in 1920. The poem is told by a survivor of a chlorine gas attack who remembers a soldier who did not put his mask on fast enough, died choking on his blood, and who now haunts the speaker's dreams.

Haunted by the World Wars

At the other end of the century, in the late 1990s, War Gothic was in a transitional moment. The most important literature and cinema to erupt from the Vietnam War had quieted down in the wake of the first Persian Gulf War. That short war had not produced much in the way of literature or film just yet (more would come in the twenty-first century). What appeared instead in the last years of the twentieth century was an obsessive return to the trauma of the First and Second World Wars. In 1998 three significant war films were released – each quite different from the other, but all borrowing heavily from the Gothic genre: *Saving*

Private Ryan, *Apt Pupil* and *Gods and Monsters*. The loudest of the three was Steven Spielberg's *Saving Private Ryan*, whose Normandy landing scene would make cinema history as the goriest spectacle of body horror ever shown in a mainstream film. This half-hour sequence is a *tour de force* of Battlefield Gothic, with blood spattering the camera lens and soldiers holding their intestines and carrying their torn limbs, and yet the film manages to repackage all this injury and trauma in a heart-warming patriotic melodrama that renders body horror henceforth nearly toothless as an anti-war aesthetic technique.[11] Revealing the distance between the innocence of the first decades and the violence-saturated last decades of the century, Spielberg demonstrates how even the most shocking scenes of bodily violation can be enlisted in the service of war-glorifying sentimentalism. Despite its brief excursion into harrowing body horror, *Saving Private Ryan* is the film that made war feel honourable again after the humiliation and soul-searching angst engendered by the Vietnam War.

In stark contrast to the flag-waving pieties of *Saving Private Ryan*, Bryan Singer's *Apt Pupil* (1998), based on a novella by Stephen King, explores the legacy of the Holocaust and the human evil it represents in a more troubling and deliberately Gothic way. A southern Californian teenager (only 13 in the original novel, played by Brad Renfro in the film) discovers a Nazi war criminal, Kurt Dussander (played by Ian McKellen), living down the street from him and begins to blackmail him into telling detailed stories of the concentration camps where he worked. The stories both awaken his own latent cruelty and revive the sadism of the old man, who tries first to kill a neighbour's cat in his oven and then to murder a homeless man. The more terrifying transformation happens in Todd (the aptly named 'apt pupil') who begins to relish his power over the powerless and graduates from killing small animals to murder.

The point of the story and film is that evil – including the radical evil that was revealed during the Holocaust – can manifest itself any time and anywhere, even in a quiet American suburb. The film unfolds with a series of classic Gothic scenes and devices – bad dreams, the intrusion of the past into the present, hallucinations, a slow descent into madness for both characters, hints of sadomasochism, the attempted cat killing – which unfold jarringly against the sunny hills of contemporary California. The film also hints at homoerotic dynamics which structure nearly all the relationships between the male characters: Todd and Dussander, Todd and his high school counsellor (whom he blackmails into silence), and Dussander and the homeless man who offers himself in exchange for a place to stay for the night. Unfortunately, this aspect of the film feels gratuitous and somewhat homophobic, hinting at subterranean connections between homosexuality and sadism. Yet the film powerfully reminds us that even in the last years of the twentieth century the evil unleashed by Nazis on their victims continued to fascinate and, in some troubling cases, to excite and attract.

Another film that was released in 1998 – also starring Ian McKellen, located in southern California, dealing with homosexuality, and probing long-repressed war memories – is the extraordinary and haunting *Gods and Monsters*. This time the war in the background is the First World War, and the story is about James Whale, the director of *Frankenstein* (1931) and *Bride of Frankenstein* (1935), ageing and enfeebled by strokes, which seem to have awakened repressed memories of the trenches. This film too is organised around an uneasy friendship between an older man, this time explicitly gay, and a younger one. Here too nightmares and mental illness are evoked by the film in order to suggest the unbearable traumas of the First World War. Unlike in *Apt Pupil*, however, the queer aspects of the relationship are introduced both meaningfully and movingly by the director Bill Condon. There are powerful analogies made between unspeakable war stories and the homosexual closet and the need for secrecy and silence about both. In addition, the experience of being an outsider, a man who loves other men, is hauntingly figured in the story by a comparison to Frankenstein's monster, who is also rejected and persecuted for what he is. Finally, the homoerotic friendship between the ageing Whale and his young gardener (played by Brendan Fraser) is both real and a Gothic ploy on Whale's part to get the younger man to murder him and put an end to his suffering. In this film, as in *Apt Pupil*, the ageing character played by McKellen is dead at the end, but the characters that he plays in each – a veteran of the trenches of the First World War and a Nazi from the Second – were far from dead at the century's close. These figures would continue to haunt the culture of war memory well into the next century.

To conclude, the twentieth century was a time of the most murderous and harrowing wars ever unleashed on this planet, and the literary genre that almost single-handedly rose to the task of showing what happens on battlefields and in the broken minds of survivors was the Gothic. Refusing reassuring myths and conventional sentiments, the Gothic provides a powerful literary toolbox for depicting both bodily injury and the many kinds of mental trauma created by war violence, offering a range of aesthetic and figurative devices for examining the impact of war on individual and collective psyches.

Other Key Texts

Ernest Hemingway, 'A Natural History of the Dead' (1932), a short story blending horror and satire in a manner reminiscent of Swift's 'A Modest Proposal', purporting to be a naturalistic-style description of corpses and the stress-induced madness of battle surgeons. Originally published in *Death in the Afternoon* (1932).

Gustav Hasford, *The Short-Timers* (1979), is one of the most ferocious and Gothic anti-war novels ever written. Hasford responded to Kubrick's watered-down adaptation of his novel (*Full Metal Jacket*, 1987) with a searing sequel titled *The Phantom Blooper* (1990), which follows the protagonist to a Vietnamese village, where he converts to an anti-imperialist stance, through a My Lai-esque massacre, and then back to the US where his home town has become uncanny and sinister.

Joe Haldeman, 'The Monster' (1986), is also a depiction of war-induced madness, in this case multiple personality disorder. The narrator is a veteran who sometimes speaks in street slang and sometimes in highly erudite English as he recounts the story of a 'humanoid' creature that has killed his friends, though an eyewitness has reported that the narrator actually killed them himself.

Third Part of the Night (dir. Andrzej Żuławski, 1971). A surreal Polish film about war madness set during the Nazi occupation. A young man is driven insane after seeing his wife and son killed by German soldiers.

Uncle Sam (dir. William Lustig, 1996). A B-quality horror film about a soldier killed in Kuwait who reanimates as a very conscious and homicidal zombie, making this among the very first horror films about the war in the Persian Gulf.

Further Critical Reading

Blake, Linnie, *The Wounds of Nations: Horror Cinema, Historical Trauma, and National Identity* (2008). Explores how horror cinema allows international audiences to engage with the trauma of history and the ways in which we identify with nation-states.

Bronfen, Elisabeth, 'Gothic Wars – Media's Lust: On the Cultural Afterlife of the War Dead' (2015). A reading of George Romero's *Diary of the Dead* (2007) in relation to WWI poetry, Ambrose Bierce, the American occupation of Haiti and the figure of the zombie as a trope for the returning veteran.

Poole, W. Scott, *Wasteland: The Great War and Origins of Modern Horror* (2019). Useful examination of the influence of the First World War on twentieth-century horror literature and cinema.

Soltysik Monnet, Agnieszka, and Steffen Hantke (eds), *War Gothic in Literature and Culture* (2015). Collection of essays on a range of War Gothic texts and topics.

Wasson, Sara, *Urban Gothic of the Second World War: Dark London* (2010). Subtle and insightful examination of British War Gothic focusing on London during the Second World War.

Bibliography

Aldana Reyes, Xavier, 'Introduction: What, Why and When Is Horror Fiction?', in Xavier Aldana Reyes (ed.), *Horror: A Literary History* (London: British Library Publishing, 2016), pp. 7–17.

Bierce, Ambrose, 'Chickamauga', in *The Collected Writings of Ambrose Bierce* (Secaucus, NJ: Citadel Press, 1946), pp. 18–23.

Bierce, Ambrose, 'A Tough Tussle', in *The Collected Writings of Ambrose Bierce* (Secaucus, NJ: Citadel Press, 1946), pp. 438–44.

Blake, Linnie, *Wounds of Nations: Horror Cinema, Historical Trauma and National Identity* (Manchester: Manchester University Press, 2008).

Bronfen, Elisabeth, 'Gothic Wars – Media's Lust: On the Cultural Afterlife of the War Dead', in Fred Botting and Catherine Spooner (eds), *Monstrous Media/Spectral Subjects: Imaging Gothic Fictions from the Nineteenth Century to the Present* (Manchester: Manchester University Press, 2015), pp. 15–28.

Eliot, T. S., 'The Hollow Men', in *The Complete Poems and Plays, 1909–1950* (Orlando, FL: Harcourt Brace, 1950), pp. 56–9.

Faulkner, William, *Soldiers' Pay* (New York: Liveright, 1997).

Hantke, Steffen, 'Troubled by Memories: The World War II Veteran as a Gothic Figure in William Wyler's *The Best Years of Our Lives*', in Agnieszka Soltysik Monnet and Steffen Hantke (eds), *War Gothic in Literature and Culture* (Abingdon: Routledge, 2016), pp. 101–16.

Hasford, Gustav, *The Phantom Blooper* (New York: Bantam Books, 1990).

Hasford, Gustav, *The Short-Timers* (New York: Bantam Books, 1979).

Hemingway, Ernest, 'A Natural History of the Dead', in *The Complete Short Stories of Ernest Hemingway: The Finca Vigia Edition* (New York: Simon and Schuster, 1987), pp. 335–41.

Hemingway, Ernest, 'Soldier's Home' [1925], in *In Our Time* (New York: Scribners, 2003).

Höglund, Johan, *The American Imperial Gothic: Popular Culture, Empire, Violence* (Farnham: Ashgate, 2014).

Hynes, Samuel, *The Soldier's Tale: Bearing Witness to a Modern War* (Harmondsworth: Penguin, 1997).

King, Stephen, 'Apt Pupil: Summer of Corruption', in *Different Seasons* (New York: Viking, 1982).

Kovic, Ron, *Born on the Fourth of July* (New York: Pocket Books, 1976).

McCrae, John, 'In Flanders Fields', in George Walter (ed.), *The Penguin Book of First World War Poetry* (Harmondsworth: Penguin, 2006), p. 155.

O'Brien, Tim, *In the Lake of the Woods* (Boston: Mariner Books, 1994).

Owen, Wilfred, 'Dulce et Decorum Est', in George Walter (ed.), *The Penguin Book of First World War Poetry* (Harmondsworth: Penguin, 2006), pp. 141–2.

Phillips, Terry, 'The Rules of War: Gothic Transgressions in First World War Fiction', *Gothic Studies*, 2.2, 2000, pp. 232–44.

Poole, W. Scott, *Wasteland: The Great War and Origins of Modern Horror* (Berkeley, CA: Counterpoint Press, 2019).

Rosenberg, Isaac, 'Dead Man's Dump', in George Walter (ed.), *The Penguin Book of First World War Poetry* (Harmondsworth: Penguin, 2006), p. 146.

Sassoon, Siegfried, *Collected Poems* (London: Faber and Faber, 1947).
Seeger, Alan, 'I Have a Rendezvous with Death', in George Walter (ed.), *The Penguin Book of First World War Poetry* (Harmondsworth: Penguin, 2006), p. 105.
Skal, David J., *The Monster Show: A Cultural History of Horror* (London: Plexus, 1994).
Soltysik Monnet, Agnieszka, and Steffen Hantke, 'Ghosts from the Battlefields', in Agnieszka Soltysik Monnet and Steffen Hantke (eds), *War Gothic in Literature and Culture* (Abingdon: Routledge, 2016), pp. xi–xxv.
Wasson, Sara, *Urban Gothic of the Second World War: Dark London* (Basingstoke: Palgrave, 2010).
Wright, Angela, *Britain, France and the Gothic, 1764–1820: The Import of Terror* (Cambridge: Cambridge University Press, 2013).

Filmography

Apocalypse Now (dir. Francis Ford Coppola, Lionsgate, USA, 1979).
Apt Pupil (dir. Bryan Singer, Tristar Pictures, USA, 1998).
Black Swan (dir. Darren Oronofsky, Cross Creek Pictures, USA, 2011).
The Boys from Brazil (dir. Franklin J. Schaffner, ITC Entertainment, USA/UK, 1978).
Bride of Frankenstein (dir. James Whale, Universal Pictures, USA, 1935).
The Cabinet of Dr Caligari (dir. Robert Wiene, Decla-Bioscop, Germany, 1920).
Day of the Dead (dir. George Romero, Laurel Entertainment, USA, 1985).
Deathdream (a.k.a. *Dead of Night*) (dir. Bob Clark, Quadrant Films, USA, 1974).
Dracula (dir. Tod Browning, Universal Pictures, USA, 1931).
Frankenstein (dir. James Whale, Universal Pictures, USA, 1931).
The Frozen Dead (dir. Herbert J. Leder, Gold Star Productions, UK, 1966).
Gods and Monsters (dir. Bill Condon, Showtime, UK, 1998).
In a Lonely Place (dir. Nicholas Ray, Santana Productions, USA, 1950).
J'Accuse (dir. Abel Gance, Pathé-Frères, France, 1919).
The Jacket (dir. John Maybury, Mandalay Pictures, USA, 2005).
Jacob's Ladder (dir. Adrian Lyne, Corolco Pictures, USA, 1990).
The Keep (dir. Michael Mann, Paramount Pictures, USA, 1983).
The Mummy (dir. Kurt Freund, Universal Pictures, UK, 1932).
Night of the Living Dead (dir. George Romero, Image Ten, USA, 1968).
Nosferatu (dir. F. W. Murnau, Prana Film, Germany, 1922).
Phantom of the Opera (dir. Rupert Julian, Jewel Productions, USA, 1925).
Predator (dir. John McTiernan, Lawrence Gordon Productions, USA, 1987).
Revenge of the Zombies (dir. Steve Sekely, Monogram Pictures, USA, 1943).
Revolt of the Zombies (dir. Victor Halperin, Victor & Edward Halperin Productions, USA, 1936).
Saving Private Ryan (dir. Steven Spielberg, Dreamworks Pictures, USA, 1998).
Silent Hill (dir. Christophe Gans, Tristar Pictures, USA, 2006).
The Sixth Sense (dir. M. Night Shyamalan, Hollywood Pictures, USA, 1999).
Waxworks (dir. Paul Leni, Neptune Film, USA, 1924).
White Zombie (dir. Victor Halperin, Halperin Productions, USA, 1932).

Notes

1. I use 'horror' and 'Gothic' interchangeably because distinctions between graphic descriptions of physical violence and the mental after-effects of that violence do not hold up well to categorical separation. Xavier Aldana Reyes, a key scholar of the horror mode, locates these two terms in a historical relationship to each other, that is, with horror as a twentieth century development of the Gothic. See 'Introduction: What, Why and When Is Horror Fiction?', pp. 9–10.
2. Wright, *Britain, France and the Gothic*, p. 12.
3. The origins of War Gothic are developed in more detail in Soltysik Monnet and Hantke, 'Ghosts from the Battlefields', pp. xi–xiv.
4. Bierce, 'Chickamauga', p. 23.
5. Bierce, 'A Tough Tussle', p. 444.
6. Faulkner, *Soldiers' Pay*, and Hemingway, 'Soldier's Home'.
7. For more on WWI Gothic fiction, see Phillips, 'The Rules of War'.
8. See Skal, *The Monster Show*, pp. 65–6, and Poole, *Wasteland*.
9. For more on the Gothic literature and popular culture of these myriad 'imperial' wars, see Johan Höglund's excellent *The American Imperial Gothic*.
10. See Hantke, 'Troubled by Memories'.
11. The term 'Battlefield Gothic' is used by Hynes, *The Soldier's Tale*, p. 26.

Chapter 11

Russian Twentieth-Century Gothic: The Irrepressible Undead

Muireann Maguire

The Russian Gothic

Long viewed by Europeans as a menacing and semi-barbarous empire, always abundant in sites of exile, confinement and suffering, Russia is the Western world's Gothic uncle: a mysterious character with a vast, unexplored estate, apparently affable but also pathologically secretive. Even for its own citizens, the country inspires sensations of mystery, danger and menace. 'Russia', warned the nineteenth-century poet Tiutchev, 'cannot be understood with the intellect alone.'[1] Instead, foreigners often first encounter Russia through fear-inspiring clichés eagerly propagated by global media: the Russian bear, the Russian winter, the endless forest, Baba Yaga the child-stealing witch, the Red Peril of communism, or, most recently, the invisible yet devastating poisons used to assassinate dissidents.[2]

Choosing to understand Russia through its literature presents us with a different set of no less terrifying archetypes, recognisable as native folklore refracted through the lens of the European Gothic tradition. Russian and Ukrainian writers enthusiastically adapted the latter in the eighteenth and nineteenth centuries for their readers. Throughout the politically fraught twentieth century, with its waves of famine, war and repression, the Gothic continued to provide a trove of metaphors for conceptualising the unspeakable. As Etkind writes, '[i]n Russia, a land where millions remain unburied, the repressed return as the undead ... in novels, films, and other forms of culture that reflect, shape and possess people's memory'.[3] The Russian and Soviet Gothic is essential today, however, not as a shadow of the Western Gothic-fantastic tradition nor as a variant of postcolonial Gothic Studies: it is a window on to the complicated and often tragic history of the Russian state itself and its relations with its immediate neighbours. From Mikhail Bulgakov's haunted apartment buildings in the early twentieth century, to Sergei

Luk'ianenko's glamorous were-tigers and grungy vampires at the beginning of the twenty-first, Russian writers consistently turn to the clichés and tropes of the Gothic to express their reality and to negotiate their unburied past.

Origins and Evolution of the Russian Gothic

The Gothic genre first spread through the Russian literary world in the 1790s by way of translations of English Gothic novels as well as of early French and German horror. Their popularity among the reading public, and their influence on Imperial Russia's emergent literary culture, is difficult to exaggerate. The writings of E. T. A. Hoffmann, in particular, are reflected in the work of almost every major nineteenth-century writer, from Aleksandr Pushkin (1799–1837) to Fedor Dostoevskii (1821–81), as well as many minor authors. Pushkin's short story 'The Queen of Spades' ('Pikovaia dama', 1833) is a richly allusive and sophisticated Gothic-fantastic tale, featuring a hero possessed by Napoleonic ambition, a vengeful spirit, madness and subtle references to the occult sciences. Of the five short fictions in Pushkin's collection *The Tales of Belkin* (*Povesti Belkina*, 1831), one, 'The Coffin-Maker' ('Grobovshchik'), is a humorous ghost story complete with dancing skeletons. His masterpiece, the verse narrative *Eugene Onegin* (*Evgenii Onegin*, 1825–33), is imbricated with Hoffmann-inspired imagery of dreamlike horror. Its eponymous hero is likened to Charles Maturin's Melmoth and to a Byronic vampire in the same breath.[4] Pushkin's mentor, the poet Vasilii Zhukovskii (1783–1852), produced no fewer than three translations of Gottfried Bürger's 1773 ballad 'Lenore', which veer gruesomely between parodying the original text and intensifying its horrific affect. Another contemporary of Pushkin, Prince Vladimir Odoevskii (1803–69), produced many Gothic-fantastic short stories and novellas, usually plotted around obsessive psychologies and supernatural vengeances. Humour, whether satirical or slapstick, is intrinsic to most early Russian Gothic writing, including the early work of Fedor Dostoevskii. While Dostoevskii's overtly supernatural stories such as the novella *The Double* (*Dvoinik*, 1846) and dark psychological tales such as 'The Landlady' ('Khozaika', 1847) or *Crime and Punishment* (*Prestuplenie i nakazanie*, 1866) owe an obvious debt to Hoffmann, their comedic element yields over time to a growing sense of tragedy.

The Double, the funniest and most influential of Dostoevskii's Gothic-fantastic fictions, describes the decline into madness of a middle-ranking civil servant who believes that a more efficient and likeable version of himself, with the same name, has joined his office. When his double is promoted above him, his downfall is swift. Inimical doubles, a theme already familiar from Hoffmann's *The Devil's Elixirs* (1815), are an almost ubiquitous trope in Dostoevskii's novels. However, he would never again express the theme as explicitly as in *The Double*, which was adapted and updated in Richard Ayoade's intriguing 2013 film of the same name. Dostoevskii's final overtly Gothic tale was 'Bobok' (1873), a satirical attack on the cupidity and lubriciousness which he perceived in Russia's rigid social hierarchy. In this story, a sleepy drunk in a city cemetery overhears subterranean conversations between recently buried corpses. Their souls are trapped in their decaying bodies; the dead are just as concerned with personal ambition and even sexual satisfaction as they were when living. None of these undead profligates expresses any long-term concern about the afterlife, although they acknowledge that the oldest corpses are unable to utter any sound except one faint, meaningless word: 'bobok'. Death is not the end for these sinners; their moral corruption has been actualised in the flesh. Dostoevskii here subverts a terrifying Gothic trope (the undead haunting a graveyard): in 'Bobok', these living corpses are normalised by their prosaically profane concerns and by the reactions of the comically naïve framing narrator.

Ukrainian Gothic is an important subgenre of Russian Gothic. As an ethnically and linguistically distinct state often dominated by its larger neighbour, familiar yet intrinsically different, Ukraine serves as Russia's uncanny Other. It has supplied a series of writers who played a major role in reconfiguring and popularising Russian-language Gothic fiction, and also the setting for many such fictions, often involving shape-shifting monsters, sorcery and blood-curdling brigands. Ukrainian writers essential to the naturalisation of European Gothic in the Slavic world include the gentleman-author Antonii Pogorel'skii (the pen name of Aleksei Perovskii, 1787–1836), the translator and critic Orest Somov (1793–1833), the playwright and novelist Oleksa Storozhenko (1805–74), the historical novelist Panteleimon Kulish (1817–97) and of course Mykola Hohol' (1809–52, better known as Nikolai Gogol). Pogorel'skii, who, not coincidentally, owned a large Ukrainian country estate, wrote the novel *The Convent Girl* (*Monastyrka*, 1833), whose orphaned heroine inherits a large Ukrainian country estate. Unfortunately, her avaricious guardian bullies, cheats and eventually kidnaps her in order to force her into marriage. The girl ultimately marries her true love after a suitably thrilling escape through the forest. This is sheer Radcliffean pastiche, replacing the wild forests of the Apennines (where another unsuitable guardian, Montoni, lurks in Radcliffe's 1794 *The Mysteries of Udolpho*) with a Ukrainian equivalent. Pogorel'skii's transposition softens the more grotesque aspects of Gothic violence, while introducing humour through the use of local colour and Ukrainian vernacular.

Gogol, although like Pogorel'skii the heir to a (small) provincial estate, took a more radical path in his mature fiction (his early works, including the horror tale 'Viy' [1835], were heavily derivative of Ukrainian folklore). Gogol created a new literary tradition that is neither European Gothic pastiche nor specifically Ukrainian in style (although it contains elements of both): his series of so-called Petersburg Tales, published between 1835 and 1842, are short fictions set in an absurd, comic, yet terrifying version of the Imperial Russian capital, St Petersburg. In the most famous of these, 'The Nose' ('Nos', 1836), a retired officer's nose bids for freedom, even claiming higher social status than its owner. In 'The Overcoat' ('Shinel'', 1842), a petty clerk starves himself for months to save up for a new winter coat, only for it to be stolen by thieves. He soon dies from the shock. The clerk's ghost persecutes the bombastic official who chose to be intimidating rather than helpful in the aftermath of the theft. Gogol's storylines are playfully, self-consciously Gothic; they achieve affect by exposing the precarity of human self-perception. Even the urban landscape of St Petersburg, a triumph of Russian political assertiveness over nature and geography, is shown to collude in human self-delusion through its misleading side streets and waterways, haunted buildings and demonic lamplighters. Gogol's stories founded the Petersburg Gothic tradition, which Dostoevskii, Andrei Belyi (1880–1934) and many other authors would later refine and expand. Tsarist Russia had other regional Gothics: Valeria Sobol's recent monograph examines literature set in the Baltic region and Finland, as well as Ukraine (all areas contested and periodically colonised by the Russian Empire) as characteristic sites of what she calls the Russian 'imperial uncanny' – a fictionalised geography 'into which the Russian Empire projected its colonial fantasies and anxieties'.[5]

As Russia entered the twentieth century, a new generation of Symbolist and modernist writers drew upon the rich imagery and motifs of their predecessors. Andrei Belyi's seminal novel *Petersburg* (1913), although concerned with the contemporary problems of political terrorism and student agitation, borrows Pushkin's image of the equestrian statue of Tsar Peter I come to malevolent life (from the 1833 poem *The Bronze Horseman* [*Mednyi vsadnik*]). The influence of Poe (via Baudelaire) and of Bram Stoker's *Dracula* (1897) on the major Russian Symbolist poets, particularly Aleksandr Blok (1880–1921), was significant in the production of a new aesthetic suffused with demons and other supernatural visitors. In the first decades of the new century, the Gothic took on a new, important and increasingly visual role in Russian society: as propaganda and satire, in the form of cartoons, political pamphlets and the lurid language of political speeches and journalism. The intensity of the use of supernatural discourse in satirical papers to whip up fear was unprecedented: Brooks writes that '[n]either before nor after (until the fall of communism) did such intense, menacing displays of monsters and ghouls feature in Russian culture'.[6] After the devastation of the First World War and the Civil War (1917–21), and an economic crisis that endured well into the 1920s, the Gothic provided a readily adaptable discourse to express the country's sense of loss and continuing fear. It also allowed writers on both sides of the political divide to demonise their opponents. The new Soviet state was founded upon principles of social justice, scientific rationalism and economic fairness. In theory, it was categorically inhospitable to Gothic writing. In practice, many leading cultural figures, including practitioners of what became (from 1934) the national literary doctrine of socialist realism, espoused traditionally Gothic themes in texts that came to constitute the canonical narrative of the Soviet state.[7] For example, the theme of the haunted house or castle re-emerged in Soviet authors' treatment of the question of property, which had been sequestered from its legitimate heirs (the people) by villainous usurpers (the aristocrats and bourgeoisie) until the Revolution. This narrative inspired a number of implicitly Gothic plotlines, notably *Cement* (*Tsement*) by Fedor Gladkov (1883–1958), which went through many editions between 1925 and 1958. While its title might seem lacking in charisma to modern audiences, Gladkov's focus on how newly enfranchised workers repossess a derelict industrial plant (here, a cement factory abandoned during the Civil War) was extremely topical, and indeed inspiring, for Soviet readers. The dystopian fantasy *We* (*My*, 1921) by Evgenii Zamiatin (1884–1937) contrasts modern, collectivised housing and old, private homes – with their secret underground rooms – on an even larger scale.

Some Soviet-era Gothic plots may be read polemically by inverting the characters' roles – were the real Gothic villains of Soviet plot not, in fact, the capitalists and nobility, but the insurgent proletariat who wrested control of homes and estates from their wronged and banished owners? Mikhail Bulgakov (1891–1940) plays with (necessarily) subtle variations on this interpretation in his many stories and novellas exploring the rights and wrongs of communal living. He returned to the theme in his most famous novel *The Master and Margarita* (*Master i Margarita*, 1940), which was too politically sensitive to be published in Russia until 1966. Until then, it circulated abroad and in secret manuscript copies (*samizdat*).

Bulgakov, although neither wealthy nor entitled, belonged to the educated middle classes and never personally supported communism. *The Master and Margarita* follows the consequences of a visit by Mephistopheles (disguised as a foreign theatrical impresario called Woland) to Soviet Russia. Much of the action takes place in a collective apartment in Moscow, commandeered and literally haunted by Woland's demonic troupe. Vampires, a shape-shifting cat demon (an homage to Hoffmann's eponymous Kater Murr), outrageous miracles and even a Satanic ball all feature in the ensuing, highly satirical comedy. It is not difficult to identify the disillusioned Bulgakov and his wife in the title characters. Margarita is a prosperous bureaucrat's wife who leaves her marriage for the Master, an ageing, self-doubting writer long silenced by his critics. Mephistopheles, restoring the Master's lost novel to him, makes the famous comment 'Manuscripts don't burn.'[8] This statement not only refutes the state police's right to confiscate and even destroy manuscripts (including some of Bulgakov's), but appears to acknowledge the Gothic trope of the found manuscript. As a result of these polemical texts and of his widely perceived lack of intellectual loyalty to the regime, and in spite of Stalin's publicly expressed admiration for his early writings, Bulgakov's career as a novelist and playwright was cruelly dogged by cancellations, censorship and critical contempt. He died from a hereditary kidney condition in 1940, working on *The Master and Margarita* to the last.

Other Gothic themes rewritten by mainstream Soviet authors include the Gothic body plotline (in which scientific or social advances aiming to improve human physiology end by creating damaged, degenerate or partially inhuman bodies), the use of Gothic monsters (exaggerated or grotesque villains) in political propaganda, and a paradoxical focus on physical death in narratives that ostensibly promote the possibility of universal resurrection. The hero of the bestselling post-war novel *A Story about a Real Man* (*Povest' o nastoiashchem cheloveke*, 1946) by the mainstream author Boris Polevoi (1908–81) is an exemplar of the Gothicised Soviet body. Aleksei, a young fighter pilot, cannot become a 'real man', that is, an avatar of patriotic courage, until after both his legs are amputated following a horrific plane crash. Although Aleksei is fêted as a true Soviet hero, his much-admired heroic body is no longer entirely human, dependent as it is on metal and leather prostheses. Similarly, Soviet stories with utopian elements, such as the novel *Happy Moscow* (*Schastlivaia Moskva*, 1936) by Andrei Platonov (1899–1951) or the many science fiction tales by the popular children's author Aleksandr Beliaev (1884–1942), often focus disproportionately on dead or dying bodies. *Happy Moscow* was written in a period of

Soviet triumphalism which Platonov originally planned to endorse. Ironically, it proved unpublishable. Its heroine is (like Polevoi's Aleksei) an amputee; her surgeon is obsessed with analysing the process of physical death. Physical extinction is a recurrent preoccupation among the characters in Platonov's fiction; this was a major factor in preventing the publication of any of his novels (including *Happy Moscow*) until the end of the Soviet regime. Beliaev's most famous novel, *Professor Dowell's Head* (*Golova profesora Douelia*, 1937), describes an ambitious scientific attempt to achieve a sort of immortality by keeping disembodied heads alive indefinitely (either under laboratory conditions or by stitching them on to the bodies of viable corpses). Despite the story's optimistic tone and the ultimate defeat of the Gothic villain of the piece (a scientist who uses murder as a shortcut to surgical fame), this fable of Promethean arrogance soon decomposes, like its re-capitated corpses, into its constituent elements.

Mikhail Bulgakov crossed several Gothic borderlines with his novella *Heart of a Dog* (*Sobach'e serdtse*, 1925), the manuscript of which was confiscated by the police and never published in Bulgakov's lifetime. Its main character is a charismatic surgeon and endocrinologist, Professor Preobrazhenskii, who successfully defends his eight-room apartment from division into smaller flats by exploiting his contacts with senior Soviet politicians (who rely on Preobrazhenskii's hormone injections to preserve their youthfulness). By transplanting human endocrine glands into a street mutt, he creates a new, interstitial being – Sharik, the former stray dog, becomes Sharikov, Soviet working-class hero, consummate snitch and disloyal bully. When Preobrazhenskii realises that his malignant creation is endangering the survival of his own pre-revolutionary enclave, he successfully reverses the operation. The true horror of Sharikov's existence is not that a dog becomes a functioning man, but that the man has the 'heart of a dog' – that he is morally worse than his canine original. Although Bulgakov's satire is evenly distributed between the bourgeois and proletarian characters in the novella, its brutally accurate parodies of recognisable contemporary types – such as the members of the house accommodation committee – made the work impossible to publish. Many real-life aspects of life in the USSR – including political purges and mass repressions, spying, an opaque and punitive justice system, and an effectively dictatorial government – lent themselves to Gothic narrative, but not of a kind that could be circulated in the author's lifetime.

What we might call 'true' Gothic – narratives with spooky settings, demonic visitors or vampires – was necessarily excluded from the positivist, rationally oriented Soviet literary space. Such narratives would not find publishers (as various stifled careers demonstrate, including the fates of Bulgakov and of Sigizmund Krzhizhanovskii, discussed in the next section). However, émigré authors and a few authors active in the transitional decades before Soviet writing ossified into socialist realism did continue in the phantom footsteps of Gogol, Dostoevskii and the Symbolist writers. The Symbolists Valerii Briusov (1873–1924) and Fedor Sologub (1863–1927), better known as novelists, wrote a number of Gothic tales of self-delusion and pathological obsession in the early Soviet years, a few of which have been translated. Their lesser-known peers Aleksandr Amfiteatrov (1862–1938), Pavel Muratov (1881–1950), Ivan Lukash (1892–1940) and Aleksandr Chaianov (1888–1937) all produced anthologies of creepy tales in direct stylistic descent from Gogol's Petersburg Tales, Hoffmann's stories and of course Goethe's *Faust*. Amfiteatrov, a prolific writer of fiction, was also a journalist, editor and classical historian (he wrote an influential life of Nero). He spent most of his life outside Russia, as his writings irritated both the Tsarist and Soviet governments. Muratov led a distinguished if peripatetic career in exile post-1922 as a journalist and art critic. He died in Co. Waterford, Ireland, where his friend and co-author, the journalist and politician W. E. D. Allen, owned a house. Lukash, a historical novelist, also penned several short stories in the Petersburg Tale tradition: 'Hermann's Card' ('Karta Germanna', 1922) is a derivative yet atmospheric updating of Pushkin's 'The Queen of Spades', while 'The Bells' ('Kuranty', 1925) describes the Soviet destruction of imperial statues and monuments in gloomy, surreal and fortunately somewhat exaggerated detail. Chaianov published only five Gothic-fantastic stories (and one utopian novella) in his lifetime, all in limited print runs during the 1920s. Trained as an agronomist, and initially appointed to a senior position in the Soviet Ministry of Agriculture, Chaianov later fell foul of a Stalinist purge against pre-revolutionary bourgeois 'experts'. He was arrested in 1930, exiled to Kazakhstan, and executed there in 1937. His explicitly Hoffmannist ghost stories are informed by his passion for Moscow's historical topography: they evoke an intricate eighteenth-century world, rich in physical detail, populated by alchemists, mesmerists, Satanists and Illuminati. In the context of Russian émigré Gothic, it would be churlish to overlook the 1938 supernatural tale by Vladimir Nabokov (1899–1977), 'A Visit to the Museum', whose émigré narrator is by mysterious means involuntarily transported from a French provincial museum to the snowy wasteland of Bolshevik Russia.

According to Brooks, the Gothic mode endured under communism because of its 'association with challenges to authority in the Russian imagination'.[9] While he has in mind propaganda posters and leaflets, the same applies to Soviet-era fiction such as Bulgakov's works and the short stories of the émigrés discussed above. In the post-Soviet period, up to the present day, Gothic archetypes have re-emerged as a literary device for processing the traumatic transition from the authoritarian communist regime to an authoritarian pseudo-democratic regime, by way of a black-market economy saturated with cheap Eastern imports and popular Western culture. In this climate, Gothic characters (rather than Gothic plotlines) have proved useful for negotiating the complex, constantly altering contemporary cultural landscape. To give a single example from the turn of the last century, the author Sergei Luk'ianenko (1968–) has gained an international fandom for his six-part *Watch* series, set in contemporary Moscow, following the latest permutations in the eternal conflict between supernatural forces of good and evil. Timur Bekmambetov's 2004 cinematic adaptation was extremely successful in Russia (with two sequels made), and sufficiently lucrative for Fox Searchlight studios to release an English-language version. Luk'ianenko's novel *Night Watch* (*Nochnoi dozor*, 1998) introduced his essential recurring characters: well-meaning vampires (who work as butchers for easy and legal access to blood) who are nonetheless destined to support the forces of evil, the Day Watch. Their counterparts form the Night Watch, a coterie of humanlike mages, witches and shape-shifters, representing virtue and protecting ordinary humans. The two Watches police each other to retain equilibrium; trouble breaks out if either side seems poised to gain an advantage. Morally ambiguous lead characters, with their multifaceted allegiances, make appropriate heroes for a morally ambiguous world. The pact between opposing Watches could be read as an ironic allegory for the Cold War, or for the current uneasy relationship between Russian and Ukraine.

In the final section of this chapter, I want to focus on two modern Russian Gothic writers – one active in the first half of the twentieth century, the other firmly in the twenty-first. Despite their very different aesthetics, both writers continue the essential qualities of Russian Gothic: grotesque humour, the fallibility of human perception and uniquely Russified monsters.

Sigizmund Krzhizhanovskii

Sigizmund Krzhizhanovskii (1887–1950), 'a Ukrainian writer with a comically unpronounceable Polish name', was active between 1920 and 1940.[10] Because none of his five novellas and almost none of his many short stories passed Soviet censorship, in his lifetime he published only occasional journalism, encyclopaedia entries (for the Great Soviet Encyclopaedia project) and a few scholarly articles. Thanks to the efforts of the Russian poet Vadim Perel'muter, who has devoted his life to publishing and promoting Krzhizhanovskii since discovering the writer's long-neglected archive, and a few determined translators and academics, his fiction is finally read and studied in Russia and abroad. Many of his short stories and novellas, in Joanne Turnbull's English translation, are now available from the prestigious *New York Review of Books* Classics series. This unexpected return from obscurity, a reversal worthy of one of his own ironic fables, is entirely justified by the quality and range of Krzhizhanovskii's work. His writing spans many genres: from theatre criticism and science fiction to comedy and satire. While he clearly draws upon a number of Western Gothic predecessors – including Hoffmann, but particularly Poe, whom he greatly admired – his style is unique. His plots are often planned around the concrete realisation of an idiom or a metaphor (for example, one story describes the plight of lovers who literally fall into their beloved's eyes). His exacting, exquisitely nuanced sentences pivot intricately around puns and neologisms. As ever in the Russian Gothic tradition, humour and tragedy are frequently interconnected.

Like Gogol and like his own contemporary Mikhail Bulgakov, Krzhizhanovskii was born in Ukraine's capital, Kiev. His family was ethnically Polish. At Kiev University, Krzhizhanovskii studied both law and philosophy. As a young man he visited Vienna and Paris; his uncle left him a small legacy; he gained minor celebrity for his public lectures on cultural topics, and in 1920 he published his first article. But the First World War, followed by the 1917 revolution, shattered the peaceful progression of Krzhizhanovskii's life. In 1922 he moved to Moscow, where (in common with many writers during this turbulent period) he experienced near-starvation, poverty and the inadequate conditions imposed on urban dwellers by Soviet housing planners. Dreadful accommodation would inspire several short stories. Krzhizhanovskii's fiction, because of its supernatural and fantastic themes and its satirical brilliance, disqualified itself from publication in contemporary journals. His work was simultaneously too realistic (because it exposed the hardships of Soviet existence) and too fantastic (with its linguistic and philosophical games) to meet the requirements of editors. In 1933 Krzhizhanoivskii was unfortunate enough to be criticised as old-fashioned and idealistic by Maksim Gor'kii, the doyen of socialist realism. As a result of this and of similar rejections, his literary career foundered. He was not even allowed to join the Soviet Writers' Union, which conveyed important privileges, until 1939. His death was hastened by multiple disappointments, long-term poverty, alcoholism and a stroke which, tragically, left him unable to read or write in his final months.

Krzhizhanovskii's particular genius lay in making the ordinary terrifying. One of the most emblematic aspects of Soviet life was the discomfort of overcrowded, noisy, communal apartments. 'Quadratrurin' ('Kvadraturin', 1925), a nightmarish fable about an unexceptional man who accepts a product sample from a mysterious visitor, is set in one such apartment. The titular Quadraturin is a paste which promises to expand a room in all directions when rubbed on every surface. Unfortunately, the hero, Sutulin (his name, from the word *sutulyi*, meaning 'hunched', implies his permanent state of self-restriction), neglects to paint the Quadraturin on the *ceiling* of his tiny cubbyhole. As his room stretches out horizontally but not vertically, it becomes ever more coffin-like; Sutulin eventually loses himself in the endlessly expanding space. Although clearly a satire on Soviet living conditions (there are plenty of entertaining cameos from Sutulin's egregious neighbours), 'Quadraturin' also taps the Gothic tradition of Gogol and Dostoevskii. Sutulin is a pitiful, easily persecuted 'little man', like Gogol's doomed clerk in 'The Overcoat'. Indeed, the comparison between rooms and coffins recalls Raskolnikov's tiny garret in Dostoevskii's *Crime and Punishment*. Characteristically for Krzhizhanovskii, his text also references European literary culture: here, the Faustian ur-narrative, in which a Satanic visitor brings a gift that will cost the hero his soul.

Other stories from this period offer a mix of classical and Gothic-fantastic plotlines and motifs. 'The Phantom' ('Fantom', 1926) is an Oedipal legend with multiple Gothic tropes: a labyrinthine hospital, underground storerooms, animated mannequins and a vengeful undead narrator. The word 'phantom' refers to an anatomical model used by obstetrics students to study the mechanisms of birth. The story's human protagonist, Dvuliud-Sklifskii, passes his final medical exams by manipulating one such phantom and its infant, which is in fact a miscarried foetus preserved in alcohol for medical use. Unfortunately for Dvuliud-Sklifskii, the creature he has delivered genuinely comes to life. Sheltered by the hospital janitor, it grows up in hiding: slimy, skeletal and still smelling of spirits. After finding a mate (a mannequin in a clothes shop), it seeks out its 'father' to kill him, since, as it informs Dvuliud-Sklifskii, when two phantoms fall in love, a human being must die. Echoes of Frankenstein and his monster are intentional. While the young doctor, Dvuliud-Sklifskii, is an innocent victim (unaware he had created a new being), his generation is not without blame. The titular phantom's youth coincides with the Russian Revolution, an unnatural birth of a different sort, and one arguably caused by the meddling of idealistic intellectuals.

Many of Krzhizhanovskii's other fantastic stories focus on individuals who are literally or metaphorically out of time with their generation. In the novella 'Memories of the Future' ('Vospominaniia budushchego', 1929), which acknowledges its debt to H. G. Wells, the hero invents a time machine for travel into the not-so-distant future. He never reveals what he sees there, except to an important visitor who appears one day unannounced (and whom the reader is clearly intended to recognise as Stalin). The visitor leaves after a long interview, looking perturbed. Soon after, the inventor vanishes for good – whether this is because he fails to return from an intertemporal jaunt, like his Wellsian prototype, or for the more banal yet equally terrifying reason that the dictator has chosen to 'disappear' him, Krzhizhanovskii never discloses.

'Autobiography of a Corpse' ('Avtobiografiia trupa', 1925) is one of several longer tales which uses the living corpse metaphor to portray the lives of intellectuals in Soviet Russia. In one of Krzhizhanovskii's rare sunnier adaptations of a Gothic theme, 'Comrade Punt' ('Tovarishch Punt', 1931), the eponymous Comrade Punt dies in his sleep at the beginning of the story. His body lies unnoticed in yet another inadequate room in a communal apartment (this room is merely the curtained-off space between two wardrobes in a passage). Comrade Punt's trousers, however, prove unexpectedly resilient: they pick themselves up, find Punt's briefcase and stride off for his office. No one there notices Punt's absence; in fact, Punt's trousers are so much more industrious and intimidating than their former owner that they soon get promoted. They are undone by their own success: because they are a pair, the office rumour mill soon generates rumours of favouritism and preferential treatment. To save themselves from mandatory separation, the trousers regretfully abandon their office and Punt's still-unnoticed corpse, preferring the safety of a dry-cleaners' where they can be anonymously reallocated to a new owner. Not even haunted trousers, this narrative implies, can withstand the forces of communism; even individualistic garments ultimately return to the collective.

Anna Starobinets

Anna Starobinets (1978–), often compared to Stephen King, Neil Gaiman and Ray Bradbury, arguably has more in common with Robert Aickman. As in Aickman's chillingly open-ended plots, Starobinets's characters passively accept, or obediently walk into, illogical and ultimately terrifying situations. In her debut collection, *An Awkward Age* (*Perekhodnyi vozrast*, 2005), the narrator of 'The Agency' ('Agenstvo') drifts into working for an enigmatic global company as an assassin. Or is this mere self-delusion to justify the inhuman revenge he takes on his ex-girlfriend? In 'The Parasite' ('Parazit'), a combination of medical and supernatural horror unifies aspects of old and new Gothic. A terminally ill child is transformed into a monstrous pupa by experimental hormonal injections. The winged humanoid that hatches out is taken for an angel by the media and the Orthodox church, but its taste for human blood suggests a rather different identity. 'The Parasite' is one of seven stories arranged around the central theme of metamorphosis in Starobinets's second anthology, *The Icarus Gland* (*Ikarova zheleza*, 2014). Starobinets's fiction typically features medical or biological horror, carefully integrated into a meticulously described realist context. She introduces cyberspace as a new locus for haunting. Her 2011 novel *The Living* (*Zhivushchii*) imagines a futuristic dystopia whose inhabitants receive compulsory implants that allow them to spend most of their time online in multiple virtual levels. The wealthier the individual, the more time they can spend in their fantasy world, and the more virtual levels they can simultaneously access. Their collectivised society is premised on maintaining a stable population of three billion live persons at any one time. Whenever anyone dies, their soul is reabsorbed by an omniscient central processor which reallocates it, after 'five seconds of darkness', to an unborn infant. All souls are tracked by numbers resembling barcodes. As in Zamiatin's *We*, an obvious influence on Starobinets's novel, not everyone has an equal right to reproduction. Any souls who manifested rebellious or criminal traits in previous lives are confined to special institutions, without appeal, as soon as they are reborn. In spite of the hyper-modern, cyber-infused context, *The Living* is predicated on a classically Gothic plot of eternal return. Everyone lives in the shadow of their own past existences (although some characters question the reality of such assembly-line reincarnation) and also in dread of somehow not re-emerging from those fateful 'five seconds of darkness'. Fittingly, when the system's harmony is eventually challenged, the threat comes from a soul that chooses darkness over rebirth.

Starobinets adds an original (and female) voice to a growing number of authors who write reflectively about late and post-Soviet culture. Several, like Starobinets, draw on elements from both contemporary horror and traditional Gothic in fictions that either satirise or allegorise Russia's recent past, notably Vladimir Sharov (1952–2018), Boris Akunin (1956–), Viktor Pelevin (1962–) and Dmitrii Bykov (1967–). Most recently, the critically hailed novelist Mikhail Elizarov won the Russian National Bestseller Prize in 2020 for his novel *Earth* (*Zemlia*, 2019), which (although not a ghost story) continues a preoccupation with post-mortem matters that would meet with the approval of Elizarov's predecessors Pushkin and Gogol: the narrator is a gravedigger and funeral worker, and much of the action transpires in cemeteries. The last word in Russian Gothic has clearly not yet been written, and it's unlikely to be 'bobok'.

Key Works (dates indicate first Russian publication)

Mikhail Bulgakov, *The Master and Margarita* (1966). Deceptively playful, yet profound, Bulgakov's greatest novel is both a *tour de force* of Russian comic Gothic and a vicious satire of Soviet corruption.

Sigizmund Krzhizhanovskii, *Autobiography of a Corpse* (or any of the other recent NYRB Classics short story anthologies, 2009–). These witty stories, full of ontological puzzles, are both an indictment of turgid Soviet bureaucracy and a varied defence of imaginative freedom, by an author who was, in his own words, 'untimely'.

Muireann Maguire (ed. and trans.), *Red Spectres: Russian Gothic Tales from the Twentieth Century* (2013) and *White Magic: Russian Émigré Tales of Mystery and Terror* (2021). Two useful and diverse collections of early twentieth-century Russian Gothic fiction, illustrating its characteristic themes.

Sergei Luk'ianenko, *Night Watch* (1998). The first book in an extended cycle which has proved to be bestselling in Russia and abroad, supernatural elements aside. The novel offers an absorbing view of Russian urban life at the outset of the Putin era.

Anna Starobinets, *An Awkward Age* (2005). Starobinets's first story collection to be translated into English: in equal parts absorbing and grotesque, it contains most of her recurrent themes of metamorphosis and psychosis.

Further Critical Reading

Brooks, Jeffrey, 'The Gothic Tradition in Russian and Early Soviet Culture' (2019). A concise and probing overview of twentieth-century Russian Gothic in art and propaganda as well as literature.

Etkind, Alexander, *Warped Mourning: Stories of the Undead in the Land of the Uncanny* (2013). The only recent monograph to use trauma theory and the concept of 'magical historicism' (akin to 'magical realism') to explore the traces of Stalinist repression in post-Soviet cinema and literature.

Maguire, Muireann, *Stalin's Ghosts: Gothic Themes in Early Soviet Literature* (2012). My monograph analyses the underlying Gothic symbols in both conformist and dissident Soviet literature written between 1920 and 1950.

Naiman, Eric, *Sex in Public: The Incarnation of Early Soviet Ideology* (1997). A quirky and original analysis of the correspondences between early Soviet cultural expression – in literature, journalism and propaganda – and Europe's cultural response to the French Revolution.

Sobol, Valeriia, *Haunted Empire: Gothic and the Russian Imperial Uncanny*

(2020). An excellent overview, using elements of postcolonial theory, of the different cultural expressions of the Gothic in different regions conquered by the Russian Empire during the nineteenth century.

Bibliography

Brooks, Jeffrey, 'The Gothic Tradition in Russian and Early Soviet Culture', *Russian Literature*, 106, 2019, pp. 11–32.

Bulgakov, Mikhail, *The Master and Margarita*, trans. Michael Glenny (London: Collins and Harvill, 1967).

Etkind, Alexander, *Warped Mourning: Stories of the Undead in the Land of the Uncanny* (Stanford, CA: Stanford University Press, 2013).

Gogol, Nikolai, *And the Earth Will Sit on the Moon: Essential Stories*, trans. Oliver Ready (London: Pushkin, 2019).

Krzhizhanovskii, Sigizmund, *Autobiography of a Corpse*, trans. Joanne Turnbull (New York: NYRB Classics, 2013).

Krzhizhanovskii, Sigizmund, *Memories of the Future*, trans. Joanne Turnbull (New York: NYRB Classics, 2009).

Krzhizhanovskii, Sigizmund, *Unwitting Street*, trans. Joanne Turnbull (New York: NYRB Classics, 2020).

Luk'ianenko, Sergei, *The Night Watch*, trans. Andrew Bromfield (London: Arrow, 2007).

Maguire, Muireann, *Stalin's Ghosts: Gothic Themes in Early Soviet Literature* (Oxford: Peter Lang, 2012).

Maguire, Muireann (ed. and trans.), *Red Spectres: Russian Gothic Tales from the Twentieth Century* (New York: Overlook Press, 2013).

Maguire, Muireann (ed. and trans.), *White Magic: Russian Émigré Tales of Mystery and Terror* (Montpelier, VT: Russian Life, 2021).

Naiman, Eric, *Sex in Public: The Incarnation of Early Soviet Ideology* (Princeton, NJ: Princeton University Press, 1997).

Odoevsky, Vladimir, *Two Princesses*, trans. Neil Cornwell (London: Hesperus Classics, 2010).

Pushkin, Alexander, *Eugene Onegin: A Novel in Verse*, trans. Stanley Mitchell (Harmondsworth: Penguin, 2008).

Sobol, Valeriia, *Haunted Empire: Gothic and the Russian Imperial Uncanny* (Ithaca, NY: Cornell University Press, 2020).

Starobinets, Anna, *An Awkward Age*, trans. Hugh Aplin (London: Hesperus Press, 2010).

Starobinets, Anna, *The Icarus Gland: A Book of Metamorphoses*, trans. Jamie Rann (Bloxham: Skyscraper, 2014).

Starobinets, Anna, *The Living*, trans. Jamie Rann (London: Hesperus Press, 2012).

Thirlwell, Adam. 'The Master of the Crossed-Out', *New York Review of Books*, 23 June 2011, <http://www.nybooks.com/articles/2011/06/23/master-crossed-out/> (last accessed 29 March 2021).

Notes

1. The title of Fedor Tiutchev's 1866 poem, 'Umom Rossiu ne poniat'', in *Stikhotvoreniia* (Moscow: Profizdat, 2012), p. 207. My translation.
2. Unsurprisingly, this latter theme is rapidly developing its own subgenre: notably, the disturbingly competent Russian poisoners pitted against British spies in Mick Herron's *Slough House* (2021), where the eponymous Slough House emerges as a modern Gothic locus; Andrei Kurkov's 2018 novel *Grey Bees* (*Serye pcheli*), which describes chemical poisoning as a potential consequence of the Ukraine–Russian conflict over Crimea; and Sergei Lebedev's novichok novel, *Untraceable* (*Debutant*, 2021).
3. Etkind, *Warped Mourning*, p. 18.
4. Pushkin, *Eugene Onegin*, p. 59.
5. Sobol, *Haunted Empire*, p. 23.
6. Brooks, 'The Gothic Tradition', p. 12.
7. For more detailed exposition of this topic, see Maguire, *Stalin's Ghosts*.
8. Bulgakov, *The Master and Margarita*, p. 326.
9. Brooks, 'The Gothic Tradition', p. 24.
10. Thirlwell, 'The Master of the Crossed-Out', n.p.

Chapter 12

The Gothic 1950s
Steffen Hantke

America in the Fifties: The Calm Before and After the Storm

For those who associate the Gothic with places and periods of turmoil, violence and paranoia, America during the 1950s would seem like an odd place and time to expect it to thrive. In the long historical hindsight of the twenty-first century, the Fifties have become enshrined as a period of prosperity and stability, the heyday of the American Century. At the outset of the Second World War, publisher Henry Luce could still worry about the nation's future. In a famous op-ed in *Time* magazine on 17 February 1941, he wrote: 'We Americans are unhappy. We are not happy about America. We are not happy about ourselves in relation to America. We are nervous – or gloomy – or apathetic.' The Fifties, taking their cue from Luce, would demonstrate that America had overcome the 'virus of isolationist sterility' and instead had 'accept[ed] wholeheartedly [its] duty and ... opportunity as the most powerful and vital nation in the world and in consequence to exert upon the world the full impact of [its] influence, for such purposes as we see fit and by such means as we see fit'.[1] Social historian Tom Engelhardt would call the achievement of this goal 'victory culture', characterising the 1950s as a period when the nation, for better or worse, had achieved a happy stasis and was resting comfortably within itself.[2] Seen in historical context, this self-confidence was both the calm *before* and the calm *after* the storm. It was tied to the turmoil of, respectively, the Great Depression, the Second World War and the difficulties of 'reconversion' to peacetime conditions after the war. It would also precede the next traumatic war – the one in Vietnam, which was, according to Engelhardt, to ring in the demise of victory culture, sparking the countercultural upheaval that was, in equal measure, to cause and celebrate that demise.

While conservative nostalgia has remained wedded to the utopian view of the Fifties throughout the years, the more critical, sceptical view, counterbalancing it at the other end of the political spectrum, is just as much a staple of how the decade is remembered.[3] This critical view may reverse the connotations of some of the decade's essential features (such as the USA's internal stability and unity, or its external hegemony). Yet it still remains safely within the reigning paradigm of a post-war America that had successfully suppressed whatever still lingered unresolved of the crises from the previous two decades. Even this more sceptical assessment of the Fifties would continue successfully to suppress the major conflicts that were already boiling beneath the surface until their eruption in the decade to follow – an eruption which, for all its disruptive power, could be both liberating and destructive in equal measure. It is this double suppression of conflicts inherent at both ends of the political spectrum – one claiming that Fifties suppression was smoothly efficient, the other that Fifties suppression was constantly failing and slipping – that takes us into the heart of the Gothic Fifties.[4]

Recognising the dialectic between the (relative) success and/or failure of suppression maps out a path that cuts across a largely canonical body of Fifties cinema. Among these texts we find some in which topical anxieties are expressed in the most transparent of metaphors; a giant radioactive creature wreaking urban destruction embodying anxieties about the Bomb is hard to miss, as metaphors go. Other metaphors are dug in more deeply as the suppression of taboo subject matter keeps pace with the increasing intensity of social anxieties; Fifties pop culture, for example, seems to find it much easier to talk about communist infiltrators than the troubling presence of wounded WWII veterans within victory culture. At first glance, it might look as though this approach – parsing the success and failure of social and representational suppression as a cultural pathology – breaks little new ground in expanding the cinematic canon of Fifties Gothic. Films most commonly associated with the decade's Gothic sensibility will continue to define the conceptual framework used to understand the decade and its culture. What this approach does accomplish, however, is to draw other texts into the Gothic's gravitational field, inviting a reconsideration of some less obvious, and thus less frequently considered, films as candidates to be added to the canon of the Gothic. With the mechanism of repression, its success and its failures, at the heart of the Gothic, this expanded concept promises to highlight the Gothic in texts most nervously guarding that aspect of themselves.

Shocking Horror: Repression? What Repression?

The greatest obstacle to reading Fifties American Gothic through the lens of suppression is that much of the decade's most iconic popular culture appears to have little inhibition in naming American anxieties explicitly and casting their representation in emphatically Gothic terms. In science fiction and horror films that imagine in lurid and shocking detail the nightmare of nuclear technology gone awry, the obsessively repeating metaphors – of giant monsters rampaging through cities, bodies gruesomely transformed by radiation, and alien invaders subverting wholesome communities – are so transparent that naming the anxieties that animated them hardly requires deep textual analysis. Even the recurring mechanisms that would regulate the oscillation between anxiety and its containment were obvious to the point of complete explicitness. From *First Man into Space* (1959) to *The Incredible Shrinking Man* (1957), from *Invaders from Mars* (1953) to *I Married a Monster from Outer Space* (1958) and from *Them!* (1954) to *The War of the Worlds* (1953), post-war triumphalism is upheld at such preposterous cost that gestures of closure and reassurance commonly end up outpaced by the spectacular imagery of disaster and abjection that precedes them. As Fifties horror and science fiction films would dramatise the see-saw between self-doubting precariousness and grandiloquent triumphalism, the dynamic fluctuation between these two poles would enact the suppression of anxiety as the very principle of narrative and ideological closure. Throughout most triumphalist celebrations of victory culture, there is always a sense that even the most thorough victory over threats and anxieties is never quite sufficient to put the audience's anxieties completely to rest.

After Susan Sontag's 'The Imagination of Disaster' (1965) set the agenda for the first wave of critical writing on Gothic cinema in the 1950s, subsequent writing on this high degree of transparency and explicitness started to go beyond the obvious Cold War context and broadened the scope of critical readings. Critics would discover anxieties in Fifties Gothic horror and science fiction triggered by the suppressed trauma of the Second World War, the rapid corporatisation of the workplace, the anonymity of mass society, the emergence of teenagers as a generational cohort, the popularity within this cohort of horror comics, the perceived proclivity of this cohort for juvenile delinquency, etc. In accord with the impact of feminist readings elsewhere, the changing roles of women in post-war America received critical attention as well. To the extent that, for example, Betty Friedan's

The Feminine Mystique (1963) looks back to 'the ghost-like situation of 1950s American housewives', it deserves, according to Rebecca Munford, the status of a 'peculiarly Gothic phenomenon'. The same is true of the more traditional texts of the Gothic from the 1950s, such as Shirley Jackson's novel *The Haunting of Hill House* (1959), which, according to Munford, were 'anticipating some of the concerns articulated in . . . *The Feminine Mystique*'.[5] Another retrospective description of the 1950s can be found at the opening of Rachel Carson's *Silent Spring* (1962) where the reader is asked to indulge in victory culture by imagining 'a town in the heart of America where all life seemed to live in harmony with its surroundings', a vision that becomes Gothic at the next turn of the story: 'Then a strange blight crept over the area and everything began to change. Some evil spell had settled on the community . . . Everywhere was a shadow of death.'[6] Environmental degradation, brought on by the use of pesticides, manifests itself as an uncanny replay of the familiar with an unfamiliar twist: 'There was a strange stillness. The birds, for example – where had they gone? Many people spoke of them, puzzled and disturbed.'[7]

While the Cold War at its most apocalyptic and abject could name its anxieties directly, Fifties victory culture would still demand from feminism and environmentalism that they take a more oblique approach. If the eerie suburban silence that Friedan and Carson are describing is that of women locked up in immaculate homes and animal life wiped off manicured lawns, it is the quieter, more oblique voice of the suburban Gothic that articulates these anxieties. The temporal delay in getting from Shirley Jackson to Betty Friedan, or getting from Rachel Carson to an explicitly environmental Gothic, is also indicative of a deeper, more efficient suppression of these issues.[8] Recognising that silence in the eerily abandoned suburbs and towns all over *The Twilight Zone* or *The Outer Limits* requires more interpretative labour. While a canonical *Twilight Zone* episode such as 'The Monsters are Due on Maple Street' flaunts its anxieties about communist subversion, reading the eerie silences before and after eruptions of mob violence as commentary on suburban housewives voiceless in their kitchens or untamed nature suffocated beneath manicured and chemically soaked lawns requires a more daring interpretative leap. As the impact of these issues gathered over time, the metaphors grew more transparent, and what used to be suppressed now rose to the surface. As victory culture silenced, marginalised and postponed engagement with these issues, Fifties Gothic would gravitate towards forms of expression not associated with the urgency of global Cold War politics and military adventure, but with the domestic sphere, with family life, and with the inner lives of characters. This form of the Gothic coincides to a large extent with what Fifties Hollywood used to call the 'woman's film', subsequently broadened and theorised by scholars under the term 'melodrama'. Two issues negotiated within the cinematic conventions of melodrama will provide examples of Fifties Gothic operating at more efficient levels of suppression: the first, how racial segregation would be erased from the post-war suburban Gothic, and the second, how the Korean War was to become the 'forgotten war' before the decade was even over.

Melodrama: Black Characters Behind White Picket Fences

Fifties America is haunted by the spectre of race, though it would take time for this spectre to be made fully visible in spaces – such as the newly emergent suburbs – that were already haunted by women's nameless problems and the silence of slow ecological collapse. *Far From Heaven* (2002), Todd Haynes's creative reimagining of *All that Heaven Allows* (1955), one of Fifties Hollywood's most prominent women's films, gets straight to the point when it turns the original lovers, doomed by class difference, into an interracial couple.[9] Horror in the wake of the 1950s is even more explicit. When a young black veteran (Edwin Hodge) becomes the victim of white mob violence in an affluent gated community in *The Purge* (dir. James DeMonaco, 2013), or when Andre Logan King (LaKeith Stanfield), lost on a suburban street at night, becomes a kidnapping victim in the opening scene of *Get Out* (dir. Jordan Peele, 2017), it is clear that suburbia's true haunted heritage is not gender or social class, but race. The true alien invader, the true monster from outer space in the suburbs, happens to be black.

The reasons for this are patently obvious. When a generation of Americans started making their way out to the suburbs after the Second World War, bolstered by the GI Bill and cheap loans, they took a large part of the tax base with them, draining cities of human, social, cultural and fiscal capital. Wartime unrest caused by the relocation of African American labour for the wartime economy provided additional incentives for 'white flight', leading to economic and legal limitations being imposed on African Americans, with so-called 'redlining' as its most egregious example. As a result, living conditions in urban areas declined to the point where social unrest would focus on urban poverty and disenfranchisement, leading to increasing law enforcement surveillance and repression. All this was to culminate in a series of urban riots during the 1960s, with the summer of 1967 as the peak of activities (Roxbury, Tampa, Detroit, Buffalo, Milwaukee, Newark).

Over the course of these two decades of suburbanisation troubled by racial tensions, it is striking to see racial themes that were still suppressed in the 1950s rising to the surface in later texts. The explicitness with which suburban paranoia is coded as racial in a film such as *Get Out* stands in contrast – at least at first glance – to how much it is pushed aside by a more urgent gender politics in Bryan Forbes's *The Stepford Wives* (1975). This is not to say, though, that race is absent from Forbes's film. It closes with a scene in the suburban supermarket where we see Ruthanne and Royal Hendry, the first black couple to have moved into Stepford.[10] Until then, all the characters in the film have been white, some even, one might say, emphatically so. While the Eberhards belong to a generation that might already be able to look back to a suburban childhood – though the film's opening makes it clear that Joanna's move to Stepford is not a nostalgic return but a separation from the urban roots of her creative energy – the Hendrys are, generationally and demographically speaking, certain to be new arrivals. In the logic of the text's examination and critique of suburbia, the Hendrys prefigure the primacy of social class over race; they are upward social mobility incarnate. In the intersectional matrix of the film, which has room for race, class and gender, race comes a distant third behind social class and gender as a social force to be reckoned with. In the film's imagery, however, this ranking of social class and gender over race is undercut. The presence of the black couple in the blindingly white supermarket (production design, costumes, actors) is a scandal far in excess of where the diegesis places its emphasis (i.e. on gender and on social class). If the Hendrys do not belong here, it is entirely a matter of their race. Their physical presence in this supermarket announces this fact, just as their presence as characters in the film elevates race from the invisibility of non-representation, or from the managed visibility of figurative representation, to the blunt fact of literal representation. More than being a comment on race in suburban America, the moment is an acknowledgement of the suppression of race in the suburban Gothic, reaching back to its beginnings in the 1950s.

With this acknowledgement, this moment in *The Stepford Wives* points back to the appearance of black characters – or rather, the lack thereof – in the suburban Gothic from the 1950s. Reading Fifties Gothic with the hindsight of these later films, we might recognise in the urban intruder who has wandered into the suburbs in *I Married a Monster from Outer Space* – a character played by a white actor – the Fifties precursor to Stanfield's character, the young black man about to become a victim of white violence in Jordan Peele's *Get Out*. Urban intruders into the suburbs are such common figures that they not only appear in

Fifties Gothic, but also figure in episodes of *The Flintstones* (1960–66), reminding the TV audience that the city is a space of crime and corruption perpetually threatening to spill over into the suburbs. As a rule, such characters are not, as in *Get Out*, black, but are, as in *I Married a Monster from Outer Space*, coded as criminal, as sexually deviant, or even as vaguely 'ethnic'. For a culture unwilling to name race, this might be a legible enough code to evoke the anxieties arising from the policing of racial dividing lines between city and suburb.

Not all suburban Gothic in the 1950s relegates blackness to a merely spectral presence by way of metaphor; black characters, though rare and rarely central, do make literal appearances. Two Fifties male melodramas about the suburbs with strong Gothic overtones that predate *The Stepford Wives* are interesting in this respect – *Rebel Without a Cause* (1955) and *Bigger Than Life* (1956), both directed by Nicholas Ray. At first glance, Ray's films share with *The Stepford Wives* the framing of race as relatively insignificant, and thus diminish its importance in the process of suburbanisation itself. And yet, much as in *The Stepford Wives*, the pronounced whiteness of the cast is broken up in final scenes that suddenly expand the significance, or stage the unexpected appearance of, black characters. In *Rebel Without a Cause*, it is the black nanny (Marietta Canty) of 'Plato' Crawford (Sal Mineo), the teenager who dies in the film's final shootout with the police. In *Bigger Than Life*, it is a black janitor – a similarly nameless and yet even more marginal character than the black nanny – who makes the briefest of appearances in the final hospital scene where the troubled white suburbanites are finally reunited.

In both films, these black characters are a stark reminder that, at the very least, there is a larger world out there where race and social class are linked more deterministically than in white suburbia. As white characters, paired up into generationally separated heteronormative couples, are allowed to walk off into futures cathartically cleansed by the act of sacrificial violence that has just occurred, the single black character is left somewhat aimless, without a place or destination, literally and figuratively. Both characters remain nameless. The black nanny remains excluded from the meticulous management of narrative and ideological closure involving all the principal characters at the end of *Rebel Without a Cause*. Similarly, the black janitor who walks through the shot in *Bigger Than Life* is no more than a brief distraction to the characters and the audience, barely visible, like a ghost. Little Richie (Christopher Olsen), the child character in the scene, might still notice him and empathise with him ('Some people work awful late . . .'), but the child's mother (Barbara Rush) immediately reroutes this empathy across class and race lines towards the immediate family drama.[11] To the extent that the black characters in both films are integrated into the discourse on social class and gender, their racial identity appears largely insignificant. Since working 'awful late' describes racial identity only insofar as race and social class conspire to assign a janitorial job to that character, even little Richie's empathetic response, drawing attention to the character yet subjugating one category to the other, could still be considered a way of suppressing race as a category. Only when these characters' blackness is itself fully recognised and reckoned with *as a racial fact* do they appear out of context; only then are they granted the power to unsettle and disturb. Only then does their presence mark the story as a Gothic tale.

Men at War: Remembering the Second World War – Forgetting Korea

While films from *The Stepford Wives* to *Get Out* show the suburban Gothic gradually inching towards explicit engagement with race, the trauma of the Korean War seems to require such radical suppression that even contemporary texts have not yet lifted the veil of amnesia. Judging by the historical facts alone, the Korean War (1950–53) should be remembered as a crucial turning point in post-war American history – one of *the* defining events of the 1950s. Apart from the fact that 'more than 320,000 Americans served in the Korean War [and] more than 33,000 were killed in action',[12] the war marked the end of a five-year period during which Americans, exhausted and traumatised by the experience of the Second World War, were rather unwilling to go (back) to war in pursuit of what their government assured them were vital self-interests around the world. Cold War militarisation geared towards nuclear conflict with the Soviet Union, by contrast, would take the somewhat abstract shape of endless military and civilian preparedness drills. Both in their mind-numbing repetitiveness and in their conspicuous lack of retroactively legitimising nuclear exchanges, these exercises would overshadow the concrete details most Americans still remembered from the Second World War. This time, though, there were no foreign mass deployments separating families, no coffins returned from abroad, no official notifications of battlefield casualties and military funerals. Though framed at times as a local manifestation of the larger Cold War scenario, the Korean War would put an end to – or serve as an antidote to – this degree of abstraction. And yet, in spite of all this, Hampton Sides writing in the *New York Times* on Veteran's Day in 2018 would reach the conclusion that the Korean War 'is still our Forgotten War, a kind of also-ran in our historical consciousness'.[13]

Hollywood did not remain entirely silent on the Korean War; Robert Lenth has counted 91 feature films on the subject before 2000, with release dates starting before the war had even concluded. But if films produced long after the Korean War would merely perpetuate the framing of the conflict as the 'forgotten war', then films made in close historical proximity to it are likely to provide insights into how this trope started. Without the safe historical distance from the traumatic immediacy of the war, films from the 1950s are likely to suppress its traumatic impact with an efficiency no longer required by later accounts. A film exemplary of the Gothic Fifties would encode the experience of the Korean War so skilfully that a contemporary audience would either be unable to recognise it or be able credibly to disavow such recognition. In fact, since the Korean War has remained the 'forgotten war' even to the present day, it would be a film in which the presence of the Korean War would remain a dubious proposition even to an audience today. One film that raises exactly these questions is *The Man in the Grey Flannel Suit* (1956).

At first glance, this might appear an odd choice – the novel by Sloan Wilson, published in 1955, explicitly mentions the Korean War as an event concurrent with the lives of its characters, while the film features no such reference.[14] This is less surprising since Tom Rath (Gregory Peck), the protagonist, is a veteran of the Second World War and not of Korea. As he struggles against small daily obstacles to define his purpose and place in post-war America, his war memories shape his personality yet also cause the destabilisation of his civilian life. Aside from the memories of killing and 'operational fatigue', Rath has kept secret a wartime romance which, having produced an illegitimate child, now intrudes into his post-war life as an embarrassment and a burden, as a social and moral obligation, and as an opportunity to reconcile wartime and peacetime identities.

The Man in the Grey Flannel Suit is conspicuously silent on the Korean War, and yet its preoccupation with traumatic wartime experiences, made manifest through several extensive flashbacks, is all the more remarkable for its historical proximity to the Korean War (it was made three years after the conclusion of the war, as compared to the eleven years that separate it from the end of the Second World War). At face value, this disjunctive chronology suggests that, just as the recently ended Korean War had made little or no impact on 1950s America, the Second World War was still as relevant, if not more so, almost a decade later. Sloan Wilson's decision to write about the Second World War is not in itself evidence of America's lack of interest in the Korean War.

Yet the massive success and subsequent canonisation of the novel demonstrate that America's interests in the 1950s – both during the decade and thereafter – were focused more on the Second World War than on Korea.

Of all possible interpretative approaches, it is perhaps easiest to argue that *The Man in the Grey Flannel Suit* dedicates all available space to the Second World War that would otherwise have been available for a critical discussion of the Korean War. This is a problematic reading because, for one, popular culture is not a zero-sum game. Obviously, Hollywood did respond to historical events, as the Korean War films that were produced and released both during and after the war demonstrate. Such a reading would also presuppose that the text is deliberately trying to change the conversation, which would assume intent on the part of publishers and film studios, which, in turn, would raise questions about who exactly wants to change the conversation so badly, and why.

A more compelling argument is that American audiences, two years after the Korean War, were not completely uninterested in Korea, but were, relatively speaking, more interested in the Second World War. If so, the Korean War would only matter to the extent that it reminded audiences of the Second World War, bridging the gap to the more distant yet more important conflict. After all, five years of reaping the dividends of the post-war peace would come to an end with the mobilisation for Korea in 1950 – a war that did look a lot like the Second World War. As far as the representational politics of *The Man in the Grey Flannel Suit* are concerned, these surface similarities between the Second World War and the Korean War do actually matter. In fact, comparisons between the two wars, made by American scholars and for an American audience, would often highlight the similarities between both conflicts: two wars halfway around the world, fought with essentially the same military arsenal, fought even by many of the same soldiers. These similarities extend even further in the cinematic processing of both wars. The 'Korean War film', Jeanine Basinger argues, 'is definitely a replay of the World War II combat film' with social and technological details, as well as some of the political issues, 'adjusted'.[15]

A brief look at *The Man in the Grey Flannel Suit* confirms Basinger's observation. The flashbacks to Tom Rath's military service – once in the Italian campaign, and once in the Pacific – replay visual iconography from the Second World War. Suffering and attrition due to the harsh winter, which was one of the central tropes of the Korean War, is aligned with a geographically and historically non-specific scene from the European Theatre (the Battle of the Bulge comes to mind). Rath's mission in the Pacific, shot with mattes and on sound stages, corresponds to the Korean War, or rather, to a fantasy that casts Korea primarily in tropical terms. Rice paddies can, in fact, be found across the Korean landscape, but the palm trees in the film stem from a broader fantasy. In that fantasy, the actual geographical features of the Second World War's Pacific Theatre and the Korean peninsula dissolve within vaguely orientalist stereotypes about Asia in circulation ever since US interests had turned to the continent.

If Basinger is correct, and the Korean War film 'replays', as she puts it, the Second World War at the movies, then the reverse might be true as well: a film about the Second World War – like *The Man in the Grey Flannel Suit* – might, in fact, replay the Korean War. This would be at the core of the film as an example of the Gothic, imagining one war as haunted by the spectral presence of another. If the individual and collective wounds of the Korean War were still too fresh after only three years, then the Second World War would provide a metaphoric analogue offering safe distance from the traumatic event. As in the substitution of generic metaphors, in which one genre expresses figuratively what another genre might not be able to express literally (for example, the Western's frontier conflicts and Indian Wars substituting for modern war), the Second World War in *The Man in the Grey Flannel Suit* may merely be a displacement of the recent trauma of the Korean War – a safely distant and already fully processed event stripped of its rawness by a triumphalist framework of 'victory culture'.

If *The Man in the Grey Flannel Suit* is, in fact, addressing the Korean War by displacing it on to the Second World War, the question arises of what makes such displacement necessary. Beyond the obviously traumatic nature of the Korean War, the film's thematic link between postwar American hegemonic politics and what the Production Code, even in the 1950s, still referred to as 'miscegenation' (i.e. the mixing of races, as in scenes of interracial romance) stands out as requiring delicate representational negotiation. This need arises from Tom Rath's wartime romance in Italy, and his illegitimate child which, having been kept secret even from himself, threatens to destabilise his post-war civilian life. The substitution of Italy for Korea takes into account both countries' respective place in the global imaginary of the Cold War. Like Italy since the Second World War, Korea would be 'crucial and unique in the emergence of the Cold War as a geographic lynchpin of US global ambitions'.[16]

The similarities between both countries end, however, with the cultural and ethnic differences between them. During the Second World War and the Korean War, six million 'Italian Americans still had ties to Italy', Alan Nadel reminds us, 'and ... the Vatican was the source of spiritual authority for over 30 million American Catholics'.[17] As the presence of an Italian American GI in *The Man in the Grey Flannel Suit* demonstrates, Italy is never really America's other – its German occupiers are. This 'obvious' difference between Italians and Germans gets replayed in Korean War films in the difference between South Koreans and their 'other' (whatever that happens to be: North Koreans, Chinese, communists). What complicates these correspondences is the conceptual framework in which this binary is enacted in the Korean War. Given the racial undertones of US non-fraternisation regulations, and an American film culture regulated by a Production Code, Tom Rath's illegitimate child with a native Korean woman would pose significant problems. The intense visual and narrative romanticising of Rath's affair throughout the film legitimises his actions to a degree that would be impossible if his paramour were marked as racially other. If displaced on to the Second World War, that troubling racial element in the affair is disavowed, while some of its other aspects are sanctioned or even encouraged as part of its romantic fantasy in service of a new Cold War colonialism. As in the suburban Gothic during the 1950s, race comes in as a force all the more compelling for being unmentionable. As a result – as *The Man in the Grey Flannel Suit* shows – talking about the Korean War three years after it ended already meant talking about forgetting it. With its strategy of displacement, the film would set the tone for a conversation that has barely changed over the years. It is no coincidence that the two most famous films about the Korean War – *The Manchurian Candidate* (dir. John Frankenheimer, 1962) and *M.A.S.H.* (dir. Robert Altman, 1970) – would barely be about Korea, but would delve deep into the unreliability of memory and the substitution of one war for another. Not by coincidence does *Mad Men*'s (2007–15) Don Draper, the series' fairly explicit stand-in for Tom Rath, discover the rare opportunity to escape from his true identity by assuming that of a fellow soldier during his service in the Korean War – a wilful act of forgetting that returns, periodically, as a threat to his assumed post-war identity. The fact that a *New York Times* commentator still referred to it as 'the forgotten war' in 2018 is ample proof that the best form of remembrance for this war is its inscription as a haunting presence on to the Gothic Fifties.

Therapeutic Unease: Gothicising the Fifties

If this framing of the Korean War as a Gothic spectre haunting American culture through a film that never explicitly mentions the Korean War feels like a stretch, the straining of its interpretative reach is a sign that, in the study of the Gothic Fifties, one methodology has gradually replaced another. Moving on from the more openly announced Gothic themes in Fifties culture, and especially the cinema of the period, to the more deeply encoded, the range of interpretations increases while the textual basis for each interpretation appears to diminish in turn. This is not to say that the more counter-intuitive readings are less valid, or that critics examining the 1950s from the vantage point of historical hindsight can legitimately claim to know better what troubled Americans during the Fifties than those Americans in the Fifties did themselves. It is to acknowledge – and to attempt to do justice to – the complexity of the period and its representational politics, and thus contribute to a more complete and accurate assessment. The limited use of black characters in Fifties films might acquire a different set of connotations when not solely dismissed as a half-hearted concession to the post-war movie audience being more racially integrated, that is, as a racist form of tokenism; a Gothic reading, instead, might recognise the destabilising power of these marginal characters, their power to haunt a narrative that pretends to achieve stability and closure by denying race altogether. Similarly, reading the culture of the American Fifties through the lens of the Gothic might return traumatic events such as the Korean War to full visibility, and, in the process, disrupt a discursive tradition, again rife with racist overtones, that is still ongoing seventy years later.

Generally speaking, the outcome of the broadening of interpretative options might be a rebranding of the 1950s, a paradigm change that finally weans us off the familiar image of the calm after and the calm before the storm, substituting for this image one that recognises the decade for the troubled, tense, nervous and anxious period that it was. If evidence for the urgency of such a historical reminder is needed, one need look no further than the most recent political instrumentalisation of the 1950s. It takes no great stretch of the imagination to see a sanitised, de-Gothicised vision of the Fifties figuring significantly in the reactionary 'Make America Great Again' agenda that still casts its pall over American politics after the change of administrations in 2021. Today, American conservatism continues to rely on a nostalgic vision of the Fifties that comes – appreciated by some, decried by others – with the full complement of the past's troubling ideological issues. For this very reason, the critical recognition of Gothic interventions in the repressive dynamic at work throughout American culture in the 1950s still matters. That the Gothic, then and now, should play a role in recognising, conceptualising, fomenting, expressing and processing what remains a precarious state of the nation is recognition of its sensibility and utility as a conceptual and artistic tool.

Key Works

Bigger Than Life (1956). Though commercially less successful than *Rebel Without a Cause*, Nicholas Ray emphasises his earlier film's Gothic tendencies, creating a story that lingers ambiguously between horror and male melodrama.
The Man in the Grey Flannel Suit (1956). Adaptation of Sloan Wilson's novel, fixing the central character and his problems as a defining statement about the decade in the public imagination.
I Married a Monster from Outer Space (1958). Low-budget science fiction and horror film with an alien invasion/impostor metaphor that, in its lack of specificity, captures Fifties suburban paranoia more accurately than thematically more self-conscious films.
The Twilight Zone (1959–64). A veritable inventory of the period's topical anxieties, looking back, like some of the best of Fifties culture, over the decade from its very end. Series creator, showrunner and writer Rod Serling's personal experiences with war also contributed to some of the period's most explicit critical commentary on racism (for example, 'The Encounter' from 1964), foregrounded in the 2019 series reboot supervised by Jordan Peele.
Short fiction by a host of pulp writers – Richard Matheson, Ray Bradbury, Robert Bloch, Fritz Leiber and others – whose work during the 1950s began to strip the Gothic of its antiquarian trappings and bring it into the modern world.

Further Critical Reading

Hoberman, J., *An Army of Phantoms: American Movies and the Making of the Cold War* (2011). An excellent detailed account of the political forces shaping Fifties culture, not just in America at large but, more importantly, within the US film industry itself; Hoberman's reading prepares the ground for further critics working to highlight Gothic elements in films and genres not commonly associated with the Gothic.
Jancovich, Mark, *Rational Fears: American Horror in the 1950s* (1996). The key text focused specifically on horror, both in film and popular fiction of the period, marking the critical engagement with social and political issues in Fifties popular culture and film beyond the agenda previously established by Sontag's 'Imagination of Disaster'.
Kaplan, Fred, *1959: The Year Everything Changed* (2009). Discussion of a wide range of Fifties American culture (from *Mad* magazine to cool jazz) that balances an account of the period's ideological repression with an appreciation of the variety and creativity of the cultural responses to that repression.
Nadel, Alan, *Demographic Angst: Cultural Narratives and American Films of the 1950s* (2018). The most incisive close readings of an idiosyncratic selection of Fifties films (*West Side Story*, *Singin' in the Rain*, *All About Eve*) in recent years, capturing the sense of the 1950s as a troubled, nervous decade. Though Nadel is not explicitly engaged in 'gothicising' the Fifties, his ability

to detect and describe anxieties in these films where one would least expect them merits praise for being itself a 'Gothic intervention'.

Sontag, Susan, 'The Imagination of Disaster' (1965). First essay-length yet major critical engagement with what was then considered the lowest form of cinematic entertainment, that is, Fifties science fiction and horror movies, as a cultural articulation of the period's Cold War anxieties; Sontag's agenda still dominates much writing on Fifties pop culture.

Bibliography

Basinger, Jeanine, *The World War II Combat Film: Anatomy of a Genre* (Middletown, CT: Wesleyan University Press, 2003).

Carson, Rachel, *Silent Spring* [1962] (Boston: Houghton Mifflin, 2002).

Engelhardt, Tom, *The End of Victory Culture: Cold War America and the Disillusioning of a Generation* [1995], rev. edn (Amherst, MA: University of Massachusetts Press, 2007).

Friedan, Betty, *The Feminine Mystique* [1963] (Harmondsworth: Penguin, 2010).

'Herbert Marcuse', in *Stanford Encyclopedia of Philosophy*, <https://plato.stanford.edu/entries/Marcuse/> (last accessed 12 July 2020).

Hoberman, J., *An Army of Phantoms: American Movies and the Making of the Cold War* (New York: New Press, 2012).

Jancovich, Mark, *Rational Fears: American Horror in the 1950s* (Manchester: Manchester University Press, 1996).

Kaplan, Fred, *1959: The Year Everything Changed* (Hoboken, NJ: Wiley, 2009).

Lenth, Robert J., *Korean War Filmography: 91 English Language Features through 2000* (Jefferson, NC: McFarland, 2003).

Levin, Ira, *The Stepford Wives* [1972] (New York: William Morrow, 2002).

Luce, Henry R., 'The American Century' [1941], reprint, *Diplomatic History*, 23.2, 1999, pp. 159–71, <http://www-personal.umich.edu/~mlassite/discussions261/luce.pdf.> (last accessed 12 July 2020).

Munford, Rebecca, 'Spectral Femininity', in Avril Horner and Sue Zlosnik (eds), *Women and the Gothic: An Edinburgh Companion* (Edinburgh: Edinburgh University Press, 2016), pp. 120–34.

Nadel, Alan, *Demographic Angst: Cultural Narratives and Films of the 1950s* (New Brunswick, NJ: Rutgers University Press, 2018).

Sides, Hampton, 'Remembering the Forgotten War', *The New York Times*, 11 November 2018, https://www.nytimes.com/2018/11/11/opinion/remembering-the-forgotten-war.html (last accessed 20 October 2021).

Sontag, Susan, 'The Imagination of Disaster' [1965], in Gregg Rickman (ed.), *The Science Fiction Film Reader* (New York: Limelight, 2004), pp. 98–114.

Wilson, Sloan, *The Man in the Grey Flannel Suit* [1955] (New York: Thunder Mouth's Press, 1983).

Filmography

All that Heaven Allows (dir. Douglas Sirk, USA, 1955).
Bigger Than Life (dir. Nicholas Ray, USA, 1956).
First Man into Space (dir. Robert Day, USA, 1959).
I Married a Monster from Outer Space (dir. Gene Fowler Jr, USA, 1958).
The Incredible Shrinking Man (dir. Jack Arnold, USA, 1957).
Invaders from Mars (dir. William Cameron Menzies, USA, 1953).
The Man in the Grey Flannel Suit (dir. Nunnally Johnson, USA, 1956).
Rebel Without a Cause (dir. Nicholas Ray, USA, 1955).
The Stepford Wives (dir. Bryan Forbes, USA, 1975).
Them! (dir. Gordon Douglas, USA, 1954).
The Twilight Zone (TV series, created by Rod Serling, USA, 1959–64).
The War of the Worlds (dir. Byron Haskin, USA, 1953).

Notes

1. Luce, 'The American Century', p. 159.
2. For a detailed explanation of the term, see Engelhardt, *The End of Victory Culture*, esp. ch. 1: 'Triumphalist Despair', pp. 3–15.
3. Tom Engelhardt's *The End of Victory Culture* is infused with this scepticism, as is Alan Nadel's *Demographic Angst*. Fred Kaplan's *1959: The Year Everything Changed* balances both ends of the spectrum, plotting social and political anxieties against the creative (at times *exuberantly* creative) responses to these very crises.
4. Underlying the argument is the close connection between the Gothic and the Freudian uncanny, supplemented by Herbert Marcuse's concept of 'surplus repression', adding an ideological dimension to the Freudian concept. On Marcuse and 'surplus repression', see 'Herbert Marcuse', *Stanford Encyclopedia of Philosophy*.
5. Munford, 'Spectral Femininity', p. 125.
6. Carson, *Silent Spring*, pp. 1, 2.
7. Ibid., p. 2.
8. Though nuclear testing does, in the strict sense, qualify as pollution, the explicit arrival of environmental horror would come with the cycle of 1970s films including *Squirm* (dir. Jeff Lieberman, 1976), *The Long Weekend* (dir. Colin Eggleston, 1978) and *Prophecy* (dir. John Frankenheimer, 1979).
9. Andrew Currie's *Fido* (2006), another film inspired by Sirk's melodramatic examination of suburban plight, takes its cue more directly from Sirk's focus on social class. A deft critical reading might succeed in teasing out a racial subtext to Currie's zombie metaphor situating itself at the intersection of race and class in the suburban space, but the film's post-9/11 context reroutes such racial concerns towards anxieties over the social impact of the modern security state.
10. Ira Levin's novel gives the Hendrys a full scene earlier on (*The Stepford Wives*, pp. 71–4), omitted from the film, in which our Gothic heroine,

Joanna Eberhardt, interacts directly with Ruthanne Hendry. The conversation with the articulate young woman, who is intensely aware of her race in her new suburban environment, ends up making Joanna feel 'very white' (p. 74).
11. Those still sceptical as to whether Ray as a director is conscious of pursuing an agenda across both films might take note of the fact that Richie is wearing a bright red jacket in that scene, a direct reference to James Dean's iconic look in *Rebel Without a Cause*.
12. Sides, 'Remembering the Forgotten War'.
13. When it comes to explaining the causes for the collective amnesia, commentators return time and again to a few central ideas: that the Korean War was only vaguely defined, conceptually blurry, not a real war but an international police action, a military intervention, or some such euphemism; that the stalemate that ended the Korean War lacked the sense of closure or dramatic resolution required for a persuasive and enduring historical narrative, foreclosing a triumphalism necessary for fond memorialisation; or that the United States, still exhausted from the effort of the Second World War, never really wanted to engage in the conflict – a lack of enthusiasm going in that directly connects to the lack of interest coming out.
14. Sloan Wilson's novel mentions the Korean War only in passing, referring to it as part of the historical backdrop, barely registering, or, in a more revealing passage early on, as 'the Korean one' (*The Man in the Grey Flannel Suit*, p. 12), as it laments that 'it was no longer fashionable to talk about the war [i.e. the Second World War], and certainly it had never been fashionable to talk about the number of men one had killed' (pp. 12–13): note how the passage represses discussion of the Korean War by projecting that repression as a lamentable fact of post-war American life on to the Second World War.
15. Basinger, *The World War II Combat Film*, p. 159.
16. Nadel, *Demographic Angst*, p. 132.
17. Ibid., p. 132.

Chapter 13

Masks of Sanity: Psychopathy and the Twentieth-Century Gothic
Bernice M. Murphy

Gothic and horror fiction has long been fascinated by individuals whose apparent lack of empathy and refusal (or inability) to adhere to conventional social norms and moral constraints means that they are capable of deeply transgressive acts, up to and including murder. As Kurt A. Kiehl observes, while the German psychiatrist J. L. A. Koch

> is credited with coining the term *psychopastiche*, or *psychopath* (meaning 'suffering soul') ... Psychopaths, under a different label or terminology, captivated attention long before Koch. Indeed, since humans first evolved, history has recorded stories of humans who display what we now understand to be the disorder of psychopathy.[1]

Edgar Allan Poe, who so often penned first-person narratives recounted by protagonists experiencing extreme and unreliable mental states, also created one of the most chilling nineteenth-century portraits of what we would now recognise as probable psychopathy. In 'The Cask of Amontillado' (1846), the narrator, Montresor, recounts how he had long resolved to 'punish with impunity' a rival named Fortunato who caused him grave (but unspecified) offence.[2] Knowing that Fortunato thinks of himself as a connoisseur, the narrator lures him to his family vaults on the pretence of having him sample a cask of Amontillado wine. Once there, Montresor chains Fortunato inside an alcove, and then walls the man in, impervious to his desperate cries. The final lines underline Montresor's satisfaction: 'Against the new masonry I re-erected the old rampart of bones. For the half of a century no mortal has disturbed them. *In pace resquiescat!*'[3]

Like several of the other fictional psychopaths referenced in this chapter, Montresor's actions are additionally troubling because he gets away with his crime. Although he clearly experiences the confessional impulse also felt by the narrators of 'The Tell-Tale Heart' (1843) and 'The Black Cat' (1843), he is an altogether more collected figure. The façade is so convincing that even Montresor's victim has no inkling of danger until his fate – like the recess in which he has been chained – has been sealed.

In his pioneering 1941 volume *The Mask of Sanity: An Attempt to Clarify Some Issues About the So-Called Psychopathic Personality*, psychiatrist Hervey M. Cleckley stated that psychopathy could be distinguished from more 'orthodox psychoses'. With the latter, he noted, there is generally a visibly altered reasoning process or 'other demonstrable personality feature' which makes those conditions readily detectable. This is not the case with psychopathy. Instead, 'The observer is confronted with a convincing mask of sanity.'[4] Using this resonant phrase as a starting point, I will now discuss some of the ways in which the concept of psychopathy impacted upon mid-to-late twentieth-century Gothic fiction, focusing on works in which human 'monsters' hide in plain sight.

The literary and filmic prominence of the 'killer among us' trope owes much to the post-WWII move away from horrors of a supernatural nature to those of a very human variety.[5] It also reflected the rapidly evolving cultural and medical debate regarding the correct way to 'treat' (or safely contain) individuals who seemed to pose a threat to those around them and to society at large. In his discussion of the frequency with which serial murderers (the most prominent variety of fictional psychopath) have appeared in cinema, Philip Jenkins notes that while such films can be traced back to 'the early days of cinema, especially in Germany', there were also many films of this type made in Hollywood between the 1930s and the 1960s.

> Multiple killers were frequent villains in films in the period during and after the second world war, and they were a mainstay of pulp fiction [...] Robert Bloch himself remarked on the post-war revival of the psychopath as a villain in fiction, and how '[p]sychopathology defied the deductive method. The psychotics emerged to confound all the bright young men and little old ladies playing detectives.'[6]

As David W. Jones observes, Cleckley's book did much to heighten public awareness of psychopathy.[7] *The Mask of Sanity* 'was ostensibly somewhat atheoretical and descriptive, but helped to establish a view of psychopathy as a psychological disposition that might well be associated with disorder and destructiveness and also might, in various manifestations, be found right across the population'.[8] The book also popularised the figure of the 'psychopath', even though Cleckley was himself 'rather doubtful about the utility of the term'.[9] Cleckley described the 'typical psychopath' in this manner:

> Alert and friendly in his attitude, he is easy to talk with and seems to have a good many genuine interests. There is nothing at all odd or queer about him, and in every respect he tends to embody the concept of a well-adjusted, happy person. Nor does he, on the other hand, seem to be artificially exerting himself like one who is covering up or who wants to sell you a bill of goods ... *He looks like the real thing* ... Although the psychopath's inner emotional deviations and deficiencies may be comparable with the inner status of the masked schizophrenic, he outwardly shows nothing brittle or strange.[10] (italics mine)

The checklist of characteristics, which Cleckley outlined and further refined in subsequent editions, was a key aspect of his book.[11] Jones highlights the extent to which the psychopathic individual's apparent 'normality' was highlighted.

> The first three characteristics are significant in emphasising the apparent normality of the presentation of the individual. As the title of Cleckley's work suggests, the appearance as a sane individual is a key feature. Such individuals often show superficial charm and good intelligence (1) – indeed, they may well be able to create a particularly good impression in social situations. They will be able to remain very calm and demonstrate an absence of 'nervousness' or psychoneurotic manifestations (3). Most crucially, of course, they have a perfectly rational understanding of the world and will not exhibit any sign of delusions or irrational thinking (2).[12]

Both Jones and Cleckley's most famous successor, Robert Hare creator of the 'Psychopathy Checklist' – observe that the arrival and aftermath of the Second World War was crucial in creating 'official' (military and medical) interest in the concept. Hare notes of the 'mad or bad' debate which dominated clinical discussions of such individuals that

> World War II gave the debate a new, practical urgency – more than speculation was necessary, First, with the military draft, the need became pressing to identify, diagnose, and if possible treat individuals who could disrupt or even destroy strict military control, and this issue drew lively public attention. But an even more ominous significance arose with the revelation of the Nazis' machinery of destruction and their cold-blooded program of extermination. What were the dynamics of such a development? How and why could individuals – even, horrifyingly, one individual in charge of a nation – operate outside the rules that most people accepted as restraints on their basest impulses and fantasies?[13]

Peter Vronsky, one of the most prominent current commentators on the subject of serial murder, has argued that the psychological aftermath of the Second World War damaged an entire generation of American men who would grow up to father sons who were much more likely to become serial killers than their equivalents in previous generations.[14] For Vronsky, the combination of a generation of American fathers who were afflicted with wartime trauma, rapidly changing social and gender mores, and misogynistic and lurid reading material targeted at men and boys all helped to create a toxic environment that facilitated an 'epidemic' of sexually motivated serial murder that would last for over fifty years. When discussing the sexually violent imagery found in many men's magazines of the 1940s and 1950s, Vronsky formulates his inquiry in decidedly Gothic terms.

> Why had the Greatest Generation and their sons fed on this sadistically depraved popular literature and imagery after the war? Why did this material even exist? What really happened to our fathers and grandfathers in that war? What dark secrets were encoded in this literature and its imagery? What made these men and their sons so angry with women?[15]

The connection that Vronsky makes between the war, misogyny and murderous psychopathy is explicitly expressed in the novel *In a Lonely Place* by Dorothy B. Hughes (1947). The protagonist is a former US airman named Dix Steele, who wanders the streets of Los Angeles at night in search of young women to strangle. As is the case in later novels of this nature, Steele's seemingly 'ordinary' façade is highlighted by an early physical description. When catching up with an old war buddy, Steele visualises himself being looked at by his friend:

> He knew exactly what Brub saw, as if Brub was a mirror he was standing before. A young fellow, just an average young fellow. Tanned, medium light hair with a little curl, medium tall and enough weight for height. Eyes, hazel; nose and mouth right for the face, a good-looking face but nothing to remember, nothing to set it apart from the usual.[16]

Steele is a cynical social climber with a talent for latching on to wealthier acquaintances. At the behest of a wealthy uncle, he attended Princeton before dropping out to join the air corps. He is also handsome and charming, and claims to be working on a book, although apart from socialising, sleeping and murder, he appears not to do much at all. Steele's misogyny makes itself apparent not only in terms of his acts of brutal sexual violence, but also in the total contempt that he expresses towards his victims. He callously reflects on the existence of one of these women: 'Her name was Mildred Atkinson and she had led a very stupid life . . . The only exciting thing that had ever happened to her was to be raped and murdered. Even then, she'd only been subbing for someone else.'[17]

For Steele, the war years were

> the first happy years he'd ever known. You didn't have to kowtow to the stinking rich, you were all equal in pay; and before long you were the rich guy ... You were the Mister, you were what you'd always wanted to be, class. You could have any woman you wanted in Africa or India or England or Australia or the United States, or any place in the world. The world was yours. That life was so real there wasn't any other life. Even when the war was over there was no realization of another life.[18]

The connection between Steele's war experiences and his compulsive violence in the present day is underlined by this sense that life has lost the sense of opportunity he experienced during wartime. Mentions of LA's 'fog' occur on several occasions, as though Steele's inner sense of disconnection is reflected in the city's atmospheric conditions. The point is reinforced by the climactic revelation that his recent crimes against women are re-enactments of the first murder he ever committed: the victim was a young woman he met while stationed in England.[19]

In A Lonely Place was not only one of the first modern serial killer novels: with Steele – who also murders a male friend so that he can use his car, clothes, money and house – Hughes had also created a character whose eye for a chance anticipated that of a much better known post-war psychopath: Patricia Highsmith's Tom Ripley, who made his first appearance in 1955. Unlike Steele, however, who is cornered by the police in the final pages of Hughes's novel, at the end of Highsmith's first Ripley novel the increasingly brazen acts of identity theft, fraud and murder undertaken by her devious anti-hero have so far gone unpunished.

Another dangerous young white man who wears a convincing 'mask of sanity' – at least for a while – is the protagonist of Jim Thompson's *The Killer Inside Me* (1952). The novel further underlines the extent to which post-war noir intersected with and anticipated themes that would come to dominate non-supernatural Gothic narratives during this period. *The Killer Inside Me* is related from the perspective of Lou Ford, a deputy sheriff in smalltown Texas who has been repressing '*the sickness*' since he was a teenager.[20] Beneath his façade of good-natured ordinariness and his penchant for folksy aphorisms, Ford is a repellent sadist who inflicts horrific sexual violence on women, although, as is the case with Dix Steele, his viciousness is not always confined to this category of victim.

In his downtime, Ford peruses the extensive library assembled by his late father, a medical doctor who realised early on that his son had dangerous proclivities. The bookcase includes

> endless files of psychiatric literature, the bulky volumes of morbid psychology ... Krafft-Ebing, Jung, Freud, Blueler, Adolf Meyer, Kretschmer, Kraepelin ... All the answers were here, out in the open where you could look at them. And no one was terrified or horrified. I came out of the place I was hiding in – that I always had to hide in – and began to breathe.[21]

Ford's relationship with his father anticipates plot strands found in the TV series *Dexter* (2006–13) and the 2012 Gothic thriller *Stoker*, both of which include flashbacks to the younger days of their psychopathic protagonists during which their 'true' nature is recognised by a father who encourages them to contain or strategically 'channel' these urges. 'The mask of sanity' conceived of by Cleckley is much in evidence throughout Thompson's novel, until Ford's rapidly escalating spiral of violent behaviour comes to a fiery and self-destructive climax (although he does succeed in murdering one of his most sorely abused female victims just before he blows himself up, thereby dying on his own hateful terms).

Ford has, up until this point, pretended to fit in with the people around him, unless it suits him to do otherwise.

> A typical Western-country peace officer, that was me. Maybe friendlier looking than the average. Maybe a little cleaner cut. But on the whole typical. That's what I was, and I couldn't change. Even if I was safe, I doubted if I could change. I'd pretended so long I no longer had to.[22]

As Philip Simpson, who sees this novel, along with *The Talented Mr Ripley*, as being key to the transition between noir and the post-war 'psycho thrillers' (as he dubs such texts) notes:

> In Ford, the reader can discern many of the characteristics of what came to be known as the serial killer: a charming, friendly, and harmless looking fellow in a position of respectability, but whose mask of normalcy conceals a twisted desire to harm other people for the most idiosyncratic of reasons. Integral to the effect that Thompson creates in the novel is the sense of intimacy between Ford's sociopathology and the reader. By the novel's end, the reader has come to understand and even empathise with Ford, simply because so much time has been spent in his psyche. Disturbingly, the narrative tempts the reader to partake of Ford's attitudes and, by implication, to assume some degree of his sociopathology. Such reader/character identification, seemingly benign in other types of fiction, takes on a disconcerting edge in the psycho thriller.[23]

As my analysis thus far has suggested, these kinds of narratives overwhelmingly focus upon young white men who are able to evade detection because of who they are and what they appear to represent. However, there is one major exception to this trend: Rhoda Penmark, the eight-year-old psychopath whose horrific actions compel her good-natured mother Christine towards drastic actions in William March's novel *The Bad Seed* (1954).

Rhoda is a disconcertingly mature child whose self-centred murders anticipate the escapades of later female psychopaths such as the manipulative high schooler Sue Anne Stepanek in the film *Pretty Poison* (1968), and the cyanide-dispensing teenager Rynne Jacobs in Laird Koenig's *The Little Girl Who Lives Down the Lane* (novel 1974/film 1976). Rhoda doesn't quite manage to fool everyone – we are told that the other children in her school 'feared and detested' her before she is asked to leave after the 'accidental' drowning of a little rival. Additionally, in a case of like recognising like, Leroy, the sleazy janitor of Rhoda's apartment building, soon figures out exactly what kind of creature she is and pays for this realisation with his life.[24] Nevertheless, by the end of the novel Rhoda has got away with three murders. Whereas Lou Ford in *The Killer Inside Me* believes that the sexual abuse that he endured as a child helped twist him into what he has become in adulthood (although, as noted earlier, there is also an inherent 'wrongness' to him), there is no suggestion here that childhood mistreatment has played a part in creating a future killer. We are left in no doubt that Rhoda Penmark had an entirely loving, comfortable upbringing with two adoring, good-hearted parents. As the novel's title suggests, she is a creature of pure, malevolent and inescapable 'nature'.[25]

As her suspicions about Rhoda's behaviour escalate, her loving mother Christine rediscovers a horrific secret about her own childhood which she has hitherto repressed. Her biological mother – Rhoda's grandmother – was a notorious serial killer named Bessie Denker. In the opinion of Christine's neighbour Reginald, a true-crime buff, Bessie got away with her crimes for many years because she cultivated every appearance of goodness:

> these monsters of real life usually looked and behaved in a more normal manner than their actually normal brothers and sisters; they presented a more convincing picture of virtue than virtue presented of itself – just as the wax rosebud or the plastic peach seemed more perfect to the eye, more what the mind thought a rosebud or peach should be, than the imperfect original from which it had been modelled.[26]

It is clear that Rhoda has inherited this same capacity for concealing her true nature: yet again, the façade of 'normality' allows the post-war psychopath to hide in plain sight.

Christine gradually accepts that Rhoda has been irrevocably 'tainted' by their shared bloodline. She resolves to end the cycle by killing them both so that this secret might never be known. Her plan is only partially successful, however: Christine shoots herself, but Rhoda is saved by concerned neighbours. In contrast to the condescending *deus ex machina* that the Hays Code demanded be tacked on to the end of the 1956 film version – Rhoda is struck by lightning, thereby receiving divine retribution – the novel offers no such neat assurance of 'justice'. As the novel ends, she sits amid a group of grieving but adoring adults. None of them suspect that she is a born killer who will surely do even more damage in future. 'At least Rhoda was spared. You still have Rhoda to be thankful for' her devastated father is told in the closing lines.[27]

I will conclude by discussing two slightly later novels in which the connection between supposed 'ordinariness' and psychopathy is again foregrounded: *The Collector* (1963) by John Fowles, and *The Vanishing* (*Het Gouden Ei*) by Tim Krabbé (1984). Both novels also further highlight the extent to which misogynistic violence had become a dominant trope in the post-war psychopath narrative. As in *In A Lonely Place*, here young women simply going about their daily lives become the targets of obsessive and sadistic male protagonists whose attempts to justify their horrific actions to themselves and to the reader only emphasise their cruelty and absolute lack of empathy.

The Collector had an important influence on later depictions of fictional psychopathy, not least because the behaviour of the psychopathic protagonist has elements in common with that of Jame Gumb from *The Silence of the Lambs* (1988/film 1991), who is also an amateur lepidopterist. Fowles's protagonist (and primary narrator) is Frederick Clegg, a young man from a working-class English background who recently worked as a clerk for the local council. Clegg has two all-consuming hobbies – butterfly collecting, and obsessively recording the comings and goings of Miranda, the beautiful art student whose family home is located opposite his workplace.[28]

As the novel's title suggests, Clegg's penchant for 'catching' beautiful creatures and keeping them for his own delectation extends beyond butterflies. A large win on the pools (a kind of lottery in which one tries to accurately guess football results) gives him the money – and the sense of entitlement – that turns his fantasies of 'capturing' Miranda and keeping her prisoner until she falls in love with him into a reality.

Clegg's American predecessor Lou Ford needled other people by spouting off banal aphorisms while also using his folksy language to disguise the seething aggression of 'the killer inside'. The language used here is also important. Clegg's account of his 'relationship' with Miranda is strewn with banal fillers and unconvincing attempts to justify his actions, which only reinforce his selfishness and lack of personal insight. For instance, he repeatedly describes her as his 'guest', a term that elides the horror and criminality of his actions. To advance his plan, he purchases a 'special' van and a cottage deep in the remote English countryside. Throughout the novel, Clegg's methodical actions contradict his claim that 'the whole idea was sudden, like a stroke of genius almost', and that without the money, he never would have acted on his sick obsession.[29] Of his new home – and the cellar concealed by the back door – he claims that once the door was closed, 'it was like down there didn't exist. It was two worlds. It's always been like that. Some days I've woken up and it's all been a dream, till I went down again.'[30]

Once he has prepared a cell, Clegg drugs Miranda with chloroform and snatches her from a London street before imprisoning her in a specially outfitted cellar on his property. However, his wilfully naïve hope that he will be able to woo her with his 'gentlemanly' behaviour soon runs up against reality: Miranda is not one of his butterflies. 'It was not like having a net and catching a specimen you wanted . . . It wasn't easy like it was with a killing-bottle. And it was twice as difficult with her, because I didn't want to kill her, that was the last thing I wanted.'[31] The repetition in those final lines is important: it suggests that subconsciously Clegg has always known that his fanatical desire to possess Miranda will have fatal consequences.

In yet another instance of toxic self-justification, Clegg blames the difference in social status which divides them for the failure of his plan. 'There was always class between us.'[32] As Clegg pathetically tries to win Miranda's 'love', his captive alternates between terror, the resolve to survive, contempt, and to begin with even a degree of pity for her captor. When the narrative switches to Miranda's perspective, it is clear that their class difference has indeed informed her perceptions of him (and may have also led her to underestimate his capacity for violence). Her initial description of Clegg emphasises the social tensions that inform their 'relationship', but also her captor's initially unthreatening demeanour:

> He's got one of those funny inbetween voices, uneducated trying to be educated. It keeps on letting him down. Dull black hair. It waves and recedes, it's coarse. Stiff. Always in place. He always wears a sports coat and flannels and a pinned tie. Even cuff-links. He's what people call 'a nice young man'.[33]

As her time as a prisoner extends to days and then weeks, Miranda gradually comes to realise that her initial survival strategies are futile, especially once Clegg begins to act upon his dangerous sexual fantasies. 'He's not human; he's an empty space disguised as a human.'[34] Eventually, after a failed escape attempt, Miranda catches pneumonia from her captor and dies. Clegg callously refuses her delirious pleas for help to the very last. His reaction to the death provides us with yet another indication of his characteristic retreat towards toxic banality: 'Well, I shut her mouth up and got the eyelids down. I didn't know what to do then, I went up and made myself a cup of tea.'[35]

Although Clegg initially claims to have considered killing himself so that he and Miranda can be buried together like 'Romeo and Juliet' – 'It would be a real tragedy, not sordid'[36] – in the opening line of the final chapter he sheepishly admits that 'As it happened, things turned out rather different.'[37] Three weeks later, Miranda's body lies buried under the apple trees in his garden. Clegg claims that he will 'never have a guest again', but, as has been the case throughout the novel, he contradicts himself soon thereafter. He already has his eye on a local shop girl, someone who 'isn't as pretty as Miranda, of course, but that was my mistake before, aiming too high ... I ought to have got someone who would respect me more. Someone ordinary I could teach.'[38] Clegg's entirely unrepentant final reflections on his 'relationship' with Miranda resemble those of Montresor, who also walled up a hapless victim below ground: 'I shall put what she wrote and her hair up in the loft in the deed-box which will not be opened until my death, so I don't expect for forty or fifty years.'[39] In contrast to Miranda's sadly abbreviated narrative – a diary of her imprisonment that chronicles the last weeks of an intelligent and self-aware young woman who thought deeply and insightfully about her life and her relationships – Clegg's closing thoughts emphasise that he has learned absolutely nothing from this episode and will likely continue to engage in the same toxic pattern of behaviour.

As well as anticipating Jame Gumb's penchant for imprisoning young women in his basement, Clegg's actions – and his sense of absolute impunity – have much in common with the final psychopath I will discuss in this chapter: Raymond Lemorne, from Tim Krabbé's 1984 novella *The Vanishing*. The first chapter is related from the perspective of a young man named Rex, who, along with his girlfriend Saskia, is on a road trip across Europe. Their drive is interrupted when Rex petulantly responds to Saskia's concern that they might run out of petrol by pulling in at a random petrol station. Saskia goes inside to buy drinks while Rex waits in the car. He is first irritated, and then increasingly concerned by her failure to re-emerge. As the wait extends for hours, and then weeks, it becomes clear that Saskia has vanished, seemingly without a trace.

We are then introduced to the man who is responsible for Saskia's disappearance. Raymond Lemorne is a seemingly everyday husband and father. However, when he was sixteen years old, he was suddenly seized with the desire to jump off an apartment balcony (and did so, breaking his arm and leg). Young Lemorne was apparently possessed by the kind of self-destructive impulsiveness which Poe defined as 'The Imp of the Perverse' (1845). Over twenty years later, and now an outwardly respectable chemistry teacher and family man, Lemorne experiences a recurrence of this inexplicable urge to do something unthinkable after he rescues a little girl from drowning. He is showered with praise for his bravery.

> The dive into the canal now felt like a stroke of luck: Lemorne tingled in his new clothes, which fit him to a tee, he revelled in the silent admiration that surrounded him at every step, and he thought, 'But would I also be capable of something evil?' He imagined the most gruesome deed he could come up with.[40]

Like Clegg, Lemorne initially tells himself that his horrific idea is strictly hypothetical: a harmless, if macabre thought experiment. However, he gradually begins to flesh out his plan by mixing up a batch of chloroform and prepping the remote rural cottage owned by his family. Lemorne realises that these actions have lent his otherwise normal life a piquancy that had previously been lacking. 'It was a game of the mind, incredibly exciting.'[41] He revels in planning an act that he knows would horrify anyone aware of his intentions. 'Hundreds of people could see him, did see him – and didn't know what they were seeing: a step towards a profoundly vile deed. He felt gleefully evil: as though he had drunk a potion of invisibility.'[42] Lemorne also has a particular kind of victim in mind: 'From the very start it had been a girl – perhaps because the child he'd saved had been a girl. But it mustn't be a child: it had to be someone who was fully aware of what was being done to her.'[43] Lemorne carries out numerous trial runs before randomly encountering Saskia and coaxing her into his car.

The final chapter outlines what happens when Lemorne contacts Rex, several years later, and offers to end his agony by telling him the truth about what happened to Saskia. Rex soon realises that he has seen him before – at the petrol station on that fateful day. 'A gentleman of about fifty, tall and well-groomed, cordial and at the same time commanding.'[44] Lemorne admits that Saskia is dead and shows Rex proof that he has been in contact with her, but refuses to reveal exactly what happened unless Rex agrees to a dreadful bargain. To know the truth, Rex will have to 'undergo the same thing'.[45] Wracked by guilt and consumed by the need to 'find' Saskia, Rex impulsively takes Lemorne up on his offer, gets into his car, and, once they return to the petrol station where it all began, willingly drinks from a coffee thermos which he knows contains a powerful sleeping draught. When Rex awakes in total darkness, it takes him a few moments to realise where he is, but then the terrible realisation sinks in. 'He was in a box, buried alive.'[46] So far as everyone except Raymond Lemorne is concerned, as the novella's chilling final line puts it, he and Saskia 'seemed to have vanished from the face of the earth'.[47]

Featuring as it does another tremendously bleak ending, and a psychopath who has entirely escaped justice – or even the faintest hint of suspicion – *The Vanishing* again underlines the Gothic resonances of the 'mask of sanity' trope popularised by Cleckley just before the Second World War began. Lemorne, like his predecessors Frederick Clegg, Dix Steele, Tom Ripley and Rhoda Penmark, epitomises the awful suspicion – validated by the twin horrors of the Holocaust and the atomic bomb, as well as the unstable, repressive and materialistic post-war world that followed – that seemingly 'ordinary' individuals could secretly harbour violent and transgressive impulses which far overshadowed the threat posed by any supernatural menace. Although Dix Steele is a serial killer, and little Rhoda, like her Grandma Bessie, is well on her way to becoming one, as we have seen the post-war psychopath did not necessarily need to rack up a substantial body count to be a profoundly destabilising presence. Such narratives underline the importance of one of the most notable conventions of mid-to-late twentieth-century Gothic: the discovery that 'normality' is an inherently unstable construct beneath which all manner of dreadful possibilities may fester.

Key Works

Shadow of a Doubt (1943). Alfred Hitchcock's film focuses on a charming, seemingly lovable local-boy-made-good whose return to his idyllic home town after many years away is at first a great source of joy to his niece (and namesake). However, it gradually becomes clear that Uncle Charlie is a relentlessly misogynistic murderer. An excellent early example of the 'mask of sanity' trope in action.

Thomas Harris, *Red Dragon* (1981). Hannibal Lecter, the most famous fictional psychopath of the twentieth century (and beyond), makes a small but pivotal debut appearance in this immensely influential gothic novel/police procedural hybrid.

Lionel Shriver, *We Need to Talk About Kevin* (2003). Shriver's controversial bestseller is a spiritual successor to *The Bad Seed*, related from the perspective of a devastated mother who believes that her teenage son was born bad, but also wonders if her own maternal ambivalence has influenced his behaviour.

Gillian Flynn, *Gone Girl* (2012). Flynn's novel is obviously an early twenty-first-century text, but her manipulative and ultimately victorious anti-hero,

Amy Eliot Dunne, is a key example of a female psychopath hiding in plain sight until she is wronged who has much in common with some of her twentieth-century predecessors.

Further Critical Reading

Jones, David, *Disordered Personalities and Crime: An Analysis of the History of Moral Insanity* (2016). An informative analysis of the origins and evolution of the concept of 'moral insanity' (now more usually known as psychopathy/ anti-social personality disorder) – the volume provides useful historical and medical context.

Simpson, Philip, 'Noir and the Psycho Thriller' (2010). Simpson's article provides a succinct overview of the 'psycho thriller' subgenre which emerged during the post-war era. He persuasively argues that these novels placed the narrative focus upon the 'internal workings of the pathological individual psyche', thereby privileging psychology over plot and frequently blurring the lines between good and evil.

Simpson, Philip, *Psycho Paths: Tracking the Serial Killer Through Contemporary American Film and Fiction* (2000). An excellent overview of the ways in which the most culturally visible embodiment of psychopathic behaviour – the serial killer – has been represented in American literature and visual media. Simpson also discusses the relationship between our perceptions of these kinds of human 'monsters' and the wider Gothic tradition.

Bibliography

Black, Will, *Psychopathic Cultures and Toxic Empires* (Edinburgh: Frontline Noir, 2019).

Cleckley, Harvey, *The Mask of Sanity: An Attempt to Clarify Some Issues About the So-Called Psychopathic Personality*, 5th edn (privately printed, 1988).

Fowles, John, *The Collector* [1963] (London: Vintage, 2004).

Hare, Robert D., *Without Conscience: The Disturbing World of Psychopaths Among Us* (London: Guildford Press, 1999).

Hughes, Dorothy B., *In a Lonely Place* [1947], in Sarah Weinman (ed.), *Women Crime Writers: Four Suspense Novels of the 1940s* (New York: Library of America, 2015), pp. 393–578.

Jenkins, Philip, *Using Murder: The Social Construction of Serial Homicide* (London: Routledge, 1994).

Jones, David W., *Disordered Personalities and Crime: An Analysis of the History of Moral Insanity* (Abingdon: Routledge, 2016).

Kiehl, Kurt A., *The Psychopath Whisperer: The Science of Those Without Conscience* (New York: Broadway Books, 2014).

Krabbé, Tim, *The Vanishing* (*Het Gouden Ei*) [1984] (London: Bloomsbury, 2003).

March, William, *The Bad Seed* [1954] (New York: Ecco, 1997).

Matheson, Sue, 'Gathering Butterflies: Lepidopterology, American Serial Killers, and William Wyler's *The Collector* (1965)', *Journal of American Culture*, 43.1, 2020, pp. 10–17.
Poe, Edgar Allan, 'The Cask of Amontillado' [1846], in *Edgar Allan Poe: Selected Tales*, ed. David Van Leer (Oxford: Oxford University Press, 2008), pp. 289–95.
Simpson, Philip, 'Noir and the Psycho Thriller', in Charles Rzepka and Lee Horsley (eds), *A Companion to Crime Fiction* (Oxford: Wiley Blackwell, 2010), pp. 187–97.
Simpson, Philip, *Psycho Paths: Tracking the Serial Killer Through Contemporary American Film and Fiction* (Carbondale, IL: Southern Illinois University Press, 2000).
Skal, David J., *The Monster Show: A Cultural History of Horror* [1993], rev. edn (New York: Farrar, Straus and Giroux, 2001).
Thompson, Jim, *The Killer Inside Me: Jim Thompson Omnibus* [1952] (London: Macmillan, 1995).
Vronsky, Peter, *American Serial Killers: The Epidemic Years 1950–2000* (New York, Penguin, Random House, 2021, ebook).
Vronsky, Peter, *Sons of Cain: A History of Serial Killers from the Stone Age to the Present* (New York, Berkley, 2018).

Notes

1. Kiehl, *The Psychopath Whisperer*, p. 36.
2. Poe, 'Cask of Amontillado', p. 290.
3. Ibid., p. 295.
4. Cleckley, *Mask of Sanity*, p. 369.
5. See, for instance, the arguments outlined in Skal, *The Monster Show*.
6. Jenkins, *Using Murder*, p. 83.
7. Jones, *Disordered Personalities and Crime*, p. 193.
8. Ibid., p. 193.
9. Ibid., p. 194.
10. Cleckley, *Mask of Sanity*, p. 339.
11. Ibid., p. 194.
12. Ibid., p. 194.
13. Hare, *Without Conscience*, pp. 26–7.
14. This is the central thesis of Vronsky's 2021 volume *American Serial Killers: The Epidemic Years 1950–2000*. The theory is also referenced in his 2018 book *Sons of Cain: A History of Serial Killers From the Stone Age to the Present*.
15. Vronsky, *American Serial Killers*, p. 110.
16. Hughes, *In a Lonely Place*, p. 400.
17. Ibid., p. 428.
18. Ibid., p. 488.
19. Ibid., p. 578.
20. Thompson, *The Killer Inside Me*, p. 138.
21. Ibid., pp. 151–2.

22. Ibid., p. 152.
23. Simpson, 'Noir and the Psycho Thriller', p. 193.
24. March, *The Bad Seed*, p. 28.
25. Thompson, *The Killer Inside Me*, p. 201.
26. March, *The Bad Seed*, p. 160.
27. Ibid., p. 217.
28. The intriguing connection between lepidopterists and psychopathy is discussed by Sue Matheson in relation to the film adaptation of *The Collector*. See Matheson, 'Gathering Butterflies'.
29. Fowles, *The Collector*, p. 27.
30. Ibid., p. 21.
31. Ibid., p. 41.
32. Ibid., p. 41.
33. Ibid., p. 122.
34. Ibid., p. 223.
35. Ibid., p. 274.
36. Ibid., p. 276.
37. Ibid., p. 281.
38. Ibid., p. 281.
39. Ibid., p. 281.
40. Krabbé, *The Vanishing*, p. 53.
41. Ibid., p. 57.
42. Ibid., p. 57.
43. Ibid., p. 60.
44. Ibid., p. 98.
45. Ibid., p. 102.
46. Ibid., p. 102.
47. Ibid., p. 115.

Chapter 14

Troubling Legacies: African American Women's Gothic from Zora Neale Hurston to Tananarive Due
Dara Downey

In Octavia Butler's neo-slavery novel *Kindred* (1979), the protagonist, Dana, a young writer living in California in 1976, finds herself repeatedly dragged back to a plantation in early nineteenth-century Maryland every time her white, slave-owning ancestor Rufus finds himself in mortal danger. Due to her skin colour, she must navigate the misery and dangers of slavery, and her inability to control when she travels in time further exacerbates the issue. What is more, each time she returns to the antebellum South, those around her become increasingly disturbed by her uncanny youth, engendering mistrust and suspicion. A few hours in 1976 seem to correspond to years in the nineteenth century, meaning that the other characters age, while she looks exactly the same. Rufus in particular thinks that Dana is 'something different. I don't know what – witch, devil', but the book itself is careful to avoid confirming whether she can command any kind of supernatural powers, despite her time travelling.[1] If anything, her movement between eras exemplifies the slave-owner's power over her, and not her own command of otherworldly forces.

Kindred therefore invokes but also denies associations with Gothic imagery that, as this chapter demonstrates, is racially inflected, and that many twentieth-century black academics and commentators saw as problematic and retrogressive.[2] It does so, however, while still making use of Gothic supernaturalism as a means of narrativising its fundamentally pessimistic view of the unexorcised presence of past violence in a present that sees itself as liberated and progressive. As this suggests, and as this chapter argues, *Kindred* is emblematic of a distinct ambivalence towards Gothic tropes and conventions in twentieth-century fiction by African American women. From Zora Neale Hurston's engagement with Southern and Caribbean hoodoo, voudou and conjure in the 1920s, to Tananarive Due's visions of successful young black women haunted by the very real presence of racialised violence in the American 1990s,

African American women's Gothic fiction walks a perilous line. These texts reject the ultimate optimism of traditional Female Gothic plots, as well as the conventional demonisation of black characters as avatars of Gothic darkness. At the same time, they acknowledge and dramatise the continuing usefulness of Gothic imagery and narrative tropes in excavating, and moving beyond, the horrific history of race relations in the Americas throughout the twentieth century and beyond.

As a set of narrative conventions that pivots upon the unveiling of horrors that result from uneven power relations, the Gothic is a useful means of giving literary shape to the legacy of enslavement in structural racism. For Teresa Goddu, 'the Gothic as a genre emerged' and developed 'in dialogue with the rise of New World slavery and the construction of racial categories'.[3] As she puts it, '[r]epresented as a house of bondage replete with evil villains and helpless victims, vexed bloodlines and stolen birthrights, brutal punishments and spectacular suffering, cruel tyranny and horrifying terror, slavery reads as a Gothic romance'.[4] Specifically, the Gothic's focus on power relations, on the difficulties of breaking free from patterns of behaviour established by and benefiting those in power, and on the past's dangerous hold over the present, renders it easily extrapolated to a wider variety of situations in which inequality leads directly to violence.[5] These elements render the Gothic form eminently applicable to depictions of slavery and racial tyranny. Indeed, nineteenth-century slave narratives by writers such as Frederick Douglass and Harriet Jacobs integrate precisely these motifs into stylistically realist accounts of imprisonment, torture and narrow escapes from the clutches of almost supernaturally powerful 'masters'.

However, before but particularly following Abolition, and on into the twentieth century, the Gothic's associations with the supernatural seemed incompatible with pleas for racial justice. Many African American writers, including Douglass, strove to distance themselves from any associations with folk magic rooted in Afro-Atlantic belief systems.[6] Such a strategy was necessitated by the fact that imaginative writers, the popular press and conservative political commentators worked hard to convert the diasporic reinventions of African religious practices into sources of Gothic terror, dwelling luridly on '[t]he fetish and demon worship, animal sacrifice, cannibalism, nudity, drumming, sexual promiscuity, and interracial "orgies"'.[7] The result of such writing was, according to Michelle Y. Gordon, 'a collective racial imaginary on which justifications for white patriarchal supremacy relied', in which, as Brenda Marie Osbey suggests, the 'impending overthrow of white power or the ritual summoning up of black power' were constructed as identical and equally terrifying to the white hegemony.[8] As Osbey points out, since at least the eighteenth century white culture has striven to establish 'the inherent magical nature of black people. That is to say, they quite often believed that blacks, so far removed, as they saw it, from themselves in historical and social and technological reality, were *naturally possessed of magical properties in their very persons*.'⁹ She attributes this to 'the inability to distinguish among folklore, popular myth and religion', which means that 'any and all belief systems particular to Africans and people of African descent, are assumed to fall into the category conveniently dubbed . . . "Black Magic"', precisely because 'such names as Voodoo and Obeah have historically been used interchangeably'.¹⁰ As a complex range of religious and folk beliefs that clash with Anglo-Protestant austerity and iconoclasm are lumped together and labelled as both naïve superstition and dangerous witchcraft, African American religious forms such as voodoo and conjure have therefore been demonised, marginalised and, via the tourist trade, commodified.

Indeed, as Toni Morrison argues, the US cultural imaginary has long exploited blackness and the thematic aspects of slavery in ways that transform real oppression and violence into figurative means of dramatising white guilt and fear. As she puts it, '[w]hat rose up out of collective needs to allay internal fears and to rationalize external exploitation was an American Africanism – a fabricated brew of darkness, otherness, alarm, and desire that is uniquely American'.¹¹ These stereotypes were exacerbated by colonial attitudes towards 'primitive' folklore. According to Gordon, practices such as hoodoo and conjure were, for enslaved populations, 'a way to ideologically order the world, negotiate bondage and exile, communicate with gods and ancestors, protect themselves and loved ones, solicit revenge or financial success, promote illness or recovery, influence love and desire, and challenge the exercise of white power in and over their lives'.¹² Consequently, as Yvonne P. Chireau demonstrates, Christian missionaries and social reformers sought to detach freed populations from the practices and beliefs that had made their lives bearable during enslavement, ostensibly because such beliefs were seen as superstition, but also because they accorded practitioners a degree of social control and agency. However, many of these same reformers, as well as academics working in the emerging discipline of anthropology, itself very much a colonial enterprise, lamented the loss of the very cultural materials they were trying to stamp out. The result was organisations such as the Hampton Folklore Society and *The Journal of American Folklore*, which sought to collect the kinds of stories that writer and ethnologist Zora Neale Hurston gathered in *Mules and Men* (1935) – stories about the creation of the world and talking animals, about mythic battles between conjurers and the devil, or about slaves calling on the devil's aid in their attempts to resist and survive the horrors of slavery.[13]

Hurston was working and writing during the Harlem Renaissance, a time of creative excitement and innovation among black artists and intellectuals in the early decades of the twentieth century, as the Jim Crow era prompted a mass migration from the rural American South to northern cities such as New York. Like Hurston, many black writers, artists and musicians made use of folklore and traditional musical forms to produce something new, while maintaining a sense of continuity and community in an unfamiliar, often hostile urban setting.[14] At the same time, in doing so, Hurston, Langston Hughes and their counterparts were treading a fine line between preserving and demonstrating the continued relevance of folklore and ritual to the African American population, and avoiding the perpetuation of racist stereotypes that depicted believers and practitioners as either superstitious dupes or demonic practitioners of cannibalism, zombieism and human sacrifice.[15] As Roger Luckhurst demonstrates, this set of Gothic tropes was built on zombie narratives written by visitors to Haiti, such as Lafcadio Hearn, William Seabrook and Wade Davis.[16] These narratives figure the rich material culture of African-derived religions as idolatrous, superstitious and abject, and as inextricable from rebellion against Anglo-Protestant 'rational' control.[17] In the process, 'in an all-out effort to affirm the superiority of European ... civilization', as Nicole Fleetwood asserts, white culture 'projected the worst fears about themselves onto Africans, [and] blackness inadvertently became the repository for all of the *prohibited* qualities that signify communion with nature, the opposite of the (English) ideal of civilization'.[18]

In many ways, twentieth-century Gothic texts perpetuated this tendency. Maisha L. Wester points out the submerged but easily indefinable 'Africanism' (to borrow Morrison's term) in well-known horror novels such as Peter Straub's *Ghost Story* (1979) and Stephen King's *Bag of Bones* (1998).[19] Similar fears of racial 'Otherness' and racially inscribed religious practices operate within (to name a small selection of texts) H. P. Lovecraft's 'The Horror at Red Hook' (1927), Fritz Leiber's *Conjure Wife* (1943), George A. Romero's film *Jack's Wife/Season of the Witch* (1973), Richard Matheson's 'Prey' (1969) and its cinematic adaptation, 'Amelia' in *Trilogy of Terror* (1975), and in the figure of the murderous vaudun priestess Dominga Salvador in Laurell K. Hamilton's *The Laughing Corpse* (1994). Less demonic are the figures of Dick Hallorann in King's *The Shining* (1977), Whoopi Goldberg's medium in *Ghost* (1990) and the Oracle in *The Matrix* (1999), who fit neatly within Osbey's formulation of the 'magical' black man or woman.

These characters feature prominently but briefly, marginalised within the frame and the plot, existing solely to produce an atmosphere of the otherworldly. Whether depicted negatively or positively, they exemplify what Fleetwood calls 'iconicity', which she defines as 'the ways in which singular images ... come to represent a whole host of historical occurrences and processes'.[20] In such images, 'the complexity of black lived experience and discourses of race are effaced. The image functions as abstraction, as decontextualized evidence of historical narrative that is constrained by normative public discourse.'[21]

From the early decades of the twentieth century, such Gothicising rhetoric led to a very reasonable 'desire, especially of working-class black people striving to advance in an ostensibly open and progressive society', to distance themselves from associations with voodoo, hoodoo and conjure.[22] It is for this reason that twentieth-century postcolonialist thinkers such as Frantz Fanon (specifically in *The Wretched of the Earth* [1961]) denounced the aura of superstition that zombie myths had built around Haiti and its inhabitants. At the same time, as Luckhurst argues, Fanon is repeatedly drawn to the image of the zombie as a powerful means of visualising the devastating effects of colonialism and capitalist exploitation throughout the Caribbean and beyond.[23] In other words, Fanon and other commentators – Hurston and her inheritors included – were caught between a fear of revivifying racist stereotypes and Gothic demonisation on the one hand, and, on the other, an awareness of the usefulness of tropes such as the zombie, the voodoo priestess and conjure practices. In line with this cautious truce, Hurston's Gothic stories remain ambivalent about that power as a means for solving day-to-day problems for women navigating the racist world of early twentieth-century America, as evidenced by stories such as 'Black Death', 'The Gilded Six Bits' and 'Spunk'. Her writing acknowledges the perils of employing Gothic tropes and plots, while demonstrating their value as vehicles for both protest and hope. Thus, while many among 'the black elite considered her folk approach demeaning', as Wendy Dutton notes, when the Civil Rights movement erupted several decades later, Hurston's project of recovering these traditions began to take on, in retrospect, an additional political urgency.[24] In the 1960s and 1970s, seeking to counter racist claims of cultural inferiority, academics and cultural commentators worked hard to demonstrate that 'slaves retained elements of West African culture as a defence mechanism that enabled them to preserve a sense of identity' and that persisted into the twentieth century.[25] As the discussion above demonstrates, however, this was also an era during which depictions of Afro-Atlantic religious practices as diabolical and murderous permeated American popular culture.

As Wester points out, while many twentieth-century black American writers were therefore careful not simply to 'mimic traditional gothic conventions, which present various problems and threats', reappropriating the Gothic with an 'awareness of its perils' could help to 'neutralize its dangers'.[26] As I demonstrate in the rest of this chapter, later twentieth-century African American women writers followed Hurston in utilising the Gothic, integrating into it elements of African-derived folklore, while struggling to avoid evoking racist stereotypes. The period 'witnessed a renaissance of black women writers and thinkers, many of whom explored spiritual themes along with questions of gender and sexuality in their work', issues highlighted by a concomitant rise in black literary criticism positing a distinctive and longstanding black culture in the 1980s.[27] These endeavours were given added impetus by the rediscovery of a number of women's slave narratives by Harriet Jacobs and Harriet Wilson, and Toni Morrison's neo-slave narrative *Beloved* (1987) was arguably the most prominent result of this new drive towards recovering black history and culture.[28]

Morrison's novel, set in the early days of Abolition, tells the story of a young woman called Sethe (who has escaped slavery while heavily pregnant) and her daughter Denver. Their house is haunted, and rendered almost uninhabitable, by the 'baby ghost' of Sethe's other daughter, who she killed in a desperate effort to ensure that her children would not be re-enslaved. Tellingly, what is most shocking and unassimilable to the characters in *Beloved* is not the supernatural, which is presented as a normal and accepted part of daily existence, but the horrors of slavery and ongoing racism in the United States.[29] In other words, the Gothic elements here reside, not in the uncanny or abject qualities associated with African American belief systems, but in the powers wielded by those who fear them. Much the same thing can be said of Ann Petry's *Tituba of Salem Village* (1964), Maryse Condé's *I, Tituba, ... Black Witch of Salem* (1986) and Michelle Cliff's *Free Enterprise* (1993), which, to varying degrees, engage with African conjure and folk magic. The characters embody supernatural sources of fear for the white patriarchy, but it is the violence and injustice that they suffer as a result that, these texts insist, must be confronted and made visible if society is to avoid repeating past mistakes.[30]

It is precisely this desire to break the power of the past over the present that animates *Kindred*. In line with Wester's thinking, however, Butler's novel also directly engages with the pitfalls of employing Gothic tropes and plots, and the awareness that, as Linda Williams asserts, '[t]here is no equivalent of the Ku Klux Klan ride-to-the-rescue for the black woman'.[31] Her victimisation does not mobilise the same meanings as that of a white protagonist, and the role of Gothic heroine (an avatar of beleaguered innocence who eventually triumphs over tyranny and privilege) is therefore by no means an easy or rewarding one for a black woman to occupy, as Butler's Dana discovers.[32] Finding herself trapped in the nineteenth century and forced to live and work in slavery, she feels that she is now vulnerable to '[h]orror stories. Except that they were true, and I was going to have to live with them for as long as I was here.'[33] The novel strongly implies that slavery as a system means that the conventional Gothic plot is far more difficult to enact than the example of her literary forebears might indicate. Early on in the narrative, Dana realises that a black woman named Alice, who is born free, and the white slave-holder's son Rufus, to whom she is bound by some mysterious connection, are in fact her distant ancestors, and that if Dana is to be born at all, she must ensure that Alice becomes pregnant by Rufus, who is determined to possess her as piece of property. Dana is put in an impossible position, needing to ensure that the present-future is made possible by the present-past, while also wanting to protect Alice. Whatever she does, there is no good outcome, and this is underlined near the end of the novel when she is forced to kill Rufus when he attacks her. She saves herself and puts an end to his increasingly despotic rule, but in the process she dooms those who work on the plantation, as they are sold, likely to an even worse 'owner'. Rufus's power, passed down through his father, cannot truly be broken, the novel suggests, because the system of slavery is far more pervasive than one man or family.

What is more, the depiction of her husband Kevin (who is white and sympathetically portrayed) makes it clear that the Gothic world of slavery does not remain safely in the past. He finds himself pulled back to the nineteenth century along with his wife when he tries to prevent her from time travelling, and it quickly becomes clear that Kevin is not subject to the same traumas and dangers as Dana is. Indeed, as a white, middle-class man, he finds himself subtly implicated in the divisions that enable the violence she sees and experiences first-hand. She worries that 'some part of this place would rub off on him', and that living too long in the nineteenth-century American South 'would endanger him in a way I didn't want to talk to him about'.[34] Nor is this merely the effect of the milieu; during their brief marriage before all of this takes place, the otherwise progressive Kevin had frequently begged her to type his manuscripts for him, despite the fact that they are both busy writers. Consequently, the possibility of his belittling and exploitation of his beloved wife haunts the narrative and the supposedly enlightened present. Indeed, we learn that Dana's aunt and uncle are unhappy that she married a white man, while Kevin's sister is overtly racist. As Dana tells Kevin after her first involuntary trip to the past, '"I feel like it could happen again – like it could happen anytime. I don't feel secure here."'[35]

While the novel therefore stresses that the 1970s are by no means free of prejudice and discrimination, much of the more overt violence is confined to the past, which Dana ultimately escapes, albeit irrevocably scarred, emotionally and physically. A similar tentative optimism is evident in Jewelle Gomez's *The Gilda Stories* (1991), which uses the trope of vampirism to dramatise the shifting but pervasive nature of racialised hatred from the mid-nineteenth century to the end of the twentieth. As Gomez herself writes in the Foreword, in the 1990s black intellectuals remained wary of the Gothic and the supernatural: 'There were those who didn't think a black lesbian vampire story – benevolent or not – was such a good idea politically. Some writer friends and activists – African American and lesbian – thought connecting the idea of vampires with vulnerable communities was too negative.'[36] To a certain extent, the novel also reflects the rapid decline of optimism after the Civil Rights movement in the 1960s.[37] The protagonist is a benevolent blood drinker who will never age, rescued by other blood drinkers named Gilda and Bird after she runs away from the plantation where she had been enslaved. When Gilda reaches the end of her life, the protagonist takes her name, and learns to move independently through the world, encountering a range of racial and gendered attitudes as the nineteenth century turns into the twentieth. In the segment set in New York in 1971, the younger Gilda talks to her friend Julius about the limitations of the Black Power movement, which had lost momentum, and which she is all too aware had sidelined women's issues. During the conversation, she finds herself almost literally transported back to the plantation, picking cotton in the merciless sun behind her sisters, struggling to drag herself out of this haunting past that looms over the 'disappointment' of the still-unequal present.[38]

Like *Kindred*, *The Gilda Stories* is therefore ambivalent about the possibilities for racial justice improving over time. In addition, while Gomez's novel is unapologetic about its supernaturalism, it does seek to distance its heroine from associations with traditional African American beliefs, while, like *Beloved*, situating these beliefs as familiar aspects of daily life rather than as frightening manifestations of Otherness. The elder Gilda, a white vampire, successfully runs a brothel with her Lakota lover, Bird, in 1850s Louisiana. A fear of '"ha'nts and suchlike. Spirits"' prompts one of the girls who works in the brothel to warn the young, nameless protagonist away from the two women, who she suggests practise 'the secret religion, vodun'. This does not worry the protagonist, however; she 'had known deep fear and knew she could protect herself when she must. But there was no cause for fear of these two.'[39] In other words, once again, the horrors of slavery are the true horrors here, not those of the supernatural, and overt associations with demonic Africanism are rejected or ignored.

Nevertheless, white superstition regarding her kind keeps her safe from their violence. She is rarely bothered while walking alone at night, a particularly perilous occupation for a black woman in twentieth-century America, because she is assumed by anyone who sees her to be 'part of the secret lore of ha'nts and spirits that lived with African people, even in Missouri'.[40] At the same time, she actively rejects such labels. In San Francisco, she finds herself examining her hair in a mirror, pleased that the image looking back at her is reassuringly human, and 'not at all the look of a ha'nt or spook as many thought her and her kind to be'.[41] She may be more than human, but not less than human. Her preternaturally long life and strength in fact allow her to engage in activities that resist systemic racism, buying companies and renting out buildings that make life better for those like her who exist outside the norms of white, straight society, creating communities in the process.[42]

Tananarive Due's *My Soul to Keep* (1997) similarly dramatises the continued danger that past racial violence poses for the present, but features far more positive attitudes towards the supernatural. The protagonist, Jessica, gradually becomes aware that her husband, David, is concealing something terrible from his past. She eventually learns that, like Gilda, he is immortal, having drunk blood in sixteenth-century Abyssinia that allowed him to join a select group of undying men who dedicate their lives to meditation and knowledge, but who become vicious killers when they feel an outsider is threatening the secret of their brotherhood. David (originally Dawit) has, also like the younger Gilda and Butler's Dana, experienced the horrors of slavery and Jim Crow in the American South first-hand. Nonetheless, as a jazz musician in the 1920s who spent most of his time practising, and later as a reclusive university lecturer, he has insulated himself from much of the ongoing violence that those outside the white 'mainstream' experienced in the twentieth-century USA.

It is Jessica, in fact, an ordinary mortal who falls in love with him after taking his class, who engages most closely with America's racialised Gothic supernatural imaginary. The house where they live in Florida has a tree that makes haunting but familiar, comforting noises after dark, which she tells visitors is 'the call of an old Indian woman's ghost'. She calls this spirit 'Night Song' and goes on to explain that 'their house was on haunted Tequesta Indian ground, like in *Poltergeist*, except their haunts weren't in a pissy mood'.[43] At the back of their house is a cave, which David tells her was once for storing arrowroot, but that she thinks of as a burial ground.[44] Here, she feels connected to her father, who was killed in a car accident when she was young, and her young daughter Kira talks to his ghost there, gaining access to knowledge of the future and ultimately joining the ancestors herself following her untimely death. Dawit's secrecy about his past is directly responsible for Kira's horrific death, from which Jessica never recovers, and which results in the breakdown of their marriage. However, the final chapters reveal that Jessica, who now uses the 'living blood' to heal sick children in Africa, later gives birth to another daughter, herself gifted with immortality, rapid healing and preternatural awareness of the future, and who struggles with her dual heritage in the later books in the series, published after the millennium.

The book is therefore ultimately optimistic, if again distinctly cautious in its optimism. As Eddie S. Glaude Jr argues, this is in line with the complexities of race relations in late twentieth-century America. He notes that, encouraged by the Reagan administration in the 1980s and 1990s, 'many embraced the language of color blindness'; however, 'what was all too clear in the outbursts of racial violence or in the persistence of racial inequality was a willful ignorance about the realities of racism that continued to haunt the nation', exemplified by the riots following the beating of Rodney King by police officers and other high-profile attacks on young black men by law enforcement.[45] By privileging 'the past as playing an active role in shaping the present', as Trudier Harris notes, 'what slavery in History denied to black Americans, slavery in literary history grants to them: the power to have a bit of control over their destinies'.[46] In the books discussed in this chapter, the supernatural makes it possible for characters to experience America's troubled racial past, to see how it continues to haunt the present, but also to hope for future change. The rise, in the twenty-first century, of supernatural Gothic fiction by and about non-white populations, by writers such as Jesmyn Ward and Stephen Graham Jones, that continues to grapple with the Gothic's problematic racial heritage suggests that this was no mere fantasy.[47] The trope of extremely longevity, channelled through vampirism, appears once again in Butler's *Fledgling* (2005) and Silvia Moreno-Garcia's *Certain Dark Things* (2016). These developments suggest that, while the Gothic past may not be susceptible to exorcism, Gothic tropes can be reappropriated as a means of undoing some of the historical erasure to which African and Native American beliefs, traditions and histories have been subjected. As Leila Taylor puts it, the 'process of dehumanization is a process of monster-making. But', she adds, 'monsters have power.'[48]

Key Texts

Zora Neale Hurston, *Mules and Men* (1935). Hurston's anthropological work under Franz Boaz; a selection of folktales from her native Florida, and her account of her initiation into New Orleans hoodoo.
Octavia E. Butler, *Kindred* (1979). The story of a young black writer in the twentieth century who is dragged back into antebellum times.
Toni Morrison, *Beloved* (1987). A house haunted by the ghost of a child killed as her mother fled slavery; we gradually learn the horrific events that led up to her death.
Jewelle Gomez, *The Gilda Stories* (1991). An account of a young, black lesbian who becomes a vampire and lives through the American Civil War, Jim Crow, the Civil Rights movement and on into a dystopian future.
Tananarive Due, *My Soul to Keep* (1997). A young journalist gradually learns that her husband is in fact an immortal blood drinker.

Further Critical Reading

Goldner, E. J., 'Other(ed) Ghosts: Gothicism and the Bonds of Reason in Melville, Chesnutt, and Morrison' (1999). Highlights the ways in which the system of slavery depended upon figuring the enslaved as congenitally less rational than the white population.
Hazzard-Donald, Katrina, *Mojo Workin': The Old African American Hoodoo System* (2012). A very detailed account of the development of voodoo, hoodoo and conjure, from slavery to the twenty-first century.
O'Meally, Robert, and Geneviève Fabre (eds), *History and Memory in African-American Culture* (1994). Collection of essays that examine the clash between American ideals of freedom and the experience and history of the United States black population.
Redding, Arthur, '"Haints": American Ghosts, Ethnic Memory, and Contemporary Fiction' (2001). Explores the use of the past and haunting in African American literature.

Bibliography

Blight, David W., 'W. E. B. Du Bois and the Struggle for American Historical Memory', in Robert O'Meally and Geneviève Fabre (eds), *History and Memory in African-American Culture* (Oxford: Oxford University Press, 1994), pp. 45–70.
Brooks, Joanna, *American Lazarus: Religion and the Rise of African-American and Native American Literatures* (Oxford: Oxford University Press, 2003).
Butler, Octavia, *Kindred* [1979] (London: Headline, 2018).
Carby, Hazel, 'The Politics of Fiction, Anthropology, and the Folk: Zora Neale Hurston', in Robert O'Meally and Geneviève Fabre (eds), *History*

and Memory in African-American Culture (Oxford: Oxford University Press, 1994), pp. 28–44.

Carpenter, Lynette, and Wendy Kolmar, *Haunting the House of Fiction: Feminist Perspectives on Ghost Stories by American Women* (Knoxville, TN: University of Tennessee Press, 1991).

Chireau, Yvonne P., *Black Magic: Religion and the African American Conjuring Tradition* (Berkeley, CA: University of California Press, 2006).

DeLamotte, Eugenia C., *Perils of the Night: A Feminist Study of Nineteenth-Century Gothic* (Oxford: Oxford University Press, 1990).

Douglass, Frederick, *My Bondage and My Freedom* (New York: Miller, Orton, and Mulligan, 1885).

Douglass, Frederick, *Narrative of the Life of Frederick Douglass, an American Slave. Written by Himself* (Boston: The Anti-Slavery Office, 1845).

Doyle, Laura, *Freedom's Empire: Race and the Rise of the Novel in Atlantic Modernity, 1640–1940* (Durham, NC: Duke University Press, 2008).

Dutton, Wendy, 'The Problem of Invisibility: Voodoo and Zora Neale Hurston', *Frontiers: A Journal of Women Studies*, 13.2, 1993, pp. 131–52.

Due, Tananarive, *My Soul to Keep* (New York: HarperCollins, 1997).

Fleetwood, Nicole R., *Troubling Vision: Performance, Visuality, and Blackness* (Chicago: University of Chicago Press, 2011).

Glaude Jr, Eddie S., *African American Religion: A Very Short Introduction* (Oxford: Oxford University Press, 2014).

Goddu, Teresa, 'The African-American Slave Narrative and the Gothic', in C. L. Crow (ed.), *A Companion to American Gothic* (Oxford: John Wiley and Sons, 2013), pp. 71–83.

Goldner, E. J., 'Other(ed) Ghosts: Gothicism and the Bonds of Reason in Melville, Chesnutt, and Morrison', *MELUS*, 24.1, 1999, pp. 59–83.

Gomez, Jewelle, *The Gilda Stories* (San Francisco: City Lights, 2016).

Gordon, Michelle Y., '"Midnight Scenes and Orgies": Public Narratives of Voodoo in New Orleans and Nineteenth-Century Discourses of White Supremacy', *American Quarterly*, 64.4, 2012, pp. 767–86.

Harris, Trudier, 'History as Fact and Fiction', in Maryemma Graham and Jerry W. Ward Jr (eds), *The Cambridge History of African American Literature* (Cambridge: Cambridge University Press, 2011), pp. 451–96.

Hazzard-Donald, Katrina, *Mojo Workin': The Old African American Hoodoo System* (Urbana, IL: University of Illinois Press, 2012).

Hemenway, Robert, 'Gothic Sociology: Charles Chesnutt and the Gothic Mode', *Studies in the Literary Imagination*, 7.1, 1974, pp. 101–19.

Hurston, Zora Neale, *The Complete Stories* (New York: HarperCollins, 2008).

Jordan, Margaret L., *African American Servitude and Historical Imaginings: Retrospective Fiction and Representation* (Basingstoke: Palgrave Macmillan, 2004).

Levy, Valerie, 'Hoodoo and Voodoo in Zora Neale Hurston's Gothic Stories and Folktales', in Monika Elbert and Rita Bode (eds), *American Women's Regionalist Fiction: Mapping the Gothic* (Basingstoke: Palgrave Macmillan, 2021), pp. 215–32.

Luckhurst, Roger, *Zombies: A Cultural History* (London: Reaktion, 2016).

Morrison, Toni, *Playing in the Dark: Whiteness and the American Imagination* (New York: Vintage, 1992).

Mullen, Harryette, 'African Signs and Spirit Writing', in Winston Napier (ed.), *African American Literary Theory: A Reader* (New York: New York University Press, 2000), pp. 623–43.

Ng, Andrew Hock Soon, *Women and Domestic Space in Contemporary Gothic Narratives: The House as Subject* (New York: Palgrave Macmillan, 2015).

Nicholls, David G., *Conjuring the Folk: Forms of Modernity in African America* (Ann Arbor, MI: University of Michigan Press, 2000).

Nunes, Ana, *African American Women Writers' Historical Fiction* (New York: Palgrave Macmillan, 2011).

O'Meally, Robert, and Geneviève Fabre (eds), *History and Memory in African-American Culture* (Oxford: Oxford University Press, 1994).

Osbey, B. M., 'Why We Can't Talk to You about Voodoo', *The Southern Literary Journal*, 43.2, 2011, pp. 1–11.

Patterson, Robert J., 'African American Feminist Theories and Literary Criticism', in Angelyn Mitchell and Danille K. Taylor (eds), *The Cambridge Companion to African American Women's Literature* (Cambridge: Cambridge University Press, 2009), pp. 87–108.

Redding, Arthur, '"Haints": American Ghosts, Ethnic Memory, and Contemporary Fiction', *Mosaic: An Interdisciplinary Critical Journal*, 34.4, 2001, pp. 163–82.

Rushdy, Ashraf H. A., 'The Neo-Slave Narrative', in Maryemma Graham (ed.), *The Cambridge Companion to the African American Novel* (Cambridge: Cambridge University Press, 2004), pp. 87–105.

Taylor, Leila, *Darkly: Black History and America's Gothic Soul* (London: Repeater Books, 2019).

Verney, Kevern, *African Americans and US Popular Culture* (Abingdon: Routledge, 2003).

Warren, Kenneth W., 'African American Literatures and New World Cultures', in Maryemma Graham and Jerry W. Ward Jr (eds), *The Cambridge History of African American Literature* (Cambridge: Cambridge University Press, 2011), pp. 730–45.

Wester, Maisha L., *African American Gothic: Screams from Shadowed Places* (New York: Palgrave Macmillan, 2012).

Wester, Maisha L., 'The Gothic and the Politics of Race', in Jerrold E. Hogle (ed.), *The Cambridge Companion to the Modern Gothic* (Cambridge: Cambridge University Press, 2014), pp. 157–73.

Wester, Maisha L., 'Keys to a Hurricane: Reading Race, Class, and Abjection in *The Skeleton Key*', *Film International*, 12.1, 2014, pp. 63–75.

Whittaker, Nicholas. 'What's So Bad About Digital Blackface?', *Aesthetics for Birds*, 14 April 2021, https://aestheticsforbirds.com/2021/04/14/whats-so-bad-about-digital-blackface/ (last accessed 21 January 2022).

Williams, Linda, *Playing the Race Card: Melodramas of Black and White from Uncle Tom to OJ Simpson* (Princeton, NJ: Princeton University Press, 2001).

Young, Jason, '"Of Moses, Mules, and Men": Zora Neale Hurston and the Politics of Folk Art', *Obsidian*, 9.1, 2008, pp. 9–19.

Notes

1. Butler, *Kindred*, p. 228.
2. With regard to my decision not to capitalise 'black' in this essay, see Nicholas Whittaker, 'What's So Bad About Digital Blackface?', *Aesthetics for Birds*, 14 April 2021, https://aestheticsforbirds.com/2021/04/14/whats-so-bad-about-digital-blackface/ (last accessed 21 January 2022). I occasionally use the term 'African American', partly for regional specificity, and partly as this was the term most frequently used by writers and academics in the final decades of the twentieth century.
3. Goddu, 'African-American Slave Narrative', p. 71.
4. Ibid., p. 72.
5. See DeLamotte, *Perils of the Night*.
6. See Douglass, *Narrative of the Life*, pp. 71–2; Douglass, *My Bondage and My Freedom*, p. 239; and Mullen, 'African Signs', p. 631.
7. Gordon, 'Midnight Scenes', p. 769.
8. Ibid., p. 773; and Osbey, 'Why We Can't Talk', p. 6.
9. Osbey, 'Why We Can't Talk', p. 6, emphasis in original.
10. Ibid., p. 6. See also Carby, 'The Politics of Fiction', pp. 34–5.
11. Morrison, *Playing in the Dark*, p. 38.
12. Gordon, 'Midnight Scenes', p. 772.
13. Chireau, *Black Magic*, pp. 129–34.
14. Nicholls, *Conjuring the Folk*, pp. 1–3.
15. See Levy, 'Hoodoo and Voodoo', pp. 221, 230.
16. See Luckhurst, *Zombies*, pp. 17–57.
17. See Gordon, 'Midnight Scenes', p. 773.
18. Fleetwood, *Troubling Vision*, p. 6. See also Wester, *African American Gothic*, p. 256.
19. Discussed in Wester, 'The Gothic'.
20. Fleetwood, *Troubling Vision*, p. 2.
21. Ibid., p. 10.
22. Osbey, 'Why We Can't Talk', p. 6. See also Young, '"Of Moses"', pp. 15–16; Chireau, *Black Magic*, pp. 134–5; and Taylor, *Darkly*, p. 147.
23. Luckhurst, *Zombies*, p. 38.
24. See Rushdy, 'The Neo-Slave Narrative'.
25. Verney, *African Americans*, p. 6; and Warren, 'African American Literatures', p. 733.
26. Wester, *African American Gothic*, pp. 1, 28. For readings of Gothic as a hostile environment for black writers, see also Doyle, *Freedom's Empire*, pp. 255–6; Hemenway, 'Gothic Sociology', pp. 106, 101; and Ng, *Women and Domestic Space*, p. 64.
27. Glaude Jr, *African American Religion*, p. 78. See also Warren, 'African American Literatures', p. 738; and Patterson, 'African American Feminist Theories', p. 100.
28. Nunes, *African American Women*, p. 22.
29. See ibid., p. 138. See also Carpenter and Kolmar, *Haunting the House*, pp. 12–13; and Wester, *African American Gothic*, p. 214.

30. Nunes, *African American Women*, p. 138. See also Wester, 'The Gothic', p. 170.
31. Williams, *Playing the Race Card*, p. 232.
32. Wester, *African American Gothic*, p. 193.
33. Butler, *Kindred*, p. 77.
34. Ibid., p. 80.
35. Ibid., p. 11. See also Taylor, *Darkly*, p. 66.
36. Gomez, 'Foreword', in *The Gilda Stories*, p. 10.
37. Jordan, *African American Servitude*, p. 206.
38. Gomez, *The Gilda Stories*, p. 176.
39. Ibid., p. 44.
40. Ibid., p. 116.
41. Ibid., p. 59.
42. Ibid., p. 186.
43. Due, *My Soul to Keep*, pp. 26–7.
44. Ibid., p. 101.
45. Glaude Jr, *African American Religion*, p. 85.
46. Harris, 'History as Fact and Fiction', p. 475; and Warren, 'African American Literatures', p. 741. See also Brooks, *American Lazarus*, p. 16; and Blight, 'W. E. B. Du Bois', p. 49.
47. See Wester, *African American Gothic*, p. 254.
48. Taylor, *Darkly*, p. 79.

Chapter 15

Medical Humanities and the Twentieth-Century Gothic
Laura R. Kremmel

The medical humanities, a term as difficult to define as the term 'Gothic' itself, is not one typically associated with the Gothic. Amid variations, most agree that the medical humanities is an academic field devoted to 1) educating medical practitioners to more ethically, accurately and humanely treat patients through humanities training, and 2) providing therapeutic outlets for patients to process and express their own medical experiences and to make those experiences accessible. While the term 'health humanities' is now often preferred for its inclusion of caregivers beyond the medical professions and states of wellness beyond those that require medical care, I use the term 'medical humanities' in this chapter because of its roots in the twentieth century.

Unlike the hackneyed anatomists of the eighteenth century or the gentlemen physicians of the nineteenth century, twentieth-century doctors, surgeons and nurses became small actors in the large system that managed them, one that could simultaneously feel like a living, breathing creature and a cold, impenetrable structure. By the 1960s a loss of individuality and humanity within medicine had begun to surface. During a panel of American medical students in 1969, students commented that 'medical education is not concerned with health, it is dedicated to the study of disease', and medical training '[stresses] not an individual human being with a disease, but rather a disease to which is attached an often vexing and more or less irrelevant personality'.[1] Medicine, while it has always been financially motivated, now turned individual doctors with their own ideals into representatives of an institution that didn't always share them.

Patient anxiety caused by the resulting dehumanisation was encouraged by the physical structure of the hospital building. The term 'clinical' is synonymous with cold, detached and unemotional. The hospitals of the early twentieth century stressed the importance of external environment – sunshine and fresh air – for patient well-being, before hospitals became progressively more specialised and industrial. Spaces once built for care were reconstructed for efficiency.[2] The result was a complex labyrinth of individual departments, working together but following their own rules, leaving the patient to be passed back and forth and ultimately feeling lost. By the 1930s, as Jeanne Kisacky writes, the hospital had become a 'medical, technological health factory', churning out diagnoses and treatments while increasing prices and decreasing charitable care.[3] The environmental benefits that the previous century fostered were abandoned by the late 1940s and 1950s in favour of artificial replication, magnifying a sense of isolation and confinement: 'The natural world became largely a view out a window.'[4] Patients could no longer interact with the world as humans but instead were part of the technological machine that medical students in the 1960s feared.

Gothic narratives, then, were given plenty to work with, including a long list of true incidents and systemic changes that seem in themselves Gothic tales. Nazi and other officially sanctioned, non-consensual human experiments denied basic humanity to those of certain races, genders, classes and intellectual abilities. Excessive use of medically approved procedures and materials such as X-rays and radium caused horrific, even fatal, suffering. Medical labels for mental illness resulted in systemic gaslighting and imprisonment. The increased use of drugs in medical and mental health removed patient agency, leaving the body vulnerable to an institution unconcerned with the human experience. A general widening of the divide between specialised medical education and public medical awareness sowed seeds of distrust. This litany of crimes impacts medicine to this day.

The Gothic's distribution of these occurrences in its fictions makes its relationship with the medical humanities contentious. If one of the goals of the medical humanities is to normalise non-normative bodies and their medical experiences, the Gothic depictions of these same bodies as threatening appears to work against that goal. If another goal of the medical humanities is to heal relationships between patients and their caregivers, the Gothic's villainisation of doctors and nurses directly contradicts that goal as well. These conflicts complicate conversations about political, societal and economic understandings of human bodies and those who control them. I argue that, while the Gothic seems to undermine the medical humanities, it also continually draws attention to the reasons why this field was and continues to be vital for ethical, reliable and compassionate medical care. In other words, the Gothic in many ways is the medical humanities' most prolific defender.

The texts highlighted in this chapter do the work of exposing the roots of medical fears while also accentuating them. Themes of medical conspiracy and experimentation reveal the increased, almost cult-like institutionalisation that facilitates them. Gothic renditions of mental institutions display the psychological trauma of the medical spaces and the stigmatisation of those within them. On the other hand, narratives of contagion call attention to the failures of medical institutions, whose control is replaced by the paranoia of a threat that lies within our own bodies and each other. All three areas of focus in this chapter are characterised by increased psychological distance between patient and practitioner, resulting in a loss of patient agency. Each area of inquiry is subsequently characterised by patients' fear of medical practitioners and their procedures, of the hospital as a network beyond control, and of other patients and their afflictions.

Conspiracy and Experimentation

Frankenstein – as a novel, character and concept – was born out of the chaotic medical and scientific innovations of the early nineteenth century, not unlike a similar obsession with discovery in the twentieth century. The scientist imagined by Mary Shelley, however, receives the kind of education of which medical humanities advocates would approve. He may be obsessed with scientific advancement, but it is the imagination and aesthetics – the humanities – of the alchemists and their romantic ideals that drive him. It is the human experience of discovery and the awe of human life that his professors attempt to teach him. James Whale's 1931 film adaptation of *Frankenstein* removes this Romantic-era education in favour of a more traditionally Gothic emphasis on class, inheritance and family lineage. The doctor – soon-to-be Baron of the house of Frankenstein – holds a dangerous place of assumed valour, even when he creates monsters in a story assumed to be so dangerous it required a warning to the audience before the opening credits. A household name for unethical and dangerous medical experimentation, the Frankenstein of the 1930s cares less for the public and humankind at large and more for his new status as a god. After giving up science for domestic bliss, this Frankenstein is allowed to live, leaving the childlike creature – voiceless now as well as nameless – to suffer.

Prior to Whale's film, H. P. Lovecraft also released a serialised story of Frankensteinian experimentation. 'Herbert West – Reanimator' (1921–22) depicts the title character's duplicitous medical career through the eyes of his assistant. Like Frankenstein, West harbours a god complex, and is obsessed with bringing the dead back to life. Unlike Frankenstein, however, West is a practising medical doctor, drawing scientific subjects from among his colleagues and trusting patients. While the Frankenstein monster is forever exiled from humanity, alone in his kind, West's creations form a collective of victims that ultimately destroy him, indicative of a larger historical collective of people subjected to medical horrors. The text is explicit in the fact that West '[takes] advantage of the disorganisation of both college work and municipal health regulations' to obtain access to the dead.[5] What's more (and what should be no surprise to those familiar with Lovecraft's biography), his early subjects are Black men, whom he clearly sees as transitional from animal experimentation to loftier goals. References to the 'African monstrosity' speak to the history of racial exploitation in American medicine that did not begin in the twentieth century but that – like the forty-year Tuskegee Study that denied life-saving treatments to Black men – certainly continued through it.[6] Though these reanimated corpses form a community, they remain the silent victims whose experiences of suffering are of no concern to their creator until they physically destroy him.

West takes advantage of the medical system, but he largely works against or outside it. Later in the twentieth century, that system itself would become central to medical horror. Doctor and surgeon Robin Cook's novel *Coma* (1977) and its film adaptation (1978) directly demonstrate both the need for the new field of medical humanities and the ambivalent attitude of the medical establishment towards it. Responsible for the creation of an entire subgenre of literature preying on anxieties about medicine – the medical thriller – Cook's first bestseller combines the female detectives of Ann Radcliffe with the mad science of *Frankenstein*, revealing systemic medical corruption on a scale not seen before. Whereas earlier Gothic examples feature medical practitioners or scientists disconnected from the larger establishment, Cook's novel is about that establishment. Individuals participate in it and administrators run it, but the extensive power of this well-oiled machine makes it both horrifying and difficult to believe. How can everyone be in on it? What's more, how can everyone be in on it while unaware of its existence? The 'it' here is the systematic inducement of coma in young, healthy patients before their organs are harvested for sale to the highest bidder. The conspiracy, run by the chief of surgery, Dr Stark, relies on the clandestine administration of carbon monoxide during surgical anaesthesia, an act that goes undetected until medical student Susan Wheeler starts asking questions.

Susan's strength – or flaw, according to medical staff – is repeatedly referred to as the 'human element': the genuine humanity that she practises towards patients and her immediate investment in their well-being.

Susan is interested in stories, not diagnoses, and her persistent questions jeopardise an underground organ market that relies on doctors *not* connecting with patients on a human level. The 'human element' that Susan brings to medicine is denigrated by her colleagues as indicative of unwanted femininity and rookie weakness, out of place amid the data collection and machine calibrations that speak for patients. Rooms such as the Intensive Care Unit, a 'surrealistic alien environment' and a relatively new medical space, graphically reinvent Frankenstein-esque laboratories – dimly lit, filled with electrical noises, bottles and bags of fluid, patients in bandages.[7] Emily Russell, in her cultural study of organ transplantation, argues that the Jefferson Institute – where coma patients go for organ harvesting – is the core of fear in the novel because its 'patients represent total loss of control over the body', but I argue that we see that loss of control repeatedly in all the hospital's various spaces, especially the operating room and ICU.[8]

Even before the reader becomes aware of criminal activity, then, *Coma* calls attention to the everyday anxieties that patients experience in medical environments. These anxieties are so common that they have been theorised and labelled 'white coat syndrome'. While the film adaptation begins with Susan's leisurely drive to the hospital, Cook's novel opens with a scene of distress as an anxious patient undergoes routine surgery. In fact, every patient in this hospital is on edge, one even commenting that he feels entirely unlike himself: vulnerable and afraid. *Coma* reaffirms their anxieties as valid; they *are* vulnerable, and they have *every* reason to be afraid. Stark does little to acknowledge patients as anything beyond materials for experiments, explaining, 'the common folk, if you will, cannot be depended upon to make decisions which will provide long-term benefits. The common man thinks only of his short-run needs and selfish requirements.'[9] The reader is the 'common man' in this scenario. As Russell suggests, the medical thriller includes jargon that alienates the reader, reminding them that they are excluded from this world on which their lives depend.[10] While the patient cues the reader's reactions to medical threats, Cook's novel also shows moments of fear for medical practitioners caught in an immoral system. The confusion and terror felt by the anaesthesiologists watching their patients slip into coma mimic the panic patients feel right before they go under. When doctors are afraid of what they have done to their patients, when their authority wavers, patient and reader trust in them is replaced by terror. The novel ends with a scene that mirrors its beginning: a female patient exhibiting horror as she is about to go under the knife. Now a patient, Susan knows Stark will use carbon monoxide to induce a coma from which she will never wake, but the similarity between the two scenes suggests that hospitals do not need diabolical conspiracies to be seen as dangerous.

Not only does Cook's protagonist exemplify the medical humanities at work – using humanistic inquiry to dismantle a system of profit that harms patients and practitioners – but his choice of popular fiction as the vehicle for his message – encouragement of *voluntary* organ donation – also endorses collaboration between the humanities and medicine. In a 2019 TEDx talk, he remarked on the power of fiction 'as a way to change public policy' and to expose problematic medical training and medicine's 'business interests'.[11] He did not study medical or even legal texts to do this; he studied bestsellers.

Fiction also exerts power over medicine in Stephen King's novel *Misery* (1987). Annie Wilkes, who rescues her favourite author, Paul Sheldon, from a near-fatal car accident, is far from the Gothic's first villainous nurse. However, she is unique in that she works alone. Cook presents the institution of medicine as a corrupt and dangerous structure, but King shows what happens when medical practitioners go rogue, eschewing the institution's power structures but also its safeguards. Annie has all the accoutrements of medicine in her home-hospital: intravenous therapy supplies, a private pharmacy of pain medications, bedpans, bandages, a wheelchair, an axe and a blowtorch. Like coma patients, Paul cannot leave his personal hospital, restrained by constant pain in a body that Annie whittles away to exploit its immobility for her own purposes.

A trained nurse, Annie reminds Paul of her generosity in saving his life, but King is not subtle in equating solo medical treatment to kidnapping and even sexual violence. In the opening scene, Annie resuscitates Paul by giving him mouth-to-mouth, an act repeatedly referred to as rape, a detail explored further by Kathleen Margaret Lant.[12] I would suggest that, unlike the detached practice of medicine that the medical humanities seeks to prevent, Annie embraces the opposite extreme in her obsession and involvement. She feels too much and becomes too attached, to the extent that she can no longer separate her needs from the needs of her patient. In this case, she needs Paul to write a new 'Misery' novel. Everything she makes him do translates to an act of rehabilitation, not of his physical body but of his body of creative work. To ease the pain of his broken legs with medication, he is coerced to burn his latest manuscript, a piece Annie finds distasteful. To prevent him from escaping before he completes the new book, she amputates his foot. Incapable of objectivity, her Foucauldian medical gaze affords her absolute power to make decisions about Paul without consent or consultation. And Paul is not the only patient over whom she has exercised this solo authority. Annie's medical training combined with her own mental unwellness make her especially unsettling as a villain. That a nurse should become a murderer subverts the cultural assumptions about a profession considered synonymous with angelic compassion and maternal selflessness. Significantly, every act of violence Annie performs involves medical supplies or procedures, and it is Annie in her nurse's uniform who haunts Paul until the very end.

Mental Institutions: Imprisoned Mind and Body

There has never been a time when mental institutions – asylums – have not been burdened by both real and imagined fears. As Annie Wilkes demonstrates, those who experience mental illness have been culturally depicted as dangerous with such regularity that whole campaigns have been dedicated to relieving the stigma caused by negative associations. There is little doubt that the Gothic's engagement with mental illness at times causes real damage to those battling this stigma. Sharon Packer credits Hitchcock's film *Psycho* (1960) with giving us the alternative to the mad scientist: just the mad, whose only medical expertise is their own experience and who could very well live next door.[13] Not only do mental hospitals and their patients elicit uneasiness, but the staff who work in mental health care have also been vilified. No area of this medical concentration has been left untouched by tales of terror and horror, making it difficult for readers to know whose side they are on.

The history of mental health care does not help. Past horrors provoke and reinforce the villainisation of mental health care in fiction, providing ample evidence of this branch of medicine's own corruption and barbarity. Involuntary treatment and indeed completely involuntary commitment prevail in mental institutions in ways that do not apply in other types of facilities, despite late twentieth-century attempts at compassionate reform. New treatments grounded in medical theory moved away from chains and straitjackets, but they resulted in no less harm. From the 1920s' rest cures and induced insulin comas, to the 1930s' electroconvulsive therapy and lobotomies, treatments dismantled bodies and minds often without patient understanding or consent.[14] By mid-century, the restraints of earlier times had been all but abandoned, and practices such as lobotomy – after a rush of popularity – fell out of favour. They were replaced by medication – anti-psychotics and tranquillisers such as Chlorpromazine – that left patients just as incapacitated without the pain or – for the most part – inverse effects. Such medications, however, disassociated the patient from their surroundings, their situations and themselves, leaving them lost and vulnerable.

The doctors and nurses who administered these medications became natural villains for Gothic works, authorities who harmed more than helped their patients, while the patients themselves – unpredictable and irrational – became dehumanised and dangerous. It is tempting to read these types of stereotypical depictions as efforts by Gothic texts to sabotage the destigmatisation of mental illness, and that responsibility should be acknowledged. I suggest, however, that the Gothic also serves the medical humanities purpose of complicating these representations by prioritising the experiences of patients and practitioners as medical Others, providing characters who can be read as more than their stigmas. An area of medical expertise and suffering that is often shoved to the sidelines or ridiculed as inconsequential – even 'not real' – is given close consideration in the Gothic texts discussed here.

A powerful narrative tool repeatedly used in Gothic depictions of mental illness is inclusivity: we're *all* mad. The Batman universe and its own nod to Lovecraft, Grant Morrison and Dave McKean's graphic novel *Batman Arkham Asylum: A Serious House on Serious Earth* (1989), challenges assumptions about mental health patients by making the masked hero one of them. More than this, Batman himself suspects that he belongs in the asylum as much as the patients with whom he interacts. This is not to say that he approves of the medical work that goes on there. Highly critical of the staff and their methods, he notes that 'it's hard to imagine this place being conducive to anyone's mental health' and accuses a doctor of 'effectively destroying [Two-Face's] personality', referring to a villain typically described as 'being of two minds' now incapacitated by multitudinous indecisiveness.[15] Making no attempt to disagree, the doctor chillingly responds, 'Sometimes we have to pull down in order to rebuild . . . Psychiatry's like that', describing mental health treatment as violent and destructive.[16] There is little evidence in the novel to suggest that any patient reaches the point of rebuilding. In fact, the hospital's namesake, Amadeus Arkham, who caricatures psychiatry by replacing science and medicine with ritual and magic, 'accidentally' electrocutes a patient while administering ECT. The excuse, 'these things happen', is acceptable to the medical community, indicative of the expendability of patients more broadly.[17]

While *Arkham Asylum* is a clear condemnation of mental health treatment and facilities, it does not equally reproach patients receiving care, nor does it present them as victims. Instead, this visually overwhelming graphic novel could be called a celebration of madness as not only desirable but also natural and unstoppable. The only characters in distress are those struggling to re-establish sanity over insanity, a hierarchy that is not valued in this world. When Batman leaves the asylum, the page's format can be read in two ways. In alternating sepia and coloured panels, the Joker says 'Enjoy yourself out there' in one panel and 'There's always a place for you here' in another. Between them, is the stand-alone phrase, 'In the asylum', meaning 'there' or 'here,' or perhaps both, a further indication of madness's lack of strict definition.[18]

While the Gothic might contribute to fears of patients with mental illness by celebrating the Joker's kind of madness in graphic detail, it often humanises the patient before exposing any dangers. Patrick McGrath's psychological Gothic novels draw on his own experiences growing up at Broadmoor Lunatic Asylum (since renamed Broadmoor Hospital), which houses the criminally insane and where his father was medical superintendent.[19] As such, they include an unusual degree of medical accuracy – not unlike Robin Cook's work – and clear compassion for mental illness patients, at the same time that they unsettle and disturb. Like *Arkham Aslyum*, McGrath's novels such as *Spider* (1990) create an uneasily close relationship between reader and protagonist, who provides a restricted view of a world warped by his own traumas. The disintegration of that view creates a disorientation shared by both character and reader, neither of whom can tell what is real. In *Asylum* (1996), McGrath illustrates the gender expectations of the 1950s that lead one unhappy woman into debilitating depression, necessitating attempted treatments involving gaslighting, isolation and containment performed by the male doctors who constantly surround and surveil her. Unlike the physical dangers of the early twentieth-century asylums, McGrath constructs states of mind that themselves become Gothic structures, ultimately facilitated by destructive social conventions considered to be healthy and sane.

Disease and Contagion

In some senses, the Gothic's depiction of mental health patients as villains, monstrous or Others encourages our fear of each other. The setting of the hospital both indicates who is dangerous and contains them in a space that makes sense for readers outside looking in. The final medical sub-category frequently borrowed by the Gothic – disease and contagion – provides no such protective barriers. In fact, disease narratives often abandon the hospital and its staff altogether, leaving those who can infect loose among those who can be infected. In Richard Matheson's *I Am Legend* (1954), we return to Frankenstein's laboratory, but this time the scientist, Robert Neville, attempts to cure or destroy the new biological threat to humanity: not a galvanised monster but infectious vampires. Since Sheridan Le Fanu's *Carmilla* (1872) and Bram Stoker's *Dracula* (1897), the vampire has been associated with science and medicine: the doctor's useless visits, prescriptions of rest or fresh air, speculative blood diseases, all within a failed narrative frame that rationalises the supernatural. *I Am Legend* takes this even further by fully replacing the supernatural with the medical and allowing it to succeed. As Priscilla Wald notes, 'it was not until the 1950s that new technologies of visualisation let researchers peer with new eyes into the mysterious workings of viruses, where they marvelled at how viruses differed from any entity they had studied before'.[20] Robert Neville, alone uninfected, determines that the infection is not caused by a virus because he *can* see it, and 'all the centuries of fearful superstition had been felled in the moment he had seen the germ'.[21] This is followed by the realisation that he knows nothing about this type of science. Medical rationale, then, provides both accessibility and barrier by simultaneously introducing information and alienating Neville from it.

And so he turns to the humanities. Observing the vampiric behaviour of the infected, Neville takes a page out of Van Helsing's book to combine what he has learned from reading *Dracula* with scientific study and brute violence. Each day, he kills the infected with stakes and other traditional vampire deterrents, all the while adding to his knowledge of bacteriology and epidemiology. Thus, if Neville is the closest figure to a doctor the novel has, he is also the biggest threat to his patients, attacking when the disease makes them most vulnerable. If he wishes to cure them, he also wishes to kill them. Medical knowledge that should serve to humanise them as patients has no such effect. Neville continues to see them as monsters to destroy.

The ending is crucial for a medical reading of *I Am Legend*, establishing Neville the doctor as a hunter, a villain and a monster. Matheson's vampires are not suave and calculating creatures of the night; they are victims of the plague, shuffling their way to new behaviours that allow them to survive in their new non-normative embodiments. The persistence of science throughout the novel collapses the distinctions between sick and healthy, the line between those constructs utterly lost. What Jen Webb and Samuel Byrnand write of the zombie is equally true of the medical vampire in this context: 'The transmission of the "virus" between us and them indicates our closeness: viruses (mostly) travel between like species.'[22] In other words, there is no use pretending that the monster is not 'us' when the science tells us otherwise. Importantly, then, the text subverts what it means to be ill, promoting redefinitions of healthy and unhealthy and a depathologisation of medical conditions deemed unacceptable because abnormal. Neville, considering himself to be healthy, is the only abnormal creature left.

It's easy to see how Matheson laid the foundation for twentieth- and twenty-first-century zombies that stray from their Caribbean roots. In fact, when Matheson caught George Romero's *Night of the Living Dead* (1968) on TV, he thought it was an adaptation of his novel: mostly healthy people in the house, unhealthy ghouls – 'those things!' – outside trying to get in.[23] From these texts, future zombies would be associated with sickness and contagion. As Charles Hoge says, *I Am Legend* 'provides the literary moment at which it is realised that monsters may be a pandemic', simultaneously showing us our own fears of becoming infected and dehumanising those who already have.[24] Romero's low-budget film, like Matheson's novel, is devoid of any reliable medical experts or establishment, the only health and safety advice being provided through public broadcasts. Despite the lack of doctors or hospitals, sickness and injury pervade the scene in the house, underlying the plot as they hide underfoot. The little girl (Kyra Schon) who is bitten by a zombie from the grave and cared for in the basement represents the unwillingness of those around her to acknowledge their own vulnerability to disease, even as they watch their friends and family rot. Perhaps the most disturbing moments in the film are when Johnny (Russell Streiner) – a man we see healthy at the beginning – bursts into the house to grab his sister, showing clear signs of infection, and when the little girl's infection takes hold and she eats her mother (Marilyn Eastman). The alienation of the mind and body from their prior identifying behaviours is indicative of a loss of selfhood caused by many illnesses that patients fear.

The zombies of the 1960s that established the medicalisation of the zombie trope coincided with a shifting definition of death in the medical community. To return to the new and dehumanising ICU graphically exhibited in *Coma*, new technologies introduced unfamiliar states of embodiment: living bodies without living brains. As Roger Luckhurst writes, 'The success of the mechanical respirator meant that the cardiopulmonary system could be sustained entirely separately from brain function. There were now patients with a complete absence of cortical activity . . . but who continued to live on within the biotechnical apparatus of the ICU.'[25] In other words, like Matheson's vampires, no longer is the zombie explicitly derived from the supernatural; as these new developments suggest, the zombie is now medically possible. Romero's notion of aiming for the head so as to kill a zombie, as Luckhurst notes, aligns with new understandings of brain death.[26] The zombie, then, becomes an object of medical study, not just a creature to be killed, for the purpose of further understanding types of death and preventing further infection. However, in the vampire and zombie narratives, rarely does this study take place in conventional medical spaces, creating a stark contrast with the tales of experimentation and organ harvesting represented by *Coma*.

The increased institutionalisation and corporatisation of medicine in the 1960s – including the American health insurance and drug industries that would become the true stuff of nightmares by the end of the century – prompted fears about the inhuman and disconnected machinery of the medical system disseminated in both the hospital and medical education. These fears would deepen for the next sixty years and show no sign of subsiding. Zombies have become more medicalised, hospitals continue to be depicted as systems of oppression, and doctors and patients take turns playing the villain. Steven C. Schlozman, professor of psychiatry and horror writer, asks,

> What if medicine itself is the real zombie? What if our current system of care, with its faceless and deadened doctors and depersonalized insurance prior authorizations and emphasis on randomized controlled trials at the expense of actual connection, is the most relevant and pressing embodiment of the walking dead in our real lives? ... you need only visit the emergency ward or a waiting room to sense the growing despair in both patient and doctor alike.[27]

The Gothic, on entering the twenty-first century, carries with it the confirmation of all the fears discussed at the birth of the medical humanities as a discipline: an Othering experience of the healthcare system, particularly in the United States, and a dehumanisation that veers into the uncanny and the abject. At the same time, the idealised cultural perception of doctors, nurses and hospitals has in many ways blocked the injustices of these systems from view, and both the Gothic and the medical humanities have adapted to disrupt these perceptions. As Luckhurst observes, the most recent miniseries adaptation of *Coma* (2012) focuses more on the capitalist health insurance industry than its 1978 screen predecessor or 1977 origin text.[28] The medical humanities has evolved into the critical medical humanities, a discipline focused less on medical education and more on the impacts of class, race, gender and disability on the experience of healthcare, areas of disenfranchisement that the Gothic has long sought to lay bare.[29] Thus, behind every evil doctor or dangerous patient in the Gothic is an actual systemic injustice that the medical humanities strives to rehabilitate.

Key Works

The Cabinet of Dr Caligari (1920). A modernist silent film demonstrating a blurring of the lines between medical care and military authority as the title character uses his patient to commit murder.

Ken Kesey, *One Flew Over the Cuckoo's Nest* (1968; film, 1975). Like *Coma*, this novel and film adaptation negatively impacted public opinion of medical facilities and practitioners, this time in the mental health fields.

Ira Levin, *Rosemary's Baby* (1967; film, 1968) and William Peter Blatty, *The Exorcist* (1971; film, 1973). Together, these novels and films represent a trend in the second half of the twentieth century of pitting medicine against religion. Unarguably, medicine loses.

Dead Ringers (1988). This film is about twin gynaecologists who become delusional and dangerous when one twin considers his patients inhuman and loses humanity himself.

Further Critical Reading

Aldana Reyes, Xavier, *Body Horror: Corporeal Transgression in Contemporary Literature and Horror Film* (2014). Includes a significant chapter on surgical horror but is of interest as a whole for its emphasis on embodiment.

Becker, Sandra, Megen de Bruin-Molé and Sara Polak (eds), *Embodying Contagion: The Viropolitics of Horror and Desire in Contemporary Discourse* (2021). A recent collection of essays, trending towards the late twentieth and early twenty-first centuries.

Belling, Catherine, 'The Living Dead: Fiction, Horror, and Bioethics' (2010). Includes an exploration of *Coma* among other texts and their broader contexts within bioethics and horror.

Wasson, Sara, *Transplantation Gothic: Tissue Transfer in Literature, Film, and Medicine* (2020). A comprehensive study of brain death and transplantation in medical history and Gothic media.

Bibliography

Abbott, Stacey, *Undead Apocalypse: Vampires and Zombies in the 21st Century* (Edinburgh: Edinburgh University Press, 2016).

Aldana Reyes, Xavier, *Body Horror: Corporeal Transgression in Contemporary Literature and Horror Film* (Cardiff: University of Wales Press, 2014).

Becker, Sandra, Megen de Bruin-Molé and Sara Polak (eds), *Embodying Contagion: The Viropolitics of Horror and Desire in Contemporary Discourse* (Cardiff: University of Wales Press, 2021).

Belling, Catherine, 'The Living Dead: Fiction, Horror, and Bioethics', *Perspectives in Biology and Medicine*, 53.3, 2010, pp. 439–51.

Cook, Robin, *Coma* (New York: Signet, 1977).

Cook, Robin, 'Fiction and Health Policy', *TEDxWesleyanU*, April 2019, <https://www.ted.com/talks/robin_cook_fiction_and_health_policy> (last accessed 8 November 2020).

Espí Forcén, Fernando, 'Anti-Psychiatry and the Arkham Asylum', in Sharon Packer and Daniel R. Fredrick (eds), *Welcome to Arkham Asylum: Essays on Psychiatry and the Gotham City Institution* (Jefferson, NC: McFarland, 2020), pp. 91–100.

Hoge, Charles, '"Crawling Out of the Middle Ages": The Deep Literary Roots of the Vampires in *I Am Legend*', in Cheyenne Mathews and Janet V. Haedicke (eds), *Reading Richard Matheson: A Critical Survey* (Lanham, MD: Rowman and Littlefield, 2014), pp. 3–17.

King, Stephen, *Misery* [1987] (New York: Signet, 1988).

Kisacky, Jeanne, *Rise of the Modern Hospital: An Architectural History of Health and Healing, 1870–1940* (Pittsburgh, PA: University of Pittsburgh Press, 2017).

Lant, Kathleen Margaret, 'The Rape of Constant Reader: Stephen King's Construction of the Female Reader and Violation of the Female Body in *Misery*', *The Journal of Popular Culture*, 30.4, 1997, pp. 89–114.

Lovecraft, H. P., 'Herbert West – Reanimator' [1921–22], in S. T. Joshi (ed.), *The Call of Cthulhu and Other Weird Stories* (New York: Penguin, 1999), pp. 50–80.

Luckhurst, Roger, 'Biomedical Horror: The New Dead and the New Undead', in Justin D. Edwards (ed.), *Technologies of the Gothic in Literature and Culture* (Abingdon: Routledge, 2015), pp. 84–98.

Matheson, Richard, *I Am Legend* [1954] (New York: Orb Books, 1995).

Morrison, Grant, and Dave McKean, *Batman Arkham Asylum: A Serious House on Serious Earth* [1989] (Burbank, CA: DC Comics, 2014).

Packer, Sharon, 'Unethical Experiments in Arkham and Elsewhere', in Sharon Packer and Daniel R. Fredrick (eds), *Welcome to Arkham Asylum: Essays on Psychiatry and the Gotham City Institution* (Jefferson, NC: McFarland, 2020), pp. 110–22.

Russell, Emily, *Transplant Fictions: A Cultural Study of Organ Exchange* (Basingstoke: Palgrave Macmillan, 2019).

Schlozman, Steven C., 'Foreword', in Lorenzo Servitje and Sherryl Vint (eds), *The Walking Med: Zombies and the Medical Image* (University Park, PA: Penn State University Press, 2016), pp. vii–ix.

Truett, Casey, Arthur Douville, Bruce Fagel and Merle Cunningham, 'The Medical Curriculum and Human Values (Part I) (1969)', in Brian Dolan (ed.), *Humanitas: Readings in the Development of the Medical Humanities* (San Francisco: University of California Medical Humanities Press, 2015), pp. 105–17.

Wald, Priscilla, 'Viral Cultures: Microbes and Politics in the Cold War', in Sarah Juliet Lauro (ed.), *Zombie Theory: A Reader* (Minneapolis, MN: University of Minnesota Press, 2017), pp. 33–62.

Washington, Harriet A., *Medical Apartheid: The Dark History of Medical Experimentation on Black Americans from Colonial Times to the Present* (New York: Anchor, 2006).

Wasson, Sara, *Transplantation Gothic: Tissue Transfer in Literature, Film, and Medicine* (Manchester: Manchester University Press, 2020).

Webb, Jen, and Samuel Byrnand, 'Some Kind of Virus: The Zombie as Body and as Trope', in Sarah Juliet Lauro (ed.), *Zombie Theory: A Reader* (Minneapolis, MN: University of Minnesota Press, 2017), pp. 111–23.

Whitehead, Anne, and Angela Woods, 'Introduction', in Anne Whitehead and Angela Woods (eds), *The Edinburgh Companion to the Critical Medical Humanities* (Edinburgh: Edinburgh University Press, 2016), pp. 1–34.

Filmography

The Cabinet of Dr Caligari (dir. Robert Wiene, Decla-Bioscop AG, Germany, 1920).
Dead Ringers (dir. David Cronenberg, Morgan Creek, Canada, 1988).
The Exorcist (dir. William Friedkin, Warner Brothers, USA, 1973).
Frankenstein (dir. James Whale, Universal Pictures, USA, 1931).
Night of the Living Dead (dir. George A. Romero, Image Ten, USA, 1968).
One Flew Over the Cuckoo's Nest (dir. Milos Forman, Fantasy Films, USA, 1975).
Rosemary's Baby (dir. Roman Polanski, William Castle Productions, USA, 1968).

Notes

1. Truett et. al., 'The Medical Curriculum and Human Values', pp. 110–11.
2. Kisacky, *Rise of the Modern Hospital*, p. 167.
3. Ibid., pp. 297–8.
4. Ibid., pp. 340–1.
5. Lovecraft, 'Herbert West – Reanimator', p. 58.
6. For a history of racial exploitation in medicine, see Washington, *Medical Apartheid*.
7. Cook, *Coma*, pp. 39–40.
8. Russell, *Transplant Fictions*, p. 192. See also Wasson, *Transplantation Gothic*.
9. Cook, *Coma*, p. 298.
10. Russell, *Transplant Fictions*, p. 212.
11. Available at <https://www.ted.com/talks/robin_cook_fiction_and_health_policy> (last accessed 8 November 2020).
12. See Lant, 'The Rape of Constant Reader'.
13. Packer, 'Unethical Experiments', p. 111.
14. Espí Forcén, 'Anti-Psychiatry', p. 93.
15. Morrison and McKean, *Batman Arkham Asylum*, n.p.
16. Ibid.
17. Ibid.
18. Ibid.
19. For more on McGrath's childhood, see the autobiographical 'A Boy's Own Broadmoor', *The Economist*, 21 August 2012.

20. Wald, 'Viral Cultures', pp. 33–4.
21. Matheson, *I Am Legend*, p. 86.
22. Webb and Byrnand, 'Some Kind of Virus', p. 112.
23. Abbott, *Undead Apocalypse*, p. 24.
24. Hoge, '"Crawling Out of the Middle Ages"', p. 11.
25. Luckhurst, 'Biomedical Horror', p. 87.
26. Ibid., p. 87.
27. Schlozman, 'Foreword', p. ix.
28. Luckhurst, 'Biomedical Horror', p. 93.
29. Whitehead and Woods, 'Introduction', p. 2.

Chapter 16

Queer Gothic Literature and Culture
Laura Westengard

Since the first Gothic novel, Horace Walpole's *The Castle of Otranto* (1764), the Gothic has included themes of transgressive sexuality. The novel begins with the death of Conrad, a young man who is engaged to be married to Isabella. After a giant helmet falls from the sky and crushes him, his father Manfred decides that he will take the place of his dead son and marry the young woman who had been positioned to be his daughter-in-law. Following this declaration, Manfred frantically attempts to control the fracturing of his patriarchal power by chasing Isabella through dark subterranean passages, imprisoning those who interfere with his plans, and dodging ancestral ghosts and giant appendages. Walpole's novel is credited with establishing the hallmarks of what would come to be known as Gothic fiction. These hallmarks include haunting, medieval castles, Catholic monasteries, catacombs, supernatural prophetic occurrences, subterranean passages, ancestral curses, terrorised vulnerable women and eroticised power dynamics. These themes and tropes recurred throughout the centuries that followed and have come to be recognised as 'Gothic', but in addition to these more recognisable Gothic tropes, eighteenth-century Gothic fiction also established the enduring and pervasive relationship between the Gothic and non-heteronormative genders and sexualities, often known as 'queer Gothic'.

Though 'queer' initially denoted oddness or peculiarity, the term later developed as a derogatory epithet for homosexuals, but by the late twentieth century queer had been reclaimed by many in the LGBT (lesbian, gay, bisexual, transgender) community as a marker of politicised resistance to the original stigma of the term. Susan Stryker notes that this use of queer first appeared on flyers at the 1990 New York Pride march after being adopted by the political protest group ACT-UP (AIDS Coalition to Unleash Power), and today it often stands for a defiant, anti-normative positionality.[1] However, queer also functions as an umbrella term that broadly represents a 'range of nonnormative sexual practices and gender identifications' both including and exceeding the meanings of lesbian, gay, bisexual and transgender.[2] The broad understanding of queer as both odd and as indicating non-normative genders and sexualities helps us understand the way the term is conceptualised in relation to the Gothic. Eve Kosofsky Sedgwick, a scholar whose career began in Gothic literary studies but who is best known as a founder of academic queer studies, frames queer as an 'open mesh of possibilities, gaps, overlaps, dissonances and resonances, lapses and excesses of meaning when the constituent elements of anyone's gender, of anyone's sexuality aren't made (or can't be made) to signify monolithically'.[3] Queerness in this sense functions as a placeholder for non-normative genders and/or sexualities and serves as a refusal to be neatly defined, pinned down or contained by any single or unchanging meaning, making it a flexible term but also potentially confusing and disturbing to those who expect tidy and predictable behaviours, identities and meanings. This refusal to remain strictly moored to the status quo reflects the disruptions of early Gothic narratives in which the inciting incidents mark a departure from 'normal' life and takes readers into the realm of the irrational, perverse and supernatural.

In *Queer Gothic* (2006), George Haggerty notes that Gothic fiction emerged before the codification of sexuality as we know it today, and that its themes of terror, fear, flight and desire all hold a sexual valence that challenge and reshape heteronormative structures. Indeed, 'social-sexual relations', he claims, 'are the most basic common denominator of Gothic writing'.[4] Eighteenth- and nineteenth-century Gothic fiction created a host of metaphors, aesthetics and settings that have resonated throughout the centuries in various forms of cultural production that contemplate, represent, condemn and celebrate queerness. Since social-sexual transgression is foundational to Gothic form and content, twentieth-century cultural producers who incorporate the Gothic often do so 'to evoke a queer world that attempts to transgress the binaries of sexual decorum'.[5]

It is important to note that although the Gothic is inherently queer, its purposes have often been conservative. Maggie Kilgour explains that the 'momentary subversion of order' that characterises the majority of Gothic narratives is followed by 'the restoration of a norm, which after the experience of terror, now seems immensely desirable'.[6] Readers enjoy the titillating details of the 'subversion of order', or the queering of the status quo, but ultimately the narrative reinforces adherence to norms by the destruction of those situations and creatures that represented divergence. In this way, Gothic metaphors serve not only as markers of disorder, but also consistently function as markers of outsider status.

Monstrosity, vampirism and ghostliness mark a character as 'other' and therefore a symbol of fear and a threat to the social order. Gothic metaphors have a dual function, however, because they represent social anxieties and desires both at once; while readers know the sexually perverse vampire is a threatening monster that will usually be destroyed in the end, in the meantime they are able to eroticise and be thrilled by the vampire's difference, which can be read as representing sexual, racial, class, ability or any other kind of 'otherness', or 'deviant subjectivities opposite which the normal, the healthy, and the pure can be known'.[7]

In *Gothic Queer Culture* (2019), I argue that the conservative aim of the Gothic performs 'insidious' trauma for queer readers and viewers who turn to the Gothic to see representations of queerness, but who must endure the underlying message that queerness is monstrous and must be destroyed for the sake of the norm. Like the term 'queer' itself, queer audiences have at times reclaimed even conservative and marginalising Gothic metaphors, a strategy that removes some of the 'linguistic and aesthetic violence committed by queer dehumanization in popular culture'.[8] Queer people are cultural creators as well, and many turn to Gothic tropes and aesthetics to explore non-normative desires and anxieties. In her study of lesbian Gothic fiction, Paulina Palmer points out that the Gothic 'confronts the writer with contradictions' since many of the features of the Gothic as a metaphor for queer sexuality are problematic. At the same time, however, the Gothic is attractive to lesbian and queer writers because of its 'tendency to question mainstream versions of "reality" and to interrogate the values associated with them'.[9] This dual function of Gothic tropes persists throughout the twentieth century, as they function as affirmation and representation, as well as devices that use queer Gothicism to further marginalise those who stray from the norm. Regardless of its contradictions, or perhaps because of them, queerness is embedded in the roots of Gothic fiction, and conversely the Gothic has become a means of creating a 'queer world' in art, literature and culture.

Gothic themes and tropes have morphed over the years to reflect shifting cultural anxieties and desires around queerness. Jack Halberstam defines Gothic as the 'rhetorical style and narrative structure designed to produce fear and desire within the reader', often achieving its aim through the deployment of excess.[10] The production of simultaneous fear and desire is a hallmark of the Gothic, and it is also a characteristic of twentieth-century cultural attitudes towards queerness, making queerness itself expressly Gothic in the public imagination. This Gothic swirl of anxiety and desire as well as the metaphors and aesthetics originating in early Gothic fiction appear frequently in twentieth-century queer cultural production – that is, cultural production created by queers as well as production that navigates queerness in its content. In early twentieth-century literature and film, for example, Gothic metaphors such as haunting, vampirism and monstrosity often served as cautionary warnings against non-normative gender expressions and sexual behaviours. Later these tropes shifted to represent psychological repression, fetishised sexuality and even empowered political resistance. The remainder of this chapter will examine examples of queer Gothic cultural production in the twentieth century, both in its conservative and reappropriated forms, by highlighting textual examples that generate simultaneous fear and desire, utilise Gothic tropes or aesthetics, and that relate broadly to non-normative genders and/or sexualities.

Since the first ancestral ghosts began wandering the halls of the Castle of Otranto, haunted houses and spectral apparitions have been persistent Gothic tropes. Terry Castle explains that lesbianism in literary history appears as 'something ghostly: an impalpability, a misting over, an evaporation, or "whiting out" of possibility'.[11] Beyond the decorporealisation of lesbians specifically, the ghostly frequently stands in for the ineffable, that which refuses to make itself clear within the rational structures of society, and the unspeakable. All of these qualities also map on to queerness in its fluidity, resistance to normative scripts and frameworks, and its taboo nature. Henry James's *The Turn of the Screw* (1898), for example, is haunted by that which cannot be spoken. The novella follows the experience of a governess who believes that her charges, Flora and Miles, are haunted by and perhaps secretly collaborating with the ghosts of a former governess, Miss Jessel, and a former valet, Peter Quint. The narrative circulates around the '"unmentionable" thing that Miles did at his boarding school, the implicitly homosexual transmission of words that remain unspecified in the text'.[12] The ghosts of this text represent the governess's vague and unconscious suspicion of inappropriate intimacies between the adults and the children of the manor that linger beyond death, as well as the reverberations of the unspeakable that are carried on through Miles's behaviour at boarding school.

Haunted houses speak to familial traumas, angst-ridden psycho-sexual development and the *unheimlich* of the Freudian uncanny. Freud's concept of the uncanny explains the eerie feeling when the known and familiar reveals itself to be strange because something that 'ought to have remained secret . . . has come to light'.[13] The hidden-away spaces of the home such as attics, basements and closets hold the secrets that threaten to burst forth at any moment, turning the domestic space into a nightmare. The 'unhomely home', Palmer notes, evokes a domestic space that, though ostensibly warm and secure, is disturbed by secrets and the return of repressed fears and desires. The implications that it evokes of a tension or clash between the familiar and the unfamiliar, the homely and the strange, make it particularly relevant to queer existence.[14]

The return of repressed desires, traumas and family secrets, those taboos that are so often hidden from the world behind the closed doors of the home, triggers the sense that a house that was once known has become strange and eerie. Of course, the figure of the closet is decidedly resonant with queer coming-of-age narratives involving the development, initial concealment and later revelation of secret sexual desires. In Gothic texts, hidden queerness represented by the uncanny, the ghostly or the monstrous often serves as a cautionary tale by making queerness the source of evil, violence and fear. Shirley Jackson's 1959 novel *The Haunting of Hill House* introduces an anthropomorphised, even malevolent, house that 'stood by itself against its hills, holding darkness within'.[15] The house appears at first glance to be the epitome of solidity in which 'walls continued upright, bricks met neatly, floors were firm, and doors were sensibly shut', but the domestic familiarity of the house quickly slips away as the protagonist, Eleanor Vance, introduces her repressed desires, grievances and regrets into the space.[16] The hauntings that emerge from the house are seemingly directed at Eleanor, who develops a nascent attraction to the confident and modern Theodora and who struggles with guilt over the death of her mother for whom she was caretaker. Eleanor's psyche is childlike and reactive, with an abundance of repressed fears and desires, which appear to give rise to the supernatural occurrences in the house. The swirl of unacknowledged queerness and unspoken guilt emerging as hauntings turn the house from steady and sensible to suffocating, overbearing and threatening. Palmer explains that the 'spectre and phantom, key signifiers of the uncanny, carry connotations of "excess" since their appearance exceeds the material, and this is another concept that connects the uncanny with "queer"'.[17] The house seems to burst at the seams with an excess of closeted content taking the form of ghostliness.

The vampire figure emerged most famously in Gothic literary history with Bram Stoker's 1897 novel, *Dracula*. Vampirism has appeared as a Gothic metaphor throughout the twentieth century, often taking on drastically shifting shapes and meanings. Across all of these iterations, however, the vampire is associated with queerness, whether as a threatening cautionary figure, an erotic outsider or a proud identity category. William Patrick Day explains that vampire legends in the twentieth century shifted drastically in response to historical and cultural contexts, and this significatory shapeshifting is aligned with the

Gothic's foundational characteristic of encompassing both the fears and desires of its moment. Day explains that early twentieth-century vampires served as cautionary tales focused on 'affirming nineteenth-century morals and controlling our baser impulses', and later vampire narratives became increasingly erotic 'initiatory tales asserting the necessity of exploring the fearful unknown'.[18] By the end of the twentieth century, the vampire had become a figure of 'liberation from the fear and terror generated by ignorance or outdated notions of sexuality'.[19] As 'Gothic social barometers', the vampire's form and function shift over time, but one factor that remains consistent is the relationship between vampirism and non-normative sexualities and genders.[20]

During the height of twentieth-century censorship in Hollywood, queerness became subtext, often represented by Gothic metaphors circulating in films. An iconic figure in twentieth-century queer Gothic cinema is the monstrous, vampiric lesbian who preys on young, virginal women. Sheridan Le Fanu's 1872 *Carmilla* introduced the figure of a strange vampire woman who appears one day following a carriage accident and proceeds to seduce the innocent and vulnerable young Laura, causing her increasing weakness and lethargy but also inexplicable fascination and pleasure. Carmilla sneaks into women's bedrooms at night and feeds from their breasts as they are unwittingly ushered into intimate romantic and erotic attachments. Twentieth-century cinematic representations of vampirism owe much to this early Sapphic vampire. Cold and repressed on the surface, part of the horror of these characters is the reveal of the perverse and evil nature underneath their icy and civilised exterior.

At times this vampirism is explicit, such as in the case of Countess Marya Zaleska in *Dracula's Daughter* (Lambert Hillyer, 1936), and at times monstrosity/vampirism is only vaguely implied as a means of coding the predatory, queer nature of the character, as with Mrs Danvers in *Rebecca* (Alfred Hitchcock, 1940) and Miss Holloway in *The Uninvited* (Lewis Allen, 1944). Countess Zaleska seeks out psychiatric help in the hope that she might be cured of her unholy urges. She makes a valiant but short-lived effort to resist the flesh of young women but soon after preys upon a beautiful woman who is brought to her art studio as a model. The model's dynamic has implications around class, economic vulnerability and sex work, while the pathologised yet incurable status of Countess Zaleska stands in for lesbian sexual desire. Queer viewers have often identified with queer Gothic characters, but in films of this period their presence is intended as a warning and a threat and they are almost always destroyed in the end (either by death or madness), as is the case with Zaleska who ultimately pays the price for her queer appetites.

Later in the twentieth century, the lesbian or bisexual vampire figure remains predatory, but her queer sexuality is more explicit. *Daughters of Darkness* (*Les lèvres rouges*, 1971) features a character based on the historical figure Elizabeth Bathory, a sixteenth-century Hungarian countess who was rumoured to have tortured and murdered hundreds of young women and bathed in their blood. In the film, an immortal Bathory arrives with her assistant at a nearly empty hotel in Belgium and eventually seduces young newlywed Valerie into abandoning her husband for a vampiric affair involving both sex and blood. In *The Hunger* (1983), elegant vampire Miriam infiltrates Manhattan nightlife with her lover John, seducing young people of all genders and drinking their blood. Eventually, she sets her sights on Dr Sarah Roberts and proceeds both to make love to her and turn her into an immortal companion.

Vampire sexuality is not confined to lesbianism, however. In Anne Rice's *Interview with the Vampire* (1976), the first novel in *The Vampire Chronicles* series, readers are introduced to one of the most famous vampire pairs, Louis de Pointe du Lac and Lestat de Lioncourt. Haggerty notes that the 'sine qua non with which this author mesmerises her readers, however, is homoerotic desire'.[21] The relationship between Louis and Lestat is one of predation and intimacy, and their bond, though fraught, is decidedly homoerotic. *Interview with the Vampire* is not the only example of homoeroticism in the *Chronicles*. Indeed, 'Lestat's devoted friend Nicholas from *The Vampire Lestat*; Armand, Daniel, and David, the central characters who emerge throughout the Chronicles – all these dazzling young men can be read as gay'.[22] These characters grapple with their inherently queer desires, and ultimately reflect the shift in the role of the vampire from villainous seducer to glamorous protagonist whose humanity is enhanced by occupying the status of 'other'. This is a distinct shift from the Gothic othering that fetishises, marginalises and ultimately destroys difference for the sake of shoring up notions of what it means to be a 'normal' human. Vampirism in Rice's *Chronicles* can be mapped directly on to the personal journey of the discovery and acceptance of queerness.[23] In this world, becoming a vampire means 'awakening and accepting one's own secret nature – whatever is there but has been repressed, especially one's sensual, sexual nature',[24] and in the late twentieth century the meaning of queer identity shifted drastically from something deeply pathologised and maligned to a marginalised identity category to be accepted and even celebrated.[25]

While vampires are arguably a type of monster, monstrosity more generally is another Gothic metaphor that often signifies queerness. In Mary Shelley's *Frankenstein, or The Modern Prometheus* (1818), Victor Frankenstein pieces together a creature with parts from 'the unhallowed damps of the grave' and the 'living animal', and the creature that is brought to life represents a type of monstrosity that queers the boundaries of humanity as well as normative procreation.[26] Because of the creature's multiplicitous difference, Frankensteinian monstrosity has been deployed to represent the threat of sexual and gender transgression, and conversely has been reappropriated as a resonant figure for some queer and transgender audiences. The dehumanising effect of monstrosity as a stand-in for gender non-conformity has a long history in the genre of horror cinema. In films such as *The Texas Chain Saw Massacre* (1974) and *The Silence of the Lambs* (1991) the killers use the salvaged flesh of their victims to construct their genders; both Leatherface and Buffalo Bill wear the scalps (and in the case of Leatherface the whole face) of their victims as a way of accessing femininity. This kind of Frankensteinian monstrosity of pieced together bits of flesh is problematically used to conflate gender variance with the monstrous and grotesque. In films such as *Psycho* (1960), *Dressed to Kill* (1980) and *Sleepaway Camp* (1983, released as *Nightmare Vacation* in the UK), the reveals that show the killer to be gender non-conforming imply that gender non-conformity itself, not murderous behaviour, is the ultimate monstrosity.

In 'My Words to Victor Frankenstein above the Village of Chamounix: Performing Transgender Rage', Susan Stryker explains her 'deep affinity' with Frankenstein's creation:

> Like the monster, I am too often perceived as less than fully human due to the means of my embodiment; like the monster's as well, my exclusion from human community fuels a deep and abiding rage in me that I, like the monster, direct against the conditions in which I must struggle to exist.[27]

Stryker's relationship to monstrosity reflects the long tradition of queer audiences recognising the dual function of queer Gothic content. The Gothic both represents non-normative ways of being and condemns those who might be deemed monstrous by cis-heteronormative standards. Conversely, queer audiences often turn to Gothicism to access admittedly problematic representations, and at times queer viewers even identify with the Gothic antagonists, thereby powerfully reframing their meaning. While the monstrosity of transgender characters in the twentieth-century horror films I describe here is certainly culpable in creating a larger trans-antagonistic atmosphere, Stryker speaks to the creativity of queer viewership in knowingly engaging with queer Gothic monstrosity with a nod to its contradictory aims and effects.

The adoption and redeployment of the marginalising projection of monstrosity on the queer body occurred during the 1980s and 1990s, the height of the AIDS crisis. At a time when the queer body was associated with disease, decay and death, the attribution of monstrosity was a means of alienating and dehumanising those who were most associated with the virus in the public imagination, gay men. The notorious reluctance of the US government even to speak the name of the virus (let alone recognise the many who were ill and dying or dedicate significant resources to stopping its spread) is directly linked with the dehumanisation of queers. Queer, HIV-positive writers, performers and artists responded to the effects of Gothic monstrosity by creating pieces that reflect monstrosity in aggressively haunting ways. Poets and writers such as Gil Cuadros and David Wojnarowicz played with the devastating effects of their own mortality and the losses surrounding them. Cuadros wrote the mixed-genre book *City of God* in 1994 as he struggled with the seemingly hopeless state of being an HIV-positive, queer Chicano living in a country that did not view him as worthy of care. Rather than avoiding or disavowing the inhumanity projected on to him, *City of God* 'revels in the negativity of monstrosity, death, decay, and loss, and deploys the darkness of Gothicism not only to acknowledge the horrors of undeniable trauma, but also to powerfully reimagine what it means to be in a place of hopelessness and alienation'.[28]

Similarly, David Wojnarowicz's writing and visual art angrily reflected his deep resistance to normative scripts and their attendant judgements projected on to the bodies of queers. The photographic depiction of those dying from AIDS-related illnesses often highlighted the 'excesses of the wasted queer body [and] were offered up to the public as the endpoint of queer identity – a monstrous confluence of non-normative desire, threat, infection, and abjection'.[29] In the series of three touching, spiritual photographs taken at the deathbed of his close friend and former lover, Peter Hujar (*Untitled (Peter Hujar)*, 1987), Wojnarowicz simultaneously refused to sanitise the ravages of the virus while simultaneously portraying the wasted queer body as a site of transcendence. Queers in the United States at this time were always already cathected to death in the public imagination, marking them as a kind of living dead creature. Wojnarowicz used his own body to reframe the attribution of undead monstrosity in pieces such as *Untitled (Silence = Death)* (1989) and *Untitled (Face in Dirt)* (1990). *Untitled (Silence = Death)* is a black and white photographic self-portrait featuring Wojnarowicz's grimacing face with his mouth stitched closed like a cadaver. The stitched mouth holds another resonance, however, since it evokes the crudely stitched together body of Frankenstein's creature, a being brought to life, given intelligence and heightened emotions, and then abandoned by all. *Untitled (Face in Dirt)*, another black and white photographic self-portrait, frames Wojnarowicz's face peeking out from underneath dirt and rock under which he seems to be buried alive, straddling the world of the living and the realm of death and marking him as undead. Both of these self-portraits highlight the sense that queer and HIV-positive people were considered vectors of death as well as forsaken as always already dead at a time when there was no viable treatment or cure for HIV/AIDS. By directing the viewers' gaze to his living face marked as undead and monstrous, Wojnarowicz offers an angry indictment of a society that has forsaken an entire generation of gay men. Both Cuadros and Wojnarowicz use Gothic monstrosity as a reappropriation and enraged redeployment of the popular association between queerness, death and a disposable, monstrous inhumanity.

As I have shown with this brief overview of several common Gothic metaphors, the Gothic serves several purposes in twentieth-century literature and culture, and those purposes are often at odds, making the Gothic a kind of battleground in which relevant anxieties and desires emerge in a swirling and incoherent blend of conservatism and anti-normativity. Since its emergence as British popular fiction in the eighteenth century, the Gothic has often functioned to define and establish what it means to be 'normal' by telling tales that marginalise, exclude and destroy those who diverge from the norm. Of course, that divergence occupies the majority of the narrative and is a large part of its appeal, making the content of these Gothic cautionary tales queer. Those with non-normative genders and sexualities have both created and consumed Gothic content and are certainly well aware that the pleasure of finding representation within queer Gothic tropes and metaphors is tempered by the damage done by associating non-normative 'outsiders' with the haunted, the vampiric and the monstrous. Queers are not simply consumers of queer Gothic literature and culture. Queer cultural producers have also turned to the Gothic to reappropriate historically damaging tropes, to express queer experiences and subjectivities, and to push back against cultural assumptions that link queerness with the threatening and the inhuman. In this function, Gothic queer literature and culture can be read not only as expressions of non-normativity but also as anti-normative creations that use the Gothic as a means of exploring imaginative new ways of existing that are not limited by cultural norms or even the confines of material humanity.

Key Works

Djuna Barnes, *Nightwood* (1936). A modernist text that includes lesbian themes paired with Gothic aesthetics and tropes.

Daphne du Maurier, *Rebecca* (1938). A Gothic tale that deploys ghosts, obsession and paranoia to allude to lesbian sexuality as well as class and gender conflict.
Rebecca (1940). Alfred Hitchcock's first American film adapts du Maurier's novel with a striking Gothic aesthetic and emphasises the lesbian-coded figure of Mrs Danvers.
The Haunting (1963). A film adaptation of *The Haunting of Hill House* that makes the novel's lesbian undertones slightly more explicit.
Rocky Horror Picture Show (1975). A decidedly campy version of queer Gothic, including allusions to *Frankenstein* and *Dracula*. Featuring Dr Frank-N-Furter, a self-proclaimed 'sweet transvestite from Transexual, Transylvania'.
Jewelle Gomez, *The Gilda Stories* (1991). A vampire story with an intersectional lens. Includes a black vampire protagonist in order to interrogate the history of United States slavery and the legacy of racism and othering.

Further Critical Reading

Fincher, Max, *Queering Gothic in the Romantic Age: The Penetrating Eye* (2007). Provides an overview of the queerness in Gothic fiction from 1765 to 1820. Helpful for investigating the roots of queer Gothic tropes.
Hughes, William, and Andrew Smith (eds), *Queering the Gothic* (2009). Models queer reading practices and Gothic reading practices for a range of texts from the eighteenth century to the present. Explores queerness in Gothic texts and the Gothic in queer texts, including both literary and pop culture examples.
Marshall, Nowell, *Romanticism, Gender, and Violence: Blake to Sodini* (2013). Reflects on the connection between compulsory gender norms, Gothic affect and violence. Makes relevant connections to contemporary political conversations around LGBTQ+ bullying by exploring queer Gothic texts from the eighteenth century to the early twenty-first century.
Rigby, Mair, 'Uncanny Recognition: Queer Theory's Debt to the Gothic' (2009). Succinct overview of the interdependency of queer theory and Gothic fiction.

Bibliography

Auerbach, Nina, *Our Vampires, Ourselves* (Chicago: University of Chicago Press, 1995).
Castle, Terry, *The Apparitional Lesbian: Female Homosexuality and Modern Culture* (New York: Columbia University Press, 1993).
Cuadros, Gil, *City of God* (San Francisco: City Lights, 1994).
Day, William Patrick, *Vampire Legends in Contemporary American Culture* (Lexington, KY: University Press of Kentucky, 2002).
Fincher, Max, *Queering Gothic in the Romantic Age: The Penetrating Eye* (New York: Palgrave Macmillan, 2007).
Freud, Sigmund, 'The Uncanny' [1919], in *The Standard Edition of the Complete Psychological Works of Sigmund Freud*, ed. and trans. James Strachey (London: Hogarth Press, 1955), vol. XVII, pp. 219–56.

Haggerty, George E., 'Anne Rice and the Queering of Culture', *Novel: A Forum on Fiction*, 32.1, 1998, pp. 5–18.

Haggerty, George E., *Queer Gothic* (Urbana, IL: University of Illinois Press, 2006).

Halberstam, Jack, *Skin Shows: Gothic Horror and the Technology of Monsters* (Durham, NC: Duke University Press, 1995).

Hale-Stern, Kaila, 'Anne Rice Confirms that the Vampires Louis and Lestat are a Same-Sex Couple with a Child', *Gizmodo*, 17 October 2012, <https://io9.gizmodo.com/anne-rice-confirms-that-the-vampires-louis-and-lestat-a-5952076> (last accessed 1 April 2021).

Hughes, William, and Andrew Smith (eds), *Queering the Gothic* (Manchester: Manchester University Press, 2009).

Jackson, Shirley, *The Haunting of Hill House* [1959] (New York: Penguin, 2013).

James, Henry, *The Turn of the Screw* [1898] (Mineola, NY: Dover Publications, 1991).

Kilgour, Maggie, *The Rise of the Gothic Novel* (London: Routledge, 1995).

Le Fanu, Joseph Sheridan, *Carmilla* [1872] (Syracuse, NY: Syracuse University Press, 2013).

Love, Heather, 'Queer', *TSQ: Transgender Studies Quarterly*, 1.1-2, 2014, pp. 172–6.

Marshall, Nowell, *Romanticism, Gender, and Violence: Blake to George Sodini* (Lewisburg, PA: Bucknell University Press, 2013).

Ní Fhlainn, Sorcha, *Postmodern Vampires: Film, Fiction, and Popular Culture* (Basingstoke: Palgrave Macmillan, 2019).

Palmer, Paulina, *Lesbian Gothic: Transgressive Fictions* (London: Cassell, 1999).

Palmer, Paulina, *The Queer Uncanny: New Perspectives on the Gothic* (Cardiff: University of Wales Press, 2012).

Rice, Anne, *Interview with the Vampire* [1976] (New York: Ballantine Books, 1997).

Rigby, Mair, 'Uncanny Recognition: Queer Theory's Debt to the Gothic', *Gothic Studies*, 11.1, 2009, pp. 46–57.

Sedgwick, Eve Kosofsky, *Tendencies* (London: Routledge, 1994).

Shelley, Mary, *Frankenstein; or, The Modern Prometheus* [1818] (Harmondsworth: Penguin, 1992).

Soltysik Monnet, Agnieszka, 'Recovering "Covering End": What Queer Theory Can Do for "The Turn of the Screw"', *Victorian Literature and Culture*, 36.1, 2008, pp. 247–52.

Stoker, Bram, *Dracula* [1897] (Harmondsworth: Penguin, 1993).

Stryker, Susan, 'My Words to Victor Frankenstein above the Village of Chamounix: Performing Transgender Rage', *GL/Q: A Journal of Lesbian and Gay Studies*, 1, 1994, pp. 237–54.

Stryker, Susan, *Transgender History* (Berkeley, CA: Seal Press, 2008).

Walpole, Horace, *The Castle of Otranto* [1764] (Oxford: Oxford University Press, 1998).

Westengard, Laura, '"Conquering Immortality": Gothic AIDS Literature as Queer Futurity in Gil Cuadros's *City of God*', *Journal of Narrative Theory*, 45.2, 2015, pp. 274–300.

Westengard, Laura, *Gothic Queer Culture: Marginalized Communities and the Ghosts of Insidious Trauma* (Lincoln, NE: University of Nebraska Press, 2019).

Filmography

Daughters of Darkness (*Les lèvres rouges*) (dir. Harry Kümel, Henry Lange, Belgium, France, West Germany, 1971).
Dracula's Daughter (dir. Lambert Hillyer, Universal Productions, USA, 1936).
Dressed to Kill (dir. Brian De Palma, Filmways Pictures, USA, 1980).
The Hunger (dir. Tony Scott, Metro Goldwyn Mayer, USA, 1983).
Psycho (dir. Alfred Hitchcock, Shamley Productions, USA, 1960).
Rebecca (dir. Alfred Hitchcock, Selznick International Pictures, USA, 1940).
The Silence of the Lambs (dir. Jonathan Demme, Strong Heart, USA, 1991).
Sleepaway Camp (dir. Robert Hiltzik, American Eagle Films, USA, 1983).
The Texas Chain Saw Massacre (dir. Tobe Hooper, Vortex, USA, 1974).
The Uninvited (dir. Lewis Allen, Paramount Pictures, USA, 1944).

Notes

1. Stryker, *Transgender History*, p. 134.
2. Love, 'Queer', p. 172.
3. Sedgwick, *Tendencies*, p. 7.
4. Haggerty, *Queer Gothic*, p. 2.
5. Ibid., p. 2.
6. Kilgour, *Rise of the Gothic Novel*, p. 8.
7. Halberstam, *Skin Shows*, p. 2.
8. Westengard, *Gothic Queer Culture*, p. 13.
9. Palmer, *Lesbian Gothic*, p. 9.
10. Halberstam, *Skin Shows*, p. 2.
11. Castle, *Apparitional Lesbian*, p. 28.
12. Soltysik, 'Recovering "Covering End"', p. 249.
13. Freud, 'The Uncanny', p. 225.
14. Palmer, *Queer Uncanny*, p. 15.
15. Jackson, *Hill House*, p. 1.
16. Ibid., p. 1.
17. Palmer, *Queer Uncanny*, p. 7.
18. Day, *Vampire Legends*, p. 27.
19. Ibid., p. 31.
20. Ní Fhlainn, *Postmodern Vampires*, p. 117.
21. Haggerty, 'Anne Rice', p. 5.
22. Ibid., p. 5.
23. See Day, *Vampire Legends*, and Haggerty *Queer Gothic*. Also, in a 2012 interview Rice confirmed that Louis and Lestat 'were the first vampire

same-sex parents', further aligning their relationship along a contemporary homonormative trajectory.
24. Day, *Vampire Legends*, p. 45.
25. See Auerbach, *Our Vampires, Ourselves*, and Ní Fhlainn, *Postmodern Vampires*.
26. Shelley, *Frankenstein*, p. 53.
27. Stryker, 'My Words to Victor Frankenstein', p. 238.
28. Westengard, 'Conquering Immortality', p. 277.
29. Ibid., p. 283.

Chapter 17

'Nightmares of the Normative': African American Gothic and the Rejection of the American Ideal
Maisha Wester

In 1919, less than a year after returning from fighting in the US armed forces alongside Allied troops, after working in factories to provide munitions and bolstering the US economy through investments in bonds, Black soldiers and citizens confronted a brutal truth: all their efforts to prove their allegiance and assimilation to dominant, white US society were fruitless. As white Americans attacked uniformed Black soldiers, firebombed Black businesses and waged open warfare on Black citizens, African Americans realised that their attempts to prove their normativity would never make them 'American'. The June 1919 bombings signalled the beginning of a 'reign of terror in the United States' to white Americans but not because of the violence African Americans suffered; rather, white Americans believed that Blacks were deserving of destruction despite evidence to the contrary.[1] Consequently, in the midst of the white terror now known as the Red Summer of 1919, many US Blacks began to question the ideals and values inherent in the behaviours, beliefs and attitudes constituent of American normativity.

African American Gothic fiction began to reject notions of the idyllic heteronormative American existence, exploring how it is a simplification requiring allegiance to alienating notions of race, gender and socio-economic class. The era was a turning point in Black Gothic literature. Nineteenth- and early twentieth-century writers such as slave narrative authors wrote literature testifying to the horrors of being denied humanity and citizenship, while their descendants wrote texts rooted in rejecting modern ideas of 'progress'. As fictions such as Richard Wright's 'The Man Who Lived Underground' (1945) and films such as Amiri Baraka's (writing as LeRoi Jones) *Dutchman* (1966)[2] reveal, all are enslaved and damned by embracing the modern, heteronormative, capitalist systems that define America.[3]

In pulling a portion of my title from Roderick Ferguson's essay 'Nightmares of the Heteronormative', I point to the ways that heteronormativity has been used as both bait and prison for African Americans. Ferguson argues that white Americans perpetually mark Black culture as 'queer' in order to further politically and economically disenfranchise Blacks. Blacks, reacting to the trauma of being deemed non-heteronormative, embraced respectability politics in which they attempted to be more (hetero)normative than even the average white American. However, in keeping with the impulses of the Gothic which gave voice to the repressed underbelly of Enlightenment thinking, Black Gothic writers challenge the normative as 'ideal'. They repeatedly reveal how assimilating to the 'normative' produces horror.

Black and American? The Psychological Costs of Assimilation

Writers such as James Baldwin reflected on the emotional, communal and psychological costs of trying to assimilate into white American culture, noting the disastrous consequences of assimilating.[4] Novels such as Pauline Hopkins's *Of One Blood* (1903), Ann Petry's *The Street* (1946) and Toni Morrison's *The Bluest Eye* (1970) repeatedly argued that the drive to conform to respectability politics results in (self-)isolation at best, and madness and death at worst. Hopkins's hero Reuel, for instance, embraces the colourism encouraged by dominant American culture only to manipulate his (unknown) sister, unwittingly committing incest in pursuit of a light, near-white bloodline. Reuel's salvation lies not in assimilating further into American culture but in returning to his Ethiopian ancestry and embracing blackness, becoming royalty in the process. Similarly, Petry's heroine Lutie utterly idolises the (white) American Dream and its figures of normativity – from naming Benjamin Franklin as her hero and role model to aspiring to the hyper-white romances depicted in advertisements – only to be coerced into murder and consequently abandon her son.[5] Morrison's novel is filled with people who aspire to white American normativity, from a well-off Black woman who prizes her finery over her family, to an impoverished mother who hates and neglects her own children for their failure to cohere to the images cast in films, to a child who loses her mind wishing for blue eyes. But as Lutie's own employers the Chandlers reveal, the idyllic normative life is also full of horrors and losses; consequently, the sacrifices the Black characters make in such novels are futile. In each case, Blacks striving to achieve (white) American normativity must invariably embrace subservience and self-effacement as part of the process.

Accepting and assimilating into the normative only helps maintain oppressive systems. After all, the normative of Jim Crow era America was violent racial segregation, the pathologisation of homosexual subjects and the acceptance of domestic violence. Baldwin explains the problem astutely:

> I'm afraid that is one of the great dilemmas, one of the great psychological hazards, of being an American Negro ... One is born in a white country, a white Protestant Puritan country, where one was once a slave, where all the standards and all the images ... when you open your eyes, everything you see: none of it applies to you.
>
> You go to white movies and, like everybody else, you fall in love with Joan Crawford, and you root for the Good Guys who are killing off the Indians. It comes as a great psychological collision when you realize all of these things are really metaphors for your oppression, and will lead into a kind of psychological warfare in which you may perish.[6]

Embracing the American normative is 'a futile and deadly undertaking' which enables our own nightmares.[7] Indeed, Fred Daniels, the protagonist of Richard Wright's Gothic story 'The Man Who Lived Underground', quips 'if the world as men had made it was right, then anything else was right, any act a man took to satisfy himself, murder, theft, torture ... he was afraid of himself, afraid of doing some nameless thing'.[8] As Hess, one of the titular characters in Bill Gunn's film *Ganja and Hess* (1973) illustrates, at best assimilating Blacks become vampires, objectifying and thriving from the labour and bodies of others.

In detailing the costs of assimilating to a problematic normativity, Black Gothic authors and filmmakers also redefine notions of terrorism. This task is important given that anti-Black violence during the Red Summer of 1919 was legitimated through political discourses which defined Blacks as (latent) terrorists. Challenging the origins of such terrorism proved an invaluable task for contemporary Black thinkers such as Richard Wright.[9] As Ira Wells argues, *Native Son* (1940) redefines terror(ism) 'not as a radical gesture performed by a profoundly alienated self – the Romantic notion of terror as the passionate expression of disaffected individuality – but as a political effect, where "terror" is the result of ingrained patterns of structural violence'.[10] Terror(ist) attacks arise first and foremost from the battering of structural violence upon the individual who warps into the monster that society prematurely deemed him.

Such assaults render Blacks terrorists of their own community. Bigger, having been warped by socio-economic oppression into 'the unconscious agent of political vengeance', first turns his rage upon his friends and family.[11] The unconscious nature of his violence alludes both to its origins as well as its ability to be (self-)perpetuated on the individual and the individual's community. Likewise, the compulsion to assimilate to an oppressive normativity is a sort of terrorist act which is initiated by a demanding white American culture, and which produces horror in the Black subject and collapse in Black communities. In rejecting the call to embrace the (white American) heteronormative, Black subjects are able to see the mechanisms of oppression and terror abounding in the normative, and (hopefully) disrupt the cycles of terrorism and loss.

Descents into Blackness/Awakenings to White Terror

Many twentieth-century African American Gothic texts embrace the trope of subterranean descent into darkness and living burial. Texts such as 'The Man Who Lived Underground', *Invisible Man* and *Dutchman* – to name a few – drive their characters down into the bowels of the earth in a flight that provides enlightening introspection which leads them to interrogate normativity.[12] Such descents in both white and Black American Gothic texts are compelled, though, by different factors. In Black texts, encounters with white violence and/or intrusions typically precede the fall into the subterranean. Fred Daniels, Wright's protagonist in 'The Man Who Lived Underground', retreats to the sewer while fleeing corrupt officers determined to charge him with a crime he did not commit. Similarly, the unnamed protagonist of Ralph Ellison's *Invisible Man* literally falls into his hole while running from a confluence of destructive social forces.

Amiri Baraka's *Dutchman* seems to disrupt this trend by beginning in the tunnels of the New York subway. The film opens with a long shot of the dark subterranean space, before roaming to scan the even darker tunnels and finally settling on Lula nearly blending with the wall and paralleled by the arriving train which carries Clay, the Black hero of the feature. However, if we consider Lulu's pursuit of Clay and the occasional white male defence of her wild ramblings alongside Clay's final, raging monologue, we realise that his journey has been likewise motivated by subtle, cultural violence. Lulu's indictment of Clay's attempts to 'fit in' – she calls him a 'liver-lipped white man', a 'would-be Christian' and a 'dirty white man' – echo the kinds of cultural and psychological violence wrought by attempts to embrace the normative. Early on in the film, Clay, jokingly critiquing the idea of plantations as 'big open whitewashed places like heaven' where slaves were 'grooved to be there. Just strummin' and hummin' all day', briefly alludes to the assaults one accepts by embracing the dominant normative. Clay's behaviour and comments suggest that dominant society has been driving him to this space for a while. Though such violent encounters do not always result in inspired, radical insight, the (temporary) exile from dominant society that results from these encounters allows the characters in question to develop a critical gaze that interrogates the dominant ideal.

As many of Edgar Allan Poe's texts illustrate, Gothic descents into the dark abyss are complex projects. His characters' descents illustrate the sense that reason is an adopted masquerade repeatedly challenged by perverse reality.[13] Uncovering the Real(ity) is not a source of relief in American Gothic texts. Rather, these moments produce horror. Literal falls into darkness metaphorise this conflict as the perverse desire to fall denotes lapses in reason. In the dark, Gothic characters of white American texts often encounter monstrous selves. Similarly, the descents of many characters in Black Gothic texts can be understood more completely in terms of Lacanian encounters with the Real. Lloyd-Smith's observation that horror is encountered '[w]here the "real" – in the sense of whatever is outside or beyond culture – comes into collision with the "symbolic" – in the sense of how things are agreed to be in culture and language' stands true for Black Gothic as well.[14] While the realisation of the protagonists is about the Real(ity) of the self, it is also about encountering and uncovering the Real(ity) of society. The consequence is not unlike the revelations of Female Gothic: such characters recognise that the ideology of progress as a lie.

Wright's 'The Man Who Lived Underground' focuses entirely upon detailing the uncanny encounter with an otherwise unobservable Real(ity). From the moment Fred descends into the sewers he begins to observe the nuanced components that make up the whole of objects, sounds and light. Hearing a car pass overhead, Fred notes 'He had never thought that cars could sound like that.'[15] Lighting a match, he similarly observes that 'it flared weirdly in the wet gloom, glowing greenishly, turning red, orange, then yellow'.[16] Exiled from the world above ground and its various organising systems, Fred can see the full, complex range of reality. Viewing for the first time the insidious nature of socioeconomic oppression and the ways it is woven into every facet of life, Fred comes to see the American normative landscape and culture as 'a wild forest filled with death', lit by 'dark sunshine'.[17]

'The Dark Sunshine Above Ground'

Religion is the first normativity that Fred reconsiders during his subterranean journey. Overhearing a choir singing, Fred observes, 'They oughtn't to do that ... Just singing with the air of the sewer blowing in on them ... He felt that he was gazing upon something abysmally obscene.'[18] Significantly, Christianity is taken as a foundational norm of American culture, yet Fred can see how it acts as a deterrent from radical change, producing Black acceptance of destructive subservience instead. Their singing is not praise of God or a testament of faith but rather their painful 'grovelling and begging for something they could never get'.[19] Both Fred and the congregation reside in the sewer wasteland of unwanted detritus; however, only Fred can see it. Meanwhile the churchgoers, captured within the net of the heteronormative, are not only blind to the ways their practice maintains the system of their oppression, but cannot accept the insight Fred eventually offers them. Later, rising from his sewer, Fred wanders in, seeking to share his redeeming message as the congregation is in the midst of song:

> *Tell me again your story*
> *The lamb, the Lamb, the Lamb*
> *Flood away my soul with your glory*
> *...*
> Many turned to look at him, but the song rolled on. His arm was jerked violently.
> "I'm sorry, Brother, but you can't do that in here," a man said.
> "But, mister!"
> "You can't act rowdy in God's house," the man said.
> "He's filthy," another man said.
> "But I want to tell 'em," he said loudly.
> "He stinks," someone muttered.[20]

The timing of Fred's appearance and his message of salvation explicitly mark him as the very 'Lamb' the church sings of and longs for. However, as a part of normative American culture, 'the Lamb' that Christian churches – even Black churches – await is explicitly white. As such, the congregation is damned by the form of salvation they seek. Wright punctuates the point with the next song the choir sings as Fred, growing frantic in his need to share his insight, is expelled from the church: 'Oh wondrous sight upon the cross / Vision sweet and divine / ... / Full of love sublime'.[21] The congregation fails to see the love Fred offers because he does not fit their image of a saviour, yet – like the saviour they seek – state agents murder him for the message he offers. Furthermore, the song predicts that such sacrificial deaths will always fail because, as the lyrics note, religious culture instructs populations to accept and praise such deaths rather than rebel against them.

Wright next indicts entertainment as a destructive distraction. Shortly after hearing the choir rehearsing, Fred encounters a packed cinema:

'These people were laughing at their lives, he thought with amazement. They were shouting and yelling at the animated shadows of themselves ... these people were children, sleeping in their living, awake in their dying.'[22] Wright's indictment of the film industry is especially poignant given the success of D. W. Griffith's 1915 *Birth of a Nation* and the explicitly racist representations of Blacks which followed it. In these early films, Blacks were either villainous as in movies such as *The Emperor Jones* (1933), buffoonish comic asides as in *Zombies on Broadway* (1945), or neutered sidekicks as in *Gone with the Wind* (1939). The only times when Black figures rose to any real revolutionary power were in horror films such as *Frankenstein* (1931) and *King Kong* (1933), and even then Blacks were only metaphorically on screen, hidden behind masks of monstrosity. Black spectators are taught to applaud the death of 'monstrous' radicals offering to topple a (problematic) society, and to applaud films whose plots feature Black submission and absence.

Dutchman also clarifies how embracing American religious and popular culture means accepting anti-blackness. While Clay's name marks him as Adam/original man, Lulu acts a demonic Eve luring Clay to his damnation through the exploitation of various narratives of cultural, romantic and economic success. Clay's first bite of an apple signals his doom as Lulu explains: 'Eating apples together, that's always the first step.' The film's focus on the apple proves telling as the fruit serves as a spiritual signifier which is also tied to Lulu's (correct) assertion of Clay's desire for cultural assimilation and acceptance. Notably, Clay's final monologue affirms this onslaught as both religious and cultural. His tirade indicts 'Christian charity' and 'Western rationalism' after defining the rage lurking in entertainers such as Charlie Parker and Bessie Smith, Black cultural artists who were appropriated by white American culture. While Lulu notes that it begins with apples, Clay's monologue ends by expressing a desire to murder 'the great missionary heart', for religion, along with the lure to become 'half-white trusties'[23] accepted into the dominant fold, colonises and entraps African Americans.

Lulu's initial seduction of Clay also recalls Baldwin's explicit points and Wright's implicit assertions about how popular film teaches Blacks to desire whiteness and reject their selves. Lulu often sounds as if she is scripting a film narrative, including characters, positioning and dialogue. In fact, Clay explicitly marks her as filmic:

LULU: Boy are you corny ... You should be on television.
CLAY: You act like you're on television already.
LULU: That's because I'm an actress.

Baldwin named the media as the means through which desires for assimilation and acceptance are conveyed, as their plots insist that Black audiences 'fall in love with Joan Crawford', an actress who functions in Baldwin's commentary as a metonym for the American normative. In the exchange above, Lulu admits to serving just this function in naming herself an actress. Importantly, the first half of *Dutchman* concludes shortly after this exchange, with Lulu seducing Clay into romantic play, in other words to perform the part of the desiring lover. The film's editing and score define his submission as disastrous. As Clay lets Lulu curl up against him, the scene cuts to a shot of the train travelling through dark tunnels and empty subway stations while an ominous, brutal marimba plays in the foreground. When the camera returns to the train, we see Lulu cuddling Clay while feeding him apples. By now, Clay's jacket is gone, his tie is loosened and his top button undone as he lounges in the seat against Lulu. Clay's dishevelled wardrobe suggests that he is quite literally coming undone.[24]

Perhaps unsurprisingly, both the story and the film indict the capitalist's idealisation of money, and the class systems and notions of luxury that accompany the ideal. Lulu, for example, repeatedly critiques Clay for his middle-class pretensions before he finally acknowledges such seeming sensibilities as a mere mask, noting that only 'Crazy niggers turning their backs on sanity' would embrace 'Money. Power. Luxury ... When all it needs is that simple act. Murder. Just murder! Would make us all sane.' The violence Clay praises should not be read literally, for soon afterwards he returns to interrogating other normative aspects of culture. The 'murder' he proposes should be read as a symbolic assault upon normative ideologies.

Wright's text is even more explicit in its rejection of capitalist ideology and redefines money as merely an agreed-upon fiction: 'The fellows in Washington sure know how to make this stuff, he mused. He rubbed the money with his fingers, as though expecting it to reveal hidden qualities ... Just like any other paper, he mumbled.'[25] The passage defines money, and all that it signifies, as a construction fabricated by national leaders. Wright ultimately rejects 'wealth' as a signifier of power, given that money lacks any real 'hidden qualities' or power on its own but rather is simple paper. Nor is this the only signifier of wealth the text assaults; Fred also steals diamonds and valuable watches along with the banknotes, items which he casts across the floor of his cave and nails to the walls in his play.

Wright marks the hope of wealth as a broken promise to Blacks in particular, though he also notes how all are betrayed by the promise. Studying the banknotes closely, Fred reads the legend,

> *The United States of America will pay to the bearer on demand one hundred dollars ... This note is legal tender for all debts, public and private ...* He broke into a musing laugh, feeling that he was reading of the doings of people who lived on some far-off planet.[26]

Fred's notion that the promise arrives from a foreign planet makes sense in light of America's history of racial disenfranchisement and the limitations to ownership and wealth imposed upon African Americans, a population who in previous generations were objectified to serve as a kind of legal tender. In Wright's more immediate era, Jim Crow politics meant that various locations did not accept money from Black hands even as the industries that drove the national economy continued to rely on Black labour. Race easily negated the pledge on the banknotes; Blacks enable the promise but cannot claim it. For oppressed Blacks, money is just one of the 'serious toys of the men who lived in the dead world'.[27] Consequently, as Clay notes, pinning your hopes on collecting quantities of it is insane.

The Hands That Pour the Acid: The Curse of White Supremacy

African American Gothic literature does not limit the call to Blacks but also reveals how white Americans invariably suffer through embracing ideas of normativity. In *The Street*, for instance, the white wealthy Chandlers suffer a crumbling family and a holiday suicide. Likewise, nightclub owner Junto cannot be with Mrs Hedges, the woman he knows is his perfect match, because both allow themselves to be governed by normative ideals of physical beauty and race. Later films such as *Tales from the Hood* (1995) posit that seemingly dominant white men are disempowered by the very form of American normative masculinity, asking 'Where does "real masculinity" reside? In upper class power? In guns? In violence? In one's sexual organs? ... The film's implied answer is, "If you have to seek a masculine identity in these props, regardless of your cultural group, you stand to lose your identity altogether."'[28] Wright's and Baraka's fictions similarly depict the ways whiteness suffers under American normativity, thus calling for would-be oppressors to awaken to their contributions to their own suffering. As Wells notes, quoting Boris Max in *Native Son*, 'There are others ... millions of others, Negro and white, and that is what makes the future seem a looming image of violence', revealing that terrorism is not a signal of external infiltration and manipulation: 'the towers are not brought down by some outward, external violence, but by a compromised foundation'.[29]

Wright's text reveals how white Americans are blind to and blinded by their oppression within a culture that wilfully dehumanises everyone. Hiding in a basement coal bunker, Fred finds himself face to face with a white man. Though the man returns six times to shovel coal, he never lifts his eyes or turns on the light, although Fred quickly locates a light bulb. Fred concludes that 'The old man had worked here for so long that he had no need for light; he had learned a way of seeing in his dark world, like those sightless worms that inch along underground by a sense of touch.'[30] Significantly, the old man's face is covered in coal dust, his eyes are watery and his cheeks are gaunt, suggesting he is not in good health and in actuality occupies a social position that renders him 'Black' in terms of his labour and class. The encounter predicts the story's conclusion in which various people reject the light Fred offers, having become accustomed to their darkness. The scene here is important because of how it connects Black oppression to (unrecognised) white suffering.

Nor is Wright's call class-contingent, for he notes how middle-class whites are also dehumanised by American normativity. Having stumbled across the vault of a jewellery store, Fred watches in disbelief as a worker steals from the safe: 'an eerie white hand, seemingly detached from its arm, touched the metal knob and whirled it ... The white hand went in and out of the safe, taking wads of bills and cylinders of coins.'[31] The event occurs shortly after Fred's encounter with the coal labourer, thereby connecting the two men despite their class differences. While the coal labourer's face and position signal his class oppression, the description of the worker here signals his fragmentation; unlike the old man, this thief never gets a face. Rather he is reduced to a mere hand which handles money. Fred returns a number of times to watch the man's doings and never sees more than his hand, and he frequently refers to the thief only as 'the white hand'. Later, while pondering the thief, Fred grows

> indignant ... he despised and pitied the man ... He wanted to steal the money merely for the sensation involved in getting it, and he had no intention whatever of spending a penny of it; but he knew that the man who was now stealing it was going to spend it, perhaps for pleasure.[32]

Fred's indignation suggests that the money in and of itself is meaningless, and therefore valuing it is a foolish delusion. The multiple scenes recount how all are alienated from and within the normative capitalist economy; even well-off white Americans are reduced to mere disembodied hands.

Fred's nightmarish vision of the Second World War amplifies the disastrous ends of embracing dominant normative culture:

To control himself, he turned on the radio ... The music ended and a man recited news events ... as he heard the cultivated tone, he looked down upon land and sea as men fought, as cities were razed, as planes scattered death upon open towns, as long lines of trenches wavered and broke ... He saw steel tanks rumbling across fields of ripe wheat to meet other tanks and there was a loud clang of steel as numberless tanks collided. He saw troops with fixed bayonets charging in waves against other troops who held fixed bayonets and men groaned as steel ripped into their bodies and they went down to die.[33]

The voice from the radio at the beginning of the vision recalls the text's previous critiques of popular culture even as the movement of the tanks alludes to various nations' willingness to destroy the vital sustenance that their citizens labour to produce. The scene climaxes with the wilful slaughter of people, unmourned and unprotested, though reduced to cannon fodder. Such passages call attention to how the white embrace of normative capitalist ideals produces profound violence regardless of the privileges of race and nationality.

The creative referents for Baraka's central female character in *Dutchman* reveal the film's concerns over white exploitation. Baraka borrows the name Lulu from a Alban Berg opera called *Lulu*, which tells the story of a mysterious young woman who suffers a downward spiral from being a well-kept mistress in Vienna to becoming a street prostitute in London. Berg's Lulu is both a victim and a purveyor of destruction, thereby suggesting that the same holds true for Baraka's character. That Lulu's monstrosity is violence against both her victim and herself becomes apparent in a number of casual asides. At one point in the midst of her attack on Clay, she cries out 'my Christ' in a tone of anguish; she seems distraught in this moment, her face near tears. Later, weaving a fantasy of her night with Clay in her room, she strangely declares, 'You'll call my rooms black as a grave. You'll say, "This place is like Juliet's tomb"', thereby signalling herself as one of the living dead.

The film's opening also marks her as both victim and villain; we first glimpse Lulu alone in a dark, desolate subway. Though cast in shadows which mark her as a frightening creature, she is nonetheless still a lone woman, without friend, community or even distraction. Though the next scene stresses her predatory nature,[34] her initial isolation also asks us to consider how she too is damned. Her stalking of Clay is suggestive of an animal in pursuit of its next meal, but we must wonder if her hunger will ever be satiated. Unlike Clay, who has other pursuits and interests to fuel him, Lulu can only watch and wait for her next victim. Unlike Clay, who retains his humanity even in his rage, Lulu ultimately loses herself to her monstrosity. In the moment that she stabs Clay, the camera centres on her contorted face. Dark circles so ring Lulu's eyes that they seem sunken in her face, and her lips twist and gape in a vicious leer, all of which is exacerbated by the camera's extreme close-up. The face that fills the frame in this moment is utterly demonic, lacking in all signs of humanity. Lulu the woman is lost.

The text's title provides the clearest argument that whiteness suffers from participation in normative systems, for 'Dutchman' is an intertextual referent, especially when read alongside several of Lulu's comments. For instance, in a rare moment of despair, Lulu notes 'How could things go on like that forever? Huh? Except I do go on as I do', thus betraying her sense of an eternal, wearying life. Lulu's decried undead state gestures back to the title's referent story, 'The Flying Dutchman', in which a slave ship is cursed to wander forever the waters around the Cape of Good Hope, bringing doom to all who spy it.[35] The subway train is a modern iteration of the doomed ship, with Lulu functioning as its arrogant but cursed captain. Though Clay's and Lulu's car carries just the two of them for the entire first half of the film, a wealth of passengers suddenly appear in the second half, once Lulu has successfully lured Clay into her arms. Clay calls our attention to the abruptness of their manifestation: 'Wow. All these people, so suddenly. They must all come from the same place', which Lulu sarcastically confirms, noting 'Right. That they do.' Given the referent story, Lulu is telling the truth despite her sarcasm, revealing that the passengers are also a product of the same ideology and culture that produces and damns Lulu. So when Clay asks, 'You know about them too?', Lulu is being honest in her answer: 'Yeah. About them more than I know about you.' Lulu and those like her are among the damned. Though she steers the ship, she, like the captain of *The Flying Dutchman*, is nonetheless bound by a greater, unseen force that ultimately governs her destiny.

Opening Our Eyes to the World Around Us

The horror of such tales stems not from the recognition of the Real(ity) lurking beneath the normative but from a seeming inability to awaken others and effect change. Fred arises from the sewers not as a horrified monster but as a man beaming with hope of such intensity that he is almost childlike. Nor does he become resentful as others refuse to heed his call but, rather, he becomes more earnest in trying to convey his message. Yet the tale concludes in a truly Gothic fashion. Fred attempts to enlighten the very officers who first led him to the sewers, but they shoot him, explaining 'You've got to shoot his kind. They'd wreck things.'[36] Fred's body is left to spiral into the darkness of the sewer, carried away by scummy water as the world above continues on, enslaved to an invisible master.

Although Clay meets a similar end, Baraka importantly notes that his death stems from different sources: 'Why is he killed? Because he wants to do that by itself you know. "I am the great black poet I'm here I'm going to express myself," you can't make change by yourself. You can either get killed, go to jail or get proud.'[37] Refusing such a fate, numerous other Black Gothic writers have taken up the call to challenge notions of the normative and thereby attack the hegemonic in their works. I have mentioned several already in the course of this essay, but we might also include independent Black horror films such as *Ganja and Hess* (1973), which I have praised elsewhere at length,[38] and marginally mainstream films such as *Eve's Bayou* (1997), which also interrogates class distinctions alongside notions of narrative stability. We might interrogate the painful, doomed romance in Gloria Naylor's *Mama Day* (1988) as a refutation of normative familial and communal dynamics. We might also look to popular horror writers such as Tananarive Due, whose African Immortal series critiques the reproduction of patriarchal structures and violence in Black communities,[39] and Gothic Afrofuturist texts such as Octavia Butler's *Kindred* (1979) to consider the importance of rejecting narratives of normativity in imagining a future free of hegemony.

In texts where the rejection of the normative is successful – such as Due's *My Soul to Keep* and Gunn's *Ganja and Hess* – it is a success achieved in the company of like-minded, driven others who can see rebellion as something other than terror(ism). And this is perhaps their first and greatest assault on the American normative ideal, for these authors refute the notion of the lone hero saving the community as a fantasy which, at best, produces a destructive pride. Rather, as Miranda desperately tries to help George see in *Mama Day*, it takes our reaching out for each other's hands to make such a revolution effective.[40] Otherwise, hegemonic narratives will merely recast us as terrorists who would 'wreck things' and so must be destroyed.

Key Texts

Hannah Crafts, *The Bondwoman's Narrative*. Written by a formerly enslaved woman in the mid-nineteenth century and rediscovered and published in 2002, the novel is the fictionalised autobiography of Hannah Crafts, a self-educated house slave who runs away to the North alongside her mistress, a beautiful young woman who Hannah discovers is passing for white. Pursued by a villainous slave catcher named Trappe, the novel details the terrors and torments Crafts endures in pursuit of her freedom. The novel notably deploys numerous Gothic conventions, rewriting well-known Gothic texts such as *The Castle of Otranto*.

Jean Toomer, *Cane* (1923). A collection of poems, short fiction and a concluding play, this highly experimental novel weaves the disparate forms into a cohesive narrative of the interracial and intra-racial oppression suffered by Blacks in the US South and North. Responding to the Great Migration and predicting Ellison's *Invisible Man*, Toomer's novel reveals the horror of the US South haunted by slavery and the US North populated by people dehumanised through their assimilation into white capitalist culture. Horror, *Cane* reveals, cannot be escaped simply by relocating.

Ralph Ellison, *Invisible Man* (1952). Ellison's masterpiece follows an unnamed narrator through horrifying misadventures – from his grotesque encounters in a Southern college to his nightmarish flight in the midst of a Harlem race riot. This complex novel reveals how migration does not provide Blacks with equality, freedom and refuge from racism; rather, they are merely damned to a different kind of Gothic existence.

Octavia Butler, *Kindred* (1979). Dana, a young Black woman, is transported multiple times from her home in 1970s California back to the pre-Civil War South where she becomes entangled in the life of Rufus, one of Dana's ancestors and a slave-owner. Repeatedly drawn back to the same slave quarters, each stay proves longer and more dangerous, until Dana is ultimately confronted with a horrible task. This book is a groundbreaking piece of Gothic Afrofuturism.

Toni Morrison, *Beloved* (1987). This award-winning novel fictionalises the harrowing story of Margaret Garner, a slave woman who killed her children to avoid them being recaptured into slavery. Recasting Garner as Sethe, Morrison deploys Gothic tropes to reveal how real existence as a Black person in America is far more horrifying than any ghost could ever be, as Sethe and her surviving daughter struggle to free themselves from the spectre of slavery and intra-racial oppression.

Further Critical Reading

Brooks, Kinitra, *Searching for Sycorax: Black Women's Hauntings of Contemporary Horror* (2018). Examining Black women in horror as both creators and characters, Brooks critiques the horror genre's representational politics while also noting how Black women have used the genre to critique white American cultural anxieties by deploying Africana folklore in their texts. Brooks explores authors such as Cheysa Burke and Nalo Hopkinson from nations across the Black Diaspora.

Harrison, Sheri-Marie, 'Marlon James and the Metafiction of the New Black Gothic' (2018). Examining the function of apocalypses in the work of Marlon James, Harrison argues that violence is central to James's disruption of essentialised ideas of race and sexuality that circulate among Black communities. As such, she argues that James's horrific endings ultimately point out an even more horrific hypocrisy among would-be radical Black populations.

Means Coleman, Robin, *Horror Noire: Blacks in American Horror Films from* the 1890s to the Present (2011). This concise volume explores Black representation in American horror film while also investigating Black authored and/or produced horror films. Tracing the long history of anti-Blackness in each era of film production, from its very beginnings in the 1890s to the late 1990s, Coleman posits that the genre nonetheless provides a representational space for Black people to challenge the racist depictions typical of the genre in dominant/white film productions.

Smethurst, James, 'Invented by Horror: The Gothic and African American Literary Ideology in Native Son' (2001). This foundational essay was one of the first to chart how 'realist' African American authors, specifically Richard Wright, addressed the racial representations dominant in American Gothic literature and film. Smethurst tracks the ways Wright appropriates and revises works such as Poe's 'Black Cat' and the climax of the 1931 film *Frankenstein* in order to speak back to texts that reduce Blackness to figures of monstrosity and terror.

Wester, Maisha, *African American Gothic: Screams from Shadowed Places* (2012). This important monograph charts the rise and developments in African American Gothic literature from its first iterations in nineteenth-century slave narratives to its late twentieth-century manifestations in novels such as *Beloved*. Arguing that African American use of the genre is a method of speaking back to oppressors, Wester also notes that Black authors are as concerned with intra-racial oppressions as they are with white antagonism. The book notably explores the various methodologies and focuses that dominated the different eras of Black Gothic production.

Bibliography

Baraka, Amiri, 'Amiri Baraka on the Background of the *Dutchman*', *MPACTODAY*, 7 June 2011, < https://youtu.be/qkhL70D2ZB0> (last accessed 22 August 2020).

Brooks, Kinitra, *Searching for Sycorax: Black Women's Hauntings of Contemporary Horror* (New Brunswick, NJ: Rutgers University Press, 2018).

Butler, Octavia, *Kindred* (New York: Doubleday, 1979).

Crafts, Hannah, *The Bondwoman's Narrative* (New York: Warner Books, 2002).

Dutchman (dir. Anthony Harvey, Gene Persson Enterprises, 1966), <https://yo utu.be/8VRoOAmtHsQ> (last accessed 20 August 2020).

Ellison, Ralph, *Invisible Man* [1952] (New York: Vintage, 1979).

Ferguson, Rodrick, 'Nightmares of the Heteronormative', *Cultural Values*, 4.4, 2000, pp. 419–44.

Fulmer, Jacqueline, '"Men Ain't All: A Reworking of Masculinity in *Tales from the Hood*, or, Grandma Meets the Zombie', *The Journal of American Folklore*, 115.457/458, 2002, pp. 422–42.

Harrison, Sheri-Marie, 'Marlon James and the Metafiction of the New Black Gothic', *Journal of West Indian Literature*, 26.2, 2018, pp. 1–17.

Lloyd-Smith, Allan, *American Gothic Fiction: An Introduction* (London: Continuum, 2004).

Means Coleman, Robin, *Horror Noire: Blacks in American Horror Films from the 1890s to the Present* (Abingdon: Routledge, 2011).

Morrison, Toni, *Beloved* (London: Vintage, 1987).

Smethurst, James, 'Invented by Horror: The Gothic and African American Literary Ideology in Native Son', *African American Review*, 35.1, 2001, pp. 29–40.

Terkel, Studs, 'An Interview with James Baldwin', in *Conversations with James Baldwin* (Jackson, MS: University Press of Mississippi, 1989), pp. 3–23.

Toomer, Jean, *Cane* [1923] (New York: W.W. Norton, 2011).

Wells, Ira, '"What I Killed for, I Am": Domestic Terror in Richard Wright's America', *American Quarterly*, 62.4, 2010, pp. 873–95.

Wester, Maisha, *African American Gothic: Screams from Shadowed Places* (Basingstoke: Palgrave Macmillan, 2012).

Wester, Maisha, 'Re-Scripting Blaxploitation Horror: Ganja and Hess's Gothic Implications', in Justin D. Edwards and Johan Höglund (eds), *B-Gothic Movies: International Perspectives* (Edinburgh: Edinburgh University Press, (2018), pp. 32–49.

Wright, Richard, 'The Man Who Lived Underground' [1945], in *Eight Men* (New York: Harper Collins, 1989), pp. 19–84.

Notes

1. Wells, '"What I Killed for, I Am"', p. 879.
2. Baraka's play premiered at the Cherry Lane Theatre in 1964 and was released as a film in 1966. My analysis stems primarily from the film text.
3. Rejection of modern capitalism is logical for Black authors, given that modern (global) capitalist systems originate in slavery.
4. Ferguson, 'Nightmares of the Heteronormative', p. 430.
5. White nightclub owner Juno lets himself into Lutie's apartment, intending to force her into sex. Lutie kills him in an enraged moment of self-defence.
6. Terkel, 'An Interview with James Baldwin', p. 5.
7. Ferguson, 'Nightmares of the Heteronormative', p. 430.
8. Wright, 'The Man Who Lived Underground', p. 56.
9. Although the terms 'terrorism' and 'terrorist' are often understood primarily in a political context as a method of engagement and warfare, the success of such political attacks depend upon the ability to achieve Gothic affect in a population. Thus to speak of terrorism is always to speak of (Gothic) terror.
10. Wells, '"What I Killed for, I Am"', p. 875.
11. Ibid., p. 881.
12. Colson Whitehead's novel *The Underground Railroad* (2016) also vacillates between subterranean flight and life above ground as the novel's heroine gradually realises that she will never access stable, normative life in the 'civilised', settled region of the United States.
13. Lloyd-Smith, *American Gothic Fiction*, p. 68.
14. Ibid., p. 114.
15. Wright, 'The Man Who Lived Underground', p. 21.

16. Ibid., p. 21.
17. Ibid., pp. 54, 57.
18. Ibid., p. 24.
19. Ibid., p. 25.
20. Ibid., p. 69.
21. Ibid., p. 68.
22. Ibid., p. 30.
23. Clay means 'half-white' metaphorically, implying that by denying their culture and embracing whiteness Blacks seem to access a small portion of social privilege. However, because they are only white on the inside, the benefits that they accrue are minimal and utterly unworthy of the required cultural, communal and psychological sacrifices.
24. Clay's movements during his monologue affirm this reading as he gathers his attire, putting his clothes back on as he rails against Lulu's assaults.
25. Wright, 'The Man Who Lived Underground', p. 46.
26. Ibid., p. 52.
27. Ibid., p. 47.
28. Fulmer, '"Men Ain't All": A Reworking of Masculinity', p. 436.
29. Wells, '"What I Killed for, I Am"', p. 874.
30. Wright, 'The Man Who Lived Underground', p. 32.
31. Ibid., p. 36.
32. Ibid., pp. 44–5.
33. Ibid., p. 57.
34. Lulu literally stalks Clay as the camera focuses on her at the rear of the car before cutting to Clay unwittingly reading his newspaper, and then cutting back to Lulu who is now positioned in a seat two rows behind Clay, still watching him, before finally advancing to his side.
35. There are numerous iterations of this legend, some of which say it was an East India trading ship not a slave ship, while others drop the regional specificity. But the primary plot remains the same: a ship carrying valuable cargo is steered to its death by an arrogant and over-confident captain.
36. Wright, 'The Man Who Lived Underground', p. 84.
37. Baraka, 'Amiri Baraka on the Background of the *Dutchman*'.
38. See Wester, 'Re-Scripting Blaxploitation Horror'.
39. Four novels compose the series: *My Soul to Keep* (1997), *The Living Blood* (2001), *Blood Colony* (2008) and *My Soul to Take* (2011).
40. *Mama Day* refutes the notion of the lone, male hero as an effective saviour. George, unable to let go of his American ideals, suffers a heart attack trying to save his wife on his own. Absent any other external actors, George's death emphasises the act of lone heroism as inherently deadly.

Chapter 18

Big Bad Wolves and Angry Sharks: The Ecogothic and a Century of Environmental Change
Christy Tidwell

Defining the Ecogothic

The Gothic, as Tom J. Hillard has argued, is 'notoriously slippery', and the *eco*gothic is no less complex.[1] Yet David Punter has written that there is one stable element in the Gothic, 'and that is fear';[2] similarly, the ecogothic is fundamentally about human fears related to the natural world. Chris Baldick's more detailed description of the Gothic says that it 'should combine a fearful sense of inheritance in time with a claustrophobic sense of enclosure in space, these two dimensions reinforcing one another to produce an impression of sickening descent into disintegration'.[3] The ecogothic, too, pays particular attention to the element of space – particularly natural spaces.

Many ecogothic narratives ask, for instance, what lurks in the forest? As Elizabeth Parker writes, 'The Deep Dark Forest is exactly that – deep and dark – and the exact source of its terrors is often mysterious, shadowy, and just out of sight.'[4] The source of terror might be the forest itself – as in Algernon Blackwood's 'The Willows' (1907) and 'The Man Whom the Trees Loved' (1912) – or it could be a monster (or witch) living within – as in *The Blair Witch Project* (1999).

The cabin in the woods, another common setting of ecogothic narratives, suggests the centrality of the ecogothic within the broader Gothic. As Bernice M. Murphy argues, '[t]he cabin in the woods is to the American Gothic what the haunted castle is to the European – the seed from which everything else ultimately grows'.[5] The cabin in the woods, provocatively described here with the language of nature, represents a space beyond civilisation, underscoring the tendency of the ecogothic to separate human and nonhuman, identifying the latter as a threat to safety and order. Insofar as forests and similar spaces exist outside human control and knowledge, they are sources of fear.

These fears are not universal, however. Murphy writes that '[e]co-horror films are most commonly found in the US and Australia, both nations established by the descendants of white settlers who set out to create a "new world" in the midst of a vast, unfamiliar, and often physically treacherous landscape already occupied by resentful native inhabitants',[6] and this indicates that the forest is frightening specifically for white settlers who do not understand the landscape and who must also deal with the people whose homes they are invading. For Indigenous inhabitants – resentful or not – the forest might not seem such a threat. And for Black people in the US the forest might represent still different fears – of white supremacy, lynching, enslavement. Most of the texts discussed here will focus on white Anglophone texts and ideas, both because that's what the broader critical conversation has tended to focus on and because there is simply not room to delve into these distinctions here. Nonetheless, they must be noted.

Although space is critical to the ecogothic, it is not all that defines it; ecogothic narratives are also often about nonhuman animals, representing them as beasts that will hunt, kill and eat humans. These narratives sometimes feature animals that might reasonably be seen as threats: great white sharks – in *Jaws* (1975), its sequels and the multitude of twenty-first-century shark movies; bears – in *Grizzly* (1976), as well as more recent films such as *Grizzly Rage* (2007) and *Backcountry* (2014); snakes – in *Ssssss* (1973) and *Anaconda* (1997); and crocodiles – in *Alligator* (1980), *Lake Placid* (1999) and *Crawl* (2019). In other cases, though, the monstrous animal is not typically a direct threat to humans: for example, rabbits in *Night of the Lepus* (1972), slugs in *Slugs* (1988), worms in *Squirm* (1976), rats in *Willard* (1971, remade in 2003) and ants in *Them!* (1954), *Phase IV* (1974) and *Empire of the Ants* (1977). This anxiety is not rational, therefore, but is a Gothic reimagining of the nonhuman.

Terrifying spaces and monstrous animals emphasise the harm that the natural world might do to us, but Stephen A. Rust and Carter Soles's definition of ecohorror offers a more complex sense of the ecogothic. Taking a fundamentally Gothic stance, Rust and Soles write that ecohorror 'assumes that environmental disruption is haunting humanity's relationship to the non-human world'.[7] Although ecohorror is often primarily identified with 'nature strikes back' narratives, Rust and Soles argue that it also includes 'analyses of texts in which humans do horrific things to the natural world, or in which horrific texts and tropes are used to promote ecological awareness, represent ecological crises, or blur human/nonhuman distinctions more broadly'.[8] Similarly, Jennifer Schell describes ecogothic literature as 'very critical of human beings and their destructive attitudes toward the natural world', noting that it tends 'to regard environmental problems with a complicated mixture of anxiety, horror, terror, anger, sadness, nostalgia, and guilt'.[9] Furthermore, Dawn Keetley and Matthew Wynn Sivils argue that the ecogothic reflects and responds to 'a culture obsessed with and fearful of a natural world both monstrous and monstrously wronged'.[10] Five out of five ecocritics agree: the ecogothic goes beyond nature-as-threat.

Ecogothic narratives also, as Rust and Soles indicate, complicate the relationship between nonhuman and human. Stacy Alaimo's concept of trans-corporeality, 'in which the human is always intermeshed with the more-than-human world',[11] is useful for understanding this complicated relationship. Trans-corporeality is not inherently good or bad; it includes beneficial relationships between human and nonhuman as well as a dangerous lack of boundaries. Within the ecogothic, the emphasis is on the latter, and David Cronenberg's *The Fly* (1986) illustrates this: as Seth Brundle (Jeff Goldblum) becomes Brundlefly, the transformation breaks down the distinctions between human and nonhuman, leaving a monstrous hybrid who begs to die. Elizabeth Parker ties this explicitly to the Gothic, noting that '[t]he Gothic is a mode famously obsessed with the transgression of boundaries – and trans-corporeality, which foregrounds the idea that there is a constant transition and flow across and between all sorts of "bodies", very much fits in with this'.[12] In other words, the ecogothic both relies upon the distinction between human and nonhuman (we are in here and nature is out there, a threatening Other) and also challenges this distinction. Within the ecogothic, both separation from the nonhuman and connection to it are frightening.

Historicising the Ecogothic

The ecogothic did not begin with the twentieth century but grew out of earlier ideas about the environment and humans' relationship to it. This history as well as shifts in environmental concerns over the century (again, primarily focusing on the US and UK) provide another way to explore key elements of the twentieth-century ecogothic.

Although the term *ecogothic* is new, the ecogothic's roots can be found in many early texts, such as William Bradford's 1620 description of Cape Cod as 'a hidious & desolate wildernes' [*sic*],[13] Mary Shelley's forbidding Arctic setting in *Frankenstein* (1818), and Nathaniel Hawthorne's demon-haunted forest in 'Young Goodman Brown' (1835). Acknowledging this history is crucial since, according to Murphy, ecohorror – particularly American ecohorror – functions by 'combining an urgent sense of present-day crisis with a much older awareness of the fraught relationship between the white colonist and the unfamiliar landscape inhabited by potentially hostile plants, animals, and humans'.[14] These early ideas about nature continue to haunt twentieth- and twenty-first-century ecohorror and ecogothic narratives.

Two other nineteenth-century ideas about the environment broadly influenced twentieth-century environmental policy and the ecogothic. One was the publication of George Perkins Marsh's *Man and Nature: or, Physical Geography as Modified by Human Action* in 1864. The book argued that humans have the ability to change the planet and set the stage for later discussions of human-caused environmental harm and, therefore, the necessity of human action to mitigate such harm. Ernst Heinrich Philipp August Haeckel's 1866 coining of the term *Oekologie*, which would become *ecology*, was also significant. Ecology builds on the Greek *oikos*, which means house or dwelling. In the context of the ecogothic, it's hard not to connect ecology's emphasis on the home to Freud's later introduction of the uncanny, or *unheimlich* (literally, 'not homely' or un-homelike). The uncanny – an eerie or frightening effect when something familiar is made to seem unfamiliar – is common to the Gothic; combining *ecology* and *unheimlich* functions to remind us that the natural world is our home, but it is not always homely, familiar or friendly. With or without Freud, ecology is important to the ecogothic for being at the root of the term itself: *ecogothic* doesn't exist without *ecology*.

In the early twentieth century, ideas about ecology focused on conservation, specifically of wilderness spaces and resources. This emphasis on conservation was a reaction to late nineteenth- and early twentieth-century developments such as industrialisation and urbanisation as well as to the losses of the period (the American bison was nearly eradicated in 1884; Martha, the last passenger pigeon, died in 1914). The first national park in the US, Yellowstone National Park, was established in 1872, and wilderness conservation became even more widespread later: President Theodore Roosevelt established many national forests, reserves, game preserves, national parks and monuments; the National Parks Service was established in 1916; and the first designated wilderness area in the world was established in 1924.

Ecogothic tales of the period responded to these ideas by exploring the dark side of the wilderness and its conservation. For instance, Algernon Blackwood's 'The Wendigo' (1910), set in a Canadian forest, represents an overwhelming and frightening wilderness, noting 'the leagues of tenantless forest', 'the merciless spirit of desolation which took no note of man', and the forest's vastness, 'smothering the little tent that stood there like a wee white shell facing the ocean of tremendous forest'.[15]

Blackwood sees the wilderness not as something worth preserving but as Other, and he emphasises its uncanny danger. One character notes that 'these woods, you know, are a bit too big to feel quite at home in – to feel comfortable in, I mean!', and another agrees, saying, 'There's no end to 'em – no end at all.'[16] Wilderness preservation is all well and good, this suggests, but it must be kept under control.

Another significant environmental issue across the twentieth century was pollution. In the early 1900s air pollution was most prominent. Beginning in the nineteenth century, thick fogs and smoke from coal burning in industrial cities caused major problems in England and the US, leading to campaigns against smoke and laws against smoke production. These had little effect, however, and the term 'smog' was invented in London in 1905 to describe this chronic problem. Several early twentieth-century ecogothic stories feature fog, smog or other atmospheric disturbances, indicating widespread concern about air pollution. For instance, M. P. Shiel's *The Purple Cloud* (1901) describes an apocalypse brought about by the titular purple cloud; Alfred Hitchcock's early film *The Lodger: A Story of the London Fog* (1927) draws on and reinforces fears of the fog by associating it with a serial killer; and *Into the London Fog: Eerie Tales from the Weird City* (2020, edited by Elizabeth Dearnley), a collection of weird and Gothic tales of the fog from the nineteenth century into the mid-twentieth century, highlights the fog's importance and its connection to industrialisation and growing pollution in this period (Dearnley notes 'the disappearance of true London fog in the years following the Clean Air Act of 1956').[17]

In the mid-twentieth century, smog was still a major issue (for example, in Los Angeles in 1943; Donora, PA, 1948; London, 1952), but concerns about other kinds of environmental harm became more widespread. After the bombing of Japan at the close of the Second World War and post-war nuclear testing on Bikini Atoll and in the American Southwest, fears about nuclear war and nuclear fallout took centre stage. *Gojira* (*Godzilla*, 1954) opens with a scene echoing the real-life *Daigo Fukuryū Maru* (*Lucky Dragon No. 5*) fishing boat, which was caught in nuclear fallout that led to the fishermen suffering acute radiation syndrome. Godzilla was designed to look like the victim of atomic bombing as well as using nuclear power himself. In the US, *Them!* dramatised these fears through a story of giant ants resulting from atomic testing in New Mexico. Nevil Shute's *On the Beach* (1957) – and the movie adaptation in 1959 – focused on the aftermath of nuclear war. Nuclear fallout pollutes the atmosphere, and air currents carry the fallout south, into the only remaining habitable regions. People must choose between dying of radiation sickness or taking suicide pills, and ultimately all of humanity is wiped out. Nuclear fears continued into the late twentieth century, with other key texts including *A Boy and His Dog* (a 1969 novella by Harlan Ellison, filmed in 1975), the Mad Max series, *Threads* (1984) and the Terminator series (particularly *The Terminator* [1984] and *Terminator 2: Judgment Day* [1991]).

While these nuclear narratives proliferated, they were not alone, and the modern environmental movement was largely shaped by narratives of pollution set closer to home. Rachel Carson's *Silent Spring* (1962) was a defining text in creating environmental change during this period. Carson argued that corporations' use of chemicals such as DDT was causing significant harm to the environment. The book was an instant bestseller, and its impact was increased (and illustrated) by Carson's appearances on television as well as before President John F. Kennedy's Science Advisory Committee and a US Senate subcommittee. Ultimately, despite many criticisms of the book and attacks on Carson herself, *Silent Spring* inspired significant social and legislative change in the USA (such as the Clean Air Act of 1963 and the movement to ban DDT).

Silent Spring also demonstrates the reach of the ecogothic. Although most of the book is factual and informative, the opening section takes the form of a 'fable for tomorrow' that tells the story of how 'everything began to change' as a result of 'some evil spell'.[18] In this imagined future, the birds, bees and fish have all died, and the world is more and more lifeless. As Carson notes, however, 'No witchcraft, no enemy action had snuffed out life in this stricken world. The people had done it themselves.'[19] Carson uses ecogothic imagery and language here to effectively illustrate the horrors humans have wrought upon themselves and the natural world. Released one year after *Silent Spring*, Alfred Hitchcock's *The Birds* (1963) turns in the opposite direction; instead of the disappearance of birds, Hitchcock illustrates a fear of their overwhelming presence. Although, as Carter Soles argues, 'the film's refusal to assign clear causation to the bird attacks ... leaves *The Birds* wanting from an ecocritical perspective',[20] it speaks to the ecogothic elements of 1960s environmental politics.

In the late 1960s the environmental movement gained even more momentum, first with the publication of the Apollo 8 Earthrise photo, which provided a new perspective on the Earth, and secondly with events such as the Cuyahoga River fire. The Cuyahoga River had caught fire many times over the previous century, but this time the public was primed to see it as representative of larger issues with polluted water. These events spilled over into massive social and legal changes in the early 1970s: in 1970 the first Earth Day took place and the Environmental Protection Agency (EPA) was established in the USA; in

1971 Greenpeace was founded and the 'Crying Indian' television public service announcement for the Keep America Beautiful organisation was launched; in 1972 multiple acts were passed in the USA to protect the environment, including a revised version of the Clean Water Act, the Marine Mammal Protection Act, the Coastal Zone Management Act and the Ocean Dumping Act. Further environmental legislation and action continued throughout the 1970s.

At the same time that these changes were occurring, ecogothic narratives flourished. Many science fiction novels explored the potential results of continuing to damage the planet, in line with Rust and Soles's expanded definition of ecohorror. For instance, John Brunner's *The Sheep Look Up* (1972) presents a near-future world in which pollution is so bad that people cannot go outside without masks, the water is frequently undrinkable, many animals are on the brink of extinction, and land and water are poisoned across the globe. These environmental issues lead to social unrest, famine and war, and the book ends with a bleak image of globally spreading pollution. In film, *Silent Running* (1972) echoes these concerns, presenting a future in which plant life on Earth is becoming extinct and specimens are grown in spaceship domes to preserve them, while *Soylent Green* (1973, based on Harry Harrison's *Make Room! Make Room!* [1966]) shows a dystopian version of urban life on Earth resulting from this kind of planetary destruction. In Japan, revealing these concerns to be global and not local, *Godzilla vs. Hedorah* (1971) – released in the US as *Godzilla vs. the Smog Monster* (1972) – connects 1970s environmental concerns with earlier ones, focusing as it does on contemporary pollution (the source of Hedorah's power) while also calling Hedorah the 'Smog Monster' and pitting it against Godzilla, the classic nuclear monster now become a defender of Earth.

The 1970s also saw a boom in animal horror. In addition to the animal horror films listed earlier, the decade included *Frogs* (1972), *Ben* (1972), *The Food of the Gods* (1976), *Day of the Animals* (1977), *Kingdom of the Spiders* (1977), *The Pack* (1977), *Orca* (1977), *Tentacles* (1977), *Piranha* (1978), *Long Weekend* (1978), *Nightwing* (1979) and *Prophecy* (1979). *Jaws* is an important example of the subgenre because many of the films that followed were basically copies of it featuring different animals; *Jaws* also led to the production of many more shark attack movies in the following decades (and an increased fear of sharks). Other 1970s animal horror movies are significant for a different reason: where *Jaws* gives no explanation for the shark attacks, these others frame their attacks in more explicitly environmental terms that coincided with the 1970s environmental movement. For instance, *Frogs* is about local pollution and the environment's response to it, while *Night of the Lepus* is about invasive species (based on reports about rabbits in Australia) and the concept of ecological balance that had gained popularity at the time.

Both types of animal horror films represented here reflect key ecogothic elements. Movies such as *Jaws* represent Gothic nature as threatening and Other, returning to the question, *What lurks in the forest?* and adding to it: *What swims beneath the ocean's surface? What beasts live near our homes?* More explicitly environmental animal horror films take up the idea that we are connected to the natural world, in one way or another. It is our intervention – our pollution, our science experiments, our expansion – that leads to animal attacks and creates a 'monstrously wronged' nature.[21] The presence of both approaches in 1970s animal horror films (sometimes in the same film) indicates a tension regarding cultural ideas about the nonhuman: it is monstrous and should be tamed, but it simultaneously needs our protection.

By the late twentieth century, environmental activism was no longer so popular and the ecogothic was less prominent. Murphy argues that this shift is explained by a 'sense that the threat of environmental catastrophe had . . . been normalised'.[22] She writes, '[i]t had become clear that the changes predicted by commentators such as Carson had already come to pass, and, in particular, that global warming, a preoccupation that only really came to the public consciousness during the mid- to late-1980s, was well underway'.[23] Although this is certainly true, a variety of distinct environmental issues came to the forefront during this period (for example, the hole in the ozone layer and the destruction of the Amazon rainforest), and one issue stands out and most clearly defines the environmental concerns of the late twentieth century: the threat of species extinction. Environmentalists focused on saving endangered animals such as the spotted owl, and these efforts were controversial (largely because of conflicts between conservation and industry). This became such a familiar issue that it was featured in movies such as *Dumb and Dumber* (1994). Furthermore, species extinction is a significant element in one of the biggest sf/horror movies of the late twentieth century, *Jurassic Park* (1993).

Illustrating the Ecogothic: *Jurassic Park*

As a story about reviving long-extinct creatures and putting them on display in a dinosaur theme park, *Jurassic Park* epitomises Baldick's definition of Gothic narratives, which 'combine a fearful sense of inheritance in time with a claustrophobic sense of enclosure in space',[24] by bringing together a prehistoric inheritance with a series of literal enclosures on an isolated island. *Jurassic Park*'s Gothic DNA, so to speak, also comes from the fact that it is a retelling of *Frankenstein* (Dr Hammond and/or Dr Wu as Victor Frankenstein, *Tyrannosaurus rex* as the Creature, etc.) and this becomes even clearer in its later iterations. In particular, *Jurassic Park: Fallen Kingdom* (2018) prominently features a misty, shadowy Gothic mansion – but with dinosaurs instead of ghosts.

The setting of *Jurassic Park* characterises it as ecogothic from the beginning. The film (and the park within the film) relies on its location on Isla Nublar, an island far from civilisation, where whatever happens occurs in secrecy. The opening scene immediately emphasises the danger of this place, focusing on the darkness, the jungle and the need for serious security measures (which fail). After a brief interlude to show off the beauty of the island and the optimistic intentions of the park's designers, the place becomes threatening again. Rain, wind and darkness create shadows where dinosaurs might lurk, and humans are ill-suited to the environment (the death of Dennis Nedry [Wayne Knight] illustrates this particularly well). As the film progresses and human control diminishes, the threat extends to the daytime (for example, with the death of Robert Muldoon [Bob Peck]) and to interior spaces (for example, the *Velociraptor* attacks in the maintenance building and in the kitchen of the visitor centre). Ultimately, the park's human spaces cannot withstand the threat of the outside and the monstrous.

The dinosaurs themselves are, however, the central threat to the human protagonists, not the island; *Jurassic Park* is, after all, a story of monstrous animals. Although these are ultimately invented and genetically manipulated creatures, the film follows earlier models of animal horror films and treats them simply as animals. This is intentional. Steven Spielberg said that he wanted the dinosaurs to be animals: 'I wouldn't even let anyone call them monsters or creatures.' And the dinosaur design drew on real animal sounds and behaviours to reinforce this approach (for example, the *Tyrannosaurus*'s roar is 'a combination of elephant, alligator, tiger, dog, and penguin sounds').[25] The film's designs for many carnivorous dinosaurs (for example, the *Tyrannosaurus*, *Velociraptors* and *Dilophosaurus*) were based on predatory animals, since the goal was ultimately to scare viewers, although there are moments when other, herbivorous dinosaurs are presented more sympathetically (for example, the sick *Triceratops* and the *Brachiosaurus* that approaches Dr Grant and the children while they rest in a tree). On the whole, however, *Jurassic Park* exploits human fears of wild animals, even if the animals in question are not ones the audience is likely to encounter.

The film also engages with contemporary ecological crises. As noted above, *Jurassic Park* was released in 1993, a moment of particular attention to endangered species as a key environmental issue. *Jurassic Park* addresses this at one remove by focusing on long-extinct creatures rather than those at risk of extinction in the present, but it is still centrally about species extinction. As I have argued elsewhere, because the film dramatises the reversal of species extinction, it 'promises that extinction need not be final' and 'is therefore not a threat', offering 'a kind of absolution for our role in ongoing species extinctions. Why should we fear extinction – or feel guilty about causing it – when it doesn't mean forever and we may have the power to reverse its effects?'[26] But this is only part of the story, since *Jurassic Park*'s de-extinct dinosaurs are indeed a threat. As a commentary on contemporary species extinctions (ones we have a hand in causing), the film tries to have it both ways. Extinction can be reversed – but it probably shouldn't be. Science will save us – but scientific overreach is also dangerous (remember, this is a Frankenstein narrative). The film also raises the spectre of our own human extinction. As with the real-world threat to humanity – climate change – the filmic threat of dinosaurs is created by us, the result of scientific 'progress' that exceeds our control.

Finally, the threat of human extinction blurs the line between human and nonhuman. It applies the logic of extinction typically applied to other species to us as well, undermining our sense of human exceptionalism. The film blurs this line in other ways, too, primarily through the *Velociraptors*, some of the most frightening dinosaurs in the movie. The *Velociraptors* are intelligent and dangerous, and there are multiple images in the film that parallel *Velociraptor* and human (the opening scene's close-up shots cutting between the *Velociraptor*'s eye and Muldoon's eye; the *Velociraptors* opening doors and communicating with each other). Although ultimately *Jurassic Park* reinforces human difference from the dinosaurs by allowing the human protagonists to escape from the island, much of the film up to that point works on breaking down those differences and challenging human superiority.

The twentieth century ended with the popularisation of a new term to describe 'the central role of mankind in geology and ecology': the Anthropocene.[27] The Anthropocene and the twentieth-century ecogothic were shaped by many of the same forces, and, from a twenty-first-century perspective, it's hard not to see the Anthropocene everywhere in the twentieth-century ecogothic. We fear the forest, which makes it easier to harvest it and use it – and its space – to build more cities and suburbs. We fear each other, which leads to the development and use of nuclear weapons. We fear animals that are outside our control (wild, mutated, de-extinct) and so they are hunted and destroyed. We fear inconvenience and economic stagnation, which leads to greater development of the land, air and water pollution, and further species extinction. Together, these fears shape both the ecogothic and the Anthropocene, making the twentieth-century ecogothic – in addition to everything outlined above – thoroughly Anthropocenic.

Key Texts

Algernon Blackwood, 'The Willows' (1907). Blackwood's novella is a classic for a reason: it creates a real sense of unease around something as seemingly innocuous as trees and connects that environmental fear to a larger, cosmic fear.

Daphne du Maurier, 'The Birds' (1952); *The Birds*, dir. Alfred Hitchcock (1963). Although du Maurier's and Hitchcock's versions of *The Birds* differ quite a bit, they both represent a key idea of the ecogothic: that the natural world is frequently beyond our understanding or control and, in that, it is dangerous.

Gojira (*Godzilla*, 1954). An iconic film about atomic fears, *Gojira* explores atomic power's effect on the environment – natural, human and built – while asking viewers both to fear Godzilla (a symbol of atomic power) and sympathise with him (its victim).

Alan Moore, *Swamp Thing* (1984–87). *Swamp Thing* illustrates the power of the vegetal world and directly responds to contemporary environmental issues in specifically ecogothic ways: the natural world is a frightening Other, nature strikes back against human polluters, and the line between human and nonhuman is blurred in frightening (but also pleasurable) ways.

The Blair Witch Project (1999). Released at the very end of the century, this film both introduces new approaches to the ecogothic and returns to older ones. Its found footage style belongs to the late twentieth century, but its representation of the scary forest and the witches within it belongs to a much longer history.

Further Critical Reading

Gothic Nature 1 (2019). This journal provides a good entry point to contemporary criticism on the ecogothic. The opening issue includes articles defining the ecogothic as well as analyses of ecogothic and/or ecohorror texts.

Keetley, Dawn, and Angela Tenga (eds), *Plant Horror: Approaches to the Monstrous Vegetal in Fiction and Film* (2016). While it focuses on just one specific subset of the ecogothic, Keetley's introduction provides a valuable structure for thinking about plant horror, and other contributors' analyses of plant horror (and ecogothic) texts are fascinating.

Rust, Stephen A., and Carter Soles (eds), ecohorror cluster in *ISLE: Interdisciplinary Studies in Literature and Environment* (2014). The introduction to this special cluster includes a frequently cited definition of ecohorror, and the cluster's articles address ecohorror and the ecogothic across multiple forms: Poe's short fiction, contemporary horror novels, horror comics and sf/horror films.

Smith, Andrew, and William Hughes (eds), *Ecogothic* (2013). The first collection specifically dedicated to the ecogothic, *Ecogothic* provides a definition of the ecogothic that is then illustrated by contributors' ecocritical analyses of Gothic texts.

Tidwell, Christy, and Carter Soles (eds), *Fear and Nature: Ecohorror Studies in the Anthropocene* (2021). This collection brings together ecohorror and the ecogothic and argues for defining the two broadly. Contributors provide readings of ecohorror and ecogothic texts, but they also question the limits of these terms, propose new ways of defining them and describe new categories.

Bibliography

Alaimo, Stacy, *Bodily Natures: Science, Environment, and the Material Self* (Bloomington, IN: Indiana University Press, 2010).

Baldick, Chris, 'Introduction', in Chris Baldick (ed.), *The Oxford Book of Gothic Tales* (Oxford University Press, 1992), pp. xi–xxiii.

Blackwood, Algernon, 'The Wendigo' (1910), Project Gutenberg, <https://www.gutenberg.org/files/10897/10897-h/10897-h.htm> (last accessed 26 July 2021).

Bradford, William, *Bradford's History of 'Plimoth Plantation'* (1898), Project Gutenberg, <http://www.gutenberg.org/files/24950/24950-h/24950-h.htm> (last accessed 26 July 2021).

Carson, Rachel, *Silent Spring* (Boston: Houghton Mifflin, 1962).

Crutzen, Paul, and Eugene F. Stoermer, 'The "Anthropocene"', *IGBP Newsletter*, 41, May 2000, pp. 17–18.

Dearnley, Elizabeth, 'Introduction', in Elizabeth Dearnley (ed.), *Into the London Fog: Eerie Tales from the Weird City* (London: The British Library, 2020), pp. 8–18.

Gothic Nature, 1, 2019, <https://gothicnaturejournal.com/> (last accessed 26 July 2021).

Hillard, Tom J., 'Gothic Nature Revisited: Reflections on the Gothic of Ecocriticism', *Gothic Nature*, 1, 2019, pp. 21–33, <https://gothicnaturejournal.com/wp-content/uploads/2019/09/Hillard_21-33_Gothic-Nature-1_2019.pdf> (last accessed 26 July 2021).

Keetley, Dawn, and Angela Tenga (eds), *Plant Horror: Approaches to the Monstrous Vegetal in Fiction and Film* (Basingstoke: Palgrave Macmillan, 2016).

Keetley, Dawn, and Matthew Wynn Sivils, 'Introduction: Approaches to the Ecogothic', in Dawn Keetley and Matthew Wynn Sivils (eds), *Ecogothic in Nineteenth-Century American Literature* (New York: Routledge, 2018), pp. 1–20.

Lewis, Simon L., and Mark A. Maslin, 'Defining the Anthropocene', *Nature*, 519, 2015, pp. 171–80.

Murphy, Bernice M., *The Rural Gothic in American Popular Culture:*

Backwoods Horror and Terror in the Wilderness (Basingstoke: Palgrave Macmillan, 2013).

Parker, Elizabeth, *The Forest and the Ecogothic: The Deep Dark Woods in the Popular Imagination* (Basingstoke: Palgrave Macmillan, 2020).

Punter, David, *The Literature of Terror: A History of Gothic Fictions from 1765 to the present day, Volume 1: The Gothic Tradition*, 2nd edn (Abingdon: Routledge, 2013).

Rust, Stephen A., and Carter Soles, 'Living in Fear, Living in Dread, Pretty Soon We'll All Be Dead', *Interdisciplinary Studies in Literature and Environment*, 21.3, 2014, pp. 509–12.

Rust, Stephen A., and Carter Soles (eds), ecohorror cluster in *ISLE: Interdisciplinary Studies in Literature and Environment*, 21.3, 2014, pp. 509–87.

Schell, Jennifer, 'Ecogothic Extinction Fiction: The Extermination of the Alaskan Mammoth', in Dawn Keetley and Matthew Wynn Sivils (eds), *Ecogothic in Nineteenth-Century American Literature* (New York: Routledge, 2018), pp. 175–90.

Smith, Andrew, and William Hughes (eds), *Ecogothic* (Manchester: Manchester University Press, 2013).

Soles, Carter, '"And No Birds Sing": Discourses of Environmental Apocalypse in *The Birds* and *Night of the Living Dead*', *Interdisciplinary Studies in Literature and Environment*, 21.3, 2014, pp. 526–37.

Switek, Brian [Riley Black], *My Beloved Brontosaurus* (New York: Farrar, Straus and Giroux, 2013).

Tidwell, Christy, '"Life Finds a Way": *Jurassic Park*, *Jurassic World*, and De-Extinction Anxiety', in Jonathan Elmore (ed.), *Fiction and the Sixth Mass Extinction: Narrative in an Era of Loss* (Lanham, MD: Lexington Books, 2020), pp. 31–48.

Tidwell, Christy, and Carter Soles (eds), *Fear and Nature: Ecohorror Studies in the Anthropocene* (University Park, PA: Pennsylvania State University Press, 2021).

Filmography

Alligator (dir. Lewis Teague, USA, 1980).
Anaconda (dir. Luis Llosa, USA, 1997).
Backcountry (dir. Adam MacDonald, USA, 2014).
Ben (dir. Phil Karlson, USA, 1972).
The Birds (dir. Alfred Hitchcock, USA, 1963).
A Boy and His Dog (dir. L. Q. Jones, USA, 1975).
Crawl (dir. Alexandre Aja, USA, 2019).
Day of the Animals (dir. William Girdler, USA, 1977).
Dumb and Dumber (dir. Peter Farrelly and Bobby Farrelly, USA, 1994).
Empire of the Ants (dir. Bert I. Gordon, USA, 1977).
The Fly (dir. David Cronenberg, USA/UK/Canada, 1986).
The Food of the Gods (dir. Bert I. Gordon, USA/Canada, 1976).
Frogs (dir. George McCowan, USA, 1972).

Godzilla vs. Hedorah (dir. Yoshimitsu Banno, Japan, 1971).
Gojira (*Godzilla*, dir. Ishirō Honda, Japan, 1954).
Grizzly (dir. William Girdler, USA, 1976).
Grizzly Rage (dir. David DeCoteau, Canada, 2007).
Jaws (dir. Steven Spielberg, USA, 1975).
Jurassic Park (dir. Steven Spielberg, USA, 1993).
Jurassic Park: Fallen Kingdom (dir. J. A. Bayona, USA, 2018).
Kingdom of the Spiders (dir. John 'Bud' Cardos, USA, 1977).
Lake Placid (dir. Steve Miner, USA, 1999).
Long Weekend (dir. Colin Eggleston, Australia, 1978).
Mad Max series (dir. George Miller, Australia, 1979–2015).
Night of the Lepus (dir. William F. Claxton, USA, 1972).
Nightwing (dir. Arthur Hiller, USA, 1979).
On the Beach (dir. Stanley Kramer, USA, 1959).
Orca (dir. Michael Anderson, USA/Netherlands/Italy, 1977).
The Pack (dir. Robert Clouse, USA, 1977).
Phase IV (dir. Saul Bass, USA/UK, 1974).
Piranha (dir. Joe Dante, USA/Japan, 1978).
Prophecy (dir. John Frankenheimer, USA, 1979).
Silent Running (dir. Douglas Trumbull, USA, 1972).
Slugs (dir. Juan Piquer Simón, Spain, 1988).
Soylent Green (dir. Richard Fleischer, USA, 1973).
Squirm (dir. Jeff Lieberman, USA, 1976).
Sssssss (dir. Bernard L. Kowalski, USA, 1973).
Tentacles (dir. Ovidio G. Assonitis, as Oliver Hellman, Italy, 1977).
The Terminator (dir. James Cameron, USA/UK, 1984).
Terminator 2: Judgment Day (dir. James Cameron, USA, 1991).
Them! (dir. Gordon Douglas, USA, 1954).
Threads (TV movie, dir. Mick Jackson, USA/UK/Australia, 1984).
Willard (dir. Daniel Mann, USA, 1971).
Willard (dir. Glen Morgan, USA/Canada, 2003).

Notes

1. Hillard, 'Gothic Nature Revisited', p. 26.
2. Punter, *The Literature of Terror*, p. 18.
3. Baldick, 'Introduction', p. xix.
4. Parker, *The Forest and the Ecogothic*, p. 2.
5. Murphy, *The Rural Gothic*, p. 15.
6. Ibid., p. 181.
7. Rust and Soles, 'Living in Fear', p. 510.
8. Ibid., pp. 509–10.
9. Schell, 'Ecogothic Extinction Fiction', p. 176.
10. Keetley and Sivils, 'Introduction', p. 11.
11. Alaimo, *Bodily Natures*, p. 2.
12. Parker, *The Forest and the Ecogothic*, p. 33.
13. Bradford, *Bradford's History of 'Plimoth Plantation'*, p. 95.

14. Murphy, *The Rural Gothic*, p. 182.
15. Blackwood, 'The Wendigo', n.p.
16. Ibid.
17. Dearnley, 'Introduction', p. 9.
18. Carson, *Silent Spring*, pp. 1, 2.
19. Ibid., p. 3.
20. Soles, '"And No Birds Sing"', p. 531.
21. Keetley and Sivils, 'Introduction', p. 11.
22. Murphy, *The Rural Gothic*, p. 192.
23. Ibid.
24. Baldick, 'Introduction', p. xix.
25. Switek, *My Beloved Brontosaurus*, p. 161.
26. Tidwell, '"Life Finds a Way"', p. 36.
27. Crutzen and Stoermer, 'The "Anthropocene"', p. 17.

Notes on Contributors

Xavier Aldana Reyes is Reader in English Literature and Film at Manchester Metropolitan University and a founding member of the Manchester Centre for Gothic Studies. He is author of *Gothic Cinema* (2020), *Spanish Gothic* (2017), *Horror Film and Affect* (2016) and *Body Gothic* (2014), and editor of *Twenty-First-Century Gothic: An Edinburgh Companion* (with Maisha Wester, 2019) and *Horror: A Literary History* (2016). He is chief editor of the Horror Studies academic book series, published by the University of Wales Press.

Scott Brewster is Associate Professor in Modern English Literature at the University of Lincoln. He is co-author, with Lucie Armitt, of *Gothic Travel through Haunted Landscapes: Climates of Fear* (2021), and co-author, with Jeffrey A. Weinstock, of *The Routledge Introduction to the American Ghost Story* (2022). He co-edited, with Luke Thurston, *The Routledge Handbook to the Ghost Story* (2017).

Kevin Corstorphine is Lecturer in American Literature at the University of Hull, and Programme Director in American Studies. His research interests lie in horror and Gothic fiction, both literary and popular, and he is particularly interested in representation of space and place, the environment, and haunted locations. He has published widely on authors including Bram Stoker, H. P. Lovecraft, Ambrose Bierce, Shirley Jackson, Stephen King and Clive Barker. He is co-editor of The *Palgrave Handbook to Horror Literature* (2018). He is currently working on several research projects including US imperialism, haunted graveyards and ecology in nineteenth-century US literature.

Janice Lynne Deitner is a PhD candidate in the School of English at Trinity College Dublin. Her thesis, funded by a Provost's PhD Project Award, explores the intersection of minds and bodies in the work of

Shirley Jackson. Her areas of research interest include horror, the Gothic, science fiction, genre periodicals and historical conceptions of gender. She is currently Postgraduate Caucus co-chair for the Irish Association of American Studies.

Dara Downey lectures in English at Trinity College Dublin, Dublin City University, and University College Dublin. Her work focuses on domestic space, labour and material culture in American Gothic fiction and popular culture. She is editor of *The Irish Journal of Gothic and Horror Studies* (online), author of *American Women's Ghost Stories in the Gilded Age* (2014), and co-editor of *Landscapes of Liminality: Between Space and Place* (with Ian Kinane and Elizabeth Parker, 2016). She is currently working on a literary biography of Shirley Jackson, as well as a longer-term project on servant figures in American Gothic.

Matt Foley is Lecturer in Modern and Contemporary Literature at Manchester Metropolitan University. He is the author of *Haunting Modernisms* (2017) and co-editor (with Rebecca Duncan) of *Patrick McGrath and his Worlds* (2019). A member of the Manchester Centre for Gothic Studies, he is the academic lead for Manchester Met's 'Haunt' project which connects Gothic scholarship to placemaking, and he is the administrator of the International Gothic Association's Allan Lloyd Smith Memorial Prizes. He works predominantly on modernist literature, the Gothic and literary acoustics.

Steffen Hantke has edited *Horror*, a special topic issue of *Paradoxa* (2002), *Horror: Creating and Marketing Fear* (2004), *Caligari's Heirs: The German Cinema of Fear after 1945* (2007), *American Horror Film: The Genre at the Turn of the Millennium* (2010) and, with Agnieszka Soltysik Monnet, *War Gothic in Literature and Culture* (2016). He is also author of *Conspiracy and Paranoia in Contemporary American Literature* (1994) and *Monsters in the Machine: Science Fiction Film and the Militarization of America after World War II* (2016). His essays have appeared in *Science Fiction Studies*, *The Journal of Popular Film and Television*, *The Journal of Popular Culture* and many other journals.

Madelon Hoedt is a Senior Lecturer in Drama at the University of Huddersfield. She is the author of *Narrative Design and Authorship in Bloodborne: An Analysis of the Horror Videogame* (2019) and has published widely on (historical) examples of horror and the Gothic in popular culture, particularly in relation to performance and video games. In her research, she is interested in issues of narrative, interactivity and experience, and she is currently working on a monograph on immersive horror performance.

Laura R. Kremmel is an Assistant Professor of English at South Dakota School of Mines & Technology. Together with Kevin Corstorphine, she is the editor of *The Palgrave Handbook to Horror Literature* (2018). She is the author of *Romantic Medicine and the Gothic Imagination: Morbid Anatomy* (2022). She has published several articles and chapters on the Gothic, medical humanities/histories, Disability Studies and British Romanticism.

Murray Leeder teaches English and Film Studies at the University of Manitoba and the University of Winnipeg. He is the author of *Horror Film: A Critical Introduction* (2018), *The Modern Supernatural and the Beginnings of Cinema* (2017) and *Halloween* (2014), and editor of *Cinematic Ghosts: Haunting and Spectrality from Silent Cinema to the Digital Era* (2015) and *ReFocus: The Films of William Castle* (2018). He has published in such journals as *Horror Studies*, *The Canadian Journal of Film Studies*, *The Journal of Popular Culture*, *The Journal of Popular Film and Television*, *Film Journal* and *The Journal of Communication and Languages*.

Emma Liggins is a Reader in English Literature in the Department of English at Manchester Metropolitan University. Her recent publications include *Odd Women? Spinsters, Lesbians and Widows in British Women's Fiction, 1850–1939* (2014) and *The Haunted House in Women's Ghost Stories, 1850–1945: Gender, Space and Modernity* (2020). Her research interests include ghost stories, haunted heritage and Victorian cemeteries. She is currently working on the American ghost stories of Shirley Jackson and writing a chapter on Susan Hill and Tracy Chevalier for a new edited collection on *Graveyard Gothic* (2023).

Muireann Maguire lectures in Russian at the University of Exeter. She is the author of *Stalin's Ghosts: Gothic Themes in Early Soviet Literature* (2012), a study of Gothic-fantastic motifs in early Soviet literature, and the editor and translator of *Red Spectres* (2013) and *White Magic* (2021), both collections of twentieth-century Russian ghost stories. Her academic interests include childbirth narrative in literature; the history of Russian-to-English literary translation; and Russian prose literature since the mid-nineteenth century. Her most recent book is *Reading Backwards: An Advance Retrospective on Russian Literature* (2021), co-edited with Timothy Langen.

Bernice M. Murphy is an Associate Professor and Lecturer in Popular Literature at the School of English, Trinity College, Dublin. She has published extensively on topics related to horror fiction and film. Her books include *The Suburban Gothic in American Popular Culture* (2009), *The Rural Gothic: Backwoods Horror and Terror in the Wilderness* (2013), *The Highway Horror Film* (2014) and (edited with Elizabeth McCarthy) *Lost Souls of Horror and the Gothic* (2017). She is the co-founder of the online *Irish Journal of Gothic and Horror Studies*. Her forthcoming monograph (also from EUP) is entitled *The California Gothic in Fiction and Film* and she was academic consultant on *The Letters of Shirley Jackson* (2021, edited by Laurence Jackson Hyman). She was made a Fellow of TCD in 2017.

Sorcha Ní Fhlainn is Senior Lecturer in Film Studies and American Studies, and a founding member of the Manchester Centre for Gothic Studies, at Manchester Metropolitan University. She is editor of the journal *Open Screens* (Ubiquity Press), and UK/EU reviews editor for the journal *Gothic Studies*. Her recent books include *Clive Barker: Dark Imaginer* (2017), and *Postmodern Vampires: Film, Fiction and Popular Culture* (2019) – winner of the Lord Ruthven Award (non-fiction) from the International Association for the Fantastic in the Arts in 2020. She has published widely on subjectivity, sociocultural history, popular culture and monster studies, and is currently leading a project on the long 1980s onscreen.

Agnieszka Soltysik Monnet is Professor of American Literature and Culture at the University of Lausanne in Switzerland. Her publications include *The Poetics and Politics of the American Gothic* (2010), *The Gothic in Contemporary Literature and Popular Culture* (co-edited with Justin Edwards, 2012), a special issue of *Gothic Studies* (co-edited with Marie Lienard-Yeterian, 2015) on 'The Gothic in an Age of Terror(ism)', *War Gothic* (co-edited with Steffen Hantke, 2016) and *Combat Death in Contemporary American Culture: Popular Conceptions of War since World War II* (2021).

Christy Tidwell is Associate Professor of English and Humanities at the South Dakota School of Mines & Technology. She works at the intersection of speculative fiction, environmental humanities and gender studies and has written about ecohorror and related topics for *ISLE: Interdisciplinary Studies in Literature and Environment* (2014), *Posthuman Glossary* (2018), *Fiction and the Sixth Mass Extinction: Narrative in an Era of Loss* (2020), *Gothic Nature* (2021) and *Science*

Fiction Film & Television (2021). She is co-editor of *Gender and Environment in Science Fiction* (with Bridgitte Barclay, 2018) and *Fear and Nature: Ecohorror Studies in the Anthropocene* (with Carter Soles, 2021).

Laura Westengard is an Associate Professor of English at New York City College of Technology, City University of New York. She is the author of *Gothic Queer Culture: Marginalized Communities and the Ghosts of Insidious Trauma* (2019). *Gothic Queer Culture* shows how queer culture adopts Gothicism to challenge heteronormative and racialised systems and practices and to acknowledge the effects of microaggression and insidious trauma on queer communities. She also writes about popular culture, performance and visual art, and contemporary US literature. She is currently researching medical archives for an upcoming book on lesser-known nineteenth- and early twentieth-century medical devices that have shaped contemporary understandings of gender and sexuality.

Maisha Wester is an Associate Professor at Indiana University, a Global Professor at the University of Sheffield (2020–24) and a Fulbright Scholar (2017–18). She is author of *African American Gothic: Screams From Shadowed Places* and co-editor of *Twenty-First-Century Gothic*. She is also the US book review editor for the international journal *Gothic Studies*. Her research focuses on racial depictions in Gothic literature and horror film, the Gothic in sociopolitical discourses, and Black Diasporic Gothic literature.

Julia M. Wright is George Munro Chair in Literature and Rhetoric at Dalhousie University and president of the Academy of the Arts and Humanities in the Royal Society of Canada. She is the author of four monographs and has edited or co-edited a further eleven volumes, most recently co-editing a scholarly edition, with appendices, of Ian Fleming's *Casino Royale* (2020). Her work centres on eighteenth- and nineteenth-century literature, especially in relation to nationalism, but she has been extending that work into contemporary television over the last decade. She has published essays on *Deadwood*, *Supernatural* and American Gothic television in general, and discusses a wide range of Gothic series in her book, *Men with Stakes: Masculinity and the Gothic in US Television* (2016).

Index

1950s America, racial contexts, 1, 207
1950s culture, 8, 9, 115, 119, 120, 135, 137, 196, 198–212, 216, 244, 251, 252
9/11 Terror Attacks, 75, 156, 211n9

A Nightmare on Elm Street (film), 145, 147–9
Abbott, Stacey, 140, 141, 157, 162, 255, 258
Addams Family, The (television series), 132, 140
African American Gothic, 3, 7, 9, 10, 11, 200, 228–41, 273–89
African American Gothic: Screams from Shadowed Places (Wester), 287
African American Women's Gothic, 9, 228, 233
Afro-Atlantic Belief Systems and the Gothic, 229, 232
Agamben, Giorgio, 138
AIDS crisis, 11, 125, 259, 266–8
Alaimo, Stacy, 292
Aldana Reyes, Xavier, 6, 95, 97n2, 125, 161n2, 179n1, 255
Alder, Emily, 17, 23, 37
Alfred Hitchcock Presents (television series), 137
All that Heaven Allows (film), 200
Alligator (film), 291, 298
American Century, 8, 33, 196
American Gothic, 8, 11, 90, 135, 198, 276, 277, 287, 290

American Gothic Culture (Haslam and Faflak), 3, 140
American Silent Horror, Science Fiction and Fantasy Feature Films, 1913–1929 (Nicolella, Soister and Joyce), 95
American's Women's Ghost Stories in the Gilded Age, (Downey) 28
Amfiteatrov, Aleksandr, 187
'An Eastern Echo' (Perrin), 25
'An Occurrence at Owl Creek Bridge' (Bierce), 170
Andriopoulos, Stefan, 135
Angel (television series), 133, 134, 139, 140
Antebellum South, 166, 228, 238
Anthropocene, 299–301
Antwerp (Ford), 57
'Apple Tree, The' (Bowen), 60
Apt Pupil (film), 174–5
Apt Pupil (novella), 171
Arata, Steven, 73
Arkham Asylum (graphic novel), 10, 250
Armageddon, 145, 151
Armitt, Lucie, 75, 76
artificial intelligence, 122, 135, 151
Asia, 206
Askew, Alice and Claude, 28
Asylum (McGrath), 10, 56, 57
atomic testing, 1, 119, 224, 294, 300
Auerbach, Nina, 162, 272
Austen, Jane, 38, 65, 69
Avenging Conscience, The: or *Thou Shalt Not Kill* (film), 5, 88–90

Index   311

'Avtobiografiia trupa'/ 'Autobiography of a Corpse' (Krzhizhanovskii), 191
Aylmer Vance: Ghost-Seer (Askew, A and C), 28

Baba Yaga, 180
Bacon, Josephine Daskam, 26
Bad Seed, The (March), 9, 219, 224
Baldick, Chris, 65, 74–6, 290, 297
Baldwin, James, 274, 275, 279, 280
Baltic region, 183
bangungut syndrome, 147
Baraka, Amiri, 11, 273, 276, 281, 283, 285, 288
Barker, Clive, 44, 45, 150, 156
Barnes, Djuna, 4, 50, 57–9, 268
'Biscobra, The' (Perrin), 25, 26
Basinger, Jeanine, 205, 206
Bat, The (film), 5, 85
Batman (comics), 97n19, 250, 251
Batman Arkham Asylum: A Serious House on Serious Earth (Morrison and McKean), 250
Baudelaire, Charles, 51, 183
Beckett, Samuel, 55
Beetlejuice (film), 93, 150
Bekmambetov, Timur, 188
Beliaev, Aleksandr, 185
Belling, Catherine, 255
Belloc Lowndes, Marie, 28
Beloved (Morrison), 233, 235, 238, 286, 287
Belyi, Andrei, 183
Benson-Allott, Caetlin, 150, 157
Berg, Alban, 283
Beville, Maria, 54
Bierce, Ambrose, 37, 166, 167, 170, 176
Bigger Than Life (film), 202, 209
Birds, The (film), 295
'Birds, The' (du Maurier), 300
Birkhead, Edith, 4, 52, 65, 66
Birth of a Nation (film), 88, 90, 279
Birth of the American Horror Film, The (Rhodes), 95, 97n2
Biskind, Peter, 153
Black Cat, The (film), 114, 116
'Black Cat, The' (Poe), 213, 287

Black Gothic literature, 11, 273–5, 277, 285–7
Black Power movement, 229, 235
Blackwood, Algernon, 3, 16, 18, 36, 37, 40, 294, 300
Blair Witch Project, The (film), 109, 145, 153–5, 290, 300
Blatty, William Peter, 255
Bloch, Robert, 42, 209, 214
Bluest Eye, The, (Morrison) 274
'Bobok' (Dostoevskii), 182, 193
bodies and the Gothic, 185
body horror, 45, 145, 150, 156, 165, 167, 170, 173, 174, 255
Boer War, 18, 168
Bogart, Humphrey, 169
Bondwoman's Narrative, The (Crafts), 285
Bookman, The, 15
Botting, Fred, 18, 53, 74, 107, 145, 157, 161
Bowen, Elizabeth, 50, 53, 60
Bradbury, Ray, 191, 209
Bradford, William, 292
Bradshaw, Peter, 83
Bram Stoker's Dracula (film), 74, 151
Brantlinger, Patrick, 73
Breton, Andre, 52, 59, 68
Brewster, Scott, 4, 28
Brexit, 1
Bride of Frankenstein (film), 118, 175
Briggs, Julia, 53, 62n6
Britain, 45, 120, 166
British Empire, decline of, 1, 16
British modernity, 3, 4, 7, 15, 16, 18, 19, 22, 37, 49, 50–3, 60, 75
Briusov, Valerii, 187
Brontë sisters, 90, 116
Brontë Charlotte, 55
Brooks, Jeffrey, 184, 187
Brooks, Kinitra, 286
Browning, Tod, 84, 168
Brubaker, Ed, 97n19
Bruhm, Steven, 73
Brunner, John, 296
Buffy the Vampire Slayer (TV show), 6, 129, 130, 131, 133, 139, 140
Bulgakov, Mikhail, 180, 184–9, 193
Burke, Edmund, 35, 68, 134

Burton, Tim, 93
Butler, Octavia, 238, 286
Byrnand, Samuel, 252

Cabinet des Dr. Caligari, Das/The Cabinet of Dr. Caligari (film), 60, 84, 88, 94, 107, 167, 255
Call of Cthulhu, The (film), 94
'Call of Cthulhu, The' (Lovecraft), 38, 39
Campbell, Ramsey, 43, 45
Cane (Toomer), 286
cannibalism, 40, 229, 231
Carmilla (Le Fanu), 252, 264
Carpenter, John, 150, 157
Carpenter, Lynette, 241n29
Carson, Rachel, 199, 295, 297
'Cask of Amontillado, The' (Poe), 213
Castle of Otranto, The (Walpole), 10, 59, 166, 259, 262, 286
Castle Spectre, The (Lewis), 103, 104, 107
Castle, Terry, 86, 262
Cat and the Canary, The (film), 5, 85, 90–2
Cat Creeps, The (film), 85, 116
Chaney, Lon, 84, 94, 116
'Chickamauga' (Bierce), 166
Chireau, Yvonne P., 230
Cho, Daniel, 133
Choisy, Camille, 102, 103, 105
Chute de la maison Usher, La (film), 94, 97n15
City of God (film), 267
Civil Rights Movement, 232, 235, 238
Cleckley, Hervey, 9, 214, 215, 218, 224
Clive, Colin, 121
clones, 139
Closed Door, The (Francheville), 108
Clover, Carol J., 148, 149, 161n16
Coffin of Flesh (de Lorde and Bauche), 108
Cold War, 125, 145, 151, 152, 157, 188, 198, 199, 203, 206, 207, 209
Collector, The (Fowles), 9, 220, 227n28
Coma (Cook), 10, 246, 247, 253–5
Coma (film), 10, 246, 247, 253–5

communism, 68, 180, 184, 185, 187, 191
Companion to the Gothic, A, 2, 74, 76
Conan Doyle, Arthur, 3, 19, 20, 27
Confessions of an English Opium-Eater (De Quincey), 131
conjure, 10, 228, 230, 232, 233
Conrad, Joseph, 49, 52, 57
conspiracy, 10, 135, 136, 138, 153, 245, 246
contagion, 10, 245
contagion and the Gothic, 251–5
Cook, Robin, 248
Coppola, Francis Ford, 74, 151
Crafts, Hannah, 285
Craven, Wes, 147, 149, 157, 162n22
Crawford, Joan, 275, 280
Cronenberg, David, 43, 150
Cthulhu 2000 (Turner), 45
Cuadros, Gil, 267, 268
Curse of Frankenstein, The (film), 6, 115, 119, 121, 123
Cushing, Peter, 119, 123
Cuyahoga River Fire, 295
cyber-gothic, 70, 145, 157, 192

Daly, Nicholas, 52, 53
Dark Shadows (television series), 137
Darvay, Daniel, 51
Das Wachsfigurenkabinet/ Waxworks (film), 91
Dawley, J. Searle, 87
Day, William Patrick, 71, 263
de Philipstal, Paul (as 'Philidor'), 86
De Quincey, Thomas, 35, 36, 131
Dead Ringers (film), 255
Deák, Frantisek, 100, 104–6, 108
Dearnley, Elizabeth, 294
Deathdream (film), 170
Der Golem/The Golem (film), 84, 115
Der Student von Prag/The Student of Prague (film), 84, 94, 115
Dexter (television series), 218
Dickens, Charles, 60, 86
Dika, Vera, 148, 161n16
Director of Public Prosecutions (DPP), 146
disease, 19, 243, 251–3, 267
Disordered Personalities and Crime: An

Analysis of the History of Moral Insanity (Jones), 225
doppelgänger, 84, 133, 138
Dostoevskii, Fedor (Fyodor), 8, 181–3, 187, 190
Down Survey, 132, 134, 135
Downey, Dara, 9, 28
Dr Jekyll and Mr Hyde (Stevenson), 36, 84, 104, 114
Dr. Jekyll and Sister Hyde (film), 124
Dracula (1931, film), 6, 93, 114, 116–18
Dracula (1958, film), 70, 119, 123
Dracula (1992, film) *see Bram Stoker's Dracula* (film)
Dracula (Stoker), 36, 52, 58, 73, 75, 94, 107, 116, 118, 152, 183, 252, 263, 269
Dracula's Daughter (film), 11, 124, 264
du Maurier, Daphne, 116, 269, 300
Due, Tananarive, 9, 10, 228, 236, 238, 285
'Dulce et Decorum Est' (Owen), 173
Dutchman (film), 11, 273, 276, 279, 280, 283, 284
Dutton, Wendy, 232
Dvoinik/The Double (Dostoevskii), 181

'East of Suez' (Perrin), 25
Eastmancolor, 121
ecogothic, 3, 11, 17, 18, 290–304
Edison, Thomas, 87, 94
Edmundson, Mark, 152, 153
Edmundson, Melissa, 17, 28
Edwardian supernatural, 3, 15–32
Edwards, Kyle, 116
Eliot, T. S., 4, 49, 53, 57–9, 167, 171, 172
Ellison, Harlan, 45, 295
Ellison, Ralph, 11, 276, 286
Engelhardt, Tom, 196, 211
Enlightenment, 7, 74, 130, 132, 138, 274
environmental anxieties and the Gothic *see* Anthropocene
Etkind, Alexander, 180, 193
Evgenii Onegin/Eugene Onegin (Pushkin), 181
Eye in the Door, The (P Barker), 171

'Facts in the Case of M. Valdemar' (Poe), 34, 36
Fanon, Frantz, 232
'Fantom'/'The Phantom' (Krzhizhanovskii), 190
Fantome de l'opera, Le/The Phantom of the Opera (Leroux), 28
fascism, 169
Faulkner, William, 4, 167
Faustian bargains, 20, 55, 115, 145, 156, 190
Fear and Nature: Ecohorror Studies in the Anthropocene (Tidwell and Soles), 301
Fear (Nesbit), 22
Felix the Ghost Breaker (film), 85, 94
female Gothic, 10, 72, 116, 119, 124, 125, 229, 277
Feminine Mystique, The (Friedan), 199
Ferguson, Roderick, 11, 273, 274
Fido (film), 211
film noir, 116, 125, 140, 169
fin-de-millennium, 7, 144–62
Fin de Siècle, 3, 15, 17, 20, 21, 36, 52, 73
Final Girl, 148, 152
Fisher, Mark, 35, 42, 45
Fitzgerald, Lauren, 72
Fleetwood, Nicole, 231, 232
Fly, The (film), 150, 292
Flying Dutchman, The, 284
Flynn, Gillian, 224
Foley, Matt, 4
found footage horror films, 7, 145, 153, 155, 156, 300
Fowles, John, 9, 220
France, 24, 97n15, 99, 124, 166, 172
Frank, Adam, 36
Frankenstein (film, 1910), 5, 87, 94, 115
Frankenstein (film, 1931), 6, 114, 115, 117, 118, 121, 122, 168, 175, 245, 279, 287
Frankenstein, or The Modern Prometheus (Shelley), 87, 103, 107, 115, 119, 122, 123, 152, 190, 245–7, 265, 266, 269, 292, 298, 299
Freeman, Mary Wilkins, 28, 37

French and Indian War, 166
Freud, Sigmund, 19, 37, 56, 66, 68, 70–72, 84, 138, 211n4, 218, 262, 293
Freudian uncanny, 19, 27, 37, 38, 50, 71, 72, 84, 86, 138, 167, 211n4, 262, 293
Friday the 13th (film), 146, 148
Friedan, Betty, 199
'From Poe to Valery' (Eliot), 58
Freund, Karl, 93
Funny Games (film), 153, 162n37

Ganja and Hess (film), 275, 285
Gaslight (film), 119
gender non-conformity, 266
German cinema, 115
German Expressionism, 5, 84, 86, 93, 94
Gerould, David, 100, 101
Get Out (film), 200–3
Ghost Road, The (P Barker), 171
ghost stories and modernism, 15–32, 54, 60, 187
Ghost Stories of an Antiquary (M. R. James), 41
ghosts, 19–32, 37, 38, 53, 57, 60, 62n6, 65, 83, 86, 92, 104, 107, 115, 145, 167, 179, 238, 259, 262, 269, 298
Gialli, 120
Gilda Stories, The (Gomez), 235, 236, 238, 269
'Glad Ghosts' (Lawrence), 21–2
Gladkov, Fedor, 184
Glaude Jr, Eddie S., 237
Goddu, Teresa, 229
Gods and Monsters (film), 171, 174, 175
Godzilla vs. Hedorah/ Godzilla vs. the Smog Monster (film), 296
Gogol, Nikolai, 8, 182, 183, 187, 189, 190, 193
Gojira/Godzilla (film), 294, 300
Goldner, E. J., 238
Golem, Der/The Golem (film), 84, 93, 115
Golova profesora Douelia/ Professor Dowell's Head (Beliaev), 186

Gomez, Jewelle, 235, 238, 269
Gone Girl (Flynn), 224
'Good Soldier, The' (Ford), 56
Gordon, Mel, 100–3, 105, 107, 108, 110
Gordon, Michelle Y., 229, 230
Gormenghast (Peake), 169
Gothic (Botting), 18, 53, 74, 107, 145, 157, 161n1
Gothic and Modernism: Essays in Dark Literary Modernism (Riquelme), 50, 51, 60
Gothic and Theory, The: An Edinburgh Companion (Hogle and Miles), 76
Gothic Cinema (Aldana Reyes), 95, 97, 125
Gothic criticism, history of, 64–80
Gothic drama, 99–113
Gothic Flame, The (Varma), 68
Gothic heroine, 148, 211, 234
Gothic media and technology, 144–62
Gothic modernism, 49–63
Gothic Modernisms (Smith and Wallace), 50, 51, 60
Gothic Nature (journal), 300
Gothic Queer Culture (Westengard), 261
Gothic Quest, The (Summers), 67
Gothic Studies (journal), 71
Gothic supernaturalism, 37, 65, 228, 235
Gothic television, 6, 129–143, 146, 150, 152, 153, 202, 218, 253
Gothic video games, 2, 44, 114, 145
Grand Guignol, evolution and history 99–113, 117
Grand Guignol, Le: Le Théâtre des peurs de la Belle Epoque (Pierron) 110
Grand Guignol, The: Theatre of Fear and Horror (Gordon), 100, 102, 105, 107, 108, 110
Grand-Guignol (play), 110, 117
Grand-Guignol: The French Theatre of Horror (Hand and Wilson), 100, 102–5, 107, 108, 110
'Great God Pan, The' (Machen), 40
Griffith, D. W., 5, 88–90, 94, 279

Gritos en la noche/*The Awful Dr. Orlof* (film), 120
'Grobovshchik'/'The Coffin-Maker' (Pushkin), 181
Gunn, Bill, 275, 285

H. P. Lovecraft: Against the world, Against Life (Houellebecq), 42, 45
Habermas, Jürgen, 130
Haeckel, Ernst Heinrich Philipp August, 293
Haggard, H. Rider, 52
Haggerty, George, 10, 260, 265, 271n23
'"Haints": American Ghosts, Ethnic Memory, and Contemporary Fiction' (Redding), 238
Haiti 168, 176, 231, 232
Halberstam, J., 73, 261
Halloween (film), 91, 146, 148
Hammer studios, 6, 109, 114, 115, 119–21, 123–5
Hand, Richard, 100, 102–5, 107, 108, 110, 112n23
Hanson, Helen, 125
Hantke, Steffen, 8, 9, 176
Hare, Robert, 215
Harlem Renaissance, 231
Harris, Thomas, 156, 224
Harris, Trudier, 237
Harrison, Sheri-Marie, 286
Hasford, Gustav, 170, 176
Haslam, Jason, 3, 140
Haunted Hotel, The (J. Stuart Blackton), 83–4
Haunted House, The (Bonis-Charancle), 108
Haunted House, The (film), 85, 94
'Haunted House, The' (Nesbit), 23
Haunting of Hill House, The (Jackson), 11, 199, 263, 269
Haunting, The (film), 269
Hauntings: Fantastic Stories (Lee), 19
Hay, Simon, 28
Hays Code *see* Motion Picture Production Code
Hazzard-Donald, Katrina, 238
Heholt, Ruth, 15
Hellraiser (film), 150, 156

Hemenway, Robert, 241n26
Hemingway, Ernest, 176
Henry, Aaron James, 132
'Herbert West – Reanimator' (Lovecraft), 245
Herbert, Daniel, 146
heteronormativity, 11, 72, 202, 259, 260, 266, 273, 274, 276, 278
Hillard, Tom J., 290
History and Memory in African-American Culture (O'Meally and Fabre), 238
History of the Modern British Ghost Story, A (Hay), 28
Hitchcock, Alfred, 28, 124, 137, 224, 249, 264, 269, 294, 295, 300
Hoberman, J., 209
Hobsbawm, Eric, 1
Hodgson, William Hope, 16, 36, 41, 45
Hoedt, Madelon, 5, 110
Hoeveler, Diane Long, 103, 104
Hoffmann, E. T. A., 8, 181, 182, 185, 187, 189
Hoge, Charles, 253
Hogle, Jerrold E., 15, 70, 71, 76, 139
'Hollow Men' (Eliot), 167, 171
Hollywood, 8, 84, 90, 144, 151, 153, 157, 161n16, 168, 169, 171, 200, 204, 205, 214, 264
Hollywood Gothic, 7, 145, 151, 153
Holocaust, 1, 171, 174, 224
hoodoo, 10, 228, 230, 232, 238
Horner, Avril, 5, 59, 60, 85
horror comics, 198, 301
horror films, 6, 7, 93, 99, 116, 118–21, 144–62, 165, 170, 171, 176, 198, 266, 279, 285, 287, 291, 296–8, 301
Horror Noire: Blacks in American Horror Films from the 1890s to the Present (Means Coleman), 286
horrotica, 121
Horton, Emily, 131
'Hound of the Baskervilles, The' (Doyle), 27
House of Usher (film), 124
House on the Borderland, The (Hodgson), 41, 45
'How it happened' (Conan Doyle), 18

Howells, Coral Anne, 71
Hughes, Dorothy B., 9, 216, 217
Hughes, William, 69, 76, 269, 301
Hugo, Victor, 91, 103, 116
Hujar, Peter, 267
Hulme, T. E., 57
human sacrifice, 25, 231
Hunchback of Notre Dame, The (film, 1923), 84, 115
Hunger, The (film), 150, 265
Hurley, Kelly, 60, 73
Hurston, Zora Neale, 9, 10, 228, 230–3, 238
Hutchings, Peter, 125

I am Legend (Matheson), 10, 251–3
'I Have a Rendezvous with Death' (Seeger), 171, 172
I Married a Monster from Outer Space (film), 198, 201, 202, 209
Il mulino delle donne di pietra/Mill of the Stone Women (film), 120
'Imagination of Disaster, The' (Sontag), 198, 209, 210
'Imp of the Perverse, The' (Poe), 223
Imperial Gothic, 73, 179n9
'A Haunted House' (Woolf), 49, 60
In a Lonely Place (film), 169
In a Lonely Place (Hughes), 9, 216, 217, 220
'In Flanders Fields' (McCrae), 172
In Our Time (Hemingway), 167
'In the Hills, the Cities' (Barker), 44
In the Lake of the Woods (O'Brien), 170
In the Mouth of Madness (film), 153, 156
India, 24–8, 39, 166, 206, 217, 289n35
insanity, 156, 225, 251
internet, 2, 44, 136, 153
Interview with the Vampire (Rice), 104, 137, 265
Into the London Fog: Eerie Tales from the Weird City (Dearnley), 294
'Invented by Horror: The Gothic and African American Literary Ideology in Native Son' (Smethurst), 287
Invisible Man (Ellison), 11, 276, 286

Ireland, 3, 132, 187
It (King), 43
Italian horror, 124, 125
Italy, 6, 120, 169, 206, 207

Jackson, Shirley, 11, 199, 263
Jacob's Ladder (film), 170
Jacobs, Harriet, 229, 233
Jacobs, W. W., 170
James, Henry, 3, 23, 24, 27, 37, 49, 52, 54, 60, 262
James, M. R., 4, 15, 16, 27, 41, 60, 64
James, Marlon, 286
James, William, 38, 39
Jancovich, Mark, 209
Jane Eyre (C Bronte), 55, 72
Jaws (film), 291, 296, 297
Jenkins, Philip, 214
Jim Crow Era, 168, 231, 236, 238, 275, 281
'Jolly Corner, The' (Wells), 24
Jones, Darryl, 20, 41
Jones, David J., 86
Jones, David W., 214, 215, 225
Jones, LeRoi *see* Baraka, Amiri
Joshi, S. T., 16, 35, 39, 40, 42, 43, 45
Jouvin, Jack, 102, 103
Joyce, James, 49, 52, 60
Jurassic Park (film), 11, 297–9
Jurassic Park: Fallen Kingdom (film), 298

Kant, Emanuel, 35
Kaplan, Fred, 209, 211n3
Karloff, Boris, 114, 117
Karta Germanna'/'Hermann's Card' (Lukash), 187
Keaton, Buster, 85, 94
Keetley, Dawn, 292, 300
Kendrick, James, 149, 157
'Kerfol' (Wharton), 24
Kesey, Ken, 255
Kiehl, Kurt A., 213
Kilgour, Maggie, 260
Killer Inside Me, The (Thompson), 9, 217, 219
Kindred (Butler), 9, 228, 233, 235, 238, 285, 286
King, Rodney, 136, 237

King, Stephen, 10, 42, 43, 156, 171, 174, 191, 231, 248
Kisacky, Jeanne, 244
Kiss of Blood, The (Aragny and Neilson), 108
Koch, J. L. A., 213
KoKo's Haunted House (film), 85
Kolchak, the Night Stalker (television series), 6, 131, 133, 134, 139, 140
Korean War, 9, 200, 203–8, 212n13, 212n14
Krabbé, Tim, 9, 220, 222
Kremmel, Laura R., 10
Krueger, Freddy, 148–9
Krzhizhanovskii, Sigizmund, 8, 187, 188–91, 193
'Kvadraturin'/'Quadratrurin' (Krzhizhanovskii), 190

La maschera del demonio/ Black Sunday (film), 120, 124
Lacanian Real, The, 277
'Lady's Maid's Bell, The' (Wharton), 26
Lang, Fritz, 50, 168
Lant, Kathleen Margaret, 248
Lawrence, D. H., 20, 50, 53, 62n6
Le Fanu, Sheridan, 252, 264
Ledwon, Lenora, 140
Lee, Christopher, 70, 119, 120
Lee, Vernon, 3, 19, 20, 49
Leeder, Murray, 5
Leiber, Fritz, 209, 231
Leni, Paul, 85, 91, 92, 94
Leroux, Gaston, 28
Les Lèvres Rouges/Daughters of Darkness (film), 265
Les Yeux sans visage/Eyes without a Face (film), 107, 124
Levenson, Michael, 58
Levin, Ira, 211n10, 255
Levitan, Kathrin, 132
Levy, Emanuel, 153
Lewis, Matthew 'Monk', 34, 67, 103, 104, 166
Lewis, Tyson, 133
Lewis, Wyndham, 60
Liggins, Emma, 3
Ligotti, Thomas, 35, 43, 45

Literary Ghosts from the Victorians to Modernism (Thurston), 60
Literary Women (Moers), 72
Literature of Terror, The (Punter), 4, 62n6, 69–72, 74, 75, 104
Lloyd-Smith, Allan, 277
Locating the Gothic in British Modernity (Wiseman), 60
'Lodger, The' (Belloc Lowndes), 28
Lodger: A Story of the London Fog, The (film), 294
Long Weekend (film), 211n8, 296
Los Angeles, 129, 130, 140, 147, 151, 216
Lovecraft Country (television series), 134
Lovecraft, H. P., 16, 33–6, 38–40, 42–4, 45, 245, 250
Luce, Henry, 196
Luckhurst, Roger, 17, 27, 231, 232, 253, 254
Lugosi, Bela, 114, 116, 168
Luk'ianenko, Sergei, 8, 181, 188, 193
Lulu (Berg), 283

M.A.S.H. (film), 207
Machen, Arthur, 36, 40, 53
Machin, James, 36, 41, 45
McIntyre, Clara, 67
Mad Men (television series), 207
MAGA (Make America Great Again), 9, 208
magical Black man/woman, 231
Maguire, Muireann, 8, 193
Mama Day (Naylor), 285, 289n40
Man and Nature: or, Physical Geography as Modified by Human Action (Marsh), 293
Man in the Gray Flannel Suit, The (Wilson), 204, 212n14
Man in the Grey Flannel Suit, The (film), 8–9, 204–7, 209
Man Who Laughs, The (film), 84, 91, 97n19, 116
Man Who Lived Underground, The (Wright), 11, 273, 275–7
Manchurian Candidate, The (film), 207
Manoir du diable, La/The House of the Devil (film), 83, 94

March, William, 9, 219
Margree, Victoria, 15, 19, 25
'Marlon James and the Metafiction of the New Black Gothic' (Harrison), 286
Marsh, George Perkins, 293
Marshall, Nowell, 269
Marxism, 1, 70, 74, 129
Mask of Sanity, The (Cleckley), 9, 218, 224
Mask of Sanity: An Attempt to Clarify Some Issues About the So-Called Psychopathic Personality, The (Cleckley), 9, 214
Master i Margarita/Master and Margarita (Bulgakov), 184
Matheson, Richard, 10, 209, 231, 251–3
Matheson, Sue, 227n28
Matrix, The (film), 151, 231
Matthews, Elkin, 69
Maturin, Charles, 55, 59, 66, 181
Maurey, Max, 101, 102
Maxa, Paula, 102, 103
MacAndrew, Elizabeth, 71
McCorristine, Shane, 19
McGrath, Patrick, 10, 56–7, 63n22, 251, 257n19
McKean, Dave, 250
McMartin pre-school trial, 147
Means Coleman, Robin, 286
medical experimentation, 245
medical humanities, 3, 10, 243–58
Méliès, Georges, 83, 87, 94, 115
'Melisande' (Nesbit), 22
Melmoth the Wanderer (Maturin), 55, 59
melodrama, 6, 84–8, 90, 93, 94, 99, 100, 101, 103, 105, 106, 112n25, 115, 116, 174, 200–2, 209, 211
mental institutions, 10, 245, 249–51
Mephistopheles, 185
Méténier, Oscar, 100–2, 105
Metropolis (film), 50, 84, 93, 122
Midnight Faces (film), 5, 85
Miéville, China, 36
Mighall, Robert, 65, 74–6
Miles, Robert, 76
millennium see fin-de-millennium

Mills, Kevin, 21
Misery (King), 10, 248
misogyny, 120, 216
Modern Weird Tale, The (Joshi), 16
modernism and the Gothic, 3, 4, 15, 38, 49–63, 165, 171
Modernism/Modernity (journal), 51
Moers, Ellen, 72
Monastyrka/The Convent Girl (Pogorel'skii), 182
Monk, The (Lewis), 67
'Monkey's Paw, The' (Jacobs), 170
'Monster, The' (Haldeman), 176
'Monsters are Due on Maple Street, The' (television episode), 199
monstrosity and the Gothic, 10, 40, 52, 73, 84, 104, 150, 246, 261, 262, 264–8, 279, 283, 287
Moore, Alan, 43, 300
Morrison, Grant, 10, 43, 250
Morrison, Toni, 230, 231, 233, 238, 274, 286
Morrow, Bradford, 56
Most Assassinated Woman in the World, The (film), 110
Motion Picture Production Code, 220
Muir, John Kenneth, 147, 155
Mules and Men (Hurston), 230, 238
multiple killers, 214
Mummy, The (film), 93, 114, 168
Munford, Rebecca, 199
Muratov, Pavel, 187
Murphy, Bernice M., 9, 290, 292, 297
My Soul to Keep (Due), 236, 238, 285, 289
'My Words to Victor Frankenstein above the Village of Chamounix: Performing Transgender Rage' (Stryker), 266
My/We (Zamiatin), 184, 192

Nabokov, Vladimir, 187
Nadel, Alan, 206, 209, 211
Native Son (Wright), 275, 281, 287
'Natural History of the Dead, A' (Hemingway), 176–7
Nazi medical experiments, 168, 171, 244
Nazis, 168–9, 171, 174–6, 215, 244

Near Dark (film), 150, 160
Neibauer, James L., 96–7
Nesbit, E., 3, 18, 20, 22–3, 27
New Companion to the Gothic, A (Punter), 2, 76
new Gothic movement, 6, 56, 119
New Weird, The: An Anthology (VanderMeer, J. and A.), 44
New York Times (newspaper), 203, 207
Newman, Judie, 73
Newman, Kim, 45, 147
Ní Fhlainn, Sorcha, 7, 44
Night of the Lepus (film), 291, 296
Night of the Living Dead (film), 10, 171, 178, 253, 257
Night Stalker, The (film), 131
Night Stalker, The (TV Show), 6, 133, 140, 142
Night Watch (Luk'ianenko), 8, 188, 193
Nightbreed (film), 150, 160
Nightmare Vacation (film) *see Sleepaway Camp*
Nightmares of the Heteronormative (Ferguson), 11, 273–4
Nightwing (film), 296, 303
Nightwood (Barnes), 4, 50, 57–9, 268
Nochnoi dozor/ Night Watch (film), 188
noir, 116, 120, 125, 140, 169, 217
'Noir and the Psycho Thriller' (Simpson), 218
non-supernatural Gothic, 217
Normandy, invasion of, 174
Northanger Abbey (Austen), 38, 65
Northanger Novels, The: A Footnote to Jane Austen (Sadleir), 65
'Nos'/'The Nose' (Gogol), 183
Nosferatu, eine Symphonie des Grauens/Nosferatu (film), 84, 93–4, 115
nuclear war/weapons, anxieties related to, 7, 145, 150–1, 198, 203, 211, 294–6, 299
Nunes, Ana, 240–1

Obeah, 55, 230
Obscene Publications Act, 146
Odoevskii, Vladimir, 181
Of One Blood (Hopkins), 274
'Oh Whistle, and I'll Come to You, My Lad' (James), 16, 64, 72
On the Beach (Shute), 294
'On the Knocking at the Gate in Macbeth' (De Quincey), 35
'On the Supernatural in Poetry' (Radcliffe), 34–5
One Exciting Night (film), 5, 90
One Flew Over the Cuckoo's Nest (film), 255
Osbey, Brenda Marie, 229, 231
'Other(ed) Ghosts: Gothicism and the Bonds of Reason in Melville, Chesnutt, and Morrison'(Goldner), 238
Owen, Wilfred, 167, 171, 173

Packer, Sharon, 249
Paco's Story (Heinemann), 170
Palmer, Paulina, 261, 263
Parasite, The (Campbell), 43
'Parazit'/'The Parasite'' (Starobinets), 192
Parker, Elizabeth, 290, 292
Patterson, Robert J., 240–1
Paulais, L., 102
'Pavilion, The' (Nesbit), 23
Peake, Mervyn, 169
Peele, Jordan, 200–1, 209
Penny Dreadful (TV show), 110
Perekhodnyi vozrast/An Awkward Age (Starobinets), 193
Perrin, Alice, 3, 23–7
Petersburg (Belyi), 209
Petley, Julian, 147
Petry, Ann, 233, 274
Phantasmagoria, 86, 149
Phantom of the Opera, The (film), 115, 125
Philips, Kendall R., 95
Pierce, Jack, 93
Pierron, Agnes, 110
'Pikovaia dama'/'The Queen of Spades' (Pushkin), 181, 187
Place of Darkness, A: The Rhetoric of Horror in Early American Cinema (Philips), 95

plant horror, 17, 23, 300
Plant Horror: Approaches to the Monstrous Vegetal in Fiction and Film (Keetley and Tenga), 29, 301
Playback (film), 2012
Podmore, Frank, 21
Poe, Edgar Allan, 5, 8, 29, 34–6, 56, 58–9, 88–9, 94–7, 107, 116, 124, 183, 189, 213, 267, 277, 287, 301
Polevoi, Boris, 185
Poltergeist (film), 160, 236
Pope Jacynth and Other Fantastic Tales (Lee), 20
Popular Novel in England, The (Tompkins), 66
pornography, 6, 120
Portlandia (TV show), 94
Postcolonial Imaginings (Punter), 73
post-colonial Gothic, 55, 180
Povest' o nastoiashchem cheloveke/A Story About A Real Man (Polevoi), 185
Povesti Belkina/The Tales of Belkin (Pushkin), 181
'Power of Darkness, The' (Nesbit), 23
Predator (film), 187
Prince, Stephen, 146
Prisoner, The (TV show), 6, 130–1, 133, 142
Psycho (film), 109, 148, 266
Psycho Paths: Tracking the Serial Killer Through Contemporary American Film and Fiction (Simpson), 225
psychoanalysis, 19, 66, 68, 70–1, 74, 76
Psychology of the Uncanny (Freud), 37, 141
psychopathy, 9, 213–27
PTSD (Post-Traumatic Stress Disorder), 167, 170
Punter, David, 2, 4, 17, 58, 62, 67, 70–7, 290
Purge, The (film), 200
Purple Cloud, The (Shiel), 294
Pushkin, Aleksandr, 181, 183, 187, 193

queer Gothic, 11, 40, 124, 172, 175, 259–72, 269
Queer Gothic (Haggerty), 10, 271
queer Gothic cinema, 11, 264
queer theory and the Gothic, 72–3
Queering Gothic in the Romantic Age: The Penetrating Eye (Fincher), 269
Queering the Gothic (Hughes and Smith), 269

race and the Gothic, 3, 10, 26, 28, 124, 200–3, 206–8, 211–14, 228–42, 273–89
Radcliffe, Ann, 12, 34–5, 68, 71, 84, 116, 182, 246
Railo, Eino, 4, 66
Ray, Nicholas, 9, 169, 202, 209
Re-Envisaging the First Age of Cinematic Horror: 1896–1934: Quanta of Fear (Jones), 95
Reagan, Ronald, 147–8, 150, 237
reality TV, 153
Rebecca (du Maurier), 269
Rebecca (film), 11, 119, 124, 264, 269
Rebel Without a Cause (film), 202, 209, 212
Red Dragon (Harris), 224
'Red Summer of 1919', 11, 273, 275
Redding, Arthur, 238
Regeneration (P Barker), 171
Revenge of the Zombies (film), 168
Revolt of the Zombies (film), 168
Rhodes, Gary D., 95, 97
Rhys, Jean, 55–7
Rice, Anne, 11, 104, 137, 265
Rigby, Jonathan, 125
Rigby, Mair, 269
Rinehart, Mary Roberts, 85
Ringu (film), 153, 155, 156, 162
Riquelme, J. P., 50, 60
Robert, Étienne-Gaspard (stage name 'Robertson'), 86
Robson, Eddie, 139
Rockoff, Adam, 148
Rocky Horror Picture Show (film), 269
Romantic Agony, The (Praz), 66
Romanticism, Gender, and Violence: Blake to Sodini (Marshall), 269–70
Romero, George A., 157–1, 176, 231, 253
Rosemary's Baby (film), 255

Rosemary's Baby (Levin), 255
Rosenberg, Isaac, 167, 177
Routledge Handbook to the Ghost Story, The (Brewster and Thurston), 28
Russell, Emily, 247
Russia, 8, 166, 180–95
Russian Gothic, 180–95
Rust, Stephen A., 291–2

Sadleir, Michael, 65
Sassoon, Siegfried, 167, 171
Satanic Panic, 147
Saving Private Ryan (film), 174
Scarborough, Dorothy, 4, 19–20, 25, 37, 52, 65–6
Schell, Jennifer, 291
Schlozman, Steven C., 254
Scott, Sir Walter, 52, 66
Scream (film), 7, 144, 152
Se7en (film), 152
Searching for Sycorax: Black Women's Hauntings of Contemporary Horror (Brooks), 286
Sederholm, Carl, 42
Sedgwick, Eve Kofosky, 72, 260
Seeger, Alan, 167, 171–2
serial killers, 120, 134, 145, 152, 156, 216–19, 224–5
servants and the Gothic, 26–7
Shadow of a Doubt (film), 224
Sheep Look Up, The (Brunner), 296
Shelley, Mary, 77, 87, 94, 103, 115, 119, 123, 151–2, 166, 245, 265, 292
Shiel, M. P., 294
'Shinel'/'The Overcoat' (Gogol), 183
Shining, The (King), 156, 231
Short-Timers, The (Hasford), 170, 176–7
Shriver, Lionel, 224
Sides, Hampton, 203
Silence of the Lambs, The (film), 152, 156, 266
Silence of the Lambs, The (Harris), 220
silent era cinema and the Gothic, 83–98
Silent Running (film), 296
Silent Spring (Carson), 199, 295
Simmons, David, 40

Simpson, Philip, 218, 225
Sinclair, May, 19, 53, 60
Sivils, Matthew Wynn, 292
Skal, David J., 125
Skoble, Aeon J., 140
slasher movies, 7, 91, 121, 144–53, 156–7, 161
slavery (US American), 9, 168, 228–31, 233–4, 236–9, 269, 286, 288
Sleepaway Camp (film), 266
Smethurst, James, 287
Smith, Andrew, 19, 30, 50–1, 53, 60, 76, 269
Smith, Anthony D., 131
Smith, Grover, 58
Sobach'e serdtse/Heart of a Dog (Bulgakov), 186
Sobol, Valeria, 183
Soldiers' Pay (Faulkner), 167
Soles, Carter, 291, 295
Sologub, Fedor, 187
Soltysik Monnet, Agnieszka, 7, 165–179
'Some Remarks on Ghost Stories' (M. R. James), 15
Son of Frankenstein (film), 117, 127
Songs of a Dead Dreamer (Ligotti), 43
Sontag, Susan, 198, 209, 210
sorcery, 182
Southern Gothic, 4
Soviet Union *see* USSR
Soylent Green (film), 296
Spadoni, Robert, 92, 116
Spain, 6, 120
species extinction, 12, 297, 299–300
Spider (McGrath), 10, 56, 251
spiritualism, 3, 19–22
Spooner, Catherine, 125, 146, 157
Squirm (film), 211, 291
Stalin, Joseph, 185, 187, 191, 193
Starobinets, Anna, 8, 191–4
Stepford Wives, The (film), 201–3, 211 n10
Stevenson, Robert Lewis, 36, 39, 84, 107
Stoker (film), 218
Stoker, Bram, 36, 39, 52, 58, 75, 116, 135, 152, 252, 263, 305
Strand, The (magazine), 20–2

Strange Case of Dr. Jekyll and Mr. Hyde, The (Stevenson), 84, 114
Strange Cases of Dr. Stanchon, The (Bacon), 26
Street, The (Petry), 274
Stryker, Susan, 259, 266
Student von Prag, Der/The Student of Prague (film), 84, 97, 115, 127
suburban Gothic, 199–203, 207
Summers, Montague, 4, 67–9, 71
'Supernatural Horror in Literature' (Lovecraft), 33–4, 37
Supernatural in Modern English Fiction, The (Scarborough), 19–20, 24, 37, 52, 65–6
Surrealists, 52, 68
Swamp Thing (Moore), 300

Tale of Terror, The: A Study of the Gothic Romance (Birkhead), 4, 52, 65–6
Talented Mr Ripley, The (Highsmith), 217–18, 224
Tales from the Hood (film), 281
Tales of Mystery and Imagination (Poe), 34
Tarr (Lewis), 60
Taylor, Leila, 237
Teaching the Gothic (Powell and Smith), 76
technology, digital and the Gothic, 5, 70, 129–43, 145
'Telegram, The' (Hunt), 18
television and the Gothic, 6, 44, 129–43, 146, 153
'Tell-Tale Heart, The' (Poe), 89, 97
Telotte, J. P., 155
Tempi duri per i vampiri/ Uncle Was a Vampire (film), 120
Tenga, Angela, 300
Terminator 2: Judgment Day (film), 150, 295
Terminator, The (film), 150, 295
'Terror of Blue John Gap, The' (Doyle), 21, 27
Terror, The (film), 93
Texas Chain Saw Massacre, The (film), 266
Théâtre Libre, 100–1

Theatre of Horror see Grand-Guignol
Them! (film), 198, 211, 291
Thing, The (film), 43, 150, 156, 161
Third Part of the Night (film), 176
Thompson, Jim, 9, 217–18
Threads (film), 150, 295
'Three Drugs, The' (Nesbit), 23
Thurston, Luke, 28, 54, 60
Tidwell, Christy, 11, 290–303, 308
Time Machine, The (Wells), 22, 191
Time magazine, 196
Tiutchev, Fedor, 195
Todorov, Tsvetan, 54, 92
Tompkins, J. M. S., 65–8
Toomer, Jean, 286
'Tough Tussle, A' (Bierce), 167
Transplantation Gothic: Tissue Transfer in Literature, Film, and Medicine (Wasson), 255–7
Transylvania, 117
Truett, Casey, 256–7
Trump, Donald J., 1
Tsement/Cement (Gladkov), 184
Turn of the Screw, The (H. James), 37, 54, 262
Turner, Jim, 44
Tuskegee Study, 246
Twentieth-Century Gothic (Armitt), 75–6
Twenty-First Century Gothic (Aldana Reyes and Wester), 3
Twilight Zone, The (television series), 199, 209, 211

USSR, 151, 186
Ukraine, 151, 182–3, 188–9, 195
'Unburied, The' (Bacon), 26
'Uncanny Recognition: Queer Theory's Debt to the Gothic' (Rigby), 269
Uncle Sam (film), 176
Uninvited, The (film), 264
Universal Studios, 6, 103, 109, 114–19, 121, 125
Unknown, The (film), 84, 94
Untitled (Face in Dirt) (photograph) (Wojnarowicz), 267
Untitled (Peter Hujar) (photographic series) (Wojnarowicz), 267

Untitled (Silence = Death) (photograph) (Wojnarowicz), 267

Vampire Chronicles, The (Rice), 11, 265
Vampire Lovers, The (film), 114
vampires, 28, 115–16, 137, 145, 150, 181, 185–6, 188, 235, 252–3, 264–5, 270, 275
Vampyr (film), 93
VanderMeer, Jeff, 36, 40, 44
Varma, Devendra 4, 68–9
Vault of Horror, The (magazine), 42
Victorian Gothic, 56, 73–4, 132, 137
   Victorian Gothic drama, 103
video (VHS), 7, 144–7, 150, 153–6, 161
video culture, 144–7
'video nasties', 146
Videodrome (film), 43, 150, 161
Vietnam War, 7, 167, 170–2, 174, 176, 196
'Violet Car, The' (Nesbit), 18
'Vospominaniia budushchego'/ 'Memories of the Future' (Krzhizhanovskii), 191
voudou, voodoo, vodun, 10, 228, 230, 232, 235, 238
Voyage in the Dark (Rhys), 55
Vronsky, Peter, 215–16

Wachsfigurenkabinet, das/Waxworks (film), 91
Waiting for Godot (Beckett), 55
Wald, Priscilla, 252
Walpole, Horace, 10, 71, 103, 166, 259
Walthall, Harry B., 88
War Gothic, 7, 165–79
war poetry, 7, 165, 171–3
Wasson, Sara, 176, 255
'Waste Land, The' (Eliot), 4, 55, 57–8
We Need to Talk About Kevin (Shriver), 224
Webb, Jen, 252
'Wedding Chest, A' (Lee), 20
Weinstock, Jeffrey Andrew, 24, 38, 77
Weird and the Eerie (Fisher), 42, 45
weird fiction, 4, 17, 33–48

Weird Tales (magazine), 16, 33, 41–2, 44–5
Wiseman, Sam, 49, 51–2
Wells, H. G., 3, 17–18, 20, 22, 52, 191
Wells, Ira, 275
Wendigo, The (Blackwood), 40–1, 293
Wes Craven's New Nightmare (film), 150
Westengard, Laura, 10–11, 259–72
Wester, Maisha L., 11, 47, 233, 273–89
Whale, James, 85, 122, 126–7, 168, 171, 175, 245
Wharton, Edith, 24, 26, 37
When the Wind Blows (film), 150, 161
White Zombie (film), 168
Whitehead, Colson, 288
Whitehouse, Mary, 147
Wide Sargasso Sea (Rhys), 55–6
Wiene, Robert, 60
Wild, Jonathan, 16
Wilde, Oscar, 49–50, 59
Williams, Anne, 71
Williams, Linda, 90, 233
'Willows, The' (Blackwood), 17, 290, 300
Wilson, Harriet, 233
Wilson, Michael, 100, 102–5, 107–8, 110–12
Wilson, Sloan, 204, 209
Wilt, Judith, 60, 62
Wind in the Rose-bush, The (Wilkins), 28
Winthrop-Young, Geoffrey, 135
Wojnarowicz, David, 267–8
Women's Weird 2: More Strange Stories by Women (Edmundson), 17
Woolf, Virginia, 49–52, 58–60, 62
World War I (WWI), 3, 7, 15, 165, 168, 173, 176–7, 184
World War II (WWII), 1, 9, 49, 169, 171, 173, 176, 196, 198, 200, 203–7, 212, 214–15, 282, 294
Wretched of the Earth, The (Fanon), 232
Wright, Richard, 11, 273, 275–82, 287

X-Files, The (TV show), 6, 131, 133–5, 137, 139, 140, 152
X-Files: Fight the Future, The (film), 152

Y2K Panic, 7, 151
Yeux Sans Visage, Les (film), 107, 124, 127

Zamiatin, Evgenii, 184, 192
Zhivushchii/ The Living (Starobinets), 192
Zhukovskii, Vasilii, 181
Zlosnik, Sue, 5, 60, 85, 96
zombies, zombieism, 137, 145, 168, 178, 231, 253, 254, 279